LIBRARIES NI
WITHDRAWN FROM STO

FROM CORRIB TO CULTRA

FOLKLIFE ESSAYS IN HONOUR OF
ALAN GAILEY

Edited by
Trefor M. Owen

D1556077

Institute of Irish Studies
Queen's University Belfast
in association with the
Ulster Folk and Transport Museum

NORTH EASTERN LIBRARY SERVICE
AREA LIBRARY, DEMESNE AVENUE
BALLYMENA CO. ANTRIM BT43 7BG

8520559 1	
RONDO	08/02/2002
U-390	£ 9.50

First published in 2000
The Institute of Irish Studies
Queen's University Belfast
8 Fitzwilliam Street
Belfast BT9 6AW
www.qub.ac.uk/iis/publications.html

in association with the

Ulster Folk and Transport Museum
Cultra
Holywood
County Down BT18 0EU

© Editor and authors 2000

This book has received support from the Cultural Diversity Programme of the Community Relations Council, which aims to encourage acceptance and understanding of cultural diversity. The views expressed do not necessarily reflect those of the NI Community Relations Council.

All rights reserved. No part of this publication may be reproduced, stored in a retrieval system or transmitted, in any form or by any means, electronic, mechanical, photocopying, recording or otherwise, without the prior permission of the publishers.

British Library Cataloguing-in-Publication Data
A catalogue record for this book is available from the British Library.

ISBN 0 85389 770 0 hbk
ISBN 0 85389 765 4 pbk

Typeset in Palatino 10pt

Printed by W. & G. Baird Ltd, Antrim

Contents

Contributors

Trefor M. Owen, editor of this volume, graduated in geography and anthropology at the University of Wales, Aberystwyth. After a short period at the School of Scottish Studies, University of Edinburgh, he spent a year as a Swedish scholar studying ethnology at the University of Uppsala before being appointed to the staff of the Welsh Folk Museum, St Fagans, where he was curator from 1971 until his retirement in 1987. Honorary Professor, University of Wales, Cardiff; Honorary Fellow of University of Wales, Bangor and University of Wales, Aberystwyth; Honorary Fellow, the Folklore Society; past president of the Society of Folklife Studies; and author of several books and numerous articles on the folklife of Wales.

Linda-May Ballard is Textiles Curator at the Ulster Folk and Transport Museum, and has written on Ulster's folklife and folk and popular culture and art.

Jonathan Bell is Head of the Curatorial Division at the Ulster Folk and Transport Museum. He has written on Irish agricultural history, museology, and popular culture.

Anthony D. Buckley is Curator in Anthropology at the Ulster Folk and Transport Museum. He has written on folk medicine in Nigeria and on ideas, social interaction and identity in Ulster.

Fionnuala Carragher is Domestic Life Curator at the Ulster Folk and Transport Museum. She has written on domestic service, and on rural and urban domestic lifestyle.

Roger Dixon is librarian at the Ulster Folk and Transport Museum. He has written on the popular press and social history.

Alexander Fenton is Director of the European Ethnological Research Centre, Edinburgh; former director, School of Scottish Studies, University of Edinburgh; and former director, National Museum of Antiquities of Scotland, Edinburgh. He has written on many aspects of Scottish rural life.

Robbie Hannan is Music Curator at the Ulster Folk and Transport Museum. He has written on Irish musical history, place-names, and the Irish language.

Patricia Lysaght is a professor in the Department of Irish Folklore, University College Dublin, National University of Ireland. She has written widely on folklore and life styles.

Michael McCaughan is Head of Transport at the Ulster Folk and Transport Museum. He has written on Irish popular and vernacular culture with special reference to maritime transport.

Christine McGregor is principal architect with Historic Scotland, in the Properties in Care division.

Megan McManus is Crafts Curator at the Ulster Folk and Transport Museum. She has written on social and economic history related to rural crafts.

Venetia Newall is a folklorist who has written widely on many aspects of folk culture, in England and elsewhere.

Ross Noble is curator of The Highland Folk Museum, Kingussie and Newtonmore, and has been involved in vernacular building research for the past twenty-five years. He has initiated several reconstruction projects over that period.

Michael J. Preston is Professor of English at the University of Colorado at Boulder. He has published *A concordance to the Middle English shorter poem, Urban Folklore from Colorado, The other print traditions*, etc.

Philip Robinson is Head of the Collections Division at the Ulster Folk and Transport Museum. He has written on vernacular architecture, social history, and linguistic heritage in Ulster.

Paul Smith is Professor of Folklore at the Memorial University of Newfoundland, Co-director of the Institute for Folklore Studies in Britain and Canada, and Associate Director of The National Centre for English Cultural Tradition, University of Sheffield.

G.B. Thompson OBE is a retired director of the Ulster Folk and Transport Museum. He has written on folklife in Ulster and elsewhere.

Bruce Walker is a senior lecturer in the University of Dundee.

Mervyn Watson is Agriculture Curator at the Ulster Folk and Transport Museum. He has written on agricultural history and anthropology.

Eurwyn Wiliam is currently Director of Collections and Education and Deputy Director of the National Museums and Galleries of Wales.

List of illustrations

page no

Sources of illustrations

The illustrations in this book are reproduced by kind permission of the following individuals and organisations: frontispiece, Spectator Newspapers, Bangor, County Down; Figures 4.1, 4.2, 4.6, 5.1, 5.2, 5.3, 6.1, 6.2, 6.3, 6.4, 7.1, 7.2, 10.1, 10.5, 10.6, 10.7, 10.8, 17.2, Trustees of the National Museums and Galleries of Northern Ireland (Ulster Folk and Transport Museum); Figures 4.3, 4.4, 4.5, 4.7, Philip Robinson; Figures 7.3, 7.4, 7.5, Mr Fred Coll, Derrybeg; Figures 8.1, 8.2, 8.3, The Highland Council, Highland Folk Museum; Figure 8.4, Donald R. Noble; Figures 9.2, 9.3, 9.4, 9.5, 9.6, Bruce Walker; Figure 10.4, from the R.J. Welch collection, Trustees of the National Museums and Galleries of Northern Ireland (Ulster Museum); Figure 12.1, Queen's University Belfast Library, Hibernica Collection; Figure 12.2, Paul Smith Collection.

Introduction

Trefor M. Owen

THE PROCESS OF ESTABLISHING THE Ulster Folk Museum was set in motion in 1958 and its first director, Dr George B. Thompson appointed in 1959. The excellent 136-acre site at Cultra Manor, a few miles outside Belfast, was acquired in 1961. Nearly forty years later the Ulster Folk and Transport Museum (as it is now called) has earned an enviable reputation on both sides of the Atlantic as an innovative open-air museum, embracing an excellent transport gallery. For many years it has also been renowned as a centre of excellence for research on the folk life of Ulster. It was this institution at an early stage in its development that Alan Gailey joined as a research officer in October 1960, becoming involved from the very outset in the formulation of the policy of the museum, as George Thompson records in his essay in this volume. In 1975 he became a keeper of non-material culture, eventually succeeding George Thompson as director in 1986. Following Alan Gailey's retirement from that post in 1996 the trustees of the museum encouraged the preparation of a volume of essays to commemorate his invaluable contribution both to the development of the Ulster Folk and Transport Museum and to the advancement of folk life studies in Ulster and beyond. In preparing the volume the editor sought the assistance of Alan Gailey's former colleagues at the Ulster Folk and Transport Museum and also of authors who were distinguished in those varied aspects of folk life to which Alan himself had contributed. As will be seen from the extensive bibliography prepared by Roger Dixon, librarian of the museum, the 103 publications listed reflect the wide range of Alan's scholarly interests centred on the museum and its activities. In addition to his involvement in the day-to-day running of the museum and the planning of its future growth, he also contributed extensively to the journal *Ulster Folklife* as its editor for many years and to the Society of Folk Life Studies as both secretary (1975–82) and president (1986–89).

The history of the efforts which culminated in the creation of the Ulster Folk Museum is the subject of Dr George Thompson's opening contribution. The Ulster Folk Museum Act passed by the Parliament of Northern Ireland in 1958 was the result of several years of active campaigning during and after the Second World War. A suitable site, commensurate with the vision of an open-air museum able to stand comparison with the best in Europe, and yet accessible, was sought and subsequently acquired at Cultra.

One of the main instigators, as George Thompson makes clear, was the late E. Estyn Evans, Professor of Geography at Queen's University, Belfast, who put forward what might be called the academic case for a new institution which would, from the outset, also have a much wider appeal to the general public in Northern Ireland. Like George Thompson, Alan Gailey was a student taught and inspired by Estyn Evans and his brand of human geography. Megan McManus' essay which follows takes a closer look at Estyn Evans and his influence on folk life in Ulster and on the development of the museum.

Two essays by Philip Robinson and Fionnuala Carragher deal with the history of buildings before their removal to Cultra. Such documentation from various sources adds considerably to the value of the buildings as exhibits, enabling their social background to be interpreted for the museum visitor. Dr Robinson rightly describes the impressive oat-milling complex of four buildings from Straid Mills, County Antrim, as the most spectacular achievement of the museum's range of open-air exhibit buildings. The corn mill was rebuilt in 1852 and the complex, as so often happened, included a corn-drying kiln. How the mill operated, as well as who operated it, is discussed by Dr Robinson. Fionnuala Carragher takes as her subject the history of the much smaller weaver's house from Ballydugan, a replica of a derelict dwelling in north-west County Down. It is seen in the context of the once dominant linen industry, and visitors to the museum, on reading her essay, can visualise its occupants and the neighbourhood in which they lived. They can also learn how such earthen-walled houses, formerly commonly found in the Irish countryside, were constructed. Both essays reflect the fact that the erection (or re-erection) of buildings as exhibits in a museum is only the first, spectacular, stage in their presentation as evidence of how their former occupants lived, emphasising how they were once grounded elsewhere in time and place.

Linda-May Ballard discusses evidence of rather a different sort, namely, dress as a historical record. Wedding gowns, which she has chosen for detailed examination, are especially important as evidence because they can frequently be dated precisely and their original owners identified. Some are preserved for sentimental reasons, but it is not often that the wedding clothes of both bride and groom survive, as they do in at least one example in the museum's collections.

These collections, among other things, contain a number of items relating to Francis James Bigger (1863–1926), who is described as a tireless promoter of all aspects of Irish culture. Roger Dixon examines his political activities and the way he sought to present the northern leaders of the insurrection of 1798 as archetypal heroes in an unfinished series of biographies which appeared in 1906.

One of the interesting features of folk life is the way the use of traditional primitive structures is revived under special circumstances before the methods used in their construction are forgotten. Such revivals often serve to preserve the practical expertise for posterity. The temporary dwelling known as a *bothóg* is a case in point. Traditionally used in connection with 'booleying' (or summer grazing) in County Donegal, *bothógaí* were later built as shelters for turf-diggers during the severe fuel shortages experienced by the Irish Free State in the Second World War. More recently, using techniques remembered from the 1940s, an example was built for use in a BBC television programme about the Great Famine. The essay by Robbie Hannan and Jonathan Bell records the evidence of one of the two brothers who built that example and supplements it with the more detailed earlier account of the *bothóg* and the practice of booleying recorded by the Irish Folklore Commission. The authors of this essay show just how remembered expertise can take its place alongside oral history as authentic evidence.

An early example of Alan Gailey's interest in vernacular architecture from his days in the Department of Geography in the University of Glasgow, before joining the staff of the museum, dealt with similar shieling structures on the Isle of Skye. In Ross Noble's essay, however, the Creel House reconstructed in the grounds of the Highland Folk Museum is rather more substantial and not unlike the kind of peasant houses studied by Alan Gailey in his article on the peasant houses of the south-west highlands of Scotland published in 1962.

The essay by Bruce Walker and Christine McGregor touches upon other topics dealt with by Alan Gailey in his research on rural settlement and agricultural improvement in the Scottish Highlands. The 'Clearances' beginning in the second half of the eighteenth century and continuing through most of the first half of the next denuded the countryside of its indigenous population to make way for a new market economy based on sheep-farming on a vast scale. This gave rise to new kinds of specialised buildings, notably woolbarns, which historians have largely overlooked in their concentration on more emotive aspects of this social revolution. The survey of this specialised form of architecture as found in the western Highlands and adjacent isles serves to remind those researchers on historical farm buildings who have concentrated on structures associated with arable economies that pastoral farming on a large scale can also give rise to its own kind of architecture. Indeed, the authors draw a comparison with similar buildings on the sheep stations of South Island, New Zealand.

One aspect of agricultural improvement in Ireland, as Mervyn Watson points out in discussing the role of the horse on Irish farms, was the growing importance of horse-powered technology with the horse remaining the source of draught power well into the twentieth century. Selective breeding by farmers at a local level aimed at producing the kind of animal most suitable for local needs, resulting in a diversity of characteristics within a single type. While traditional ploughs find their way into folk museum collections and become the object of scholarly study, the animals which once drew them are often ignored: after all, horses die and cannot be studied retrospectively. The disappearance of the horse from the Ulster farm, it is interesting to note, was the subject of an article published by Alan Gailey in 1966 in which he reviewed the topic from a different angle, using government statistics to highlight regional differences in the retention of traditional practices.

Another topic on which Alan Gailey has worked is touched upon in Eurwyn Wiliam's essay on concealed horse skulls, a phenomenon to be found on both sides of the Irish Sea. As in Mervyn Watson's essay the significance of the horse in rural society is examined. Eurwyn Wiliam's subject, however, calls for a different approach involving the examination of twenty-seven instances recorded in Wales and the assessment of prehistoric and folklore evidence in order to explain this esoteric practice. He raises a basic question confronting folklorists, namely, whether the centuries-long gap in the evidence for existence of a custom signifies a distinct break in continuity or merely the disappearance of the evidence.

Paul Smith and Michael J. Preston in taking up the subject of Christmas Rhyme chapbooks printed in Ireland make an interesting contribution to the field of Irish folk drama which has been one of Alan Gailey's research interests. Behind their work is the tantalising question of the relationship between the written text and the actual performance. Having collected copies of all known chapbooks containing texts, they have devised their own method of studying the material systematically so as to discover the relationship between the surviving chapbooks and to establish a specific printed tradition with a known degree of variation to which oral texts may be compared. On the basis of their investigation they are able to propose a printing history and to outline a Belfast tradition.

Anthony Buckley, too, in dealing with Orange and masonic ritual, is conscious of Alan Gailey's work on Irish folk drama as he sets out to study the rites involved. Secrecy, he notes, is found in both drama and ritual; and to consider the nature of ritual from the viewpoint of the anthropologist, he introduces a novel theme by comparing ritual and theatrical forms of drama, using Spielberg's adventure film *Raiders of the Lost Ark* to exemplify the latter.

One field of study which has become popular during the last two decades is the ethnology of food. The universal tendency throughout Europe to abandon traditional diets and meal-times in favour of fast food and so-called TV dinners has awakened a keen interest in the historical background. Alexander Fenton views the changes in attitudes to food which have taken place in Scotland over 300 years. The seasonality of supply and the 'spring hunger' known in most European peasant societies have now been virtually eliminated by the ready availability of food from all parts of the world throughout the year. This state of affairs was preceded by the introduction of new crops, notably the potato, and by increased productivity which minimised the periodical years of scarcity which too often resulted in famine. The growing awareness of health considerations in food consumption and the increasing possibility of conscious choice, for the first time in the experience of the bulk of the population, brought about a uniformity of diet related not to local tradition and supplies but to the operation of a world-wide market.

Whereas Alexander Fenton takes the whole of Scotland into his purview in discussing long term changes in diet, Patricia Lysaght goes to the other extreme and selects a well documented small community, living on the now deserted Great Blasket Island. It is still possible to study in considerable detail the provision of food through land-based activities based on livestock and tillage and supplemented by hunting and gathering, as frequently happened in peasant communities. The consideration of sea-based sources of food in this island community, is the subject of another paper shortly to be published. Between the two essays we shall have a balanced view of a food economy based almost entirely on local resources. Dr Lysaght prefaces her treatment of the subject in the present volume with an account of the harsh island environment and the once stable social organisation of its former inhabitants, enabling the reader to see the economic activity on the land in its true perspective, and the provision of a constant supply of food as its main concern.

In her essay Dr Venetia Newall deals with Shetland, another island culture and economy prone to much greater outside influence than the Great Blasket. Because of its strategic geographical location and its accessibility to the North Sea trade routes used by Hanseatic merchants, not to mention its abundant fishing grounds, Shetland has, over the centuries, attracted the attention of rival interests. Dr Newall looks specifically at the influence the Dutch, relatively late-comers on the scene who came to fish for herring in the summer months and engaged in trade with the islanders. By the middle of the sixteenth century up to 2000 Dutch boats were involved in this lucrative commerce. After a period of decline the Dutch herring trade revived in the second half of the nineteenth century before ceasing after the First World War. At one time, indeed, the entire population of Lerwick could speak Dutch. Dr Newall examines the evidence for Dutch influence on the culture of Shetland as revealed by such diverse features as its architecture, its sword dance, lace-knitting designs, place-names and dialect.

Nearer home, cross-channel links across the Irish Sea are the subject of Michael McCaughan's essay dealing with early steamship enterprise in the first half of the nineteenth century when traffic with Liverpool became increasingly important. Mr McCaughan examines the technological and financial considerations involved in the development of what became a regular service operating to fixed timetables. This he follows with a detailed study of one of the steam-boat companies founded, as he put it, 'on a national wave of steamship mania' to take advantage of what could have proved a lucrative enterprise. Alas, the County of Down and Liverpool Steam-Boat Company collapsed after only three years, and its pride, the steamship *Victoria*, sailing under new ownership, foundered off the Isle of Man three years later.

This final essay reminds us of the important place of maritime life in the Ulster Folk and Transport Museum as it exists today. Alan Gailey's invaluable contribution to the development of the museum, building on the success of his predecessor, has been matched by his wide-ranging publications in the field of folk life studies. The essays presented in this volume reflect both the breadth and depth of his scholarship and the high regard in which he is held by his colleagues in this field.

1

The Road to Ballycultra

G.B. Thompson

In Northern Ireland the year 1960 saw not only the dawn of a new decade but in the annals of the Ulster Folk and Transport Museum it was the year that Alan Gailey, fresh from gaining his doctorate at the University of Glasgow, became the museum's first curatorial appointee and was, in time, to become its second director and its longest-serving member of staff.

Two years earlier, with the passing of the Ulster Folk Museum Act by the government of Northern Ireland, a long-standing dream was about to become a reality. The board of twenty trustees established by the Act, representative of central and local government and the Queen's University of Belfast, and headed by its first chairman, Alderman Robin Kinahan, appointed the museum's first director, George B. Thompson, in January 1959. Though coming from a curatorial post in the Belfast Museum and Art Gallery, he assumed a role that was to remain essentially administrative and thus the appointment of a colleague to take responsibility for initiating a programme of research and collection was paramount.

Alan Gailey took up duties as the museum's tentatively-named research officer on 1 October 1960. Having, like George Thompson, studied for his primary degree in the the School of Geography at the Queen's University of Belfast, created and headed by Professor Estyn Evans, Alan was already familiar with, and knowledgeable in, local folk-life study. His academic mentor was, in an Irish context, a pioneer in the field, and those of his students with the requisite interest and aptitude inevitably became disciples. A fortunate few, of whom Alan is one, were to be offered, with the establishment of the Ulster Folk Museum, an opportunity to translate discipleship into full-time careers.

As a foundation member of staff, Alan was prominently involved in the formulation of the policy by which the museum was to develop and function, and he merits a substantial share of the credit for the successes sub-

sequently yielded by the policy's implementation. However, if the Ulster
Folk Museum Act of 1958 and the start of Alan's career in 1960 represented a beginning, it also saw the culmination of a long, often difficult and
frustrating, period of planning and promotion. As the title of this paper
indicates, it was a period which could be likened to a journey begun over
half a century ago, a journey involving the negotiation of many difficulties
and obstacles along the way, but ending at last in the townland of
Ballycultra in north County Down. In 1960 Alan became a fellow wayfar-
er and it is appropriate, therefore, in a volume commemorating his career,
to document a brief review of the events and circumstances which
spawned the institution wherein that career was pursued.

While today one cannot be precise as to how and when the idea of a
folk museum in Northern Ireland evolved, there can be little doubt that
two events in the late 1920s were of major significance.

In 1928 the Queen's University of Belfast appointed Emyr Estyn Evans,
a graduate of the University College of Wales in Aberystwyth and a
scholar of exceptional ability and vision, as its first lecturer in Geography.
The following year the first section of a new building for the Belfast
Museum and Art Gallery, neighbouring the university, was opened to the
public. These two events, appearing at first to be unconnected, were destined, in the decade which followed, to become increasingly related, and
one consequence was the emergence of plans for a folk museum in
Northern Ireland.

At Aberystwyth, Evans studied under Professor H.J. Fleure, the first
holder of the chair of Geography and Anthropology, established in 1917. It
was reflective, therefore, of Fleure's tuition that in coming to Ireland Estyn
Evans recognised a fertile field for the comprehensive study of habitat and
heritage, and applied himself to investigating it by field observation and
archaeological excavation to such effect that he gained an unparalleled
knowledge and understanding of Ireland's personality. In the years
leading from his arrival at Queen's University to the outbreak of the
Second World War he was well on his way to laying the foundations of
geographical, archaeological and folk studies in Northern Ireland and to
become, inevitably, a leading proponent of the proposal to establish a folk
museum in the Province.

With the opening of the new Belfast Museum and Art Gallery in 1929 a
resultant updated statement of policy identified ethnology as a special
field. It seems reasonable to assume that while there was no specific reference to a folk museum the idea was already in mind, for some years later,
when presumably the work of commissioning a new building had been
mostly completed, the deputy curator, Sidney Stendall, travelled to
Scandinavia to study established folk museums.

The outbreak of the Second World War in 1939 prohibited immediate
progress, though in 1942 Sidney Stendall, having now succeeded Arthur
Deane as curator of Belfast Museum and Art Gallery, produced a new

policy document for post-war implementation. This document noted for the first time the creation of a folk museum as a major objective, and in Estyn Evans, already familiar with Scandinavian prototypes through having seen them at first hand, Stendall had an enthusiastic and influential co-advocate.

Notwithstanding the predominance of war news the folk museum proposal caught the attention of the local press and in a letter to the editor of the *Belfast News-Letter*, penned on 17 November 1942, Estyn Evans sought to heighten folk, journalistic and public interest. He wrote:

An Open-Air Museum

Sir: May I draw public attention to the importance of the news items which have appeared in the Belfast papers recently regarding proposals to establish an open-air museum in the city?

Those who have seen, in happier days, the folk museums of Copenhagen, Oslo and Stockholm will understand the remarkable interest they have aroused among the peoples of Scandinavia, and the part they have played in the cultural and artistic life of the northern nations. It is significant that the museum movement went hand in hand with the reconstruction of rural life, and if Northern Ireland would seek to emulate the achievements in agricultural reorganisation which have given the Scandinavian countries their high place among the nations of the world, it cannot afford to neglect the cultural and traditional aspects of national life. One might go further and say that to attempt to copy the results without understanding the methods would be to court disaster.

The amount of material available for assembly in an open-air museum is abundant, but in a few years' time the opportunities may have passed. From the educational point of view, the importance of the folk museum needs no emphasis, but it might be pointed out that the inherent attractiveness of a well laid out site would result in a popularity similar to that of an open-air zoo. Finally, it is obvious that the open-air display should be developed in association with the admirable indoor collection of the Municipal Museum at Stranmillis.

Yours etc., E. Estyn Evans

In the pre-war years, the more Estyn Evans came to know the Province's cultural landscape through extensive field observation and archaeological excavation, the more concerned he became about the almost complete neglect of Irish studies at Queen's University. It was a discrepancy emphasised by the fact that the Irish Folklore Commission in Dublin, established in 1935 by Professor Seamus Delargy, was already on its way to gaining international recognition. So, in 1939, Estyn Evans and several associates, including George Paterson, curator and virtual founder of the Armagh County Museum, applied, via the Queen's University vice-chancellor, to the Senate for support to initiate folklife study at Queen's and to provide facilities for archival storage. However, with war clouds gathering, the

Senate felt able to make only a token gesture of approval by way of an annual grant of £25 for a five-year period. The resultant disappointment provoked an appeal to central government through Dame Dehra Parker, Parliamentary Secretary to the Minister of Education. She relayed the appeal to J.M. Andrews, the Minister of Finance who, in turn, brought the appeal to the notice of Lord Craigavon, the Prime Minister, but by now war had been declared, and consequently the government response was limited to an indication of willingness to consider the appeal more fully when hostilities had ended.

The return to peacetime normality after 1945 was gradual rather than immediate; wartime constraints and material shortages lingered on. Nevertheless, in September 1945, Sidney Stendall re-submitted to the Libraries, Museums and Art Committee of Belfast City Council his 1942 post-war development plan. This included the creation of a new Department of Antiquities and Ethnography and the appointment of a departmental keeper whose duties would include the development of plans for a folk museum.

Progress towards setting up the new department was inevitably conditioned by the procedures and pace by which the city's bureaucratic machine functioned, and three years were to pass before the department was established with a keeper in post. Significantly, the appointee – the author of this paper – was a graduate fresh from Evans's School of Geography, at Queen's.

In the interim, negotiations with the Transport Committee of the City Council succeeded in ear-marking a site for the proposed folk museum in the Belfast Castle estate. This comprised an area of five acres including the castle's former stable buildings.

Like all good executives, Sidney Stendall recognised a likely opportunity when he saw one, and was poised to take advantage of any that might arise. Thus, in 1949, he felt that an outstanding chance to advance his plans had come his way when he was invited by the Ministry of Education to assist a sub-committee formed in connection with the Festival of Britain to be held in 1951. The Festival was to be a nationwide celebration of British victories and achievements, a means of shaking off post-war doldrums, and a focusing of the nation's gaze towards a bright new future. Stendall's proposal, therefore, that the development of the folk museum be adopted as the Libraries, Museums and Art Committee's contribution to the Festival was approved in January 1950.

By today's standards the statistics by which Stendall supported his proposal appear modest in the extreme. Capital and running costs for the twenty-five weeks of the Festival were assessed at £6174, which would be off-set by an estimated income of £1100 coming from visitors averaging 250 per day, paying an admission charge of 6 pence (2.5p) a head and purchasing guide books! Nevertheless, these estimates appear to have caused some concern and gave rise to speculation about the possibility of finding financial assistance from other quarters. Significantly, the local authorities beyond Belfast were seen as likely sources both of objects of interest and grants-in-aid. Even more significantly, the minutes of a meeting in August 1950 of the Libraries, Museums and Art Committee record a suggestion that since the proposed folk museum 'would illustrate the way of life and folklore of the people of Northern Ireland and would be in the nature of a state museum', the cost of its establishment should not fall entirely on the city. Here, then, was a new perspective which, if more reflective of civic economy than imaginative reappraisal, was eventually to have a funda-mental influence on the future progress of the folk museum plan. Furthermore, the minuted definition of the museum's function was to prove later to have been a remarkably accurate forecast of the function as defined in the 1958 Ulster Folk Museum Act.

However, other factors were to have a more immediate effect on Sidney Stendall's proposal. A folk museum centred on the stable buildings at Belfast Castle involved structural alterations, and under General Defence Regulations, still in force in the war's aftermath, the use of building mate-rials required government authorisation. Consequently a request for approval was denied, since materials, steel in particular, were still in short supply, and so the emergence of a folk museum as a Festival of Britain feature fell victim to post-war constraints.

In the history of the folk museum project, the year 1951 proved to be a major watershed. First, the Keeper of Antiquities and Ethnography was given leave to follow in the footsteps of Estyn Evans and Sidney Stendall and travel to Scandinavia to observe folk museums at first hand. It was an experience which not only strengthened his enthusiasm for the concept but convinced him that the proposed Belfast Castle site was seriously inadequate and that if the folk museum advocates could be persuaded to reassess spatial requirements, deferment, if not abandonment, of develop-ment at the castle site would be a blessing in disguise. Furthermore, in 1951 Belfast was to host the Annual Conference of the Museums Association, and the following year was to see the welcome return to the city, after an interval of 50 years, of the British Association for the Advancement of Science. Inevitably preparations for these events resulted in the folk museum project being kept in cold storage, and with Sidney Stendall's retirement at the end of 1952, hopes of unfreezing it seemed to be dashed indefinitely. However, with the arrival in 1953 of Stendall's suc-cessor, W.A. Seaby, pessimism was to give way to renewed optimism sooner than expected. Like his predecessor, Bill Seaby had also visited Scandinavia and was, therefore, already inspired by the folk museum format. Soon after his arrival in Belfast he sought to inject new life into the local project, and with characteristic energy and enthusiasm, initiated what was to become the final promotional phase.

The five-acre site at Belfast Castle was still seen as the location for the folk museum, and a revision of cost estimates prompted an application to the Northern Ireland Tourist Board towards an anticipated expenditure of £10,500. However, the Ministry of Commerce, responsible for Tourist Board affairs, felt that folk museum development fell beyond the provisions of the Tourist Traffic Act, and suggested as an alternative that an approach be made to the Ministry of Finance for funding from a new post-war source, the Ulster Land Fund.

The Land Fund had been established in 1948 with capital of £1 million. Its function included the payment of death duties where the government had accepted property in lieu of money. Furthermore, it would provide for the acquisition of land, buildings and chattels to preserve or improve the natural beauty or amenities of an area – the flora, fauna, geological, architectural or other scientific or historical features. The implementation of Fund objectives could result from direct government action or by grant-aiding other approved bodies.

Meanwhile, Dame Dehra Parker, now a government minister, had not forgotten the pre-war overture made to her regarding the development of folklife study in Northern Ireland. Consequently, she wrote to Estyn Evans to suggest that since, in 1939, the government had indicated a willingness to re-consider the matter after the war, the time had come to try again.

To provide for a more structured and consolidated promotion and expansion of public interest in folklife study, and to give added support to the folk museum proposal, a group of leading proponents came together in 1953 to form the Committee on Ulster Folklife and Traditions under the chairmanship of Estyn Evans. Foundation members included Dame Dehra Parker and Dr Brian Maginess, whose later appointment as Minister of Finance, while depriving the committee all too soon of his membership, provided it with an interested and sympathetic ally at ministerial level.

As Minister of Finance, Dr Maginess funded the Committee on Ulster Folklife and Traditions with a grant spread over four years. Though of more modest size than the committee would have wished, the grant provided for the appointment of a field officer, Mrs Katherine Harris, and, in 1955, for the launch of the annual publication *Ulster Folklife* under the editorship of R.H. Buchanan. The committee also achieved a considerable expansion of public interest, and, at the same time, amassed a substantial amount of archival material through building up a Province-wide body of voluntary collectors and correspondents. Though the committee as such ceased to exist in 1961, happily it was immediately reborn as the Ulster Folklife Society.

While corporate responsibility for folk museum development was still centred in Belfast City Hall, the eyes of its advocates were becoming increasingly directed towards central government. So, in 1953, a deputation from the Libraries, Museums and Art Committee sought and were granted a meeting with the Minister of Finance, Dr Maginess. A proposal was submitted to him that the folk museum should be regarded as a national rather than a municipal development, but within the context of a

Northern Ireland national museum.

The deputation succeeded in their mission to the extent that in March 1954 the minister appointed a committee under the chairmanship of Sir Roland Nugent to consider and report on the feasibility of establishing a folk museum in Northern Ireland. The committee comprised seven members representative of central and local government and the Queen's University. Not surprisingly, the university's nominee was Estyn Evans. Bill Seaby, though not a committee member, was, nevertheless, called upon for specialist advice.

The Committee's Report reached the minister five months later and included a somewhat pointed reference to the likelihood of a folk museum being established in the Republic of Ireland, coupled with a warning that such a development could accelerate the process by which objects of interest and significance to all those who valued Ulster's past could pass into the ownership of people and institutions outside Northern Ireland – a forecast probably aimed at Unionist sensibilities!

The Nugent Committee Report was, on the whole, a commendable document endorsing not only central and local government funding, but also emphasising the folk museum's educational potential. However, it still envisaged the Belfast Castle site as the most favourable location. Furthermore, the folk museum's curator would be subject to the control and supervision of the director of the Belfast Museum and Art Gallery. This watered-down concept of national status, together with adherence to the Belfast Castle site was, eventually, to become something of a stumbling block. However the report was favourably received by the minister who submitted it to the Cabinet in October 1954, with an added memorandum recommending the preparation of legislation to set up an authority responsible for establishing a folk museum on a national basis. He advocated that central government should make available to the authority a capital grant of £20,000 from the Ulster Land Fund and an annual grant of £2000 from general resources.

While at last the establishment of a folk museum seemed to be simply a matter of time, and the willingness of the Cabinet to sanction a commitment augured well for eventual parliamentary approval, the very important question yet remained as to whether or not local authority reaction would be favourable. Traditional reservation elsewhere in the Province about Belfast seemingly monopolising new developments could well give rise to opposition. Furthermore, as George Paterson of Armagh County Museum astutely observed in a letter to Estyn Evans, it would be very inadvisable to progress the folk museum proposal too far ahead of local authority opinion, thereby coming belatedly to seek financial support for what might be seen as a *fait accompli*. George Paterson also voiced strong reservations about the suitability of the Belfast Castle site in terms both of location and size. He was well tuned-in to local opinion and his warning should have been taken seriously. Instead it appears to have gone unheeded in certain quarters and his prediction came perilously close to coming true.

In an almost ill-fated attempt to win local authority support an invitation was issued by the Libraries, Museums and Art Committee to representatives from across the Province to a meeting in Belfast City Hall in November 1955. The fifty-seven individuals who attended, instead of being wooed by a persuasive submission, were asked to agree to a predetermined decision to form a Folk Museum Association whose president, vice-president and council members had already been identified. It was a serious misjudgement of the Ulster personality, causing resentment by which the folk museum project could have suffered a major setback. Fortunately there were those present whose initial hostile reaction gave way to constructive thought and, in rejecting the suggested association, the assembly agreed to setting up an advisory committee with a stronger and more broadly-based local authority presence. The committee's task was to consider yet again the folk museum proposal as a joint central government, local authority, undertaking, and to envisage its development on a scale more commensurate with the rich content of the folklife it was to illustrate. Any remaining ruffled fur at the City Hall meeting was later unruffled when, at the concluding dinner hosted by the Lord Mayor, the Minister of Finance proposed the toast 'the future success of the folk museum' and publicly confirmed central government support.

The members of the advisory committee soon got to work with a commendable sense of purpose and with a welcome determination to conceive the folk museum on a much larger scale than hitherto. Since it was intended that their conclusions and recommendations would be submitted to central government for legislative endorsement, their deliberations benefited greatly from having on hand the advice of a very capable and influential senior civil servant, Kenneth Bloomfield who, in 1954 had been secretary to the Nugent Committee. Thus he was already a knowledgeable and committed folk museum proponent whose abilities were to see him become later in his career Sir Kenneth Bloomfield, Head of the Northern Ireland Civil Service.

Such was the advisory committee's wish to see the development of the folk museum expedited, that within a week of its foundation it was considering a memorandum prepared by one of its most enthusiastic members, T.B. Graham, Town Clerk of Bangor. Among its proposals was that the museum site should be sixty to eighty acres in extent, that capital cost would be of the order of £120,000, and that local authority input towards recurrent expenditure could initially and realistically be fixed at the produce of 1⁄4d in the £1 of net annual value.

In less than two months the advisory committee's conclusions had been crystallised to the extent that in January 1956 Kenneth Bloomfield was able to submit to it draft legislation which, with little alteration, was to become passed as the Ulster Folk Museum Act by the Parliament of

Northern Ireland in 1958.

The unfortunate two-year delay between first draft and final legislation was caused by the finance portfolio changing hands twice in fairly quick succession. While it would have been fitting if Dr Brian Maginess, still Minister of Finance in 1956, and the man who had already persuaded the Cabinet to accept the project in principle, had been able to steer folk museum legislation through to the statute book, his transfer to the Attorney Generalship precluded it. His successor, George B. Hanna, was Minister of Finance for less than a year, and so the responsibility for submitting the Folk Museum Bill to parliament fell to the new minister, Terence O'Neill.

The 1958 Ulster Folk Museum Act placed the development of the museum with a board of trustees, twenty in number, under the chairmanship of Alderman Robin Kinahan, later Sir Robin Kinahan. Five members, including the chairman, were appointed by the Minister of Finance, three were appointed by each of the three local authority associations – county, municipal and rural. Belfast City Council, because of its long involvement with the project and the special part it played in its promotion, was allocated four trusteeships. The Province's second city, Londonderry, appointed one trustee, as did the Queen's University which, not surprisingly, nominated Estyn Evans.

The act envisaged a capital expenditure, including site purchase, of £80,000, a third less than the amount suggested by the advisory committee. Half the capital would come as a grant from the Ulster Land Fund, the remainder to be raised on loan. As proposed by the Advisory Committee, local government throughout the Province would, collectively, contribute annually the product of 1/4d in the £1 of rateable value, to add to the fixed annual grant of £3000 from central government.

The trustees met for the first time on 30 October 1958 at Chichester House in Belfast. By January 1959 they had appointed a director, G.B. Thompson, who took up duties the following April. Attention then turned to selecting and purchasing a site. It was assumed, somewhat naively as it turned out, that this would be achieved in, at most, a few months. It was generally accepted that, as in other countries, the museum should be located close to the main centre of population, and the southern outskirts of Belfast seemed, strategically and environmentally, the most favourable area. Unfortunately the cost of land there was already at a level whereby the purchase of sixty to eighty acres was beyond the museum's entire capital resources. Thus, the search for a suitable site at an affordable price came to extend over a wider area and was to last for two-and-a-half anxious and frustrating years.

Meanwhile, in the absence of a permanent home, and with little by way of material possessions, it could be said that, initially, the folk museum existed wherever the chairman, trustees and director happened to be. The director started work in April 1959 as a subtenant in part of a fourth-floor office in downtown Belfast. His periodic meetings with the chairman, Robin Kinahan, were in any of the offices which he, a prominent businessman, occupied in the course of his several company chairmanships. During his term of office as Lord Mayor of Belfast, trustee meetings were held in the splendour of the Lord Mayor's parlour.

Primary staff appointments eventually necessitated a move from the fourth-floor office in the centre of Belfast, to a rented, unfurnished terrace house at 53 University Street. It was there that in 1960 Alan Gailey began his museum career and it was there that news arrived of a possible site, Cultra Manor, being offered for sale in north County Down, overlooking Belfast Lough, and a modest eight miles from Belfast. An initial discreet visit revealed Cultra Manor to be an estate of 132 acres surrounding a large Edwardian house whose formal setting was encircled by an outer perimeter of undulating pasture-land. It was as close as one could hope to being ideal for folk museum development. Furthermore, an overture to the estate agency handling the sale disclosed an asking price comfortably within the museum's resources. Consequently, in December 1960, the trustees unanimously agreed to purchase Cultra Manor. However, with a final destination in sight it seemed that problems were not wholly at an end and that the last stretch of the journey was to prove more time-consuming than anticipated with negotiations for the purchase becoming more difficult and prolonged than anticipated. Nevertheless the trustees' determination was such that in March 1961 the purchase was completed. The embryo Ulster Folk Museum had, at last, a permanent home wherein structural and functional development could begin.

The journey embarked on so long before by the museum's founding fathers, notably Estyn Evans and Sidney Stendall, was infinitely longer and more full of incident than they could possibly have envisaged at the outset. In its later stages, when the original destination at Belfast Castle had been superseded by later developments, the journey was diverted to become something of a mystery tour, and the mystery as to where it would end was to remain unresolved beyond the museum's formal establishment in 1958. However, with the purchase of Cultra Manor the final destination became known, and good fortune decreed that those who first conceived and advocated a folk museum for Northern Ireland survived to see it not only established but permanently located.

Although Sidney Stendall, an Englishman, returned to England when he retired in 1952, at least once a year he re-visited the city where he spent forty-two years of his working life in Belfast Museum and Art Gallery, progressing from assistant curator in 1910 to director in 1942. Thus, he lived to see his cherished folk museum project become a reality, to see the Keeper of Antiquities and Ethnography, whose post he had created in 1949, become the museum's first director, and to put his stamp of approval on the Cultra Manor site.

Estyn Evans became a foundation trustee, having been nominated as the Queen's University's representative. In 1968 he succeeded Sir Robin Kinahan as board chairman, a position he occupied with characteristic distinction for the next six years. George Paterson, whose innate reserve made him less prominent as one of the folk museum's original proponents, was nonetheless an influential force in its promotion and it was fitting that he, too, became a foundation trustee.

Bill Seaby's trusteeship was not to last throughout his time in Belfast, due presumably to increased professional demands following the nationalisation of the Belfast Museum and Art Gallery which became the Ulster Museum by act of parliament in 1961. However, it should be acknowledged that the establishment of the Ulster Folk Museum owes much to his initiative in reviving a dormant, if not moribund project, following his arrival in Belfast in 1953.

While the purchase of Cultra Manor meant that in a figurative sense these pioneers had completed the journey that was to lead to Ballycultra, the folk museum's small staff, by now seven in number, had yet, literally, to travel the last few miles to become occupants of their permanent headquarters. Alterations were first necessary to convert Cultra Manor from domestic to institutional use. However, the resultant delay offered none of the frustrations of earlier interruptions, since the disconcerting element of uncertainty had now been eliminated. So, in 1963, the small group of museum personnel transferred themselves from Belfast to Ballycultra, and basic development work began in earnest. It could be said, therefore, that the end of one demanding journey initiated the beginning of yet another involving the no less demanding task of converting an objective, so long and so determinedly pursued, into a structural and functional reality.

2

Some Notions of Folklore, History and Museum Interpretation: A Time for Reappraisal?

MEGAN MCMANUS

THE ULSTER FOLK AND TRANSPORT MUSEUM, now part of the National Museums and Galleries of Northern Ireland, is a major open-air museum and a major local resource for the community, and was established in 1958. Although furnished to represent a set date of around 1900, and despite the later addition of a transport gallery, the museum had its roots in the discipline of folklife. Estyn Evans was a prime mover not only behind the establishment of the Ulster Folk Museum, but also the Ulster Folklife Society and the journal, *Ulster Folklife*. These achievements make him the single most influential figure in folklife in Ulster. Because of his importance in setting the pattern for the museum and for later scholars, it is worth examining his work, the development of his ideas and his methods, and the implications of these for the development of folklife in Ulster and its interpretation within the museum. The paper looks particularly at the representation of trades and crafts.

Evans's background has been described well elsewhere but a short summary may be helpful. Emyr Estyn Evans was born in Shrewsbury in 1905. In 1922, he went to the University College of Wales at Aberystwyth to study geography and anthropology under Professor H.J. Fleure and graduated in 1925. Sir John Myres of Oxford offered Evans a place for postgraduate work in archaeology. However, Evans had developed lung problems and after attending a sanatorium near Ironbridge, he convalesced in Wiltshire with Dr R.C.C. Clay, who was a keen amateur archaeologist. Evans came to Ireland in September 1928 to take charge of the new Department of Geography at Queen's University of Belfast.

In 1931 Evans was awarded a distinction for his MA thesis entitled 'Some late Bronze Age industries in Western Europe'. Estyn went on to revive the Ulster Journal of Archaeology, and until 1948 this was issued from his department. He also started work on his first major book. By 1955 Estyn had established the journal, *Ulster Folklife*, and then worked towards the establishment of the Ulster Folk and Transport Museum. In 1960 he went on to create an Anthropology Department at Queen's University in Belfast.[1]

Irish Heritage – the first major book on folklife – was published in 1943, and was followed by a series of articles. In 1952 he published Mourne Country, and in 1957, there followed another major contribution to folklife in the form of a book, *Irish Folk Ways*. However, Evans presents the most clearly codified statement of his perspectives in 1973, when The Personality of Ireland was published, the result of the Wiles lectures at the Queen's University of Belfast.

A large proportion of Evans's work is clearly in the field of archaeology, but he describes himself as an anthropogeographer in the style of Carl O. Sauer and H.J. Fleure.[2] It is important that we understand what this means since the connotations of the word anthropogeographer have changed. Fleure, like Evans, was a charismatic teacher. He has been described as a zoologist by training, who had subsequently turned to anthropology, pioneering the study of human physical types in England and Wales.[3] However, Glyn Daniel describes both Fleure and Evans as important figures in the establishment of distributional and ecological studies in archaeology. Daniel sees this development as one of the key advances in archaeological technique made between 1900 and 1950. He points out that, prior to this, archaeologists had regarded antiquities as art or commonplace objects and that there was no attempt to study find spots in their geographical and ecological relationships, nor to map the distribution pattern of a type of antiquity or all the antiquities of a period.[4]

Sauer spells out the work of the anthropogeographer clearly. He states that a geographer must be aware of the dependence of life on the physical environment, of ecology and the relationship of this to the spatial distribution of arts and artefacts. This will explain their history.[5] The key questions of the anthropogeographer of the time are: How are associations of particular artefacts distributed spatially? What was the nature of the environment in which these distributions were placed? What does the interrelationship between these factors tell us about the long past?

Evans, the archaeologist and anthropogeographer, was also, like many academics of the period, influenced by the ideas of Darwin and by anthropologists who drew on the work of Darwin. One key concept, which is very influential in Evans's work, is the idea of survivals developed by Taylor in his book *Primitive Culture*, namely that characteristics which do not appear to fit in the present are survivals from a distant past.[6] This leads to the assumption that looking for survivals in the present can unravel the prehistory or history of people. Evans frequently indicates that for him Irish culture is of particular value because it is a repository of survivals from previous eras. For example he states:

Yet this Ireland is not only a treasure house of old ways, unrivalled in Western Europe but a working culture of the highest scientific interest.[7]

For Ireland has preserved to a remarkable degree the customs and social habits of the pre-industrial phase of western civilisation.[8]

The outstanding interest of Ireland for the student of European origins lies in the fact that in its historic literature, language and social organisation, as well as in its folklore and folk customs, it illustrates the marginal survival of archaic elements of the Indo-European world.[9]

Evans's concern with survivals has two other corollaries. The first is that he views Ireland as a peasant society. In 1942 he states, 'In essentials Ireland is and has been a peasant society'.[10] It is part of the Atlantic culture of the European oceanic fringe and as such essentially pastoral in nature. The importance and significance of this is restated in 1957 when he writes:

> The retention of many of the attributes of a peasant society is the key to the survival of the folk ways with which we are concerned in the following chapters. Even the Great Famine, which marks a grim watershed in social and economic history, did not entirely obliterate them, though it had far reaching effects that it might be regarded as the end of prehistoric times in Ireland.[11]

Evans outlines the characteristics of the peasant society as a society which is first and foremost concerned with the maintenance and continuity of society. Peasant societies place special value on blood ties in extended family groups. Peasant families are large. Childbearing is part of the ritual seen as necessary for success with stock and crops, and barrenness in wives is regarded as unnatural and disgraceful.[12] Peasant societies are only to a limited extent drawn into the world of money; they have a permanent link with the soil, periodic gatherings for exchange and social intercourse, and seasonal festivals celebrating major points in the agricultural cycle are important.[13]

Evans also regards the practice of sympathetic magic as important in peasant societies. This idea, taken from the early anthropologist, J.G. Frazer, is defined as the symbolic carrying out of certain deeds in order to promote success in another field. It is based on his law of similarity and the idea that an effect resembles a cause, and that an effect can be produced by imitating it.[14] Evans uses this concept to explain the importance of childbearing in women.

The second corollary follows from the first, namely that his area of interest is mainly rural. Like Fleure, Evans regards isolated rural communities as poor in material resources, and placing their efforts in poetry and oratory and song – arts in which the poorest labourer can often compete on fairly even terms with his richer neighbour – rather than great buildings, sculpture or orchestral music, which demanded large equipment.[15]

Evans's concern with the everyday, with very broad sweeps of time and his acknowledgement of the unwritten record of the past, dovetailed well with the developing discipline of folklore. In 1846 the English folk-lorists had adopted the definition of the subject put forward by William Thoms, emphasising 'the traditional beliefs, legends and customs current among the common people' and 'the manners, customs, observances, superstitions, ballads, proverbs etc of the olden time'.[16] Early folklorists focused on non-material culture, mainly story and legend. In 1955 folklore was defined by the Arnhem conference as the spiritual tradition of the folk, particularly oral tradition. However, from the 1940s many scholars took the view that the definition needed to be widened in order to include material culture. Scholars began to use the term folklife to mean all ele-ments of traditional life, including the oral element of folklore.[17]

As with the content, Evans's work on method also reflects his roots in archaeology and anthropogeography. He pleads for a study of human experience chorologically, chronologically and typologically.[18] He asks too for a trilogy of regional studies based on habitat, heritage and history. Habitat is defined as the total physical environment. Here Evans eschews the growth of statistical method in geography as being applicable only to short time-spans and incapable of illuminating the most precious elements of culture. Heritage is defined as man's cultural inheritance from a prehis-toric past, his oral traditions, beliefs, languages, arts and crafts.[19] This is a definition similar to that used by anthropologists for culture. The impor-tant differences are that anthropologists would include items such as cus-toms and norms but not the notion that cultural characteristics are inher-ited from a prehistoric past.

History is defined as the written record of the time. Evans's attitude to history is a product of the period in which he worked. Historians are crit-icised for studying elites. They have been slow to break away from the study of parliament and constitution. They attach little importance to the archaeological record. The story they tell is blurred by the prejudices of the men who write it. Historians have focused on political relations between England and Ireland, economic distress and religious cleavage.[20] In *Irish Folk Ways* Evans remarks that the fact of something being described in the eighteenth century is more important to the historian than its presence in the twentieth. This is a comment on the paucity of the historical methods of the time.

Very little is said about the method needed for his trilogy of studies. However, what he does advocate are two methods which were critical to the development of archaeology, that is the geographical mapping of the distribution of typed cultural features and the importance of field obser-vation. Evans states that he has studied techniques for using tools and that, by assisting, he has learnt more than books can teach; he is on the whole advocating a field study approach generated in archaeology. He is not, at this stage, advocating the field survey techniques of the sociologist or the participant approach of the anthropologist. Evans writes:

Our knowledge of the Irish countryside will advance only through field-study and the mapping of our findings. The time has not yet come when one can prepare maps of cultural distributions, but this is the end in view... We need maps of house-types and styles of furniture, of farm implements and the lay out of fields and fences, of boat-types, of dialects and superstitions, and so on; and we must study these distributions both against the physical and spiritual environment of Ireland and against the wider background of their overseas connections.[21]

Evans's selection of content is entirely consistent with his theoretical perspectives. The topics relate to the rural and to the everyday. Studies are placed against the backdrop of geology, geography and prehistory. Specific elements are singled out. Material elements include the house – in particular the distribution of the central and gable hearth, types of thatch and hearth furniture. There is work on farm buildings and fences, cars and carts, spades and ploughs and home-made things. The emphasis is on the material item as a form rather than the result of a process. In fact, Evans comments that the archaeologist Gordon Childe has a near Marxist insistence on the significance of technological and economic change. In *Irish Folk Ways* the construction of churns is described and a distribution map of churn types given. Bread sticks are presented as an evolutionary sequence. Bread irons are shown to illustrate regional types. He does consider the blacksmith, but separately. The blacksmith is important to Evans as a maker of edge tools. He points to the forge as a gathering place, to the blacksmith as a focus of magical activity and to his social importance rather than as a maker of bread irons. In fact, we know that blacksmiths rarely made edge tools from the eighteenth century; we know that in the nineteenth century two-thirds of a country smith's work was in horse-shoeing and the rest in the repair of agricultural equipment and the making of gates. These are items that became accessible and necessary after wrought iron became cheap in the 1840s and roads acquired hard surfaces. It is earlier that the blacksmith worked with an expensive and comparatively scarce raw material. Basket makers are described as concentrated around Lough Neagh and in the Suir Valley. The role of the Industrial Workshops for the Blind in training these craftsmen is outside the scope of the study as is the long established relationship of rural basket makers with city dealers. The spade is singled out for attention because of the huge variety of regional forms. The shovel, a more standard implement, and one which frequently provided a viable economic context for spade production, is not. In agriculture, Evans singles out harvest and seedtime as well as ploughs and spades. He also deals with non-material culture. Festivals and fairs, customs and beliefs are singled out.

The influence of Evans on folklife can be seen in the early volumes of the journal, *Ulster Folklife*. There are articles on beliefs and customs, techniques and the distribution of house types. As Buchanan points out, in its first decade, *Ulster Folklife* published articles on community life and lore, folk medicine, time and seasons, myths and popular oral literature. Only in the fields of human life, recreation and historical and religious tradition were there none.[22]

Evans's great contribution is that he enabled us to look at the world of the everyday around us. He made us aware of its value. The rural focus and the context of a huge sweep of time mean that we were able to do this freed from the clutter of conflict, the horror of famine, notions about the recent past or ideas such as nostalgia for a Celtic world. The question was not, 'What is the present?' Or, 'What was a short period of the past like?' The question was, 'What does the present tell us about the long distant past?' Evans's work also imbues a sense of the aesthetic. Perhaps his greatest contribution in the future will be his interdisciplinary approach. We must remember, too, that in his ability to adopt radical notions about concept and method in archaeology he was a forward thinker. This is what we must learn from.

The years between 1928 (when Evans came to Northern Ireland) and 1958 (when the Ulster Folk and Transport Museum was founded) were dynamic for the social sciences in general. Anthropologists rejected the evolutionist view. They began to look at the local as well as the exotic. They began to explore the use of empirical method and participant observation. The question of how to explain human behaviour became more important than charting the exotic or establishing sequences. Sociologists formulated new techniques for approaching the study of complex societies. The intellectual toolkit that a curator or folklife student can use now, is not the toolkit of fifty years ago.

Fashions in ideas change. There is no doubt that the contemporary student can have difficulties with some of Evans's work. For example, Evans made it quite clear that he followed Fleure in rejecting the notion of pure race. However, he did believe that a physical anthropological study in Ireland, analysing head forms and blood types, would be a means to establish vestiges of those prehistoric people responsible for innovation. His supervision of such a project led him to remark that the physical characteristics of the Old Stone Age people that first settled Ireland may be found in a small proportion of living Irishmen.[23] Some of their skills such as the building of curraghs and ancient rituals linger today.[24]

Similarly, some ideas may be rejected as environmental determinism. For example, the idea that the drumlins of southern Ulster with their steep sides, confused drainage of winding streams and lakes, made the drumlin country a considerable obstacle to movement, and, with other physical factors, helped to isolate the north from the rest of the country in early times.[25]

In any case, the genesis and intermingling of new ideas did not take long to filter into folklore. In 1955, in a critique of folklore rather than folklife, Buchanan stated that while the study of survivals could yield valuable insights, and while this study could yield material valuable to other disciplines, such material could only be accepted with reservations. He stated that folk belief outlines were not clear and concepts were not precise. Folklore could only give a clouded image of the past and could not have a place in exact science. Buchanan pointed to the definition of folklore advanced by Margaret Murray as 'the intimate life of the folk of every class, that background of our daily life which we miss so much when we are cut off from it', including not only concrete tangible objects but '... the sights and sounds of daily life... things so small that they are not recorded in history, poetry, biography or other serious literature'. Buchanan pleaded for a greater inclusion of cultural context in folklore and quotes Opie as saying 'Folklorists are interested in the embers of an earlier thought and way of life glowing in a period when the unknown bonfire from which they came has long burnt out.' Buchanan concludes with an appeal for context, meaning the synchronic and scientific study of contemporary communities.[26]

In 1965, Sigurd Erixon of the Nordic Museum in Sweden wrote an article explicitly charting the manner in which folklife had developed in responses to changes in the humanities generally. He stated that early folklife studies had been typological in nature and dominated by the concept of evolution. By 1930 this had been replaced by an attempt to see folklife against a background of movements and dispersals – the diffusionist approach of Evans. The influence of the functionalist school which was concerned to ask how customs furthered cohesion and solidarity in society, led to the establishment of synchronic studies and set period short historical research. Erixon pointed out that while in the 1920s folklife was concerned with the rural peasantry as bearers of folk culture, it had later become accepted that some urban communities contained folk traditions. Erixon advocated systematic case studies of both individuals and communities and stated explicitly that folklife was also concerned with the mechanism of change. The inability of functionalist studies to deal with either conflict or change had, of course, quickly been established as a criticism of the school of thought.[27]

How did the Ulster Folk and Transport Museum draw on thought in folklife to interpret the way of life of the people of Ulster past and present? Open-air museums have always been more than repositories of antiquarian objects or works of art. They have been as much concerned with the collections as with the nature of their role in the community. At an early stage, Thompson states, the museum is as essential as any other community development and the true purpose of a folk museum must be based not only in the past and present but also in a vision of the changes that await us in the future.[28] This latter statement is significant because while folklore has been concerned with the past in the present and with enriching the present, it has not generally concerned with the idea of the future.

The questions and problems that students of folklife have addressed in defining the scope of their study are not necessarily the same as those of a curator concerned with interpretation of the subject matter to a community within a given context. There are obvious difficulties in saying to a man from Antrim that his recent past contains relics from the prehistoric period. I cannot say to this man that his cultural heritage consists of a series of distribution maps. There was an obvious tension between the need to represent items that were significant to the anthropogeographer with a long time perspective and the need for a museum to place interpretation within a fixed time period. What ideas then did the folk museum draw upon?

From Evans came the lesson of the importance of the environment and the idea that the purpose was to illustrate differences between regions. There was also the idea of the importance of agriculture and of the need to illustrate regional variations in vernacular dwellings. From Evans too came the idea that the museum was of importance internationally for its representation of the heritage of part of the Atlantic province of Europe. From folklife there came the idea that the urban as well as the rural should be represented and the incorporation of delineated, short time perspectives. From the Swedes there came the idea that the pace of contemporary urbanisation was now fast and that factors such as the development of the European Economic Community meant that there was an urgent need to preserve or rescue features of individual societies.[29]

How would the museum do this? The aim was to establish an Ulster landscape in miniature. The open-air museum would consist of three sections, an area of farmland with dispersed farms, and second, an area of closely grouped dwellings or farmsteads – a clachan. This would show evolution in the landscape and provide a setting for the display of regional vernacular architecture. The dwellings would originate at different times but be furnished roughly as they would have been in 1900, so linking the interpretative need for the synchronic with the broader time perspectives. However, it was recognised fairly early in the collecting process that it was difficult to delineate the urban from the rural since the products of a Falkirk foundry or a Scottish pottery could easily find their way into an Ulster farmhouse. It was also recognised at an early stage that a representative collection might be hard to obtain. At this stage, collections management issues, namely the separation of handling and reserve collections, were not addressed.[30] The third section was to be a village or service centre to be modelled on a synthesis of surveys in contemporary and recent Ulster. The museum would be a living museum insofar as services such as spade making would be located in the farm areas and other services such as weaving in the village. There would be craftsmen to demonstrate traditional skills and thus bring the little settlement truly alive.[31] The building of three galleries to set the context would complement the open-air museum. One would show crafts and social life, one would show textiles, costume and the linen industry, and the third would focus on agriculture and rural life.[32]

How much of this programme has been achieved? The museum now has in excess of twenty-nine buildings in the open-air museum. Following Evans, there is representation of both hip-roofed and gable hearth houses. One gallery, rather than three, was built, but the museum houses extensive transport galleries on another site. The museum has a rural area and has built not a village, but a town. Very few studies of nucleated settlements have been undertaken to back this. The living museum concept has not thrived. At one stage the museum had a spade-maker, a blacksmith and a damask weaver. At present it has a working farm, a tweed weaver and a working print shop. Exhibits are largely static. Attendants, trained to cook and spin, supply activity. In the town displays, mass-produced products have largely driven out products that depended on a discriminating knowledge of local materials. It can be argued that the resultant museum represents an uneasy compromise between the demands of the public for an interpretation based on easily understood, specific time periods, and the need to represent ideas rooted in the development of folklore. At the same time the intellectual and social context in which we operate is changing.

Gearoid Ó Crualaoich and Diarmuid Ó Giolláin have stated that the position of folklore studies in both the north and south of Ireland reflects the official ideologies and the governing regimes in both regions. They have pointed out that in both, to some extent, folklore is perceived as a precious heritage from another time and from outside our space, and as somehow not directly a product of or subject to the effects of historical process or the political conflict. They have defined folklore, following Gramsci, as the conceptions of the world and of life implicit to a large extent in determining time, space and strata of society, and for the most part in opposition to the official conceptions of the world that have succeeded one another in the historical process in Ireland. For them it is the world-view of non-elite or popular groupings. It is not tied to any setting, rural or urban, or to any era. In this, they challenge Irish folklore to move away from the notion that it is something beautiful and quaint, with additional overtones of the old-fashioned, and frequently Gaelic in origin. They question the commonly-held belief that the value of folklore lies in the preservation of the harmless but homely wisdom of olden times or its usefulness as entertainment for children and unsophisticated tourists.[33] We may agree or disagree with these authors, but they are highlighting the need for a fundamental reappraisal of the ideas that govern our actions.

At the same time, there comes from the community a demand that we reappraise our interpretative practice. The school use of the museum has led to a need for a greater representation of history. Our visitors are interested in the minutiae of daily life and are as likely to ask about the earth closet as the cruck truss. They are as interested in the lives of the inhabitants of a house as the layout of the wall and nature of the floor. The museum now plays a pivotal role in the 'Education for Mutual Understanding' programme which seeks to build relationships between Catholic and

Protestant communities by bringing them together to engage in heritage-linked creative activities. Schools and other groups are beginning to reiterate Evans's plea that we provide a practical knowledge of technology that will facilitate a creative link with the environment and a sympathetic view of the human past. There is, too, a greater understanding of the tool of drama and music in the exploration of issues and ideas. Cross-community groups are looking to the museum to be a living host for the practice of traditional techniques such as horse-ploughing or the dissemination and auction of rare breeds. Artists, craft-workers and hobbyists look to our collections and to our knowledge of period skills and techniques for ideas that they can link with the creation of something new or with the exploration of the idea of the sustainable community – all needs that an open-air museum can be uniquely placed to meet. The idea that we can not only show the past in the present but that the present and the past can be a springboard for creativity in the future is becoming established. There is an expectation, too, that we should develop a coherent policy regarding the representation of the Troubles. Actor-based studies and community partnership exhibits may be ways to tackle this. The existence of demand is not, in itself, a reason for supply. However, the nature of the open-air museum as a unique resource for the community and the challenges of the period in which we live, suggest that it is time to look again at both our ideology and interpretative practice. This must be done in a systematic way and have regard for the past as well as the huge array of concepts and methodologies available in the present. The establishment of the Ulster Folk and Transport Museum as part of the new National Museums and Galleries of Northern Ireland presents an ideal opportunity to do just this.

Notes and references

1. Evans, Gwyneth, 'Estyn', in E.E. Evans (ed) *Ireland and the Atlantic heritage: selected writings* (Dublin, 1996).
2. Evans, E.E., *The personality of Ireland: habitat, heritage and history*, (Cambridge, 1973), p 1.
3. Campbell, John, 'Ecology and culture in Ireland', in E.E. Evans (ed), *Ireland and the Atlantic heritage: selected writings* (Dublin, 1996), p 226.
4. Daniel, G.E., *A hundred years of archaeology* (London, 1950), pp 302–8.
5. Sauer, C.O., *Agricultural origins and dispersals*, Bowman Memorial Lectures, The American Geographical Society (New York, 1952), p 1.
6. Taylor, E.B., *Primitive culture* (London, 1871).
7. Evans, E.E., *Irish heritage: the landscape, the people and their work* (Dundalk, 1949) p 5.
8. Ibid. p 6.
9. Evans, E.E., *Irish folk ways* (London 1957), p xiv.
10. Evans (1949), op. cit., p 10.
11. Evans (1957), op. cit., p 10.
12. Ibid.
13. Evans (1949), op. cit., p 11.

14. Frazer, J.G., *The golden bough* (London, 1890).
15. Evans (1949), op.cit., p 8.
16. Thoms, W.J., writing as Ambrose Merton in *The Athenaeum*, 1846.
17. Buchanan, R.H., 'A decade of folklife study', *Ulster Folklife*, 2 (1965).
18. Evans (1973), op. cit., p 10.
19. Evans (1949), op. cit., p 3.
20. Ibid., pp 11–13.
21. Ibid.
22. Buchanan, R.H., 'A decade of folklife study', *Ulster Folklife*, 11 (1965), pp 63–75.
23. Campbell (1996), op. cit., p 229.
24. Evans (1957), op. cit., p 6.
25. Evans (1949) op. cit., p 19.
26. Buchanan, R H, 'The study of folklore', *Ulster Folklife*, 1 (1955), pp 8–12.
27. Erixon, Sigurd, 'Folk-life research in our time', *Gwerin* no. 6 (1962).
28. *The Annual Report of The Ulster Folk Museum*, 1958–60 and 1960–61.
29. Ibid.
30. Thompson, G.B., 'The Ulster Folk Museum collection', *Ulster Folklife*, 5 (1959), 9–13.
31. Thompson, G.B., 'The development of the open-air museum', *Ulster Folk Museum Yearbook*, 1965–6.
32. Cornforth, John, 'A view of Ulster rural history', *Country Life* (7 May 1981).
33. Ó Crualaoich, G. and Ó Giolláin, D., 'Folklife in Irish studies', *The Irish Review*, 5 (1988).

3

Heroes for a New Ireland:
Francis Joseph Bigger and the
Leaders of The '98

Roger Dixon

FRANCIS JOSEPH BIGGER was born in Belfast in 1863 into a prominent Belfast Presbyterian family. He was educated at the Royal Belfast Academical Institution, of which his grandfather was a founder, and was devoted to the study of Irish archaeology and Ulster history. He revived the *Ulster Journal of Archaeology* and was a prolific writer and a tireless promoter of all aspects of Irish culture, especially folklore and folk music, and he advocated learning the Irish language. He was elected a Fellow of the Royal Society of Antiquaries of Ireland in 1896.

An article written about him in 1916 described him 'as comparable with St Patrick himself',[1] and this is typical of the kind of reverence he inspired in his admirers who ranged from politicians like Roger Casement to writers and poets such as Joseph Campbell.

Bigger died in 1926 and is still remembered today for his very public support for Irish nationalism. His extensive library and the major portion of his papers were bequeathed to Belfast Central Library, but small collections exist elsewhere and the Ulster Folk and Transport Museum is lucky to hold quite a number of unique items relating to this fascinating man.

For more than a quarter of a century Francis Joseph Bigger acted as Ulster's apostle of Irish culture. Through the use of that culture he sought to promote the idea of Ireland as a separate nation to England and to bind Catholics and Protestants together in a new unity. He believed that Ulster in particular was divided by two powerful forces, namely religion and the English influence, and he set out to help to create a common heritage formed of language, myth, cultural identity and a common enemy, the English. At a speech in Clogher in 1909, he declared: 'I cannot see a solitary reason why we should love the English Nation. She is and has always been our most bitter enemy'.[2]

Bigger's efforts to create a united cultural identity have to some extent been covered elsewhere[3] but his political work is perhaps less well known. Like many others, he had become interested in Irish nationalist politics through his involvement with the Gaelic League. It was through it that he made the acquaintance of Roger Casement, Douglas Hyde, Alice Milligan, Bulmer Hobson and many others who were to play such an important part in the creation of an Irish Republic. Bigger's ability to organise and his known influence in legal, academic and local government circles in Belfast were to be of great value to the Gaelic League in the North of Ireland. Alice Milligan, the poet who was a fervent Gaelic Leaguer and nationalist, bombarded him with requests for help for League events. The following extract from a letter written to him by Milligan in 1910 was typical of the kind of request he received.

> The projected pageant and play should be arranged at once. You should write to W.B. Yeats and get himself to keep himself free for the date in March. He should undoubtedly be here and Dr. Hyde also. Do all this and many other things without waiting for the Lord Mayor. I hope you are on good and approachable terms with the new one![4]

Indeed Bigger the 'fixer' was constantly at work on behalf of the League, organising increasingly large gatherings culminating in a huge event at the Ulster Hall. Cathal O'Byrne recounts that, 'During his term as President of the Gaelic League in Belfast, Mr Bigger decided that the Gaels had stayed quite long enough in the lanes and back streets and as nothing was too good for the Gaelic League they should have a big show in the Ulster Hall... A big success it proved.'[5]

In matters of a more directly political nature he could also be relied upon to play his part. In July 1905 a young nationalist activist, Stephen Clarke, was arrested in Ballycastle for distributing an anti-recruitment pamphlet which had been written jointly by Alice Stopford Greene, Roger Casement and Bulmer Hobson. When he was sent for trial to Belfast Assizes, Hobson and others naturally approached Bigger to organise his defence. Hobson tells us:

> In all political trials it was the practice for the Government to pick the jury carefully; so Bigger, who had an extraordinary knack of knowing nearly everybody, very genially went about talking to men whose names were on the panel from which the jury would be selected. In the result we were sure of five members of the jury when the trial started. They were a canny lot, and managed to reach an agreement which saved loyalist faces while giving us an acquittal. Their verdict was guilty but with no seditious intent. So Stephen Clarke was discharged, and the trial, fully reported in the press, was the best propaganda we could have had.[6]

This gives ample evidence not just for Bigger's political sympathies at the time but also his abilities as a fixer. Certainly for anyone in a tight corner Bigger was a very useful man to have on their side which was why a number of nationalist political and cultural groupings sought his help. One such was the Dungannon Clubs established by Bigger's friends, Bulmer Hobson and Denis McCullough. Its name and its constitution would have struck an immediate chord with Bigger as Hobson tells us in his autobiography that the name Dungannon Clubs was adopted for the new venture, because:

> ... it recalled the Dungannon Convention of 1782, when the armed Volunteers of Ulster had met to proclaim that English interference in Irish affairs could no longer reconcile Catholic and Protestant.By recalling that noble period in the history of Ulster, we hoped to appeal to a tradition that had by no means died out, and the time did not seem to be inopportune. The Orange junta that had controlled the province for a century was showing every sign of senility.[7]

The Belfast secretary was Denis McCullough and the constitution he helped draw up for the clubs, particularly the first three clauses, represents very closely Bigger's own aims and objectives. These clauses were:

1. That this Club be called 'The Dungannon Club (No.1) Belfast'.
2. That it be open to all Irishmen who endorse its propaganda.
3. That its objectives are:
The building up of Ireland
(a) Intellectually – by educating the people by means of schools, classes, lectures, publications, etc. The establishment of libraries and every means calculated to educate the country.
(b) Materially – by the fostering of existing, and the starting of new industries by the exclusive use of Irish manufactures and produce.
(c) Physically – by the popularisation of physical culture and training by the spread of our national games, and by the training of the boys of the country.

By the time the Dungannon Clubs manifesto was issued Bigger was already actively promoting the objectives stated in clause three, for in addition to his abilities as a fixer and general organiser on behalf of the League he also had considerable talent for rousing others in support of the cause by both writing and lecturing. Of the many lectures he gave his favourite was entitled 'The hills of holy Ireland'. Despite its innocuous title it was in fact a diatribe against the iniquities of British rule in Ireland down the centuries. His delivery of the lecture at the Linen Hall Library brought him into conflict with that institution's governing body of which he was a member. The minutes to the Lecture Committee of 1907 leave us in no doubt as to their feelings, stating that

> Without expressing any opinion on Mr Bigger's statements as to English government in Ireland, the committee are of the opinion that any lectures calculated to rouse party and religious bitterness are not in the interest, or for the welfare, of the society; and had they been aware that the title 'The Hills of Holy Ireland, was to be used as a pretext for ventilating political

prejudices, they would not have given their sanction to such a lecture being
delivered under the auspices of the society.[8]

The pamphlet was eventually published by the Catholic Truth Society and
enjoyed considerable popularity for many years.

In his political writings, Bigger generally preferred to deal with the past
rather than attempt to analyse the current situation. The flight of the earls,
the land war, and the plantation of Ulster were among his favourite subjects and he covered them time and time again in publications such as *Sinn
Fein* and *The Gael*. However, it was the 1798 rebellion and its northern leaders in particular who provided both him and the Dungannon Clubs with
their greatest inspiration. The men of 1798 appealed to Bigger on two
accounts. There was his genuine interest in local history and his fascina-
tion with a period that, although it remained embedded in folk memory,
seemed by the 1890s to belong to a world as fabulous as Camelot.
However, as a propagandist for the nationalist cause he also saw that they
presented the perfect inspirational heroes for a new Ireland: although they
were Protestants, they had stood for liberty and equality and called for the
unity of Catholic, Protestant and Dissenter. Perhaps most importantly of
all they had been willing to take up arms against England and in many
cases sacrificed their lives for Irish independence. Bigger with his
undoubted gift for inspiring people with an interest in their own past saw
clearly the potential that these men had for winning Protestants in particular to the cause of Irish independence.

Following the centenary celebration of the 1798 rebellion in which
Bigger was closely involved, he set out to write a series of biographies of
the northern leaders of the United Irishmen with the express purpose of
creating suitable heroes for the nationalist cause. In all he completed six
biographies covering the lives of William Orr,[9] Henry Monro, Henry Joy
McCracken, James Hope, Thomas Russell and Samuel Neilson. During his
lifetime he was considered to be the foremost authority on the 1798 rebellion in Ulster and according to Dr Crone, 'everyone who knew anything
on the subject always declared that there was no man in Ireland better fitted to the task'. Certainly Bigger himself considered that he was uniquely
well placed to write these biographies as he says in the preface to that of
William Orr:

> It has fallen to me, brought up in the country of the northern leaders of the
> insurrection of '98 related to several of them, familiar with their homes and
> haunts, acquainted with the scenes of their deaths, a frequent visitor to their
> graves, their people and my people known and connected with each other,
> their names household words – it has fallen to me, after the lapse of a cen-
> tury, to be a chronicler of their lives and actions.[10]

That these were to be highly partisan works Bigger leaves us in no doubt
and clearly sets out his purpose in writing them, stating that:

> My sole desire has been to redeem from the obloquy and scorn that alien
> feeling has poured forth, and place in the niches they are well entitled to

occupy, men whose every action was noble, self-sacrificing, and patriotic in the highest sense. One and all sacrificed everything held most dear for the ideal set before them, national freedom and regeneration.

They may have lived before their age, but the seed they sowed and nourished with their blood has sprung up and borne fruit a thousand-fold, and their actions will ever continue to influence the life of the people until every creed and party within the four seas of Ireland are welded into a common nation, one and indivisible.[11]

In the biographies Bigger treats these men very much as archetypal heroes and their lives are given what we today might recognise as the Hollywood treatment. In fact, the biographies are quite repetitive, with the same or similar phrases used time and time again. The heroes have a happy childhood, and loving parents, with the old homestead and countryside described in cinematic detail, as in the case of the Orr family home, where:

... undulated woods, ploughed uplands, and wide spreading lawns stretch down the valley to where the towers of Antrim nestle by the shore of Lough Neagh. Along its margin, embowered in foliage, lie the ruins of Shane's castle, with the old round tower nearer hand, and the great double fort of Rathinra just across the burn, whilst right across the vista Lough Neagh gleams and glistens in the sunlight, or is reddened by the glory of the sunset topping the hills of Tireoan and Tirconail.[12]

His heroes grow to become brilliant students, good at games and usually show hints of future glory by carrying out heroic acts as boys. Munro, for instance, rescues people from a fire and is described by Bigger as being first up the ladder and into the burning building. On reaching manhood the hero is not only popular with all but also exceedingly handsome. Russell is 'a model of manly beauty' with 'majestic stature', yet 'with benevolence that beamed from his fine countenance'. Munro is formed by nature with most perfect symmetry and Orr is strong and athletic, handsome and comely with a figure a sculptor might copy. So we have the hero set in his idyllic homeland and growing into a tall, broad-shouldered, handsome and universally popular man. The hero then goes on to have a successful career and in most cases a happy marriage; Orr, we are told, has 'a beautiful young bride and revelled in the fullness and joy of life and the ample bounty bestowed upon his household'. At all times Bigger is at pains to show that his heroes are men of substance who would have a great deal to lose by upsetting the status quo. It is at this stage in the hero's career that he first notices the injustices being perpetrated in his country. Bigger describes the country as being rack-rented by corrupt landlords with Catholics and Protestants being equally abused but kept divided by dishonest landlords.

The hero then sets out to right these wrongs and become a champion of the people. In the biography of Monro we are told that 'this happiest of homes could not make Henry Monro deaf to the wave of agony that rose daily from the mass of the people of Ireland, brow-beaten by the petty

squireens whose touts and spies prayed upon them', and when he witnessed this, 'he left wife, friends, business, everything to face danger and
death for his devotion to Ireland'.

The actual rebellion of 1798 is not dealt with in detail in any of the biographies but we are left in no doubt as to the righteousness of the rebels'
cause and the iniquity of their opponents. The behaviour of the crown
forces is shown to be unspeakable and worse, in fact, than anything before
or since. In the biography of Russell he tells us that, 'the people were given
over to a military terrorism than which nothing more brutal and revolting
is recorded in history'.

In contrast, Bigger ignores all atrocities committed by the nationalist
side and he tells us that 'there never was a popular uprising so free from
excesses' and blames any criticism of rebel behaviour on government
propaganda which he claims set out to create a 'mythology of Nationalist
excess'.

Naturally, throughout the rising Bigger's heroes behave with absolute
courage and chivalry. Even in defeat they never desert the cause and
remain steadfast 'like the Spartan band who stood firm when all was lost'.
In defeat, the hero is then betrayed by that most notorious of all the figures
of Irish folklore, the informer. Bigger recognises the importance of the role
of informers and devotes more attention to them than to any other figure
in the biographies, with the exception of the hero. The following extract,
concerning Billy Holmes, who gave information leading to the arrest of
Munro, is typical of Bigger's coverage:

> It is said that Billy Holmes got £50 for betrayal of Monro. Whatever the
> amount they got a considerable sum of money and with it they bought a
> better place at Burren. But they were despised and loathed by the whole
> people. Orange and Green, Catholic and Protestant and anti Patriot alike
> detested those who were capable of such an act. In the whole history of
> Ireland's century-long struggle acceptance of the informer's pay has been
> the unforgivable sin condemned alike by all parties, by all classes and by all
> creeds. The land of Burren has long since passed from the Holmes. Billy's
> brother James was badly handled one market day at Ballynahinch and
> years after was nearly killed by the people in Lisburn market. From the
> effects of his treatment there he never recovered. They were called by every-
> one The Monro Holmes and were afraid to even put their name on a cart
> and used a fictitious one when going to markets. Billy and Margaret
> Holmes were buried in Dromara Protestant Churchyard within a few yards
> of the south wall close to the new transept. Their neglected grave is marked
> by a plain field stone without any inscription to call the detested name to
> memory.[13]

Bigger frequently uses religious imagery and Biblical quotations to brand
the informer's role and raise the status of the hero to a Christ-like position.
Orr's betrayer, for instance, is described as receiving, 'thirty pieces of sil-
ver like another Judas'. In fact, the Judas image is used in the description
of almost all the informers in marked contrast to the saintly images

reserved for the heroes.

Following on the heroes betrayal comes his martyrdom. Having set the scene with silent grieving crowds kept back by armed soldiers, the hero gives his glorious speech before dying a swift and painless death. Russell, we are told, preserved a settled serenity of countenance to his last moment, and told his persecutors that, 'I die at peace with all mankind. Gentlemen may God almighty bless you all'. Thus, says Bigger, 'died one of truest and bravest who have given their lives for the independence of Ireland'. Munro, he tells us, actually jumped off the gallows platform, thus hanging himself and sparing the executioner the ignominy of having to kill a hero. In the case of Orr's executioners, Bigger again draws comparisons with Christ by telling us that his executioners 'acted unwittingly just as the Roman soldiers acted' and that the infamous Judas, Samuel Turner (the man who informed on Orr) bartered his soul for gold.

After the execution comes the hero's burial where, as we would expect, religious references abound, and in Orr's biography mourning crowds 'rushed from their homes to wait on the roadside in tears and anguish' and then spent all night guarding the dead body with an almost idolatrous care. The very ground in which the hero is buried becomes holy and is 'consecrated afresh and made a doubly sacred spot and the grave will become a place of pilgrimage for all true lovers of Ireland'. By contrast, the grave of the informer will be a neglected and accursed spot avoided by all.

In the two biographies in which the hero is not executed, Bigger shows less enthusiasm. In the case of Hope he merely annotated Hope's own autobiography and, interestingly, his biography of Neilson is probably the most balanced and carefully researched work. Perhaps Neilson's death from yellow fever in America the year after the rebellion ended was not sufficiently martyr-like to inspire Bigger's hero worship.

The first of the biographies, that of William Orr, was published in Dublin in 1906; it was subtitled 'The Northern Leaders of the '98 (No.1)' but it was to be the only one of the series to be published. Bigger was involved in numerous other projects to promote Irish culture, ranging from editing the *Ulster Journal of Archaeology* to building labourers' cottages, and no doubt the time involved in preparing the other manuscripts for publication deterred him. In addition, the situation in Ireland was becoming increasingly fraught with a new uprising about to create a fresh set of martyrs for the nationalist cause. However, his interest in the leaders of the '98 rebellion never abated and at times became almost an obsession, particularly in regard to his often macabre searches for the bones of hanged rebel leaders such as Henry Joy McCracken.

In the run-up to the 1916 rebellion, Bigger continued to make strongly political speeches while claiming to have no political interest. His speech to the Lusk Aeridheact is typical:

Ireland will never take her rightful and proper place among the progressive

countries of the world until she has national freedom and independence
and until her people speak the native tongue. Much has been done and is
being done still for the restoration of the language. Upon the political hori-
zon also the day of promise has dawned. The people of this country are in
a state of tension wondering what is going to happen and feeling hopeful
that the right thing should happen; and I have come here from Belfast to tell
you that we want no divided Ireland; the North should stand by the South
and East by the West to build up a prosperous independent nation upon
Irish lines, according to Irish ideas.[14]

Also, his campaign against the importation of English goods and culture
continued unabated. His speech in Clogher in 1909 was typical of that
campaign in it he stated that:

> ... he and another visited a National School in Clare last September. It was
> a Convent School. They were conducted round the school. There were
> English advertisements on the walls, such as Colman's Mustard, Fry's
> Cocoa, and maps with advertisements on them. He inquired where the
> Industrial Map of Ireland was. They said they had one, and that they would
> look for it. And where did they find it. Behind the door (laughter). It was
> similar case with all the National Schools of Ireland. If he went into the
> schools around Clogher he wondered would he find advertisements for
> Fry's Cocoa on the walls, and he would wonder more if he found the
> Industrial Map of Ireland there. This was a map published by the Gaelic
> League. Where such advertisements as the ones he had just mentioned
> were it was not a very Gaelic district to say the least of it.
>
> He had not come there to plead for any creed or class, any one people or
> another. His class was to be Irish and he did not care which side was taken
> up as long as it was Irish, and for the good of Ireland.[15]

Although probably not actively involved in the organising of the 1916
rebellion himself, a number of Bigger's very close associates, particularly
Sir Roger Casement and Denis McCullough, were. Casement's long
friendship with Bigger is commented on by all Casement's biographers
but Bigger's very close association with Denis McCullough, the Belfast
Republican leader, is less well known. Perhaps in the young McCullough
he saw echoes of the leaders of the '98 rebellion and indeed their relationship came to a dramatic conclusion – which would not have been out of
place in Bigger's own biographies – when the security forces raided his
house in search of McCullough, who, after 1916, had become a wanted
man. Bigger, however, with his wide circle of contacts, was tipped off and
was able to telephone his home from his office and warn Bridget, his
housekeeper, to get McCullough out. This she accomplished with her
usual efficiency, hauling the young man out of bed, bundling his clothes in
a bag and then literally pushing him through a hole in the hedge on to
Fortwilliam golf course as the security forces arrived at the front door.
McCullough successfully made his escape, and Bigger had the hole in the
hedge made into a little archway, and in the archway he placed a wooden
cross in memory of Denis McCullough's delivery.

However, despite McCullough's escape and Bigger's romantic gesture, things were not turning out in the north as either had planned or wanted. McCullough got to Dublin but found that he could never return to Belfast. His last and only surviving letter to Bigger dated 25 April 1924 is tinged with sadness and regret. He writes:

> As Johnny Clarke used to say 'The clouds are darkening over the hills of Ulster again, but yerra! what's the good of talkin?' I hope you are as well as usual and that you will look me up when in Dublin as I cannot go to Belfast to look you up. Much as I would like to do so. I get lonely for the Blue Hills and for the ould times whiles. Give my love to Brigid and tell her Cooley has a kick left in him yet. With every good wish as always, your friend, Denis McCullough.[16]

For Bigger, seeing his dreams of romantic nationalism turn into the reality of civil war in the South and full-scale sectarian conflict in the North, must have been devastating. The 1920s could have been dangerous times for someone like Bigger who had so openly identified himself with Irish nationalism. However, he was, as always, lucky in his friendships. Prominent men like Sir Robert Baird, proprietor of the *Belfast Telegraph*, Sam Coughran, minister of Sinclair Seamen's Presbyterian Church, and many others all stood by him.

He continued to write on local history, but in these later articles he turned away from the romantic portrayal of nationalist heroes and English iniquities to concentrate on less politically controversial subjects and appears to have abandoned all intentions of publishing the rest of the northern leaders of the '98 series.

Interestingly, after 1920 his articles ceased to appear in the nationalist press and almost all his later work was for Belfast unionist papers such as the *Northern Whig*, the *Newsletter* and the *Belfast Telegraph*. However, despite this, there is no strong evidence to suggest that he ever lost entirely his belief in the nationalist cause. The creating of the border enraged him and, acting in his usual idiosyncratic way, he simply refused to cross it and spent his later vacations in Scotland or continental Europe.

Bigger himself may have turned away in his later years from the romance of the men of '98, but the legacy he helped to create lives on. United Ireland commemoration societies flourish and a whole raft of publications have appeared to mark the bicentenary of the 1798 rebellion. The vast majority of these publications treat the rebellion in a balanced and scholarly manner; however, among these new works has been a reissue of Bigger's life of Orr, so his portrayal of romantic revolutionaries may yet inspire a new generation. There is even talk of publishing all six of the biographies, something that even Bigger, with his boundless energy and enthusiasm, was unable to achieve during his lifetime. In a sense, the project has more to do with the enduring popularity of the men of '98 than necessarily any real regard for Bigger as a historian. However, it does suggest that Bigger, even if he was a somewhat unreliable historian, had the mak-

ings of a first-rate propagandist. He possessed an unerring instinct for
choosing popular themes and a remarkable ability to inspire ordinary people who otherwise would have found little to interest them in their own
country's history.

In a sense Bigger's death in 1926 marked the end of an era of great hope
for Irish culture and nationalist politics in Belfast. His friend and admirer,
the nationalist MP Joe Devlin, tried to keep the spirit alive by acquiring
Bigger's house, Ardrigh. But the great days of Casement and Hyde attending ceilidhes there were gone forever and Devlin soon gave it up.

Bigger's brand of romantic Irish nationalism and his hopes of uniting
Protestant and Catholic in a common cultural identity already seemed
hopelessly naive and old fashioned by 1926. However, despite Bigger's
part in Nationalist politics being down-played in his latter years, his role
was never entirely forgotten by either side as the dramatic blowing up of
his gravestone by loyalists in 1971 proved.

Notes and references

1. Quoted by J.S. Crone in *Francis Joseph Bigger in remembrance* (Dublin, 1927) p 27.
2. Published speech, journal unknown. Bigger scrapbook No.3 – Bigger archive,
    Ulster Folk and Transport Museum.
3. Dixon, Roger, 'Francis Bigger, Ulster's Don Quixote' *Ulster Folklife*, 43 (1997);
    Dixon, Roger, 'Apostle of the Living Legend: Francis Joseph Bigger' in *Fin de
    Siecle – Arts and crafts and the Celtic revival in Ireland Northern Perspectives* (1998).
4. Bigger archive, Ulster Folk and Transport Museum.
5. O'Byrne, Cathal, *As I roved out*, Belfast (1946) p 201.
6. Hobson, Bulmer, *Ireland, yesterday and today* (Tralee, 1968), p 25.
7. Ibid.
8. Quoted in Killen, John, *A history of the Linen Hall Library 1788–1988* (Belfast,
    1990), p 86.
9. Bigger, Francis Joseph, *The northern leaders of '98* (No.1) (Dublin, 1906). The
    other biographies were never published and remain in manuscript form in
    Belfast Central library. I am grateful to Belfast Public Libraries for granting
    permission to publish extracts from them.
10. Ibid., p 6
11. Ibid., p 7
12. Ibid.
13. Bigger, J.F., Biography of Henry Munro, unpublished manuscript from the
    Bigger archive, Belfast Central Library.
14. 'No Divided Ireland Wanted', *Irish News*, 24 June 1913.
15. Published speech, journal unknown. Bigger scrapbook No. 3, Bigger archive,
    Ulster Folk and Transport Museum.
16. Bigger archive, Ulster Folk and Transport Museum.

4

Water Power and 'Strong' Farmers: The Weir Family of Straid Mills, County Antrim

PHILIP ROBINSON

IN 1982 THE ULSTER FOLK AND TRANSPORT MUSEUM acquired an oat-milling complex of four buildings from the townland of Straid, two miles south-west of Ballymena, County Antrim (Figure 4.1). After removal to Cultra, its re-erection was completed fifteen years later (Figure 4.2). Technologically, this group of four buildings (a row of millers' houses, a kiln, the mill itself and a grain store and stable) is the most spectacular achievement of the Ulster Folk and Transport Museum's range of open-air exhibit buildings. However, the completeness of the original mill proved to be only part of the value of the project, for surviving documents and family papers revealed a fascinating story of how water power had been harnessed to make much more than a livelihood. A strong rural family dynasty grew from this small centre of corn (oat) milling.

The Weirs of Straid Mills[1]

The first record of any member of the Weir family to come to this site from Scotland in the seventeenth century is of a John Weir, farmer of Straid, who died in 1697. His descendants continued farming in this area until the middle of the twentieth century.

How long the mills at Straid had been operated by the Weirs is not clear. John Weir's gravestone, dated 1697, has a range of images of mortality and other symbols carved on both faces. Among these is a 'Miller's Mace' – the trade symbol of a miller. The record of the marriage of Robert Weir (born 1770) to Elizabeth Orr-Warden indicated that he was a farmer having a lint mill and two oat mills at Straid. They had three children, Hugh, James and Mary. Elizabeth died in the first decade of the nineteenth century and Robert remarried in 1815, to Martha Telford. They had a family of nine;

Figure 4.1 The Straid Corn Mill Complex in situ. The water-wheel is on the back gable
of the mill building to the right (UFTM L1612/1/7)

four girls and five boys. Alexander, the youngest son, was born on 27 June
1830.

By the 1850s Alexander had assumed the responsibility for the running
of the Straid farm and mills, and inherited them after Robert's death in
1859. It was in all probability Alexander who supervised the rebuilding of
the corn mill in 1852.

Alexander married Rose McKay in 1852. After Robert's death,
Alexander and his family remained in the main house and his mother and
one unmarried sister, Eliza, moved to one of the other houses on the farm.
A brother, Samuel, remained with Alexander for a few years until he
obtained his own farm at Tullygowan.

Most of Alexander's brothers and half-brothers settled in the area in
their own farms. Alexander, although the youngest son, appeared
throughout his life to look after the affairs of his family and those of many
of his neighbours. He kept meticulous records and accounts of the day-to-
day running of the farm and mills, some of which have survived to the
present day (see Figure 4.4).

The whole enterprise at Straid played an important role in the community, both economically and socially. A number of local people were
employed in the mills. It was a place of constant activity, day and night.
After a day's work many locals gathered in the boiler house at the rear of
the main house, in front of a large peat fire – often twenty or more.

Figure 4.2 The Straid Corn Mill Complex, after reconstruction at Cultra (UFTM L3272/4)

The complex with its farm, power supply, mills, blacksmith's and carpenter's shops, was virtually self-sufficient. Prior to the First World War, Alexander's sons, Robert and John, utilised the water power to operate a turbine which provided electricity for the house, and by a system of pulleys and belts could drive some of the farm implements, the thresher, corn crusher, butter churn and sharpening stone. This was quite a novelty in the area and attracted many sightseers.

By the 1930s the mills were operating at a greatly reduced level, due to competition from larger mills. The war years, 1940–45, saw a temporary increase in the volume of work for both the corn and flax mill. There was a demand for linen which was used to cover the wings of Wellington bombers. Both mills, however, finally ceased operating shortly after the war.

By this time the numbers of the family living in the area had diminished. One of Alexander's sisters, Margaret, had married and emigrated to Australia in 1852. Later in that century and in the early part of the twentieth, many of Alexander's brothers, married sisters, half-brothers and their families emigrated, mainly to Australia and New Zealand and some to America. There some continued in the farming tradition, others moving into business or the professions.

Of Alexander's own family, which numbered nine, one son died in infancy, and another son, James, and a daughter, Dinah, died in the 1880s, both unmarried. Two sons emigrated: Alexander with his family to

1. FARMHOUSE
2. CARPENTRY SHOP
3. SMITHY
4. FLAX SCUTCH MILL ('WEE' MILL)
5. FLAX SCUTCH MILL ('BIG' MILL)
6. CORN MILL
7. CARTSHED AND STABLE WITH STORE OVER
8. MILLERS' HOUSES
9. CORN-DRYING KILN
10. WEIGH-BRIDGE

Figure 4.3 An 'industrial' complex at Straid, Ballymena, County Antrim

Canada, and William to South Africa. Another son Hugh, a farmer, married and lived with his family near Straid Mills, but all his family died unmarried. Robert, a bachelor son, inherited the farm after Alexander's death in 1915 and lived there with his spinster sister, Annie. On Robert's death his brother John, who had spent a large part of his life travelling abroad, moved to the Straid. John died in 1956, and his only son, involved in medical practice elsewhere, eventually disposed of the farm. So for 300 years there had been Weirs farming and milling at Straid. By the 1890s they had reached a dominant position in the life of the district, but finally the lure of the professions or the colonies overcame the last of these links with the land.[2]

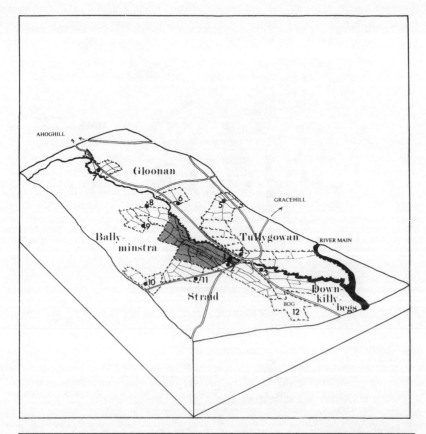

KEY	FARM	TOWNLAND	AREA (ACRES)
1	ALEXANDER WEIR (Straid Mills Farm - shaded area)	STRAID and BALLYMINSTRA	43 23
2	JOSEPH PORTER, to HUGH PORTER (1886), to JAMES WEIR (1902)	STRAID	43
3	JAMES WEIR, to ROBERT WEIR (1879)	DOWNKILLYBEGS	25
4	JAMES and SAMUEL WEIR, to ALEXANDER WEIR (1882-1890), to JOHN CAMERON (1896)	TULLYGOWAN	59
5	JAMES WEIR	TULLYGOWAN	17
6	WILLIAM CATHCART, to SAMUEL WEIR (1865), to ALEXANDER WEIR (1891)	GLOONAN	7
7	JOHN WEIR, to JAMES SMALL (1865)	GLOONAN	28
8	JAMES WEIR, to DAVID WEIR, JUNIOR (1879)	BALLYMINSTRA	18
9	DAVID WEIR	BALLYMINSTRA	10
10	HUGH WEIR, DAVID WEIR (1869), to WILLIAM MILLAR (1886)	BALLYMINSTRA	12
11	DAVID WEIR, to DAVID ROGERS (1902)	STRAID	17
12	ALEXANDER WEIR	DOWNKILLYBEGS	(MOSS)

Figure 4.4 Weir family farms in the Straid area, 1860–1905

Straid Corn Mill

The datestone over the door to the Straid Corn Mill reads 'A.D. 1852 R. Weir'. In that year Robert Weir obtained a new lease of the Straid Mills farm from the O'Neill estate, and set about reconstructing the mill which

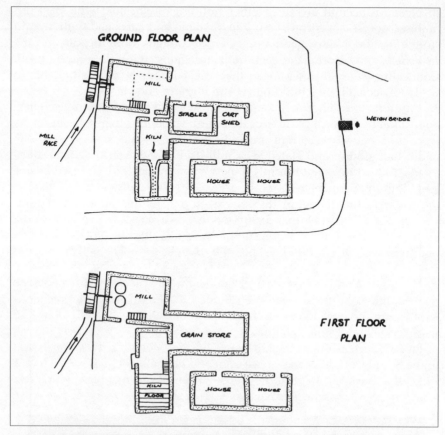

Figure 4.5 Sketch of Straid Corn Mill

had been on this particular site since at least 1754.

The rebuilding of 1852 left the mill complex much as we see it today –
a stone, two-storey slated mill with a large water-wheel outside. The
wheel is 18 feet in diameter and is of the type known as 'overshot', where
the water is carried out over the top of the wheel to fall onto the far face of
the wheel. Overshot wheels are generally more efficient than breast shot,
but require a greater fall or 'head' of water. Inside the mill the axle drives
a bevelled cast-iron cog wheel known as the 'pit wheel'. The pit wheel
rotates in a vertical plane, reflecting the motion of the water wheel outside.
The bevelled cogs on this interlock with a wallower or bevelled gearing
which drives a larger 'spur wheel' with wooden cogs fixed to the same
shaft. The wallower gearing and the spur wheel both rotate in a horizontal plane, and the function of the spur wheel is to interlock with the 'stone
nuts' – the gearing which drives the millstones. At various points along
the moving shafts, belt drives are taken to power the elevators, shakers,
sieves, fans, winnowers and sack hoist.

Next to the mill are three other buildings associated with the corn milling process – a corn-drying kiln, a stable and cart-shed with a grain store in the floor above, and a pair of mill cottages. Both the kiln and the cart-shed/grain store have been built up against the mill building itself. Connecting internal doors mean that at each floor level it is possible to walk between all three buildings without going outside.

When the buildings are examined closely, it is possible to detect alterations that have taken place over the years. The mill cottages, for instance, were once one-storeyed and probably thatched, while they are now one and a half storeys and slated. The mill itself shows some signs of alterations. Indeed it was not simply a 'new' building in 1852. Re-used beams and blocked openings in the walls give a clue to the period before 1852.

A map of the district in 1813 marks on the site the 'Strade Mills', and the 1833 first edition Ordnance Survey map also marks a 'corn mill' on the site of the present mill.[3] According to the 1833 Valuation Notebooks,[4] this corn mill was an old building, possibly thatched, but in good repair and with the following dimensions: 34 feet long, 23 feet broad, and 7 feet 6 inches high. With the exception of the height, the plan measurements are precisely those of the present mill. Indeed the 1860 Valuation Notebooks (describing the post-1852 mill) refer to a mill building, 11 yards long, 7.5 yards wide and 2 storeys high.[5]

In 1835, according to the Ordnance Survey Memoirs, the water wheel at the Straid Corn Mill was breast-shot and only 13 feet high with 2 feet, 8 inch wide buckets.[6] In 1860 the water wheel was 16 feet high with 4 feet wide buckets. This wheel drove two pairs of stones – 'always the two work

Figure 4.6 The stone floor in the Straid Corn Mill, before dismantling (UFTM L/1774/34)

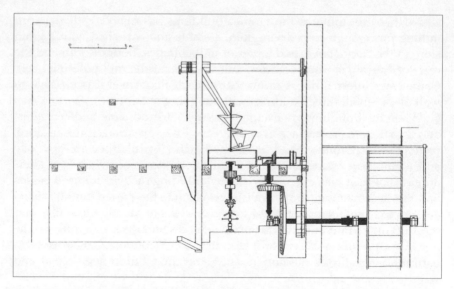

Figure 4.7 Straid Corn Mill: section showing drive to one of three sets of stones

together' – for eight months of the year, sixteen hours daily, with one stone shelling and one stone grinding (see Figure 4.6). In 1889, the mill was only working three to four months a year for eight hours a day grinding oats, rye and wheat. By this time there were three pairs of stones, as now, with one for shelling and two grinders.

According to older custom, and the 1852 lease, the tenants of the O'Neill estate in the surrounding townlands were bound to take their corn to the Straid mill, and to give one sixteenth of the grain to the miller as toll or 'multure'. A nearby corn mill on the same stream was providing what in 1881 Alexander Weir felt was unfair competition, so that he had to charge only the same toll, namely one fortieth of the grain. As a result of a petition to the O'Neill estate agent on the basis of this complaint, Alex Weir obtained a considerable rent abatement. In 1930, when the mill was still operating, account books reveal that one sixteenth multure was then being charged again, although when it was re-opened during the 1939–45 war years, a money charge of two shillings per hundredweight was introduced. In those years, strangely enough, coke was brought from Ballymena to fire the drying kiln, while throughout all the earlier years turf was used.

Water power at Straid

Although Robert Weir obtained his lease of the Straid Mills farm from the O'Neill estate in 1852, he had already been working the farm and the mill on a year-to-year agreement. The earliest known lease for the mill was made out in 1754 to John Miller, so its term was probably 99 years. Exactly when the Weirs took over the lease of the farm is not certain. They were there by 1824, but they must have been working the mill considerably before 1700, or have had some association with it. The feature which made this farm so desirable was the potential of its site. It was adjacent to a good 'head of water' on a tributary of the river Main, and being close to bridging points of the nearby rivers, soon became a focal point for the locality. The corn mill, certainly in existence in 1754, was by 1813 supplemented by a flax scutching mill, the site then being known as 'Strade Mills'. However, by the outbreak of the First World War in 1914, it was the variety of uses which Alexander Weir had found for the water power which was truly remarkable. Not only were there three water-powered mills, one for corn and two for flax scutching, but almost every conceivable device whose drive or motor could be powered from the mill race, was. First of all, a side race from the main mill race (just below the mill dam) powered the 'wee' scutch mill. Further down the main race, a second side race powered a potato washer. Inside the farm's weather-boarded smithy, the same side race could be used to turn a belt-driven grindstone and a wood-turning lathe. Beyond these on the main race, the water could be diverted in two directions. One branch could power either the 'big' scutch mill or the corn mill. The alternative branch from the mill race drove a turbine which (by means of belt drives) could turn a saw-mill beside the farm's carpentry shop, a small domestic-scale corn grinder, a milk churn, a corn thresher, and even the pump to force water up from the well to the domestic water tank above the farmhouse kitchen.

Fortunately, Alexander Weir's initiative and practicality has endured, not only in terms of these industrial archaeological remains, but in his accounts and notebooks. For such a complex to have survived is rare enough, but when this is backed by a considerable body of documentation, the result is a unique case history of rural life and industry in Victorian and Edwardian Ulster.

Notes and references

1. Some of the information on the Weir family history comes from a collection of family papers donated to the museum by Dr and Mrs J Weir of Antrim. I am indebted to Miss Anne Weir for the additional detail.
2. Anne Weir, 'The Weirs of Straid Mills' in *Field Excursions in Ulster, 2: Gracehill and district, county Antrim*, Ulster Folklife Society, 1983.
3. Ordnance Survey Six Inch Sheets, County Antrim, first edition, 1833.
4. Public Record Office of Northern Ireland (PRONI), VAL 1.B 1833 Valuation Notebooks, Parish of Ahoghill.
5. Public Record Office of Northern Ireland (PRONI), VAL 2.B 1860 Valuation Notebook, Parish of Ahoghill.
6. *Ordnance Survey Memoirs of Ireland, Parishes of Co. Antrim VIII, 1831–5, 1837–8, Ballymena and West Antrim, Vol. 23*, (Parish of Ahoghill), Angélique Day and Patrick McWilliams (eds), (Belfast, 1993), pp 13, 31.

The Ballydugan Weaver's House

FIONNUALA CARRAGHER

THE BALLYDUGAN WEAVER'S HOUSE in the grounds of the Ulster Folk and Transport Museum was opened to the public on 19 May 1967. The Ballydugan house was the museum's fifth exhibit building and its official opening was marked by a gathering of staff and invited guests. In recognition of the historical importance of the Ulster linen industry, Sir Graham Larmor, the chairman of the Ulster Linen Guild, was the first to enter the house. He was greeted with the evocative, rhythmic sound of a working linen handkerchief loom operated by Robert McEvoy, who was one of the few surviving handloom weavers in Ulster; he came from Shankill townland, near Lurgan in County Armagh (Figure 5.1).

Robert McEvoy was an employee of the long-established linen firm of William Ewart & Sons Ltd, of Waringstown, County Down and Belfast.[1]

The Ballydugan Weaver's House is distinctive because of its association with the once-dominant Ulster linen industry and in particular with the skilled craft of handloom weaving but less obviously because the house is a 'replica' building (Figure 5.2). Unlike previous museum exhibition buildings, the Ballydugan house was not removed from its original site but was built in the Cultra folk park. The exhibit house was modelled upon a derelict stone and earth-walled weaver's house from the northwest corner of County Down, close to the county boundary with County Armagh. The original house was situated on a small side road leading off the long, straight main road that goes between the mill village of Gilford and the larger market and linen town of Lurgan (Figure 5.3).[2]

The weaver's house lay close to the boundary between the two rural townlands of Ballydugan and Bleary and the house was in Bleary townland; it was on land owned by a local farming family, the Blane family of Bloomvale House, Bleary. It was located by the museum in 1965 when it had laid derelict for several years and was used as an agricultural store. The postal address was Ballydugan and therefore the house was called Ballydugan by the folk museum.[3]

Figure 5.1 Mr Robert McEvoy weaving in the Ballydugan House, at the exhibit's opening in the Ulster Folk and Transport Museum, 1967 (UFTM L336/18)

Background information relating to its previous occupants was uncollected at this time as the museum's priority was to survey the house as a model for the reconstruction of a vernacular mud walled house. However, later oral information and recent research has confirmed the name of Gibson as the family who lived in the house. Members of the family had been linen 'cambric' weavers. In the 1901 census household returns, a James Gibson aged sixty-four years and a widower, is described as a cambric weaver. Likewise his two daughters, Elizabeth, aged forty and Ellen Jane, aged thirty are described as cambric weavers. All members of this small household were able to read and write and were born in County Down.[4]

The Gibson family belonged to the Church of Ireland and therefore to the local parish of Knocknamuckley and its Church of St Matthias which is situated in Ballygargan townland in County Armagh. Knocknamuckley parish was established in October 1837 and it incorporated several townlands from the older County Down parishes of Tullylish, and Seagoe in County Armagh. The County Down portion of the Knocknamuckley

Figure 5.2 Ballydugan Weaver's House in the Ulster Folk and Transport Museum, early 1970s (UFTM L436/9)

parish lay within the barony of Lower Iveagh. But both Bleary and Ballydugan belonged to the catchment area of the Lurgan Poor Law Union in County Armagh.[5] In the nineteenth century, Bleary townland formed part of the large local estate belonging to the absentee landlord, Alexander J.R. Stewart, a member of the aristocratic Londonderry family. In 1921, the Blane family purchased Bloomvale House, a large two-storied stone farmhouse dating to the late eighteenth or early nineteenth century, and its associated outbuildings and farmland. It originally belonged to the Gaskin family who were farmers and part-time wholesale linen merchants; but by the later nineteenth century, Bloomvale was the home of the Dobson family, who through marriage had inherited the property.[6]

In contrast, Ballydugan townland did not form part of a large estate; its main proprietors were the Whittle and Wallace families who did not live locally and seem to have been largely based outside the locality, mainly in Dublin.[7] In their place, a scattering of Protestant clergy, land agents and professional families served as a local gentry and just below them were a number of respectable 'strong farmers' who provided employment for a variable population of casual agricultural labourers and unemployed cottiers or weavers. The 'strong farmers' and their sub-tenants consisted of families whose English and Scottish ancestors had been established in the district following the Ulster Plantation and its subsequent disruptions, the Cromwellian land forfeitures, dispossessions and later settlements. Before

Figure 5.3 Ballydugan Weaver's House, County Down, model for the house in Ulster Folk and Transport Museum (UFTM L1089/3/f16)

the Plantation, Ballydugan and its neighbouring townlands had formed part of the older, medieval Irish sub-division of Clanconnell belonging to the Irish family of Magennis, the Lords of Iveagh.[8] By the early eighteenth century the surname Magennis all but disappears from the north-west of County Down and in the Ballydugan/Bleary locality new surnames, such as Adamson, Calvert, Dynes, Levington and Skeath had become well established.

The townland name of Ballydugan can also be spelled as Ballydougan and it is an anglicisation of a local surname 'O'Duigean's/Dugan's place'. Bleary has been translated as meaning 'O'Leary's place' but this is an unconvincing anglicisation and a more likely explanation is that the name simply means 'a portion of land' from the Irish word *bladhraigh*.[9] However, the surname Gibson which is associated with the weaver's house was not a common surname within the populous Ballydugan and Bleary town-lands, although it is a well-known Ulster surname which is mainly identi-fied with County Down; the surname can be of either Scottish or Irish origin.[10]

In the nineteenth century, the Ballydugan locality was a rural landscape of low drumlin hills and fields; it was an enclosed cultivated and fertile countryside of a few large farms and numerous weavers' 'patches' or small-holdings. Other local buildings included a few schools and Orange halls. The main churches were situated in neighbouring townlands; the nearest Presbyterian meeting house was in Ballynagarrick townland and there was a Quaker meeting house in Moyallen. The Catholic church was in Clare townland near Gilford. The main Church of Ireland church was situated in Tullylish townland and there were also long-established churches in the nearby villages of Gilford and Waringstown. The Knocknamuckley parish church in County Armagh was a nineteenth-century addition; its church building was completed and consecrated in February 1853.

There were few streams in the locality and water was mostly obtained from farmhouse wells or from domestic water butt barrels. One acknowledged problem facing householders was the difficulty in obtaining turf for fuel because by the early 1830s the local bogs were almost exhausted. Instead, turf had to be fetched from the Montaighs area in County Armagh at a distance of some nine miles and imported coal transported via the Newry canal to landing places along the river Bann. The cost of carriage was expensive for the poorer residents of Tullylish parish. In the 1830s, a baronial valuation for Tullylish parish recommended that the cost of carriage for both turf and coal be reduced. This valuation also lists thirteen main residents of Ballydugan, two of whom lived in houses valued over five shillings.[11] The two wealthier occupiers were farmers, namely a Robert Adamson and a Richard Mills. The Adamson family can be identified with Hollymount House in Ballydugan, a Georgian farmhouse with substantial outbuildings and a garden. The Adamsons were an established Presbyterian family of strong tenant farmers and linen merchants who were active in the church life of Ballynagarrick Presbyterian congregation.[12]

Ballydugan townland was home to the locality's most notable landmark, Shane's Hill, height 341 feet, but this modest hill is an obvious lookout point with excellent views of the surrounding countryside. Throughout the nineteenth century Shane's Hill was a gathering place for a variety of open-air meetings. During the early decades of the century, it is mentioned as a meeting place for a local secret agrarian association called the 'Tommy Downshires' and in later decades as a venue for evangelical meetings.[13]

The 1834 Ordnance Survey account of the parish of Tullylish gives but brief mention of Ballydugan and Bleary townlands because there were no mills or gentleman's seats in these two rural townlands. Equally, both townlands were at some distance from the banks of the river Bann where several important and prosperous bleach and linen mills were located. However, in general terms, Tullylish parish is noted in the memoir as populous with a total of 10,498 inhabitants, the majority of which belonged to the established church. Small-holdings were between three and ten acres and most 'cottages' were stone built, thatched and with three or four rooms on the ground floor. The ordinary diet for cottiers was plain and it consisted of potatoes, meal, milk, butter and bacon. Both linen production and agriculture provided employment but the hand-spinning of linen yarn by women was being replaced by factory production. Both coarse and fine linens were produced in the parish, including *duck*, a coarse strong linen which was used for sailcloth and the finer household and dress linens, such as damask and cambric. A few specific customs were briefly recorded; 'there still exists a custom of lighting fires on St John's Eve; and on the 24 June, the Freemasons assemble with the insignia of their order and march around a portion of the country'.[14]

Cambric is a fine, plainly-woven linen cloth and by the nineteenth century, it was mainly used to make up handkerchiefs and, to a lesser extent, as a dress material. Its name dates from the sixteenth century and it was derived from the linen manufacturing and fortress town of Cambrai in French Flanders. The weaving of cambric was introduced into Ireland during the early 1700s, and in 1737 a cambric manufactory was established in Dundalk, County Louth with government support through the Linen Board. Skilled workmen were brought over from France to settle in Dundalk.[15] By the 1750s, Lurgan and its environs were strongly associated with the weaving of fine linens and in particular with the weaving of plain fine cambric and the patterned diaper and damask table linens. The district lay within the 'linen triangle' between the towns of Dungannon, Lisburn and Newry, and this district maintained its reputation for fine linen well into the twentieth century.[16]

During these early decades of the linen industry, the manufacture of linen was largely a domestic business; flax was grown locally and scutched or bought from itinerant yarn merchants. Locally-grown flax was spun into yarn by female members of the household and then woven into cloth by the farmer or weaver, his sons and any apprentices who may have boarded with the family. Disposal of the 'brown' unbleached linen was either by direct sale in the local market or through a recognised middleman, such as the independent 'jobber' or to a linen draper or bleacher. As a member of a distinctive workforce, the handloom weaver in eighteenth-century Ulster has earned a lasting historical reputation for possessing a lively and pugnacious spirit. This was shown by the varied interests of weavers, for instance, regular attendance at local fairs and markets, the establishment of local reading clubs and participation in the gambling pastimes of cock-fighting, horse-racing, and 'coursing' with hounds. Religious and political allegiances were strongly supported largely through the grass roots and usually sectarian politics of local agitation and oath-bound societies.

Regarded by the eighteenth-century agricultural reformer, Arthur Young, as poor or indifferent farmers, weavers often farmed a small patch of land to provide food for their families when times were hard and to earn some extra cash in better times. Possession of a small patch of land allowed a welcome degree of flexibility for a weaver and his family because food prices could fluctuate according to the season and during a trade depression the price for his cloth would be poor. The food he could grow on his small farm could save him when the price of oatmeal and potatoes got too high in the markets or when the price of cloth was reduced. By the nineteenth century the growth of factory methods of production was detrimental to the social status and independence of the rural male linen weavers. Many weavers gave up weaving, emigrated or settled for employment under a manufacturer, thereby accepting a cash wage, and the associated strict work discipline, which included regular fines for misdemeanours.

In the nineteenth century, this vulnerable class of weaver/cottiers was among those to suffer under the Great Famine of 1845–49. In west County Down, local distress was severe and it was worsened by unemployment due to a depression in the linen industry, the spread of epidemic disease, rising food prices and not least by the inadequate, poorly-managed relief provided by the Lurgan workhouse. By the end of 1846, the workhouse was filled to capacity with 805 paupers and its high weekly death rate throughout the following months was to draw censure from the Poor Law Commissioners in Dublin.[17] In February 1847, a contemporary (anonymous) correspondent to a Presbyterian church newspaper, *Banner of Ulster*, wrote specifically of the hardship experienced in the Shane's Hill area of County Down. The once 'Sturdy Independence' of the inhabitants who had opposed 'high rents and oppressive landlordism' was now wanting and in its place the horrors of 'penury, starvation and death'. Families had sold furniture for food and some were found reduced to living on 'raw turnips as their only food' and 'The Pestilence is aboard'. Individual tragedies were reported. In March 1847, a local coroner's court returned a verdict of death by starvation and cold on one John Williamson of Ballydugan. And in April 1847, the case of a Ballydugan man, a weaver named Thomas McMurray, who had died of the fever, was reported: his body had lain in the house for five days before a coffin was obtained through the private charity of a Mr Robert Mills of Clare townland. The death rate in the workhouse was high, although private church-led charity had undertaken the establishment of soup kitchens and parish relief funds. The reporter also accused the absentee landlords of the townland, namely a Mrs Whittle and Miss Wallace, of forwarding only paltry subscriptions to the Tullylish parish relief funds which, considering the extent of the distress on their property, amounted to 'a mockery of charity'. In response to this bitter charge, one Presbyterian minister, Thomas Lowry, a resident of Ballydugan, stated that the ladies' contribution was larger than many other proprietors in the parish and private arrangements had previously been made by them to forward money for seed purchase to their poorer tenants.[18]

The Great Famine inflicted death, sickness and impoverishment on people living near to Shane's Hill, but the recovery during the 1850s was steady and in this locality a marked population decline is not associated with the Famine but with the later decades of the nineteenth century and the gradual demise of the rural handloom weaver.[19] Patterns of emigration from the locality have not been researched but it is likely that people moved to urban centres such as Lurgan, Gilford and Belfast or further afield to the USA and Canada.[20]

By the 1860s, Lurgan and its hinterland was celebrated for its cambric and muslin production and its ancillary hem-stitching and handkerchief factories. Lurgan was described as the 'cradle of the Irish cambric industry' and its main employers and local workforce praised. Handkerchief manufacture began in the Lurgan district during the 1820s and by the 1830s also included hem-stitching concerns.[21] Factories were usually situated in the towns but one later exception was the rural embroidery and hem-stitching factory built in 1865 in Ballydugan by the Blane family. This factory later incorporated a Swiss embroidery school and provided employment, mainly for local women, up to the late 1990s.[22] By the late nineteenth century, handloom weavers who worked in their own homes were invariably supplied with yarn from a local linen agent to weave into cloth in return for a wage. The 1830s saw the older hand shuttle replaced by a new flying shuttle for linen looms which, because it was lighter to handle, encouraged women to become weavers. The following decades of the nineteenth century also witnessed the introduction of the power-loom weaving of linen, which was eventually to sound the death knell for the domestic hand-loom weaver. Boys, women and girls could be trained to operate power looms but unlike a hand-loom weaver they did not require to undergo a long apprenticeship. However, the highest quality of linen cloth, such as damask, was still produced on the hand-loom but by the early twentieth century hand-woven linen was a luxury product with a shrinking export market and its ageing workforce of hand-loom weavers could not demand decent wages.

In external appearance the Ballydugan weaver's house has several features of a characteristic Irish vernacular dwelling: it is a long, low, single-storey house of three bays or rooms, whitewashed both internally and externally, and is thatched with wheat straw. It has a slightly off-centre brick chimney and four windows along its front side and four windows at the back. The house has no back door but its front door has a shallow, brick-built porch. The number of windows is generous but four of the eight windows are needed to light the weaving workshop and not the ordinary living space within the house. The weaving workshop is notable for its high, open ceiling; the extra height of the ceiling was required to accommodate the height of the linen looms.[23]

There were sunken traces of the foundations of four looms on the floor of the original Ballydugan house and these looms may be safely presumed to have been for the smaller cambric handkerchief and diaper looms. Two old looms – a tall Jacquard damask loom and a handkerchief loom – were, by the early 1970s, acquired by the museum and placed in the house. From

January 1968 to the late 1970s, John McAtasney was employed by the
museum to demonstrate hand-loom weaving on a Jacquard loom in the
weaver's house.[24]

Internally, the Ballydugan house consisted of a bedroom, central
kitchen/living room and a roomy beaten-earth floored workshop for the
linen looms. The kitchen had a central hearth with a boarded full-length
screen and bench on its inner side serving as a protective 'jamb' wall
between the hearth and the front door. There was also a timber-boarded
open half-loft above the open hearth, suitable for storage purposes or
perhaps as extra sleeping accommodation. The floor of the weaving shop
is of beaten earth while the bedroom has a pine-boarded floor and low,
boarded ceiling. The weaver's house was dated as belonging to the second
half of the nineteenth century but its exact year of building remains
unknown.[25]

Throughout recent centuries, local stone was the most readily available
material for building Irish vernacular houses but 'mud' or clay (tempered
earth) was also widely used, especially in areas where building stone was
scarce and timber resources had become depleted. By 1700 this relative
lack of timber led to a dependence on imported timber and on wood salvaged from local bogs for use in the construction of smaller rural houses;
an associated phenomenon was the disappearance of late medieval traditions of timber house-framed carpentry.[26]

A tradition of vernacular earthen houses in Ireland has been traced
back to medieval Ireland, probably as an innovation within the Norman
Pale of south-east Ireland. The drier weather enjoyed in this part of the
country helped to ensure the survival of many substantial earthen farmhouses.[27] In the northern counties the early history of this building tradition remains obscure 'but at the Plantation it was certainly widespread
and may have been the dominant type'.[28] Vernacular earthen house types
are also known from the continent and from Britain; the most celebrated
English examples are the sixteenth or seventeenth century 'cob' houses of
Devon and Cornwall.[29] Earth and clay have been used for building purposes from the earliest times, but the extent of use of clay within buildings
varied in conformity to individual and local circumstances. Clay was a
versatile material whose use was often graduated from the partial or complete building of solid load-bearing walls, merely to its use as a wall filling
or bedding material for stone course work.

But the main defining feature of clay or earthen-walled houses is that
treated or 'tempered' earth is used as a mass material and often for load-
bearing walls usually on stone foundations. To guarantee stability the
external clay walls were often of great thickness (up to 1 metre wide) and
were sometimes faced with fieldstone. The upper triangular parts of
gables and side walls of the house were difficult to build up with clay and
frequently layers of sod courses or roughed-out blocks of earth were used
instead, examples of brick or stone gables were also common. In the

weaver's house the front and rear walls are of mud with stone facings and the corners of the house are of stone. The interior walls and gables were mud-walled.[30] Mud walls were by necessity given an external finish of lime rendering to weatherproof them and protect them from vermin but this practice also served to make many mud-walled houses indistinguishable from neighbouring stone houses. Internal partition walls within buildings could be made from the range of existing materials.

Various familiar constructional methods or 'recipes' used for building clay-walled houses existed throughout Ireland but ideally the clay source should be located close to the proposed house site. A sufficient amount of clayey earth was dug up and pounded and mixed up with some water to a smoother texture and then left to 'sour' for several days. Chopped straw or a similar fibrous material was also well mixed into the mixture to bind the clay. Hard, laborious work was required in the digging, local transportation and in the physical preparation of the clay for use as a building material, and historical accounts stress the communal nature of house-building. The main building skills were within the reach of the ordinary householder but they required knowledge of the right method of clay preparation and care and patience in gradually building up the main walls from the prepared clay/tempered-earth in layers. The wall surfaces were trimmed smooth by using a spade, hay knife or similar tool. The use of wooden 'shuttering' to hold the mud in place while building up walls was known but does not seem to have widely practised in Ireland.[31] Patience and good weather was essential because at least a week was needed between building the wall layers, to allow for settlement and drying of the mud. A small house could take several months to complete and larger houses may have taken well over a year.[32] Skill was also needed when inserting the hearth and chimney and the door and window openings. Construction of the chimney roof required the skill of a competent brick-layer and a house carpenter, but cheapness in construction was one of the main advantages of a mud-walled house because family and friends could undertake most of the building work.

In Ireland, clay-walled houses were known from the midlands and down the broad sweep of the east of Ireland. Specific Northern Irish examples have been recorded from the Lagan valley in County Down and from the southern low-lying, Montaighs flood plain of Lough Neagh, in County Armagh.[33] In the nineteenth century, mud houses were often associated with a poorer, unpretentious stock of housing and they rarely exceeded two storeys in height but could be found in both rural and urban contexts.[34]

Despite their association with poverty and peasantry, Irish 'mud' houses did represent an efficient use of local resources and labour. When well-built and maintained, an earthen house or cabin provided a warm and comfortable home. The longevity and comfort of clay or mud-walled houses has been defended by commentators from both past and present perspectives: solid earthen walls provided good insulation, allowing for coolness in the summer and warmth in the winter months. Modern views also note the aesthetically simple, harmonious appearance of vernacular 'earthen' houses in the landscape. The 'environmental friendliness' of these earthen houses which 'breathe' is admirable and they use a ubiquitous resource as a prime building material, which is pre-eminently biodegradable.[35]

The last two occupants of the Ballydugan house were two elderly spinster sisters called Elizabeth (known as Lizzie) and Ellen Jane Gibson. The Gibson family paid rent to the Blane family for the house. As required, the Blane family undertook repairs on the house, such as hiring a thatcher to repair the roof. Apart from a small surrounding patch of grass and its hedge there was no land attached to the Gibson holding. When last lived in, the house did not have electricity or piped water; there was a turf fire and drinking water was obtained over the road from the nearby pump in the yard of Bloomvale farm. The weaving workshop had become the scullery. Most household groceries and other goods, including turf for the fire, were available from carts and vans that had regular rounds in the locality. By the early 1940s both sisters were elderly and Lizzie was mostly house-bound, although Ellen Jane could undertake some occasional domestic work for a local teacher. Visitors to the Gibson sisters included female relatives who came down by bus from Belfast.[36] Both sisters had a long life and their burials are recorded in the parochial burial register for Knocknamuckley church. First, an entry for a Lizzie Gibson of Bleary who died on 5 December 1946 aged eighty-four and a later entry for Ellen Jane Gibson of Bleary who died on 5 January 1963 aged ninety-two. A separate baptismal record gives the name Elizabeth Gibson who was born on 29 March 1861 to James and Margaret Gibson of Bleary.[37]

After the death of Ellen Jane, the Gibson house was used as a store and in recent years it has been 'blocked up' but it still stands with one gable end facing the road. The chimney has been removed and the roof is of corrugated metal sheeting. The house is now surrounded by modern urban housing developments and its rural character is muted. Likewise, other reminders of the linen weavers of this northern corner of County Down have mostly disappeared, as local livelihoods are now dependent on agriculture, various contracting-type employment, and jobs in local towns or further afield in Belfast. However, the presence of the Ballydugan house in the Ulster Folk and Transport Museum is a continuing tribute to the once-dominant and prosperous Ulster Linen Industry.

Acknowledgements

I wish to thank the following for their help in the preparation of this article: Miss Muriel Blane, Bleary, County Down; Rev B.T. Blacoe of St Matthias' Church, Knocknamuckley and Arthur Paterson of the Select Vestry, Knocknamuckley, County Armagh; the late Philip Wilson of the Craigavon Heritage Museum, Pinebank House; Gerald MacAtasney, Belfast; Mr McConkey, Ballydougan; Ian Adamson, Bleary, County Down.

Notes and references

1. Comment on the opening of the weaver's house, 'Mr McEvoy who is one of only five men in a Belfast mill who can work such a loom', *Irish News*, 20 May 1967. The linen firm of Ewarts was founded in the early nineteenth century and by the twentieth century the firm, by then a public company, owned several spinning, weaving and bleaching concerns.
2. The weaver's house is on Calvertstown Road, off Plantation Road, Bleary.
3. Early Folk Museum references are varied and refer to a weaver's house from near Lurgan or Waringstown but by the 1970s the name Ballydugan was used and has now become established.
4. Public Record Office of Northern Ireland (PRONI) Census of Ireland 1901, Enumerators returns.
5. Mann, G.G., *Historical notes on the parish of Knocknamuckley* (Lurgan, 1937). Lurgan Workhouse was built in 1840 and it accommodated 800 inmates.
6. Bloomvale house is now a listed building and it is presently the home of the Ballydougan Pottery.
7. Whittle is a rare surname in Ireland, although in the early nineteenth century a Stafford Whittle was the gentleman proprietor of Thistleborough House, Glenavy, County Antrim. A Mrs Elizabeth Whittle and a Miss Wallace (who may have been related, in the early 1830s Ballydugan formed part of the Wallace estate) are listed as living in number 38 Eccles Street, Dublin, *Thom's Irish Almanac and Official Directory for 1850* (Dublin, 1850), p 719. Alexander R. Stewart was the landlord of Ards in County Donegal. The family seats were at Ards, near Letterkenny, County Donegal and at Laurencetown House, Gilford, County Down; this family was a cadet branch of the Stewart family of Mount Stewart County Down, the Irish seat of the Marquess of Londonderry.
8. Atkinson, E.D., *An Ulster parish being a history of Donaghcloney* (Dublin, 1898), pp 20–23.
9. Information via the Northern Ireland Place-Name Project, the Queen's University of Belfast. There are two townlands in County Down named Ballydugan; the other Ballydugan townland is outside the county town of Downpatrick.
10. Bell, Robert, *Book of Ulster surnames* (Belfast, 1994), p 76.
11. PRONI, Val.1B 350. Valuation book, Tullylish Parish.
12. Nimmons, J., *Newmills congregation 1796–1947* (Lurgan, 1948), pp 13, 27, 28. Thomas and James Adamson were listed among the first elders of Newmills Presbyterian Church, in Ballynagarrick townland; in the 1860s a Robert Adamson persuaded the landlord, Mr Whittle, to grant land for Ballydugan

school, where a Sunday school was later established. Ibid, p 28. The school building is now the local Young Farmers Club.

13. Presumably the hill was named from the famous sixteenth-century Irish chieftain, Shane O'Neill. The view from the slopes is still impressive but the hilltop is now fenced off and encloses a DOE water plant building. John McCartan, a linen merchant and land agent for the Bishop of Dromore was asked about the 'combination' called the Tommy Downshires. 'They met [several years ago] on Shane's Hill to protest against a local [unnamed] agent and to demand rent reductions but there had been no recent combinations', Devon Commission, 1844, Q. 89 p 302.

    In the 1870s the local Presbyterian minister, the Rev. James Orr, held prayer meetings on Shane's Hill during the summer months. Nimmons (1948), op. cit., p 31.

14. Day, Angélique and McWilliams, Patrick (eds) *Ordnance Survey Memoirs of Ireland, Parishes of Co. Down vol. 12, 1833–38* (Belfast, 1992), pp 140–7. By the middle of the nineteenth century there were no masonic halls in either Ballydugan or Bleary but Bleary had at least one Orange hall. Bleary townland had strong Orange links dating back to the Peep O Day boys and the Battle of the Diamond in 1795, when the 'Bleary boys' were among those who fought against the Catholic Defenders; after this sectarian fight the first Orange lodge in Ireland was reputedly established. In the early twentieth century a small Hibernian hall (now derelict) was established in Ballydugan townland largely due to a population shift of local Catholics from the nearby Clare townland.

15. Crawford, W.H., *The handloom weaver and the Ulster linen industry* (Belfast,1994), p 5. The Dundalk factory lasted for about ten years and a cavalry barracks was later built on is site near to Dundalk Bay.

16. The term 'linen triangle' is a modern, academic phrase coined by W.H. Crawford, historian of the linen industry.

17. MacAtasney, Gerald, *The Famine in Lurgan and Portadown* (Belfast, 1997), pp 45–66.

18. *Banner of Ulster*, 19 and 26 March 1847 and 20 and 30 April 1847.

19. Crawford, W.H., 'A handloom weaving community in Co. Down', *Ulster Folklife*, 39 (1993), pp 1–14.

20. During this period the city of Belfast and mill towns and villages of Ulster were expanding and attracting rural migrants.

21. Crawford, W.H., *The Irish linen industry*, UFTM exhibition booklet (1987), pp 21–22.

22. A local entrepreneur, Mr James Blane, farmer and local spirit grocer, established the factory and it was later managed by his son Christopher. During the early decades of the twentieth century the factory received funding from the Department of Agriculture and Technical Instruction and employed a Swiss emigrant to teach Swiss machine embroidery. This family is related to the Blane family of Bloomvale. The factory is still in business but it is no longer wholly a family firm.

23. UFTM leaflet on Ballydugan weaver's house, 1970s.

24. Gailey, Alan, 'Damask weaving in the museum', *Ulster Folk and Transport Museum Yearbook, 1968–69*. Mr McAtasney is now employed at the Irish Linen Centre, Lisburn.

25. The weaver's house does not appear on the 1830 Ordnance Survey map. Alan Gailey dated the house to the middle of the nineteenth century on the basis of

its later purlin roof and brickwork.

26. Buchanan, R.H., 'The Planter and the Gael, cultural dimensions of the Northern Ireland problem', in W.F. Boal and J.N.H. Douglas (eds) *Integration and division, geographical perspectives on the Northern Ireland problem* (London, 1982), p 63.

27. Danaher, K., *Vernacular architecture in Ireland* (Cork, 1975), p 9.

28. Buchanan (1982) op. cit., p 53.

29. Brown, R.J., *The English country cottage* (London, 1979), pp 147–58.

30. UFTM leaflet, Ballydugan weaver's house.

31. McCourt, Desmond, 'Weavers' houses around south-west Lough Neagh' in *Ulster Folklife*, 8 (1962), p 43. Also see, O'Hare, P., 'The use of mud as building material constructing a single-unit dwelling at Currow, Co. Kerry, in *Sinsear*, 8 (1995), pp 133–45.

32. Brown (1979), op. cit., p 151.

34. Gailey, Alan, *Rural houses of the north of Ireland* (Edinburgh, 1984), p 55.

35. MacDonald, Frank and Doyle, Pegin, *Ireland's earthen houses* (Dublin, 1997).

36. Information given to F. Carragher by Miss Muriel Blane, September 1998.

37. Church records, Knocknamuckley parish, select vestry. The ages for the Gibson sisters in the parochial records are a close but not an identical match to the 1901 census records, which may have been rounded to give even numbers and younger ages.

6

Material Evidence:
Dress as a Historical Record

LINDA-MAY BALLARD

Rites of passage are familiar territory for the folklorist, and of these, marriage is perhaps the most popular subject for research. Books on the subject prove to be of endless interest, and several exhibitions, including the monumental Love and Marriage in Europe[1] have engaged (if that is not an unacceptable pun) many of the most eminent European researchers in attempts to interpret this important occasion.

Irish folklore provides a great deal of evidence for the folklorist. There are oral accounts of matchmaking and runaways, of marriage divination and of a wide range of traditional celebrations, some regional, some almost universal, which attend the event of a marriage in Ireland. From these oral accounts, the staple diet of a research folklorist, a particular image of the traditional wedding begins to appear. In presenting an exhibition, however, the folklorist must draw on material as well as on non-material sources, and it may be that here a dichotomy appears. The textiles collection of the Ulster Folk and Transport Museum includes a superb selection of nineteenth-century wedding gowns. The most regularly-represented fabric is silk, and the changes in shape of these gowns illustrate speedy responses to changes in contemporary fashion. The dresses are in a range of colours, and the popularity of tones of mauve can be accounted for by the dominance of the shades of mourning on the fashion scene of the British Isles. Another rite of passage has made its presence felt on the event of a marriage. These dresses do not at first glance correspond with the image conjured by oral traditions of the event of marriage in local society in the course of the same era. The initial reaction is to assume that the dresses and the folklore do not in fact correspond, but that they belong to the same era but to different regions and social groupings.[2] Research and a well-documented collection illustrate that the answer is not so straightforward.

The collection includes three very important contemporary outfits, all from the late 1850s, which show this point to perfection. One is a dress of oyster silk, worn by Matilda Carson of Belfast when she married Alexander Finlay of Holywood on 22 September 1858 in Second Holywood Presbyterian Church in County Down. This couple were of the affluent middle class, but it is in the colour of the gown (oyster) rather than in its style that the social class of the bride is most clearly represented. At this date, a bride wanted to have a better return from the investment in her wedding gown than to wear it only once, and Mrs Finlay would in fact have been expected by her contemporaries to wear her wedding gown to evening parties which they would arrange in her honour subsequent to her wedding. The dress in question includes all the typical features of the fashion of the time, wide bell-sleeves under which sleeves, no doubt of fine Irish lace, would have been necessary, a full skirt supported by a crinoline and trimmed with fringing and a dropped shoulder line. It also features a detachable bodice which can be removed to reveal one much less demure, intended for evening wear.[3]

The second dress of the trio was worn when Jane Graham, a farmer's daughter from the Ballinamallard district of County Fermanagh, married a Mr Mooney in Magheracross Parish Church on 9 July 1859. Jane's silk dress bears many similarities to Matilda's, but the most immediately apparent distinction is in its colour, for Jane chose for her wedding day a very fine blue and grey check pattern. The general shape of both dresses is very similar, but the characteristics in Jane's are less pronounced. Her dress illustrates clearly that when they could afford it, young women of Ulster made every effort to acquire a silk wedding gown which would continue in wear long after the wedding, and Jane's preference for blue instead of white is evidence of a practical streak to increase the wearability of her gown. It is worth noting that nineteenth-century travellers in Ireland frequently comment on the standard of dress which they observed, particularly in the north of the island. For example, John Barrow, writing in 1835, remarked: ' But though the people were well dressed, and exceedingly decent in their manner, we passed on both sides of the gap some very wretched habitations…',[4] suggesting that there may have been a visible discrepancy between standards of dress and other evidence of general standards of living. Jane Graham appears to have been from a family which was comfortably off, and likely to have enjoyed a general standard of living higher than that reported by Barrow from Donegal. Her dress illustrates that fabrics of the highest quality could be obtained in many parts of the country, that young women were sufficiently interested in fashion to have these made up into attractive garments, and that local dressmakers could reach the standards to which the clientele aspired.[5]

At about the same time, the daughter of the keeper of the East Light on Rathlin Island married a Mr McFaul, one of the local blacksmiths. The East Light was itself the first established on the island. Its foundation stone was

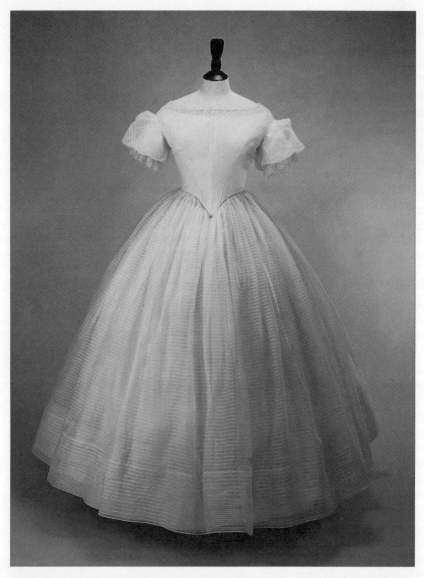

Figure 6.1 Muslin dress worn by bridesmaid Kate Stevenson at her sister's wedding,
163. The two-piece dress was worn over petticoats and supported by a hooped crinoline. The bodice is boned and back lacing (UFTM L4681/1)

laid in 1849, and in 1856 it first offered protection to shipping navigating
very dangerous waters in a main route.[6] Mrs McFaul's wedding ensemble
is of very great interest. It features a skirt of shot purple silk, its full shape
in the general fashion of the time; its waistband, bearing witness to many
extensions, suggests that it remained in wear for very many years. The
skirt was teamed with a black mantle, for which pieces and even scraps of

silk had been saved. This, too, is reminiscent of the other two dresses in the trio, like them featuring bell sleeves and fringed trimming. Her straw bonnet with purple silk ties also survives. The ensemble makes several very important points. A decade after the Famine, on remote Rathlin, the wife of an artisan could aspire to own a silk outfit, and was clearly aware of the fashion trends of her era. Her choice of colours was astute, for the black mantle was to be one of the staples of the later nineteenth-century wardrobe, and Queen Victoria was to make purple one of the shades appropriate for court wear (and therefore for fashionable dress) in the second half of the century.

Between them, then, these dresses add considerably to the understanding of marriage and folk tradition in mid nineteenth-century Ireland, and to our awareness of the standards of self-presentation to which local women could aspire. But not everyone chose to wear silk. In 1812, a farmer's daughter from Glenwherry, County Antrim, was described on her wedding day as 'a modest-looking young girl about seventeen. She was dressed in a white calico gown and ribands, and had a fan in her hand'.[7] This bride clearly chose the colour most regularly thought to symbolise purity, and, in bridal terms, virginity. At this date, when a bride wore white, this colour was also often worn by her bridesmaids, and Ellen Stevenson made exactly this choice on her wedding day in 1863 (Figure 6.1). Although the bride's gown does not survive, the delicate dress of white muslin worn by her sister Kate is part of the collection of the Ulster Folk and Transport Museum,[8] as is the spade mill owned by the family of her father, John. The spade mill is re-erected in the museum grounds as a working exhibit, and the dress further illuminates the way of life and the expectations of the associated family.

Oral lore, written documents and material culture may all combine to assist the folklorist in interpreting the past, but photographs also have an important part to play. W.A. Green's photograph showing the arrival of the strawboys at a wedding may perhaps have been staged, but it does not appear to have been falsified (Figure 6.2). A white-dressed, veiled young woman may frequently have taken the floor with a strawboy, and this continued to be the case until the 1960s, particularly in parts of Fermanagh and perhaps to the south. Nowadays, the strawboys are again beginning to be popular at weddings, as many folk customs undergo revival. Photographs of rural couples also suggest that among the less affluent, the principals, bride, groom, and perhaps best man and bridesmaid may have acquired finery for the occasion, but the rest of the guests – even the parents of the bride – often did not.

Until the 1840s, many Irish weddings took place in the home of the bride, or sometimes in the dwelling of the officiating priest. This may have helped to establish the popularity of Showing Sunday, on which bride, groom, bridesmaid and best man went to church together to display their wedding finery. The occasion was the Sunday following the wedding, and may have involved a degree of public display that the wedding had in fact taken place, but it is usually described as the opportunity for the bride to show off her outfit to the congregation. In churches where the men and women were usually segregated, this might be the only occasion on which a married couple sat together in church. As the crinoline gave way to the bustle, the gasps to greet the first brides daring enough to wear this fashion in any given area can only be imagined, but the appetite for fashion held good, and as the 1860s gave way to the 1870s there are clear signs that the new fashion was eagerly embraced and widely worn. The outfit chosen by Margretta Adams for her wedding to Robert Dunlop in 1877 is particularly interesting. This wedding took place in the drawing-room of Ashville, in Antrim, on 28 August; presumably it was by special licence as by this date these provisions would have been essential under the law. The dress was made by a Miss Thompson, whose premises were at Carlisle Circus in Belfast, and who was clearly capable of creating gowns in the latest fashion. This example of her work features the violin-shaped bodice popular at the time, together with magnificent frogging of silk rope.[9] Associated documentation provides another interesting detail of an aspect of social change, for the beautiful tan Irish poplin of which the dress is made was the wedding gift of the bride's brother-in-law, James Mitchell of Monaghan, a draper. At this date, it was perfectly acceptable to give personal gifts to a bride for her wedding presents, a tradition which persisted in rural Ireland until the 1950s, by which time most brides marrying in the towns and cities expected to receive household items only. The dress also

Figure 6.2 Strawboys at a Sligo wedding, early twentieth century. The straw masks disguised the young men who sought to dance with the bride and her attendants, bringing them good luck and fertility if they were well-treated (WAG 1957)

provides further evidence of the standard and range of fabrics for which provincial women could obviously rely upon their local drapers.

Surviving wedding dresses show us that good quality silks and skilful dressmakers were widely available in nineteenth-century Ireland, but close study of an early twentieth-century dress reveals a surprising detail (Figure 6.3). On 18 January 1912, Samuel Corbett, another draper, this time

Figure 6.3 Jane Eliza Sprott's dress is of rayon with silk lining. The fashion is typical of the years 1910–12, and the bridegroom's outfit is also typical of men's dress of the era (UFTM L3225/1)

from Portadown, married Jane Eliza Sprott. Her wedding dress is very typical of the fashion of that date, and is in oyster-coloured rayon. The lining is of silk. Clearly, when man-made fabrics first became available, the fashion conscious preferred them to more established, natural materials.

A good collection of wedding gowns is an invaluable asset to the folklorist intent on interpreting this fascinating aspect of life in the past through visual display. It is worthwhile noting that these dresses chosen by brides in the past may confound some of the expectations which other sources may help us, unwittingly, to formulate. These wedding gowns are therefore of great importance in their own right, but they have additional significance as they incidentally illustrate several issues of past social and economic life. They also show the clear contrast between the conspicuous display of the dress, or at least, the best dress of many women in the past and the dress of contemporary men. In addition to the gown worn on her wedding day by Matilda Carson, the collection of the Ulster Folk and Transport Museum includes the suit worn by the bridegroom, Alexander Finlay. This is of plain black wool, and only the subtlest details of the tail coat and trousers set them apart from similar garments of several other decades. For evidence of the dress of less affluent rural bridegrooms, we must turn once again to oral sources:

> A man from Foygin, Donaghmore [County Tyrone] acquired a very good coat. It is believed he received this special coat from uncles who had earlier emigrated to New York. The coat was so special that he never wore it, except when he was getting married. For at least twenty-five years after this

Figure 6.4 The fashion for motoring veils has influenced bridal fashions, shown in this picture taken by Newcastle, County Down photographer, Conn, c.1912. Perhaps the young people have hired a car for a day's excursion following the wedding, as was popular at the time (UFTM L3132/5)

(1807s–1890s) all the neighbouring small farmers would go to him to bor-
row the coat for their own marriages. The practice fell into disuse because
it became a liability for a young man to be seen going to visit the house, as
the neighbours automatically concluded that he was planning marriage.[10]

It is not quite clear from the story whether the coat was sent home from
America, or left behind. Many brides received their wedding dresses, or
the money with which to buy them, as gifts from sisters and other close
relatives and friends who had emigrated. Some bridegrooms enlivened
their outfits by wearing colourful waistcoats, and one surviving mid nineteenth-century example has its lining inscribed 'My darling husband's
wedding waistcoat'.[11]

Surviving wedding accessories also provide evidence of past tastes and
skills (Figure 6.4). The collection of the Ulster Folk and Transport Museum
includes bridal head-dresses illustrating the symbolic importance of the
orange blossom, which, like many other tokens associated with courtship
and marriage, betokened fertility. Lace veils bear witness to the skills of
local needlewomen and to the demand for their products. Fine quality
embroidered and otherwise decorated shoes preserve evidence of a range
of crafts. The material evidence of items such as wedding dresses may
stimulate and support extensive and rewarding possibilities for research.

Notes and references

1. See *Amour et mariage en Europe, aspects de la vie populaire en Europe, 1975, Actes
    Colloque International*, intro. Roger Pinon, Musee de la Vie Wallonne, Liege,
    1975. I am indebted to Dr R.A. Gailey who first drew this to my attention some
    years ago.
2. In the early 1990s, an exhibition entitled 'Tying the knot' was displayed at the
    Ulster Folk and Transport Museum. The response of one curator, seeing the
    unexpected opulence of the gowns, was to exclaim, 'But where are all the dress-
    es of the poor?' It may be worth pointing out that the very poor may have dis-
    pensed with the formality of the wedding ceremony altogether. See Ballard, L-
    M., *Forgetting frolic* (Belfast, 1998), p 127; also McLoughlin, D. 'Workhouses and
    Irish female paupers 1840–1870' in M. Luddy and C. Murphy (eds), *Women sur-
    viving* (Swords, 1989), p 128.
3. Ulster Folk and Transport Museum accession number 331.1972. A similar solu-
    tion to a slightly different problem was found by a bride from Lisburn a centu-
    ry later. When Miss Carol Chambers married Mr John Diamond on 22 April
    1953 she wore a rather extravagant gown acquired from the modish Renee of
    Belfast. The gown features a bolero top which when removed revealed a neck-
    line more suitable for evening wear, and the dress continued in use for some
    time after the wedding.
4. Barrow, J., *A tour round Ireland* (London, 1836), p 116

5. Ulster Folk and Transport Museum accession number 372.1969.
6. Clark, W., *Rathlin, disputed island* (Waterford, 1971), p 136.
7. Gamble, J., *A view of society and manners in the north of Ireland* (London, 1813), p 94.
8. UFTM accession number 1152.1987.
9. UFTM accession number 526.1972.
10. Archive of the UFTM.
11. UFTM accession number 509.1976.

The *Bothóg*:
A Seasonal Dwelling from County Donegal

ROBBIE HANNAN AND JONATHAN BELL

TRANSHUMANCE HAS BEEN PRACTISED in County Donegal since at least the
seventeenth century.[1] Throughout Ireland, the practice of moving livestock to hilly areas for summer grazing was known as *buailteachas*, or 'booleying'. By the nineteenth century, the tenants of the Gweedore estate in
north-west Donegal were described by their landlord as having 'an Arab
mode of life, not having a fixed residence'. He claimed that they would
move three times a year, between the coastal plain, the off-shore islands,
and the inland hills.[2] Oral evidence suggests that this movement was in
fact significantly modified by the landlord's approach to estate management,[3] but the movement of cattle to the hills, in either summer or winter,
meant that the construction of temporary shelters continued well into the
twentieth century. In Gweedore, the most common type of temporary
dwelling was the *bothóg* (Figure 7.1). Fred Coll of Derrybeg, Gweedore,
gave the following summary of the use of *bothógaí*.

> Some people that were living in this area here that's away from the shore,
> that had no rights to grazing at the shore... would have what they called
> the *bothógaí*... The *bothógaí* were constructed of sod in the mountain, dry
> sod, in a dry place... They would construct it into a bank... The man of the
> house would probably go up at that time... and look after the cows – herd
> the cows, and whatever number of sheep they had up there too.

> There was a number of people that had nothing more down here than *both-*
> *ógaí*, and it used to be a great thing in past times... if your people lived in a
> *bothóg*, they would be up casting to you. 'Sure what the Hell are you talk-
> ing about, sure your grandfather lived in a *bothóg*'... which was a slur
> then... My own [great]grandfather on my mother's side lived in a *bothóg*,
> and it was said to me... After he got married, he had no land [and he had
> to]... go up into the mountain there and just make this *bothóg* and try to
> make do with just his wee cow and his couple of hens, and try to hack a liv-
> ing out of the side of the mountain... Those who stayed on in areas like that
> and went out and cut... the 'cuts' they called them, established a right to
> them.

Figure 7.1 *Bothóg* in north-west Donegal, c.1900 (UFTM L440/19)

The following, much more detailed, extract of an account of bringing cattle to high ground for summer grazing and the construction of a *bothóg*
was collected by Seán Ó hEochaidh, of the Irish Folklore Commission,
from Niall Ó Dubhthaigh, who was born in 1874 in the townland of
Bealtaine, which is about a mile from *Gort an Choirce*, in the parish of *Cloich
Cheannfhaola* in north-west Donegal. The full text can be found in
Béaloideas, 13 (1943), pp 132–56.[4]

It is reproduced here with the permission of Professor Séamas Ó Catháin,
Head of the Department of Irish Folklore, University College, Dublin.

Irish text

Le trácht ar shean-nósaí – sin sean-nós amháin ar chualaidh mise trácht air
nuair a bhí mé mo ghasúr, agus nach gcluin tu lá iomráidh thall ná i bhfos,
thíos ná thuas air anois, – sin an grás a bhí ag daoine fad ó shoin a dhul 'un
t-sléibhe 'un buailteachais ins a't-Samhradh, agus pilleadh arais 'na bhaile
i dtráthaibh na Samhna le n-a gcuid eallaigh… Na talta a bhí thart i gcoir
na fairrge anseo againn fad ó shoin… Mín Lárach, Machaire Rabhartaigh,
Árdaí Mór, agus an ceanntar thart soir go Cill Ulta. Bhí na talta sin an-
bheag, cumhang. Bhí talamh maith ann, an méid a bhí ann de, ach bhí gan-
ntanas mór inghilte ortha. Ní rabh inghilt ar bith ná talamh garbh thart
comhgarach acú a dtiocfadh leófa a gcuid eallaigh a scaoileadh amach
ortha, mar bhí acú i n-áiteacha eile fríd a' pharáiste. A dh'aindeoin go rabh
siad ceangluighthe thíos anseo ag na cladaigh, bhí ceart acú ó na tighearnaí a gcuid eallaigh a chur ar inghilt ar na sléibhte i bhfad ar shiubhal – sin
thart suas fá bhun an Earagail, agus ó sin thart siar go Mín na Cuinge. Ba
leis na tighearnaí talaimh a bhí ins an áit seo – ba leófa na sléibhte, agus

thugadh siad-san cead dó na daoine a gcuid eallaigh a chur ar inghilt ansin ar feadh a' t-Samhraidh, dá mba mhian leófa sin a dhéanamh…

Cha dtiocfadh leis an mhuinntir seo a théigheadh 'na chruic leis na h-ainmhidhtí an Samhradh a chaitheamh thuas ansin gan dídean nó foscadh beag a bheith acú, agus áit a ndéanfadh siad a scríste, agus greim bidh réidh ann, agus thógad siad bothógaí beaga fód, agus ba sin an cineál áruis a ndéanfadh siad comhnaidhe ionntú ar feadh an t-Samhraidh.

Mar dubhairt mé, ba dh-é an grás a bhí ins an taoibh seo de'n tír,'achan trí theaghlach a dhul isteach le chéile. Rachadh na fir suas ansin agus thóg-fadh siad an bhothóg, agus nuair a bheadh 'achan rud réidh acú-san chuir-fidhe suas na h-ainmhidhtí leis na cailíní. Bhíodh cuid de na bothógaí seo an-mhór – chomh mór agus go dtiocfadh leófa cúpla bó a thabhairt isteach ionntú i n-a gcuideachta héin. Cha dtugadh siad isteach go minic iad amach ó mur mbeádh ceann acú le breith, agus thugadh siad isteach iad sin le deoch the a thabhairt daofa. Cha gcuirtidhe na h-ainmhidhtí óga a choir na bothóige a' chor a' bith. Bhíodh siad thart comhgarach do'n bhothóig'san oidhche, agus nuair a thiocfadh bodhránacht an lae lá thar na bhárach, d'éireóchadh na cailíní, agus chuirfeadh siad suas taobh an t-sléibhe arais iad, agus d'fhanóchadh siad ansin go socair suaimhneach ar feadh an lae go dtigeadh an tráthnóna arais, agus snámhadh siad anuas leó chuig an ísleacht tráthnóna, agus d'fhanadh siad thart comhgarach do na bothógaí ar feadh na h-oidhche…

Nuair a bhéadh siad ag 'ul a thógáil ceann de na bothógaí seo, rachadh fir an bhaile suas, agus a gcuid spádaí agus piocóidí leófa, agus dá bhfe-icfeadh siad bruach nó ardán beag deas graibhéil nó gainnimh a bhéadh i n-áit deas thirim, rachadh siad chuige, agus gheárrfadh siad taobh an bhruaich seo ar shiubhal, agus dhéanfadh siad é a chomhthromú go dtí go ndéanadh siad áit mhór fharsainn ansin. Chonaic mise mé héin ballógaí na mbothóg seo, agus bhí siad tuairim ar dheich dtroigh ar leithead. Bhí an taobh a rabh an bruach ansin déanta, agus ní rabh a dhath acú le tógáil ach na beanna, agus taobh-bhalla amháin. Fóide móra abair agus scrathacha a bhíodh ins na ballaí seo. Ní rabh moill ar bith fóide móra go leór a bhaint thart fá na bothógaí. Dá mb'fhéidir daofa ar dhóigh ar bith é, thógfadh siad na bothógaí seo ins a' chruth go mbéadh a n-aghaidhe ó dheas, agus na beanntracha thoir agus thiar. Bhéadh áit fuinneoige (nó poll beag a dhéanfadh ionad fuinneoige) ins an taoibh ó dheas, agus doras ar an taobh-bhalla. Ba dh-é an taobh ó thuaidh cúl na bothóige ansin. Ba mhaith leofa i gcomhnuidhe an ghaoth tuaidh a sheachtnadh dá mb'fhéidir daofa é ar dhóigh ar bith. Ba léir leófa go mbéadh na bothógaí ní ba sheascaire dá mbéadh a gcúl ins an áird ó thuaidh. Chuireadh siad ceann ar a' bhothóig ansin, go díreach ar an nós chéana a gcuireann muid ceann ar na toighthe ceann-tuigheadh atá againn go dtí an lá indiú. Bhéadh mullach na bothóige níos airde ná na taobhanna, agus cleith na bothóige a' sleamhnú síos rud beag ar an dá thaoibh. Chuirfeadh siad taobháin de ghiúmhas breagh poill ar an bhothóig ansin, agus len-a dtuaigh bhainfeadh siad slis-

neacha, agus dhéanfadh siad an rud a dtugann muid creataí ortha de sin –
na slisneacha beaga éadtroma a théid treasna ar na taobháin. Chuireadh
siad iad seo ó chionn go cionn na bothóige, agus ansin bhí a gcuid
scrathacha bainte acú réidh le cur i n-a mullach sin.

Bhaineadh siad na scrathacha seo, an dóigh chéana a mbaineann muid
iad dó na toighthe ceann-tuigheadh atá againn – tuairim ar ceithre troigh
agus fiche ar fad, agus dhá throigh go leith ar leithead, agus ghlacfadh sé
beirt d'fheara láidre scraith acú seo a thógáil suas ar bhothóig. Cuirfidh
siad bata astoigh ins a' scraith seo, agus cuirfidh siad suas rompú í go dtí
go rabh sí ar fhíor-mhullach a' toighe. Agus ansin leigtear síos go deas
suaimhneach ar mhullach na gcreataí ar an taoibh eile í. Agus ní bhaintear
bogadh astú. Bhail, chumhdóchadh siad an bhothóg le scrathacha mar sin
a' chéad uair, agus dá mbeithidhe gan a dhath a chur oirthí ach sin, bhéadh
sí comh díonmhar le buidéal.

Bhainfeadh siad ualaigh mhóra mion-fhraoich ansin le n-a gcuid cor-
rán – mion-fhraoch a mbéadh dubh-chíb fríd: agus níl tuighe ar bith a thig
a chur ar theach atá comh díonmhar ná comh seasmhach le sin. Sheasfadh
tuithe de sin dhá bhlidhain gan deór a leigean isteach. Tuighe throm de seo
a chuirfeadh siad ar na bothógaí, agus beagán súgán thall agus i bhfos i n-
a mhullach sin ar eagla go dtiocfadh gaoth mhór a bhéarfadh ar shiubhal
an tuighe, agus bhíodh siad comh neamh-mbuaidheheartha astoigh ansin
agus dá mbéadh siad i gcuisleán a' rí. Mhairfeadh na bothógaí sin bliadhantaí agus bliadhantaí.

Bhail, ansin, bhí fir bhláthmhara i gceart síos anseo fa'n Árdaí Mhóir,
agus ba ghráthach leófa-san sciathógaí cocháin a dhéanamh a chuireadh siad
ins na dorsa i n-áit comhla. Bhíodh siad seo tuairim ar chúig troigh ar airde
agus tuairim ar thrí troigh nó mar sin ar leithead. Bhí siad déanta de shlat-
acha sailéoige go díreach mar tchídhfeá comhla ar dhoras. Bhíodh bacáin de
ghiumhas poill sáithte isteach i leathtaoibh an dorais a choinneóchadh an
sciathóg seo daingean, agus nach leigfeadh dó tuitim amach. Ins an oidhche
ansin chuirfeadh siad maide nó beirt leis an sciathóig seo a choinneóchadh
daingean í ins an oidhche ar eagla go dtiocfadh a dhath ortha i ndiaidh a
dhul a luighe. Le cois na sciathóige seo chuirfeadh siad cúpla uchtán fraoich
ins a' doras dá mbéadh oidhche fhuar ann, agus bhéadh siad comh seascair
astoigh ansin agus dá mbéadh siad astoigh sa chortha.

A chois na binne thiar de'n bhothóig bhí áit na teineadh. Chan mórán
de áit teineadh a bhí ann, ach bhí sé maith go leór agus ghníodh sé cúis
bhreagh fá choinne na teineadh le linn an ama de'n bhliadhain a bhíodh
ann. Ba bheag an teinidh a bhíodh a dhíoghháil ortha, ach amháin san oidhche, agus fhad agus a bhíodh siad a dhéanamh réidh greim bídh. Bhíodh
an teinidh seo ar an teallach go díreach mar tá sí againn ins na toighthe a
bhfuil muid ár gcomhnaidhe ionntú. Teinidh bhreagh mhónadh, agus
smutáin giumhais a bhíodh acú. Rachadh an toit suas go díreach le taoibh
na binne, agus ní rabh similéir ar bith ann ar chor a' bith, ach poll mór cru-
inn déanta thuas ar fhíor-bhárr na bothóige. An méid de'n toit ansin nach

rachadh amach ar an pholl sin rachadh sí amach ar an doras. Is annamh a bhíodh siad ag éileamh fá'n toit nó bhí tarraint bhreagh ins na poill seo. Bhí dhá úrsáid ins a' pholl seo – bheireadh sé tréan soluis do'n mhuinntir a bhéadh astoigh nuair a bhíodh an doras druidte acú, agus bhí sé a' dhéanamh úsáid fuinneóige chomh maith leis an toit a bheith ag 'ul amach ann. Dá mbeadh rud beag toite acú ach oiread, ní chuirfeadh siad suim ar bith ann, nó ba léas leis na seandaoine go rabh an toit folláin ag duine.

Bhí poll beag de áit fuinneóige ansin ins an taobh-bhalla ó dheas, mar dubhairt mé. Ní rabh gloine ar bith acú le cur ins na fuinneógaí seo, agus i n-áit an ghloine bhéadh croiceann caorach cartuigh ionntú, agus thiocfadh tréan soluis fríd an chroiceann seo ins na fuinneógaí ach amháin nuair a bhíodh siad ag 'ul a luighe san oidhche, go sáitheadh siad beairtín maith fraoich nó a leithid sin isteach ionntú...

Na h-urláir a bhí ins na bothógaí ins an am a rabh mo mháthair ionntú, ní rabh leacacha ná brící ná a dhath de'n t-seórt sin ann, nó cha rabh iomrádh ar bith ar chement go cionn leath-chéad bliadhain 'n-a dhiaidh anseo – ach i gcuid mhór áiteacha siar ins an áit a rabh na bothógaí seo, bhí árdáin bheaga thall agus i bhfos, agus bhí siad lán de sgainniogán deas mín, agus sin an t-urlár a chuireadh siad i gcuid mhór de na bothógaí. Bhí áiteacha eile ansin a rabh an chré ghorm comhgarach, agus d'imtheochadh siad agus bhainfeadh siad cúpla ualach de'n chré seo, agus m(h)easgfadh siad suas í mar dhéanfá le aol nó cement, agus chuirfeadh siad suas le dhá órdlach de'n chré ghorm sin isteach ins a' bhothóig ó chionn go cionn. Ghlacfadh sé seachtmhain nó mar sin leis an urlár sin a chruadhadh agus a thriomú, agus nuair a bhéadh sin tirim níl a'n urlár ins a' chonndae a bhéadh ní bhfhearr ná é.

Ba dh-é an t-urlár buailte a bhí ariamh ina a' pharáiste seo urlár de chré ghorm. Ní rabh na leacacha ró-fhóirsteanach do na buailtíní; bhí siad róchruaidh, agus bhrisfeadh siad barraidheacht de na buailtíní. Ach má tá an t-urlár cré ghuirm cruaidh héin, tá umhlú beag ann, agus ní bhriseann sé oiread buailtín. Bhail, sin an seórt chéana urláir a bhíodh ins na bothógaí acú, dá mbéadh an chré ghorm ar dhóigh ar bith comhgarach daofa nuair a bhéadh siad ' tógáil na bothóige. Tá mé cinnte go bhfuil cuid de n h-urláir sin le feiceáil thiar i lorgacha na mbothóg go dtí an lá indiú.

Bhí an bhothóg seo uilig i n-a h-aon seamra amháin. Bhí sí tuairim ar ocht dtroigh ar fad agus a' leithead dá réir. Is annamh a bhíodh ainmhidhe ar bith astoigh acú amach ó múr dtugadh siad isteach cúpla bó bainne nuair a bhéadh siad ar bhéalaibh ghamhna a bheith acú; nó dá mbeadh ceann acú tinn, bhéarfadh siad isteach iad seo ceart go leór.

Bhéadh smutáin bhreaghtha giumhais sínte thart i gcoir na mballaí acú ansin, agus turtógaí nó leacacha faofa, agus a gcuid soithighbainne suidhte thart i gcoir na mballaí ar na maidí sin. Sin an áit a mbeadh an chuinneóg agus an pigín agus an gogán, agus tobáin, agus achan soitheach eile a mbíodh a dhíoghbhail ortha – choinnigheadh siad go deas glan órdúil ar na maidí seo iad.

Translation

Talking of old customs – there is one old custom which I heard of when I was a boy which you never hear tell of anywhere now. That is the custom people had long ago of going to the mountain for summer grazing and returning home again with their cattle around Halloween.

The lands around the sea here a long time ago – Mín Lárach, Machaire Rabhartaigh, Árdaí Mór, and the area eastward to Cill Ulta, those lands were very small and narrow. There was good land there, what there was of it, but there was a severe shortage of grazing. There was no grazing or rough land near to them where they could let their cattle loose on it, as there was in other places throughout the parish. Although they were tethered down here at the shore, they were allowed by the landlords to put their cattle to graze on the mountains in the distance – that is up around the foot of Errigal and from there over to Mín na Cuinge. It was the landlords who were in this place who owned the mountains and they gave the people permission to put their cattle to graze there for the duration of the summer if they wished.

These people who used to go into the hills with their cattle could not stay there without having cover or shelter and a place where they could rest and prepare a bite of food, and they would build little sod huts, and that was the sort of dwelling in which they would live throughout the summer.

As I said, it was the custom in this part of the country for three families to move in together. The men would go up then and they would build the *bothóg*, and when they had everything ready the animals would be sent up with the girls. Some of these *bothógaí* would be very big, so big that they could bring a couple of cows in them along with themselves. They would not often bring them in except one of them was ready to calve and they would bring the likes of those in to give them a hot drink. The young animals would not be let near the *bothóg* at all. They would be close by the *bothóg* at night and at dawn the next day, the girls would get up and put them up the mountainside again. They would stay there calmly and peacefully during the day until evening would come again, and they would dawdle down with them to the lower ground in the evening and they would stay close by the *bothóg* during the night.

When they would be going to build one of these *bothógaí*, the men would go up with their spades and picks and if they would see a bank or a nice little height of gravel or sand in a nice dry place they would go there and cut the side of the bank away and they level it then so they would make a big wide area there. I myself saw the ruins of these *bothógaí* and they were approximately eighteen feet long and ten feet wide. The side where the bank was (already) made and they had nothing to build except the gables and the side-walls. These walls would be made of large sods of turf and scraws. There was no difficulty in cutting enough large sods in the vicinity of the *bothógaí*. If it was at all possible for them, they would build these *bothógaí* so that they would be facing south and the gables east and west. There would be a place for a window (or a small hole which would take the place of a window) on the southern-facing side, and a door on the side-wall. The side facing north would be the back of the *bothóg* then. They always liked to avoid the north wind if they possibly could. It was clear to them that the *bothógaí* would be more cosy if the back of them was facing north. They would put the roof on the *bothóg* then exactly in the same way we put a roof on the thatched-houses we have today. The top of the *bothóg* would be higher than the sides and the horizontal of the *bothóg* would slide down somewhat on the two sides. They would put purlins made from fine bog fir on the *bothóg* then, and with their axes they would cut slivers, and they would make what we would call the ribs of the roof with that – the small light slivers which go across the purlins. They would put these from one end of the *bothóg* to another and then they had their scraws cut ready to put on top of them.

They would cut these scraws the same way we cut them for the thatched houses we have – about twenty-four feet in length and two and a half feet wide, and it would take two strong men to lift one of these scraws on the *bothóg*. They would put a stick inside this scraw, and they would put it up before them until it was on the very top of the house. Then, it is let down nice and gently on the top of the ribs on the other side. And there is not a budge out of them. Well, they would cover the *bothóg* with scraws like that first of all, and if they were to put nothing on it but that, it would be as water-proof as a bottle.

They would cut big loads of fine heather with their sickles – fine heather with black sedge through it; and there is no thatch you could put on a house which would be as weather-proof or as permanent as that. That sort of thatch would last for two years without letting in a drop. It was heather such as this that they would put on the *bothógaí* and a little bit of straw-rope here and there on top of that in case a gust would come that would carry off the thatch, and they would be as unperturbed in there as they would be in the king's castle. The *bothógaí* would last for years and years.

Well, then there were really fine men down there around Árdaí Mór, and they used to make straw screens which they would put in the door-way in place of a door-leaf (Figure 7.2). These would be about five feet high and three feet or so wide. They were made of sally rods just as you would see a door-leaf on a doorway. There would be pegs of bog pine pressed into one side of the door which would keep this screen secure and would prevent it from falling out. At night time they would put a stick or two against this screen which would keep it secure during the night in case anything thing would come on them after going to bed. As well as this screen they would put a couple of armfuls of heather in the doorway if it was a cold night, and they would be as snug in there as they would be inside in the (meal) chest.

Figure 7.2 Oral testimony suggests that this may be *Bothóg Mhary Móire*. Note the door made from *súgán* (straw rope) (UFTM L440/2)

The fire-place would be in the west side of the *bothóg*. It was not much of a fire-place but it was good enough and would do well for the fire at that time of year. They did not need much of a fire, except at night, and when they would be preparing a bite of food. The fire would be on the hearth exactly as it is in the houses in which we live. They used to have a fine turf fire with pieces of bog wood. The smoke would go straight up the side of the gable, and there was no chimney there at all, but a large round hole made up at the very top of the *bothóg*. The smoke which did not go out the hole would go out the door. They seldom complained about the smoke for there was a good draw in these holes. There were two props in this hole – it would give a plenty of light to those who would be inside when they would have the door closed and it also served as a window through which the smoke could escape. If they had a small amount of smoke for that matter, they would not pay any attention to it for the old people regarded smoke to be good for a person.

There was a small hole for a window in the south-facing side wall, as I said. They had no glass to put in these windows, and instead of the glass they would have a tanned sheep-skin in them, and plenty of light would come through this skin in the windows except when they would be going to bed at night, they would shove a good bundle of heather or the like in them.

The floors in these *bothógaí* when my mother was in them, there were no flags or bricks or anything like that, nor was there any mention of cement for fifty years after that here, but in many parts over where these *bothógaí* were, there were little heights here and there which were full of nice fine gravel, and that is the floor they would put in many of the *bothógaí*. There were other places then where there was blue clay nearby, and

Figure 7.3 *Bothóg* built as a shelter for turf cutters in a bog near Gweedore railway station, in 1989. Photograph courtesy of Fred Coll.

they would go and take a couple of loads of this clay, and they would mix it up as you would do with lime or cement, and they would put up to two inches of this blue clay in the *bothóg* from one end to the other. It would take a week or so for that floor to harden and dry out, and when it would be dry there is not a floor in the county which would be better than it.

It was the beaten floor that was always in this parish, a floor of blue clay. Flags were not very suitable for flails; they were too hard, and they would break too many of the beaters of the flails. But if the floor of blue clay is hard itself, there is a bit of pliancy with it, and it does not break as many beaters. Well, that is the same sort of floor they used to have in these *bothógaí*, if the blue clay was any way near to them when they would be building the *bothóg*. I am sure that some of those floors are to be seen in the traces of the *bothógaí* to this very day.

This *bothóg* consisted of one room. It was approximately eight feet long

Figure 7.4 *Bothóg* built in *Doirí Beaga*, by Fred Coll. The *bothóg* was used in a BBC Timewatch programme in 1995. The actors in the photograph were local people.

and its width accordingly. They would rarely have animals inside unless they would bring in a couple of milch cows when they would be on the point of calving; or if one of them was unwell, they would bring these in all right.

They would have pieces of wood stretched out near the walls then, with clumps of grass or flat stones under them and there milking vessels would be positioned around the walls on those sticks. That is where the churn, pail, and the wooden vessel, and the tubs and every other vessel they would need would be [kept] – they would keep them nice and clean and orderly on these sticks.

Recent history

The valuable account translated here, describes one type of temporary dwelling, but other dwellings and shelters were also constructed. Fred Coll remembered a larger type of structure known as a *cró*, and *bothógaí* could vary a lot in construction and use. Some were too small to be used as dwellings, and were intended to provide day-time shelter for turf cutters or livestock herders in wet weather. One small structure, built in 1989 in a bog near the disused Gweedore railway station, had roughly the same proportions as a sentry box, or watchman's hut (Figure 7.3). The front wall was built up of sods, and the interior, which was circa three feet square, had space only for a seat made from a single plank.

The speed at which a *bothóg* could be constructed was well illustrated by Fred's sister Bríd, who told of a young couple leaving Gola island in the morning, to be married in the chapel at Derrybeg. As soon as the young couple went off in the boat, the men of the island took spades and began to build a *bothóg* for them to live in. When the newly-weds arrived back that evening, the *bothóg* was complete, there was a pot of potatoes boiling on the fire, and a celebration dance was held that night in their new home.

Fred Coll claims that *bothógaí* were last constructed in numbers during the Second World War. The Irish Free State remained neutral during the war, but there were severe fuel shortages because of disruption to international trade. The government responded to this emergency with a massive drive to increase the domestic production of turf. Shift working was introduced on large bogs, and workers built *bothógaí* for shelter.

The most recent *bothóg* in Gweedore (Figures 7.4 and 7.5), was constructed by Fred Coll and his brother for the BBC, for use in a television programme about the Great Famine. The brothers remembered the techniques of building, from the War. The project provided an invaluable opportunity for recording a very distinctive type of dwelling, and was also a unique testimony to the extreme poverty endured by millions of Irish people in the recent past, and their ingenuity in overcoming it.

Notes and references

1. Graham, J.M. 'South-west Donegal in the seventeenth century', *Irish Geography*, 6, (1970).
2. Hill, Lord George, *Facts From Gweedore*, (ed. E.E. Evans) (Belfast, 1971), p 28.
3. Testimony of Mr Fred Coll (UFTM tape R89.97).
4. Ó Dubhthaigh, Niall (collector Ó hEochaidh, Seán) 'Buailteachas i dTir Chonaill', *Béaloideas*, 13 (1943). A translation of this can in found in *Folk Life*, vol 22 (Leeds, 1983), pp 42–54.

Figure 7.5 Interior of Fred Coll's *bothóg*, showing the fireplace

8

Creel Houses of the Scottish Highlands

R. Ross Noble

THE FOLLOWING IS AN ACCOUNT of the construction, in 1997, of a house type which was prevalent in the Central Highlands of Scotland until the late eighteenth century. The work is part of an on-going research project at the Highland Folk Museum, whereby a farm township or *baile* of circa 1700 is being reconstructed. This four-year project began in 1996, and is funded by the Highland Council, Moray Badenoch and Strathspey Enterprise, and the European Regional Development Fund. It stems from an early experiment in building turf houses carried out by the Highland Folk Museum in the 1980s.[1]

The methodology used in the project is as follows. The township of Mid Raitts, near Kingussie, is being systematically excavated and the reconstruction work on the museum site is based on the layout, floor plans, hearth positions, etc. of the original buildings. To this evidence is added the ethnological research gathered by the museum over a long number of years, including fieldwork, documentary evidence, and, of course, the physical evidence of building parts held in the museum collections. The project director is a structural engineer, who interprets the foregoing sources of evidence in terms of their ability to produce viable structures. The ensuing buildings are a synthesis of that debate, with the major proviso that nothing is built which directly refutes the archaeological evidence.

The workforce is drawn from the local population, and embraces a range of skills, few of which were relevant to the project. The first six months of the project were spent in mastering the basic skills of handling and using the building tools of the eighteenth century – adze, side-axe, cross-cut saw, pit saw, draw-knife and hand augers – and the learning process is continuing as I write. The timber for the project was, at the outset, standing trees, and all the turf has been cut on site. The thatching materials have mainly been grown on site, or gathered locally.

The project is now in its third year, and six buildings have been erected, together with the associated head dyke, animal pens, stackyards and pathways. Each building represents a different element in the building tradition of the area – feall houses, caber houses, single and multiple-bladed crucks, walls with alternating stone and turf construction, roofs thatched with oat straw, heather and broom. The publication of all the research findings is still some way off, but it is apposite that this first account should appear in a volume of essays presented to someone who has been at the forefront of research into vernacular building traditions, and who was one of the first modern scholars to draw attention to Highland creel houses.[2]

The creel house

When such a house is to be built, the first thing done is to construct a coarse frame of wood, corresponding to the dimensions of the house, in length and breadth; then upon this frame to fix standards inclining inwards at proper distances, which rise to the height of the intended wall, and are kept in a firm position by being morticed in a tree above, of the same dimensions with the tree below. These standards are closely wove with wickerwork to keep the sods from falling in; which being built on the outside, finish the walls of a creel-house as it is called.[3]

This early nineteenth-century description of a creel house by James Robertson DD is one of several valuable accounts relating to the construction method. Elsewhere in the report he records that the local term for building turf is 'feal' and that thinner turves, used for roofing material are 'divots' Fifty years earlier, Alexander Shaw gives an almost identical account of the method in Glenmoriston, except that he adds, 'But many of their houses have no fail at all'.[4] The inn at Glenmoriston, according to James Boswell, was built of thick turfs, and thatched with thinner turfs and heath: 'Where we sat, the side-walls were "wainscotted", as Dr. Johnson said, with wicker, very neatly plaited'.[5]

Even the houses of substantial farmers, tacksmen or even landowners could be 'mud, wattled huts'.[6] Certainly in the inventory of materials used to build 'the principall onsett and steidding of the mainis of the saidis landis of Deluorar Ane hall or fyre hous' there is a reference which might suggest that this sixteenth-century gentleman lived in a creel house: 'twelf scoir staikis or cassokis in the haill hous for uphalding of the faill wallis yairof'.[7]

Pictorial evidence exists as well. A late eighteenth-century drawing of the township of Lynwilg, near Aviemore, shows what appears to be a creel house either ruined or undergoing repair (Figure 8.1) The left half of the building shows three exposed couples, and wattle panels between them. The right hand side of the building is roofed, and partly faced with turf. This illustration also reveals a wattle fence round a kailyard, giving a clear indication of the technique. In a treatise on sheep management, Sir George

Figure 8.1 The township of Lynwilg, near Aviemore, showing possible creel houses.
Artist unknown, c.1771.

Stewart Mackenzie illustrates the construction of a sheep cot, based on the
traditional highland cottage, which has wattle walls.[8] There are a number
of late nineteenth-century photographs of buildings in the Lochalsh and
Kintail districts of the West Highlands, which reveal survivals of this technique.[9]

A barn which has survived to the end of the twentieth century with one
wattle panel and a gablet surviving has just been taken into care by the
National Trust for Scotland. On other parts of the building, wooden lou-
vered panels have replaced the original wattle.

Reconstruction

The timing of the reconstruction of the creel house meant that the workforce had already considerable skill in cruck-making and in the building of
turf walls. One of the major constraints in the case of the former activity
was the quality of the timber. Traditionally, most crucks for the principal
buildings in a township would have been made from one piece, for additional strength. This meant that trees with naturally curved trunks or
limbs would have been selected for the purpose. In the earlier turf house
experiment at the Highland Folk Museum in the 1980s, the museum had

been fortunate enough to be able to acquire such trees from a neighbouring estate, and the advantage gained through having less timber to convert has been previously documented.[10] The current project is using timber from the museum's own woods, which consist of pine plantings from c.1920. These are considerably straighter, and yield few pieces suitable for single-bladed crucks. All the crucks in the creel house, therefore, are scarf-jointed at the wall-head level. The jointing pegs or trenails (tree nails) are mainly of birch or ash, and shaped by means of a drawknife.

The process of cruck-making has become quite refined in the course of the past two years. The work of converting the timber is done at the edge of the woodland. The tools used are a two-man cross-cut saw, a side-axe and an adze. Two men can prepare the timber for a couple – a pair of crucks – in about twelve hours (less if the wood grain is kind). The basic size and shape of each component, crucks and collars, is roughed out at this stage. This reduces the volume of timber to be transported by about 30 per cent, and, since it is the water-laden sapwood which is being removed, the weight is reduced by up to 50 per cent.

At this stage, the timber is transported to the jointing and assembly area, within the township and close to the construction site. The transportation is carried out by slipe with a single Clydesdale mare as the power unit. The slipe or sledge has been copied from one in the museum collection and has proved to be very efficient. The heavy end of the timber rests on the slipe and is secured by ropes or a chain. The horse then drags the timber to the desired location, easily manoeuvring round standing trees, and tackling some steep gradients.

At the assembly point the timber is laid out in accordance to a pegged template and the scarf or half-lapped joints created with the same tools as previously listed with the addition of a set of hand augers (half-inch to two inches) for the various peg holes. The components of the couple are then transported, as before, to the house site, and assembled on the ground with the base resting on stone cruck pads. At this point, the couple is normally raised into the vertical position by a team of men, or by horse power, using a lifting stick to reduce the amount of force required. The upper collar is connected by rope to the top of the lifting stick, which is then raised manually to an angle of about 30 degrees from the horizontal. The stick is then pulled upright, lifting the couple with it. By the time the stick is beyond the vertical point, the couple is at an angle whereby the full effect of the horizontal force of the hauling team is applied. A back stop post, again linked to the upper collar by rope, prevents the couple from travelling beyond the vertical.

In the case of the creel house, however, an additional experiment was initiated before the couples were raised. Among the visitors who have come to view the re-construction work have been a number of country craftsmen. One of these, with a lifetime's experience in fencing, pointed out that it was traditional to char the base of strainer posts before putting them in the ground, to reduce the level of rot occurring through rising damp. Since couples would be in contact with moist turf, would this not have a similar advantage in preserving them? Thus the bottom section of each couple was charred before the couples were raised into position.

Turf used in this project has all been cut on site from areas of rough pasture. In the interest of efficiency most of it has been gathered with the help of a mechanical turf cutter, and transported to the building site by tractor and trailer. However, as part of the experiment, one house was built without these modern aids. The turf for this building, a feal house, was cut by spade and transported by horse-drawn slipe. This suggested that normally it required three men cutting and one operating the horse to keep two men supplied with building turf. Just under an acre of turf was required to build the feal house, including roofing turves (divots). In a creel house of comparable size, that quantity of turf would be reduced by 25 per cent to 30 per cent, highlighting one of the obvious advantages of this form of construction. The inner basket frame allows for a narrower wall of turf without loss of stability.

Whereas the workforce had, in the first year, become familiar with the woodworking and turf-building skills required for the project, the only 'wattling' experience within the team was one craftsman who had attended a traditional basket-making course run by the museum. It was decided therefore that the first set of wattle panels used in the creel house would be contracted out. Willow hurdles, made to specification, were acquired from an English hurdle maker, as were some standard split hazel hurdles. The latter were used as a pattern by staff of the Highland Vernacular Buildings Trust (HVBT) to begin the process of acquiring the skill themselves. In the end some 25 per cent of the external 'basket', together with the wattling for internal divisions was carried out *in situ* by staff using both split and unsplit hazel (Figure 8.2).

The creel house is a fairly substantial building, with internal dimensions of over 16 metres (52 feet) long and 5 metres (16 feet) broad. This required a total of seven couples, giving an eight-bay house, with each bay approximately 2 metres. These were all erected on stone pads as the first stage of construction. Previous experience had shown that it was not necessary, or indeed sensible, to build the complete stone 'foundation', which is a feature of the archaeology of these buildings, at this stage. One of the most significant structural points in such houses, where the walls are not intended to be load bearing, is the point where the wall interfaces with the lower purlin. This purlin sits on top of the lower collar beam of the couple, and it is crucial that that purlin takes the place of a wall plate, allowing the collar to distribute the downward thrust of the roof into the couples, and not the wall. Given the asymmetrical nature of rough-hewn crucks and purlins, it is much easier to have the purlins in place and then build the wall up to meet them.

In one of the other reconstructions, it proved possible to completely

Figure 8.2 The creel or basket work, showing both willow and split hazel

roof the structure including the laying of divots, without constructing the walls at all. This had the practical benefit of allowing the workforce a sheltered environment for the wall-building phase of the construction, the longest part of the house-building process. It was even possible to have a fire burning on a hearth during the building work – a boon in the rather chilly environment of the Central Highlands of Scotland.

The lack of necessity for this stone 'foundation', with the exception of base pads for the couples together with a few stabilising and packing stones, raises the question of why it therefore occurs in all the buildings. It appears that the real function of these stone footings is to provide the buildings with a damp-proof course, preventing the earthen floor from drawing moisture from the living, growing turf which comprises the walls. Perhaps a later phase of the experiment might allow for a structure to be built without such footings to further test this theory.

To return to the creel house and the importance of the wallhead position, the construction of the 'basket' adds another factor to the equation. Some descriptions seem to suggest that the lower purlin is an integral part of the 'basket' with the standards being 'mortised' into it. However that means that considerable stress is placed on these standards by the weight of the turf leaning against them. The structural solution which was used in this experiment was to have each bay supplied with framed panels of wattle attached to the outer face of the purlin. A comparable longitudinal member was then required at the base of the panel, situated slightly in from the outer face of the cruck to create a vertical elevation for the panel. The position of this lower 'base purlin' then determined the height and depth of the stone footings, and the starting point for building the turf outer skin. The inner face of the footings, as shown by the archaeology, was slightly forward of the inner face of the cruck pads, where they could be recognised.

It was at this point that the first exciting discovery of this experiment emerged. As the panels and the outer skin of turf were put in place, a series of shallow alcoves appeared in the inner wall, between the couples. These were 400 mm deep, and 400 mm up from the floor level, and ideally suited to function as built-in furniture, either as storage space or, with an additional padding of turf or other soft material, seats (Figure 8.3). Visitors to the house during this construction phase, when no other furniture was in place, were instinctively drawn to using these wall recesses as seats. Perhaps there is a greater significance in James Boswell's choice of words than has been realised when he wrote, 'Where we sat, the side walls were wainscotted… with wicker'.

In an inn such as this one in Glenmoriston, such seating would have been of great benefit. With large pieces of furniture such as kists and a box bed in the main 'fire room' or living quarters, the creel house in the museum can easily accommodate 10–15 seated adults.

A second discovery leading to a need to re-evaluate our understanding

Figure 8.3 Interior of the creel house, showing the alcoves, or seats, created between the crucks by the construction method

of the written evidence concerning creel houses occurred when the end walls were being constructed. In each of the buildings raised previous to this, the main structural element had been a single hip cruck, curving from the roof-tree, where it met the outermost couple to rest on a pad at the centre point of the end wall. The project director was less than keen to use this form of bracing in the creel house. He reasoned, first, that in as large a building as this, with seven couples, he would prefer additional bracing against lateral movement. Second, he raised a difficulty previously encountered. The inner face of the stone footings of these houses are squared at the corners, but the outer face of the end walls appears often to be curved. This makes complete sense in terms of wind and rain deflection. The difficulty arose from trying to build round-ended turf walls with only one vertical stress relief in the centre.

The solution put forward by the project director was to have two timbers running from the roof-tree to two points which trisected the end wall. While there was nothing obvious in the archaeology of Raitts which totally negated this – cruck pads have not been easily identifiable at all, and certainly no obvious hip cruck pads have been found. However, the evidence from the few standing buildings in Scotland which still have end crucks points to one single blade in a central position. But in these examples the crucks are inserted in stone walls, which are relatively square faced on the outside, and which are at least partially load-bearing. It was agreed, therefore, that the documentary evidence would be re-examined to see if a justification could be found.

One of the names given to end crucks in Scottish building terminology is 'tail fork'. In the previously cited account of the possible creel house at Deluorar we have reference to: 'Ane hall or fyre hous haifing fyve treen cuppillis yairintill and twa taillforkis… twa chalmeris… haveing four trein cuppillis and twa taill forkis… twa aitt barneis and ane beir barne ilk ane yrof haveing fyve trein cuppillis and twa taill forkis'.[11]

Until now, I have always assumed that these tail pieces, or end crucks, 'forked' off at right angles from the roof tree; but the term 'tail fork' would certainly sustain another interpretation in that it could literally be a forked branch extending from a single point at the roof to two points along the wall footings. It was decided, therefore, to experiment with this form of end bracing.

Unfortunately, large forked limbs were not available, and two separate timbers, joined together at roof level with a scarfed joint, had to suffice. Following the advice of the project director, the ends of these branches projected over the footings, and rested on a stone in the ground. A second stone was fixed against the end of the branch to prevent movement. When the turf was erected the part of the branch beyond the stone footings was almost totally absorbed within the wall. This left only the evidence of two large stones protruding from the ground just beyond the wall to show the novelty of the construction method. Subsequent fieldwork suggests that such boulders are often a feature of township sites, including Raitts. These could easily be interpreted as 'tumble' or otherwise disturbed stones, but as a result of this experiment should perhaps be examined more closely in future. A number of visiting archaeologists have stated that they recognised the feature, but had attached no significance to it until now.

The construction phase of the experiment concluded with the laying of cobbles in the byre end, the building of an internal partition between the byre and the fire room, the establishment of a hearth and smoke canopy, and the thatching of the roof. Of these tasks only the first has proved to be completely straightforward.

By the time the team began working on the internal partition and the smoke canopy, they had gained a degree of proficiency. Working mainly with unsplit hazel, which was kept supple by immersion in a pond on the neighbouring golf course, it proved to be a relatively easy task to split this with a froe and weave it round upright stakes of birch or alder. The smoke canopy was created as one would a basket – a basket almost 2 metres long and 1 metre wide at the lower end. This reduces to half the width at the point where it meets the smoke hole. The problem lay not with the wattle structure but with the daub which was intended to overlie it.

In accordance with the principles of the project, the aim was to use local materials whenever possible, and the excavation at Raitts had indicated that a clay pit was a feature of the township. However, sourcing local clay proved difficult, and when a seam was finally found, in the Dell of Spey near Kingussie, the quality was rather poor. It was decided, however, to proceed with this material. The clay was mixed – sometimes by hand, and for comparative purposes in a cement mixer – with straw and cow dung from the museum farm. The resultant mix was foul, thick and very difficult to apply. It also took several weeks to harden off. The addition of a little lime to the mixture improved the hardening qualities, but did not make the application with a trowel much easier. In the end a rather unprepossessing wall, full of undulations and rough finishes was achieved, but it certainly did little to enhance the character of the house. The smoke hood has not been clay rendered to date, in the hope of finding a better source of clay.

The problem with the hearth was less consequential and more amusing. Excavations at Raitts and elsewhere in the Highlands had shown that many hearths were served by an underfloor duct which brought in a steady draught of air. This was successfully achieved in an earlier reconstruction by a duct branching off the byre drain, just inside the front door. In the case of the creel house, however, it was decided to take a duct directly from the foot of the turf wall to the hearth. It gave the desired draught, but, unfortunately, proved to be a 'des res' for a family of rabbits who moved in as soon as it was built. Because of constraints arising from modern health and safety procedures, the eviction of these tenants proved quite difficult, but it is unlikely that we have uncovered something which would have been an issue in the eighteenth century, when the township's dogs would have dealt with the matter without ado.

None of the staff at HVBT had experience of thatching. In the summer of 1997, therefore, a master thatcher was engaged as a coach. Duncan 'Stalker' Mathieson is one of the last thatchers working professionally in Scotland using local techniques. In the three months of his residency, he thatched the feall house with oat straw, with several members of the HVBT team (including the project director) acting as his assistants. That team then thatched a barn with oat straw on their own, with 'Stalker' supervising, and have since gone on to thatch a third building in the same material, without supervision, and with a gratifyingly successful outcome.

Oat thatch has a fairly limited lifespan, however, and was not the most popular roofing material for substantial buildings, where heather was preferred. This was the favoured option for the creel house. Before tackling such a large roof with a new material, it was decided to thatch a small outbuilding, using the instructions imparted by 'Stalker' during his time on site. A source of long-stemmed heather was found (with difficulty, because of modern moorland management techniques), and a fourth successful roof covering was created. The only problem was that the thatch was almost a metre thick by the time the ridgeline was reached. This was acceptable in a small building, but would have put unacceptable strains on resources (heather and manpower), to say nothing of the roof timbers, on the creel house. A modified technique was developed, which used 50 per cent less thatching material, and involved sealing the ridge with clay – a known practice in some parts of the Highlands.

The result has not been a success. The roof leaks like a sieve, in apparently random spots. There is no obvious fault line, such as the joint between clay and heather, and it is presumed that the problem lies with the amount of heather laid, and the way it has been put down. The roof is holding water, rather than shedding it. It was hoped that bringing 'Stalker' back in the summer of 1999, to have a second attempt at thatching this roof, would have solved this situation. One problem is that Duncan Mathieson is over eighty years old, and becoming less able to work on roofs. This highlights the immediacy of the need to train new thatchers in Highland techniques.

In the meantime, the HVBT thatchers are having better luck in reviving the obsolete technique of thatching in broom, by a process of trial and error and reference to ethnological source material.

Furnishing and plenishing

Despite the problem with the thatch, and partly because it was not recognised as being as serious as it turned out to be, work began in the summer of 1998 to fit out the interior of the creel house. The reference source for the furniture and fittings were the collections at the Highland Folk Museum, and the creators of the new pieces were the workforce of HVBT, with all their acquired skills. Stools and chairs were shaped by adze and side axe. Legs were produced using axe and drawknife. Occasional demonstrations of the use of the shave horse or the pole lathe quickly turned into a veritable production line, while staff with a bent for whittling or chip-carving found themselves, on wet afternoons, making spoons, ladles and other treen items.

By this time HVBT had four – and for a time, six – young school-leavers on a two-year traineeship funded by the Highland Council in conjunction with the European Social Fund. Much of their training in traditional craft skills – wood-turning or stone-carving – resulted in birch or alder bowls, decorated bake-stones and querns, all destined for the creel house. Stone cruisie moulds were copied from the lighting collection, and new cruisie lamps were fashioned out of sheet metal. The test pieces for the trainees were spoon boxes, salt boxes and small kists.

The largest items of furniture are the box beds, which not only provide sleeping accommodation, but also serve as the room dividers. The beds are all based on a box bed in the museum which has an inscription 'DMP 1702' on the lintel over the door, and a series of other early eighteenth- century dates on one of the front panels. It is not clear whether 1702 is the date of manufacture, or perhaps records a marriage of some other event. 'DMP' is almost certainly a MacPherson, as the bed is known to have come from a MacPherson township. There is a similar bed in Biggar Museum, with a provenance which relates it to the second half of the seventeenth century. It is fairly certain, therefore, that this bed type was in use in the Central Highlands at the outset of the eighteenth century.

The 1702 bed, as it survives, appears to be half of a double unit, joined lengthwise by mortise and tenon joints. It is fairly low, just under five feet from the ground, and the bottom rail of the door shows signs of heavy wear, indicative of people climbing on it. It seems likely that the roof of the box provided another bed space. At some later date a cornice has been added, to hold an upper mattress in place. So the bed is in fact a two-tier piece of furniture, which in its full form must have been able to accommodate eight adults, or fewer adults and a greater number of children.

In the creel house, four box beds have been fitted (Figure 8.4). One is in the main living space (the 'fire room' as it was known in Gaelic) Two are placed end-to-end, with a door-width gap between them, forming a couple of little corridor bedrooms leading to the 'room' at the end of the house. These four beds, together with one side-wall of the house, form a further room – the closet or milk house, entered by the doorway in the corridor. Even if some of the upper bed units are used mainly for storage, and the bed in the room used mainly for *rites de passage* as oral tradition and other evidence suggests, there is still ample sleeping accommodation for a fairly large family.

The corridor bedrooms are quite commodious, thanks in particular to

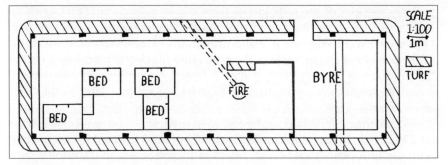

Figure 8.4 Creel house in the Highland Folk Museum

the wall recess, referred to earlier. A simple curtain screen would create an acceptable private space, certainly by early eighteenth century Highland standards, where many people simply slept on palliases on the floor of the 'fire room'. Captain Burt, thought to have been a military engineer in a tour of duty in the Highlands in the 1730s, refers to this several times, and during one visit to a house near Loch Ness, he counted nine people sleeping on the floor, both children and adults.

The other large pieces of furniture are kists and aumries, again copied from items in the furniture collection. Kists vary in shape and size, and in some cases provide additional bench seating or work surfaces. The aumrie in the closet has wickerwork sides for the storage of dairy products. Birch saplings were used in this instance as the wattling.

The fitting-out of the byre end has yet to be tackled. Little evidence has yet been found for the system of trevicing used at this period. Some postholes have been found in excavations, which suggest a wooden structure of some sort, and possibly little different from what can be seen in surviving byres from a century later, at Auchindrain, a preserved township in Argyll.

Conclusion

A great deal of valuable information has already been garnered from this experiment in reconstruction, and a great deal more will emerge in the coming months and years. Mistakes have been made, and are being identified through the occurrence of problems, such as the leaky thatch. An attempt to insert roof lights in the thatch has exacerbated this problem, with rot reaching the wattle panels immediately below these gaps in the thatch.

Because this is part of a larger experiment, it will be possible to compare the structural soundness of creel buildings against other forms of turf buildings, adding considerably to the body of knowledge about this tradition of earth building, which was once so significant in north-west Europe. Trainees from HVBT are spending six weeks in the spring of 1999 in Iceland, where they will take part in the restoration of a turf church.

Apart from the technical knowledge being gained, the creel house, and indeed the whole township of Baile Gean, (Township of Goodwill) will give visitors to the Highland Folk Museum an unparalleled experience in interpretation of the lifestyle of Scottish Highlanders at a time before the clan system began to disintegrate. At its simplest, because all the furnishings and plenishings are replicas, it suddenly becomes apparent that our ancestors did not live in houses full of dark, heavily patinaed, antiques. Indeed, as one visitor remarked, 'this furniture could have come from Ikea yesterday!' The scale of the creel house, the commodious living space, and the privacy of the corridor bedrooms, will all help to correct misconceptions about these people all living in squalid 'smoking dunghills'.

Acknowledgements

I am grateful to George Dixon for drawing my attention to the 'List of structural and agricultural timbers in Stratha'an' and, even more importantly, transcribing it from Scottish Secretary hand. I am also grateful to my son Donald for the plan drawing of the creel house.

Notes and references

1. Noble, R.R. 'Turf-walled houses of the Central Highlands', *Folk Life*, 22 (1983–84), pp 68–83.
2. Gailey, R.A.'The peasant houses of the south-west Highlands of Scotland' *Gwerin*, 3 (1962), p 238.
3. Robertson, J., *General view of the agriculture of Inverness* (London, 1808), p 58.
4. Scottish Record Office (SRO) *Board of Trustees Papers, NG/1/7/4 1754* , p 68 (quoted in Allen, N.G., 'Walling materials in the eighteenth century Highlands', *Vernacular Building*, 5 (1979), p 3.
5. Boswell, J., *The journal of a tour to the Hebrides*, (R.W. Chapman, ed.) (Oxford, 1979), p 246.
6. SRO, *Annexed Estates Papers E741/30/4*, (quoted in Allen, op. cit., p 4.)
7. SRO, 'List of structural and agricultural timbers in Stratha'an' *Seafield Muniments GD 248/13/6*, (c.1585).
8. Walker, B. and McGregor, C., *Earth structures and construction in Scotland* (Edinburgh, 1996), pp 36–7.
9. Ibid., p 39.
10. Noble (1983–84), op. cit., pp 74–5.
11. SRO, op. cit., p 7.

Buildings Associated with Post-Clearance Sheep Roumes in Lochaber, Lochalsh, Skye and the Sma' Isles

Bruce Walker and Christopher McGregor

The Highland Clearances, during which whole communities of the indigenous population were 'cleared' from the land are well documented.[1] The published material tends to cover emotive subjects such as absentee landlords, social injustice, estate economics, eviction, emigration, pre-clearance settlements and buildings, landowners attempts to set up new towns and rural industries. In every case, the clearance of people to make way for sheep is a prime topic, yet little or nothing has been written on the building types associated with the setting up of large-scale sheep farms.

The gap in our knowledge is partly due to the way we study buildings, that is, separating the estate buildings from those of the tenants, and partly from misconceptions as to the nature of sheep farming. Many people seem to think that sheep spend their entire life wandering at will on mountainous terrain, and that the only structures associated with their husbandry are dikes, fanks, stells and washing-stages. Even the washing-stage, a popular subject in nineteenth-century genré painting, is seldom mentioned. The fact that many mixed farms have specific woolbarns is often missed and many researchers seem to think that all sheep farms have similar accommodation regardless of the size of the flock.

The situation described above has resulted in a researcher's blind spot which has obscured the existence of a range of buildings supporting the fundamental reason for the entire exercise, that is, the production of wool and its storage, in good condition, until it can be transported to a suitable market.

On the smaller mixed farms, occupied mainly by tenant farmers, and where the numbers of sheep are reasonably small, it is usually possible to store the baled fleece in a space not in use from the time of shearing until the wool is taken to market. This accommodation can be provided in byres, root stores or barns as these buildings are mainly in use over the winter. Some even have woolbarns provided, but none of the spaces are large enough to promote comment from the casual visitor.

The large sheep roumes, where the flock can be counted in the tens of thousands, requires an immense space to store the baled fleece. In a situation like this, the estate often erects a woolbarn capable of storing the entire production. The cost of this enormous building may be partly off-set against better prices for the wool as the wool stock may be held until the market is favourable to the vendor.

The range of structures associated with sheep roumes comprises:

- field dikes – enclosing the areas where sheep overwinter or where lambing takes place;
- head dikes – protecting traditional townships from the sheep on the rough grazing;
- fanks – for holding, sorting, controlling and marking sheep. Later examples also incorporate a sheep dip;
- sheepcots – for protecting ewes and young lambs from predators at lambing time;
- smearing houses – for preparing substances to be rubbed into the skin and the roots of the wool to prevent problems with maggot;
- stells – to provide shelter from the wind on areas of exposed grazing;
- washing stages – usually projecting into running water where the sheep can be washed to remove some of the smearing mixture prior to shearing;
- woolbarns – where fleece can be stored in dry conditions from the time of shearing until the market is favourable or until the wool is required for a local weaving industry.

Of the above-mentioned structures, the sheepcots, smearing houses and woolbarns have not been recognised by building historians mainly because the original function changed before historical interest developed and there was a general reluctance to add fuel to the sheep versus indigenous population debate. Smearing houses ceased to be functional after the introduction of sheep dip. Those standing away from the other buildings could be converted to any function from shepherds accommodation to a general storage space. Those built into the ground floor of woolbarns are often converted to byres or stables depending on whether the estate returned to a form of mixed farming or concentrated on sporting activities after the decline in sheep and wool prices. Sheepcots often change to field barns after a return to mixed farming in the 1870s.

Attention was drawn to the woolbarns in a somewhat convoluted way. Mrs Elizabeth Beaton, then an inspector of historic buildings at Historic Scotland, identified a group of buildings in Lochaber and the Sma' Isles as being similar to the bank barns found in the Lake District of England. After consultation with Dr Ronald Brunskill, an expert in these structures, during which the scale of these buildings was not mentioned, a report was prepared for internal circulation within Historic Scotland. Geoffrey Stell, of the Royal Commission on the Ancient and Historic Monuments of Scotland was approached regarding the possibility of the RCAHMS carrying out a survey of these structures. This proved impossible at the time but funding was found to allow the Scottish Buildings Study Group at Dundee University to carry out the work. The survey of the Lochaber structures took place in October 1984 and March 1985 and those on the Sma' Isles of Canna and Eigg in March 1986.

The 1984–85 survey group comprised: Miss Ray Marshall BSc, Monifeith; Fraser Middleton BSc, Broughty Ferry; Adrian Neville BSc, Belfast; Lawrie Orr BSc, Falkirk; Keith Renton BSc, Edinburgh; and Gordon Wallace BA, London. The 1985-86 group comprised: Douglas Cawthorne BSc, Thurso; Stuart King BSc, Arbroath; Donald McIntyre BSc, Marborough, Wiltshire; Miss Pauline Russell BSc, Edinburgh; Ronald Terry BSc, Broughty Ferry; and Michael Wilkie BSc, Dundee. Both groups worked under the direction of Dr Bruce Walker.

Historical background

Towards the end of the eighteenth century agricultural improvements were being considered in the Highlands of Scotland. James Anderson, writing in 1785, points out that the mixed farming, so popular in Lowland Scotland, was not feasible in most areas of the West Highlands.

> The western parts of the Highlands of Scotland are for the most part extremely steep, rugged and mountainous... forming dry healthy pasturage for sheep, and would afford much greater profit to the owners if depastured with sheep, than with cattle. The islands likewise, which are at present possessed of a breed of sheep carrying finer wool than any in Europe, and which could easily be preserved without debasement, or even improved, so as to yield even greater quantities of wool, of a quality superior to any that is yet known would, in many cases, yield a return, if stocked with such sheep, perhaps tenfold greater than if pastured with cattle. Yet on account of the laws that, under the severest penalty, prohibit the carriage of wool by sea, but under regulations that cannot possibly be complied with in these countries, the natives have in general hitherto been obliged to rely on cattle as their principal stock, and thus forgo one of the chief advantages that nature has conferred upon them. Those fine-wooled sheep are suffered to stroll about neglected, in small numbers; and no natural benefit has yet been felt from the wool, though it might, if raised in sufficient quantities, lay the foundations of woollen manufacturers of certain kinds, that would be unrivalled in other markets – a manufacture of SHAULS... made of this wool, is just now in its infancy here, which may perhaps in time grow to be an object of some importance, or other manufacturers of a kind for which such fine wool is fitted, if the laws should be so framed as to admit of a reasonably free commerce in this article. At present however, the natives, from never having been able to derive much advantage from that wool, scarcely know anything of its value in a commercial light; And, should they come to

discover its value, if the present laws shall remain in force, there is reason
to fear it may be converted to the benefit of rival nations, by improving their
manufactures, rather than our own. For, as the risk is really smaller to
smuggle wool at present to France and Holland, by means of the smuggling
vessels which frequent these coast with spirits, than it is to send it to any
part of Scotland, it is natural to think, they would embrace that as their
surest and best market for this commodity.[2]

Anderson also reports a rumour that smugglers were 'paying an anker of
brandy for each stone of wool'[3] which is in value, more than ten times the
rate paid in Lowland Scotland.

Other writers shared Anderson's views. The *Caledonian Mercury* of 18
March 1771 reports: 'The lands [of Ardnamurchan] are also very popular
for sheep store farms'.[4] The term 'store' in this context, refers to 'farmstock
reared or bought in for breeding or fattening'; the sheep farm being known
as a 'store-roume' or 'storeroom'[5] and the sheep farmers as 'storemasters'.[6]
Other contemporary publications confirm a change in the law, the decline
in cattle rearing and arable farming and an increase in the number of
sheep.

Once wholesale sheep farming was adopted on a farm or estate it tended to exclude the commercial rearing of cattle, as the richer low pasture,
suitable for cattle, was required for overwintering the sheep and for lambing in the spring.[7] On the large sheep farms, cattle stocks were reduced to
a few milk cows to supply the inhabitants.[8]

The change from cattle to sheep and the clearance of the inhabitants is
well documented but the impact on the landscape in terms of new buildings is less easy to assess. Taking the parish of Ardnamurchan as an example: there were eleven slated houses in the parish before 1780; one in
Ardnamurchan district, five in Sunart, two in Moidart, and three in
Arisaig. These are likely to be the houses of the lairds. A further seventeen
slated houses were erected in the next seventeen years; one in
Ardnamurchan, four in Sunart, four in Moidart, and eight in Arisaig.[9]
These are likely to be the houses of the estate factors, schoolmasters and
clergy.

Further down the social scale the position is similar. Prior to 1797 there
were five cottages in Ardnamurchan 'built or cast with lime'; seven in
Sunart, five in Moidart and ten in Arisaig.[10] The term 'cast with lime' refers
to roughcasting or harling and not to a shuttering technique of building
masonry. The numbers of slated and masonry houses and cottages may
seem low but in many upland parishes in east-central Scotland there were
no slated houses in the mid nineteenth century and less than 45 per cent
of cottages were constructed with masonry walls.The prosperity associated with the erection of slated houses and masonry walled cottages in the
last years of the eighteenth century can only derive from the introduction
of sheep farming.

Wool production begins to increase dramatically.

An account of wool sent coastwise from the Port of Fort William for three years preceding the 5th day of January 1792

	cwt	qrs	lbs
From 5 January 1789 to 5 January 1790	2,737	3	24
From 5 January 1790 to 5 January 1791	2,653	2	8
From 5 January 1791 to 5 January 1792	3,593	2	1
Total	**8,985**	**0**	**5**

Or, 41,930 stones, at 24lbs English to each stone. Two thirds of the wool are white, and one third is tarred. The greatest part of the above wool is sent coastwise to Liverpool and other ports in England.[11]

The reporter calculates a little more than six fleeces to every stone[12] giving a sheep population in excess of 250,000 excluding spring lambs.

The Scots merchants were slow to realise the potential of this new trade and it was not until 1817 that an annual sheep and wool sale was established at Inverness,[13] although this was the wrong side of the country for the Lochaber sheep farmers.

Farming journals continue to give advice on ideal layouts for farm buildings through to the 1830s. This includes advice on improving both the pasture and the stock. Many dealing with mixed farms suggest the provision of a separate woolbarn, giving the farmer the option of retaining the fleece if market prices are poor. Even with all this activity and the 'clearance' of large tracts of the countryside, it was the 1870s before 'substantial improvements' are reported in all districts.

A report on the Glenorchy district of Argyll is typical, and summarises the situation on one estate:

The proprietor of New Inverawe wrote 13.8.1877 regarding the improvement made on his estate. About 40 years previous there were only thatched houses, undrained fields, and a lot of waste ground. Now almost all buildings are slated... the thatched buildings are the exception, so far certainly as new erections are concerned.[14]

The rearing of sheep and cattle, rather than the raising of crops, being the occupation of the farmers, it could not be expected that much could be done in the improvement of land here as in countries depending on crops and culture. However, drainage money, as it is called, was applied for by many proprietors.[15]

The change from indigenous thatched buildings to 'improved' slated buildings in the 1830s relates to the publication of 'Designs of Farm Buildings drawn up under the direction of a committee of the Highland Society of Scotland' published in 1831.[16] This publication is one of the few to include designs for a 'mixed hill farm'. This design provides the clue to the early use of the large barns found in Lochaber as it has a special room designed for the storage of wool. The text reads: 'A room is designed for holding wool, which by some may be thought unnecessary, as the barn or cow-house is frequently made use of for holding it till sold: but it sometimes happens that in bad markets, the wool is left over a year: in this case a house for it is necessary.'[17]

The provision of a timber-floored room 23 feet by 15 feet, for the storage of fleece on a medium-sized mixed-farming hill-farm, gives some indication of the requirement on a large estate devoted almost entirely to sheep farming and lacking other agricultural buildings. A similar situation exists on the sheep stations of New Zealand where the terrain is similar to that of Lochaber. *Historic sheep stations of the South Island*[18] illustrates similar-sized woolbarns to those surveyed in Lochaber on sheep stations with similar-sized flocks. The New Zealand woolbarns are constructed of timber and corrugated iron while those in Lochaber are either masonry or mass-concrete.

A search was made for specific references to woolbarns in Scotland but this proved unproductive, possibly due to the adverse publicity given to sheep farming by the 'anti-clearances' lobby, or due to the small number of estates with massive flocks of sheep. A possible example was located by Professor J.B. Caird of Dundee University, in the form of a specification. The 'Specification of Barn and Smearing House to be erected at Skirinish Farm, Skye in 1872'[19] does not identify the type of barn, but its relationship to a smearing house suggests it may have been a woolbarn. 'Smearing' was the application of a fat/tar solution often made with poor quality butter and tar. The solution was rubbed into the base of the fleece on the living sheep to prevent maggots establishing themselves in clotted wool. The specification is interesting in that its date makes it almost contemporary with the later alterations to the smearing houses and woolbarns in Lochaber, rather than the date of their first erection. It is however contemporary with the mass-concrete smearing house and woolbarn at Glencripesdale, to be discussed later. Unfortunately, the drawings referred to in the specification have not been located and therefore the exact form and dimensions of the structure are not known.

Discussions with shepherds from various parts of Scotland established the following criteria regarding sheep shearing and fleece storage:[20]

1. It is essential to keep the fleece dry during storage.
2. Sheep should be shorn when the fleece is dry as it is difficult to dry the fleece after removal from the sheep.
3. The body heat of the sheep can be utilised to dry the fleece. This is done by keeping the sheep under cover overnight prior to shearing.
4. The wet climate of the West Highlands makes it almost essential to have provision for drying the sheep as described in item 3.
5. It makes good economic sense to be able to store the fleece until the market is favourable.

6. Storage is essential between the time of shearing the fleece and its removal from the farm.
7. Owing to the unpredictability of the weather it is easier to organise transport after the shearing is completed rather than in advance.
8. Storage sheds close to a pier or sandy beach simplified transport arrangements in the nineteenth and early twentieth century.
9. Many estates tried to introduce the manufacture of woollen goods as a local industry and they would wish to retain a suitable quantity of fleece for their own use.

Sheep farming was obviously highly profitable as in 1848: 'The store farmer now occupies the place of a very superior order of tenants called Tacksmen'.[21]

In 1872 William Macdonald reports on the country of Inverness: 'Good commodious slated farm steadings... have increased considerably, year by year';[22] and 'Surface draining has been largely executed [1869] in Badenoch, Lochaber, Glenelg, Glengarry and other high parts of the country with a view to improve sheep pasture;'[23] 'Sheep farming has been brought to great perfection, perhaps more than in any other part of Scotland'.[24]

Unfortunately the sheep and wool trade declined somewhat in the 1870s.[25] About the same time mass concrete was introduced into Lochaber as a building material.[26] These two happenings are not directly related but, as much of the alteration work on the older woolbarns is executed using this material and provides cattle byres in the ground floor of these structures, the change can be neatly attributed to the decline in the sheep and wool trade.

The decline in sheep farming is further supported by the introduction of new crops. In 1872, William Macdonald notes: 'There is not county in Scotland that has a higher percentage of its arable land allocated to potatoes than Inverness-shire'.[27]

The reporter is referring to arable land and not to sheep farms but a few years later in 1897, J. Cameron Lees reports: 'At Keppoch, Mr Macdonald had an excellent crop of peas'.[28]

Even with these new crops there was very little cereal grown in Lochaber. Philip Gaskell calculates that the Achrannich Estate used 341 bolls of meal between 1855 and 1859; of this, 276 bolls (81 percent) were brought in from outside. A similar situation is known to have existed on some of the more fertile islands such as Eigg.[29] This explains the minimal provision of threshing machinery even in the largest of the converted barns.

Consideration was given to the suitability of the large Lochaber barns for hay-making as practised in the large cruck-framed barns of Lochalsh in recent years.[30] Not only were the Lochaber barns unsuitable for this purpose, due to their masonry walls and slit ventilators, but further research

Sketch of the Sheep Cot lately erected at Coul

Figure 9.1 Sheepcot (George Stuart Mackenzie, 1809)

into the Lochalsh barns, with their wattle walls or banks of louvred ventilators, established that these structures were originally erected as sheepcots. Sheepcots were erected to protect ewes and young lambs from foxes and dogs[31] but the large well ventilated space would also make an ideal store for holding fleece. Changes in the type of farming from sheep to mixed agriculture has resulted in their being adapted to hay-making as described by O'Malley.[32]

The barn structure is illustrated in a nativity scene painted by William Bell Scott in 1872.[33] The people and animals are necessary for the subject matter and do not reflect the original function but the structure and construction are accurately represented.

The sheepcot function is described by Sir George Stuart Mackenzie in 1809. The cot described is based on the construction of a typical Highland cottage of the period (Figure 9.1). The cot comprises the skeleton of a cottage, that is, the cruck frames, wattle lining and thatched roof. The cottage would have had turf walls built against the wattle in the form of eighteenth-century creel houses.[34] This structure, considered as typical of the period, illustrates the significant change and importance of the masonry-walled cottages mentioned previously. As a protective structure, the cot would function well as it would keep the sheep or other contents dry and secure while allowing a free circulation of air. Mackenzie's description reads:

> Cots may be very easily and cheaply constructed after the manner of Highland cottages, where birch trees or others having a natural bend, or branches of any large trees can be got. The framework is constructed as follows:

> Two trees or large branches, are laid together, so that the distance between the thick ends maybe 12 or 14 feet. The small ends are then morticed together and fastened with a wooden peg. About four feet below this a piece of wood is laid across, morticed and fastened; the ends projecting about a foot on both sides. Small projecting pieces are also fixed at the height where the roof is to begin. These parts are now called couples and when a sufficient number have been prepared, they are set up at the distance of ten feet from each other. They are now joined together at top by straight trees being laid

along into the forks made by the crossing of the ends of the couples. Similar pieces are laid along the sides resting on the projections, and the whole are fastened by means of pegs, similar to what ship carpenters call treenails. To form the roof, small straight trees, usually birch or Scotch firs, are laid across the rails, the thick ends being nailed to the lowermost rail. A rail is also fastened along the inside of the couples near the bottom. On this and the lower roof rail are nailed spars, which are placed close together, but not so as to exclude a free circulation of air. In the front, spaces are left open at intervals. The thatch consists of heath, which is the most durable of all others. There is some art required in laying it on, although the operation appears to be very simple. The first layer consists of heath, having the thick roots cut off, and nicely arranged and fastened down by long pieces of wood tied with willow twigs to the framework. The heath is then laid on without regard to roots, except having them inmost. The thatch is laid on thicker and thicker towards the top, where it is fastened by means of a thin sliced turf laid along. The whole is distinctly seen in the plate which represents the framework and the appearance of a cot which has been constructed as already described.

Moveable cots may be made, with frames filled with straw or heath, by means of wickerwork; the sides being made of wickerwork alone.[35]

A number of these cots survive in Lochalsh and were the subject of a survey in the 1970s.[36] Probably the best-known example is the one on the Balmacara Estate and owned by the National Trust for Scotland.[37]

It is intended to describe a number of sites where there are sheepcots, smearing houses or woolbarns giving specific references to the actual site or site local. A number of additional structures reported in the Historic Scotland inhouse document, and subsequently found to be unrelated to sheep farming, have been omitted from this paper. Copies of the complete manuscript report giving reasons for the above omissions are held by the Royal Museums of Scotland: Country Life Archive, the Royal Commission on the Ancient and Historic Monuments of Scotland: National Monuments Record for Scotland; and Historic Scotland: Historic Buildings Inspectorate.

Achnacon, Appin, Argyll (NN118566)

In 1791, the parish of Appin is described as follows:

... by far the greatest part of this extensive parish is mountainous, and well adapted for sheep... There is little grain raised... in the higher parts of Appin, since sheep flocks have been found beneficial. Many of the sheep farms are very extensive and, considering the height of the hills, produce excellent grass, and, of course, very good sheep, perhaps among the best in the western districts.[38]

All the black cattle bred are principally intended for common family use. There are 25,000 sheep in the parish, or perhaps many more, and they are daily on the increase.[39]

Figure 9.2 Woolbarn, now Leishman Mountain Rescue Centre, Glencoe

The reporter also mentions the completion of a new road through Glencoe.[40] This may have occasioned the proposed new farm and inn at 'Achnacoan Shealling.'[41] It is uncertain whether the inn was built, but in 1870 Achnacon is described as: 'A small but neat mansion house situated in the south of Appin and about half a mile east of the Parish Church, Property and residence of C Stewart'.[42]

The Ordnance Survey of the same year shows a layout similar to that existing today.[43] A few years later in 1878, the farm is mentioned again: '… at the mouth of Glencoe, is the tenement of Achnacoan, Invervagin, Etc. possessed by Messrs S & W Farish at a rent of £398. A grand sheep tenement of the same class as those around it…'[44]

The steading at Achnacon is now the Leishman Mountain Rescue Centre, Glencoe, (Figure 9.2) converted to the purpose under the auspices of the National Trust for Scotland, who own the 1390-acre farm.[45] The building that survives is a long rectangular two-storey structure with a gable slated roof. The long south elevation is built into the slope of the ground to allow ground-floor access to both floors. Unfortunately there is no record of the building's internal features prior to its remodelling and the existing structure incorporates twelve-pane case-and-sash windows and multi-paned glass doors in the fenestration which are out of character with this class of structure. The upper floor still retains some tall slit ventilators on the north side. The interior has been completely remodelled removing all traces of former fittings. Externally the masonry rubble walls have been whitewashed. The building was not surveyed by the Dundee team as there appeared to be little to be gained from the exercise.

Achranich, Morvern, Argyll (NM704474)

In 1794, the state of the agriculture in Morvern is described as: 'The uniting of farms began long ago and seems to be gaining ground in proportion to the avidity for high rent and the rage for sheep stocks;'[46] and 'the farms as presently possessed are 32 in number of which 17 are in the hands of gentlemen tacksmen, and for the most part stocked with sheep; 5 in lease to shepherds; and 10 occupied by small tenants'.[47]

The calculations of stock for that period suggest 14,000 South country-bred sheep and 2500 black cattle.[48] This proportion changes in favour of more sheep and by 1843 the sheep population is reckoned at 29,000 while the cattle number reduces to 690.[49] Sheep and wool are considered to be the main product. In 1851, the large barn at Achranich is built,[50] probably as a smearing house and woolbarn. According to Philip Gaskell, who has carried out extensive research in the Ardtornish Estate Office, the mansion house is the work of Alexander Ross of Inverness[51] but there is no record of the architect for the barn. The Ordnance Survey of 1872[52] shows the barn in its present position but lacking the courtyard development to the south. Concrete construction is introduced into Morvern in 1871,[53] and Samuel Barham, the estate master of works erects a number of mass-concrete buildings on the estate in the 1870s and 1880s. A report of 1878 reads:

> Mr Smith, Achranich, keeps his lands in his own hands, and had a deer forest and a sheep stock of white-faced. There are also some Highland cattle.54 The deer, sheep and Highland cattle are all hardy and are unlikely to require covered accommodation suggesting that the byre occupying the ground floor of the barn structure may be much later as all the alteration work carried out to create the byre is of mass-concrete construction.

The courtyard development in its present form appears on the 1900 edition of the Ordnance Survey.[55] This suggests that these new structures, which are all of mass-concrete construction date from the 1880s and 1890s and may be contemporary with the byre. A survey was carried out on 16 October 1984 by Ray Marshall, Adrian Neville, Keith Renton and Gordon Wallace.

The woolbarn is a large, three storey neo-gothic structure with a single storey aisle projection along the ground floor of the north facade (Figure 9.3). The overall dimensions of the main block are 32.5 metres by 7.5 metres by 7.0 metres high at the eaves and 10.8 metres at the ridge; the aisle adding a further 5.4 metres to the width of the ground floor. The building is dated 1851 on a plaque over the east gable doorway. The Italian gothic character of the building is similar to the style of the Achranich boathouse, 1853 and the first Ardronish Tower, 1856-66.[56]

The barn sits close to the Rannoch and the old farmhouse of Achranich. It is positioned against a slight slope which may originally have provided ground floor access to the first floor. The subsequent construction of a courtyard on this side of the building and the reorganisation of the floor levels to provide two tall storeys and an attic leaves this a supposition. The application of harl to the south elevation hides any further clues that might survive.

The re-organisation of the floor levels results in some peculiar detailing. The new upper floor bisects the original upper storey windows resulting in considerable changes to the fenestration. The new byre floor and changes to the facade are formed using mass concrete. The upper floors are of tongued-and-grooved boarding over timber joists supported on rolled steel joists (RSJs). The six intermediate stanchions supporting the RSJs, between the gables are irregularly spaced possibly to accommodate the spacing of the stalls for the cattle.

The original walling is of squared pinned rubble and the splayed tops to the upper storey window openings are formed by corbelling two stones to meet at the apex. The roof is slated and is provided with three ridge ventilators. Rafter ends project at the eaves and this aesthetic is carried to the gables with false rafter ends showing under the barge boards. The aisle projection is now roofless but a photograph showing it intact appears in Gaskell.[57]

Evidence of the original internal form was recorded and an attempt at reconstruction made. When new, this building must have been the largest and most splendid structure in Morvern parish.[58]

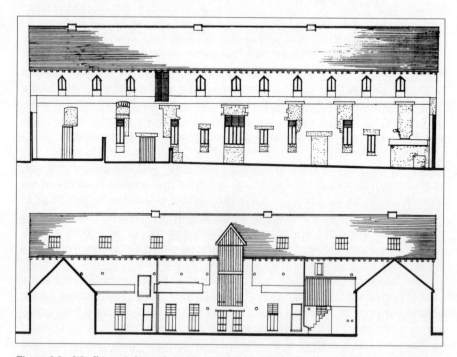

Figure 9.3a Woolbarn, Achranich (top) north facade; (bottom) south facade to courtyard

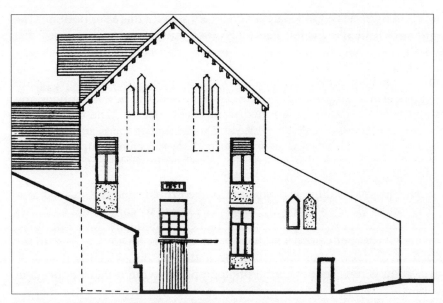

Figure 9.3b Woolbarn, Achranich, east gable

Glencripesdale, Morvern, Argyll (NM662593)

In general terms the economic background to this property is similar to that of Achranich but whereas Achranich was in private ownership in the eighteenth century, Glencripesdale was part of the Duke of Argyle's property.

In 1770 an Argyle Estate paper reports Glencripesdale as having 100 cows and 100 sheep.[59] There is little information on this estate for the next hundred years, but in 1869, Glencripesdale sold off its detached sheep farm of 13,500 acres.[60] In 1871, the remainder of the estate is sold to the Newton family from Warwickshire who, later the same year, buy the adjacent sheep farms of Laudale and Liddesdale making an estate of 23,500 acres. The new estate is intended to function as a sporting estate.[61]

In 1872, Glencripesdale is described as: 'a farmhouse situated at the mouth of the glen of the same name. There are suitable offices and servants houses attached. Mr Robertson, occupier and tenant, Property of Mr Newton.'[62] In 1878: 'The Glencripesdale estate belonging to Rev.W & H Newton, is occupied as follows: Glencripesdale, by Messrs Robertson at a rent of £850. The stock consists of blackfaced sheep. Laudle, with a stock of blackfaced and Liddesdale with whitefaced sheep are in the proprietors hands'.[63]

The Newtons built a large no-fines concrete mansion house that same year at Ordnance Survey reference NM662590.[64] There is a smearing house behind the present farmhouse and a silo-byre, built in the early 1900s, also in mass-concrete.[65] The estate appears in a sale notice in the 1920s issued by Harrods Ltd, London. It is described as: 'An excellent residential and sporting estate lying alongside Loch Sunart. Situated in one of the prettiest parts of the Highlands and standing in approximately 7,500 acres of hill and moorland and a small amount of arable land'.[66]

The mansion and adjoining offices are described in detail. The farm-house is:

> … in excellent condition and containing nine rooms, kitchen, scullery, bath-room (hot and cold).
>
> Adjoining cottage with four rooms. Cottage and Bothy near Gardens. Range of Farm Buildings and bothy room. Also a cottage for keeper or shepherd at Camusallach… between 50 and 60 acres arable and semi-arable land situated near Farm and Buildings.
>
> The farming is let on a lease for twenty years from Whitsunday 1922, with the provision of a mutual break every five years. The first break takes place at Martinmas 1927, the vendors being under no obligation to take over the tenants sheep or other stock…

The survey was carried out on 6 March 1985 by Fraser Middleton, Lawrie Orr, Keith Renton and Gordon Wallace, but concentrated on the silo byre a building type more commonly found in Stiermark, Austria than in Scotland.[67] The smearing house was a small two-storey structure with a blocked fireplace on the ground floor. It had been stripped of all fittings and distinguishing features.

Kilmalieu, Ardgour, Argyll (NM897556)

Ardnamurchan is a particularly large parish, part in Argyll and part in Inverness-shire. It is subdivided into four districts: Ardgour and Ardnamurchan in Argyll, and Arisaig and Moidart in Inverness-shire. Something of the general situation has already been outlined in the historical background to the subject. In 1872 the Ordnance Survey notes:

'Cilmalieu: a farm steading and dwelling house, slated and in good repair. Property of A Forbes Esq, Kingairloch'.[68]

The English meaning of Cilmalieu is given as: 'A Burying place of some Iona saint'.[69] The 1875 Ordnance Survey map shows Cilmalieu as having a similar layout to that surviving today but with some minor differences. The barn is shown as forming the south side of an enclosure. There is another shorter building against the north side, but this has since been removed.[70] In 1878, Kilmalieu and Gair of Kilmalieu are occupied by A.H. Bill and Mrs Bill at a rent of £200. The stock consisted of Blackfaced sheep.[71]

The 1900 Ordnance Survey map shows the removal of the building and enclosure to the north of the barn and the formation of two smaller enclosures to the south and west. The barn was reroofed with shingles between 1964 and 1967. About this time the owners persuaded the Ordnance Survey to change the spelling of the name to Kilmalieu as they had been using that spelling for some considerable time.[72] The survey was carried out on 18 October 1984 by Ray Marshall, Adrian Neville, Fraser Middleton and Lawrie Orr.

The barn is a long, rectangular, two-storey structure, with a peind roof (Figure 9.4). The overall dimensions are 26 metres by 6.4 metres. It is sub-divided by two internal gables that are carried to the underside of the roof. The long north-west elevation is built into a slight slope, insufficient to allow direct access from the upper ground level but sufficient to allow carts to be loaded and unloaded through each of the three entrances. The central entrance is reached by a timber forestair and the three upper com-partments are linked by doors in the internal gables. There is also a central access to the upper storey in the south-east elevation. The upper storey is ventilated by eight slit ventilators in each of the long elevations.

The ground floor has been altered at various times. The central com-partment has two wide entrances formed with RSJs. The byre to the south-west is reasonably intact but has a central support to a floor beam that dis-turbs the present layout giving the impression of a compromise layout. The stable to the north-west has been remodelled to utilise a former cart/gighouse bay, the entrance to which is through an arched opening in the north-east elevation.

The building is constructed of whitewashed rubble. The intermediate floors are of timber supported in mid-span on RSJs. The ground floor has brick paviors in the stable, and concrete paving elsewhere. The building probably dates from the mid nineteenth century.

Drumnatorran, Ardnamurchan, Argyll (NM820626)

This is a more traditional steading dated 1828 and farmhouse, 1834.[73] In 1845, Archibald Clark comments on the well-managed farm, farmhouse

Figure 9.4 Woolbarn, Kilmalieu

and offices of 'Drimnatorran'.[74] The Ordnance Survey describe it as: 'A large farm-steading, dwelling house and offices, two storeys high. Situated a short distance northeast of the Parish Church. Property of Sir Thomas Riddell Bart, Strontian'.[75] The layout is similar to that existing today. A rectangular enclosure is shown a little to the east of the existing sheepfold, its use is not known.[76] The Ordnance Survey 1875 edition shows a rectangular court of buildings within the enclosure[77] but both buildings and enclosure disappear before the 1896 edition is published.[78]

In 1878, D Clark, reporting on the agriculture of Argyll, comments: 'On the Sunart Estate, across Loch Sunart, there are some large sheep tenements, but it may be enough to mention the following: Drimnatorran (sic) possessed by W.Kilpatrick and J Mulligan jun... Rent £571... carries stock of Cheviot sheep...'.[79]

Access for a detailed survey was refused but the structure takes the form of a traditional U-plan steading 33 metres by 22 metres overall, comprising three gabled ranges, each approximately 7 metres wide. The court is open to the north-west and is built into a hillside allowing ground floor access to the upper floors of all three ranges.

The roofs are slated, the walls harl-pointed rubble with tooled granite dressings. The upper floors are lit and ventilated by alternate louvred windows and tall slit ventilators. A heated henhouse is built against the west gable of the court. This is a common feature in Scottish farmhouses as hens will not lay eggs if they are cold. The lower floor of the steading contains stables and byres. Abutting the north-east range is a large roughly semi-circular sheep-fold approximately 24 metres by 16 metres and comprising six sections. The well is located slightly to the east of the fold.

This is probably the earliest steading in the group and contemporary with the mixed/sheep farm designs mentioned earlier.[80] It is also similar to many of the mixed/sheep farms of the eastern Highlands and although it is capable of storing large quantities of wool in the extensive upper storey, it is far less specialised than buildings such as Achranich.

Ranachan, Ardnamurchan, Argyll (NM789613)

The 1872 Ordnance Survey note: 'Ranachan or Rannochan: This name applies to a small one-storey slated house on the northern side of Loch Eight. Proprietor, D Cameron Esq, Inverallot by Fort William'.[81]

The house is situated a little to the north-east of the woolbarn and has obviously been rebuilt between 1872 and 1900.[82] Ranachan is also mentioned in the same 1878 report as Drumnatorran: 'on the Sunart estate... there are some large sheep tenements... Ranachan, possessed by Charles McArthur. Rent £200... Stock, Cheviot sheep'.[83]

The survey was carried out on 16 October 1884 by Fraser Middleton and Lawrie Orr.

The building is a large rectangular two-storey gabled structure of more than one build. The overall dimensions are 23.6 metres by 10.3 metres. The ground floor has a double pile plan, the result of an extension to the south. The original building is 6m wide and comprises two compartments on the ground floor separated by a central cross-passage. The upper floor is entered by a masonry forestair on the west gable.

The extension is constructed in 60 centimetre masonry rather than the 90 centimetre masonry of the original structure. The extension effectively doubles the ground floor accommodation which comprises byres to the west end stables to the east of the passageway. The upper floor is treated as a single volume yet the forestair has been extended to accommodate a second gable entrance suggesting some form of subdivision in the past. A ramp has been constructed in the north-east corner to allow access for carts. This entrance breaks the eaves line and is protected by a large peined roofed dormer. There are also loading trapdoors over the passage and above the centre of the north west compartment. All the windows light ground-floor compartments and face north and east.

Abutting the building to the north is a large sheep fold and fank. The fank is approximately rectangular and measures 19 metres by 55 metres. A single-storey timber and corrugated iron shade, 21 metres by 45 metres, stands inside the west wall facing the fank and sheep dip. The dip stands above ground level making it necessary to lift the sheep in bodily. This is probably because the fank stands on an outcrop of rock, the slope of the surface allowing the sheep in the dip to clamber out at a higher level. The dipping of sheep by lifting them bodily into the dip is still being practiced in some areas.[84] The fold is divided into four main enclosures with four smaller enclosures round the fank.

Cliff, Moidart, Ardnamurchan, Inverness-shire (NM739694)

In 1872 Cliff is described as: 'a large farm steading about 25 chains west of Sheil Bridge. It is slated and in good repair. The property of Lord Howard of Glossop, Glossop Hall, Derbyshire'.[85]

The Ordnance Survey shows a U-shaped steading open to the south with gables to the roadside. A rectangular block of corresponding length to the north range occupies the south side of the road. A detached block is shown at right angles to the roadside block at its western end.[86]

The 1901 Ordnance Survey shows the U-shaped block extended to the west to form a second courtyard open to the west. The detached blocks to the south of the road are linked to form an L-shape. There is a new building on the north side of the road to the north-west of the new courtyard and a second new building parallel to the east range of the original U-shaped block.[87]

This building now forms a large, high quality dwelling house as the result of a complete conversion leaving little or no evidence of the original functions or fenestration, apart from some tall slit ventilators on both floors of the south facade.

The new dwelling appears to occupy the north range of the original U-shaped block. It is a long, two-storey, gabled structure with slate roof, raised skews and harled walls. The fenestration comprises regular banks of twelve-pane case-and-sash windows with double and tripartite examples in the west gable. Entrance is from the north through a single-storey gabled porch with round-arched doorway.

The later block to the east has been retained as outhouses and garage but the rest of the group has been either demolished or slighted to form screenwalls round a south-facing garden. The building was not examined in detail as the owners were not present and could not be contacted. The road has been altered to bypass the group to the northeast. This building may have been very similar in character to Drumnatorran but on a flat site.

Dalilea, Moidart, Ardnamurchan, Inverness-shire (NM735693)

Dalilea House is said to have been rebuilt after destruction in 1746.[88] This is likely to be the house shown on the Ordnance Survey map of 1875 and 1901 as the present house is considerably larger and dated 1907. In 1872: 'Dalelea (sic): This name applies to a large stone edifice with outbuildings, situated about 55 chains southeast of_____. It is two storeys high, slated and in good repair. The property of Lord Howard of Glossop'.[89]

The outbuildings comprise three detached ranges round a five-sided court.[90] The west range is the only one still surviving and is small in scale when compared to the later steading. There is also a small sawmill to the east of the outbuildings. This also survives but in a converted form as a threshing mill.[91]

The 1901 Ordnance Survey map shows that the outbuildings described above had been demolished and a roughly rectangular court built immediately to the east of the retained range. The barn forms the east range of this group. At this time the name is spelt 'Dalelia'. The Dalilea shepherd, Anthony Buckley, informs us that the barn is used for storing wool, hay or straw depending on the time of year. The lower floor is used as a fodder store for the cattle in the byre to the north. The intermediate floor which formerly defined the woolbarn has been removed leaving a single volume. There was no evidence of any other function other than the woolbarn over the fodder store.

The barn was surveyed on 17 October 1984 by Ray Marshall, Fraser Middleton, Adrian Neville and Lawrie Orr. It is a small rectangular gabled building of two storeys, crudely buttressed on the west facade facing the steading court (Figure 9.5). The rear of the building is set into rising ground to the east allowing ground-floor access to the upper floor. The overall dimensions are 14.65 metres by 6.25 metres, providing a similar wool storage area to that provided at Ranachan. The walls are constructed of whitewashed rubble and the gabled corrugated iron roof oversails the eaves and skews. There are three ridge ventilators. The upper floor is lit and ventilated by five slit ventilators in each gable. There are opposing doors, approximately in the centre of each long elevation. The lower floor has a door under the west door of the upper floor. This is flanked by windows suggesting that the lower floor may have been used as a smearing house or stable but the lack of drainage channels and evidence of stalls precludes the latter.

Callert, Kimallie, Inverness-shire (NM092603)

Sheep were first introduced into this parish in 1764[92] and by 1793 the value of the land had tripled.[93] A contemporary report reads: 'The greatest part of the parish consists of high grounds; and, as the heaths yield excellent grass, it is well calculated for sheep'.[94]

At the time, the parish is described as supporting 6,000 head of cattle, 500 horses, 1,000 goats, and 60,000 sheep.[95] Sheep farmers occupy three-quarters of the parish[96] and much of the low pasture is retained for winter and spring grazing for the sheep.[97] The arable land on a sheep farm is allocated as follows:

> The following is the average number of English acres, under the different sorts of grain, on each of the sheep farms:
>
> 13 acres are under 12 bolls of oats
> 4 acres are under 3 bolls of barley
> 10 acres are under 14 bolls of potatoes
> Total 27 acres in tillage
> 34,973 acres in sheep pasture

Figure 9.5 Woolbarn at rear of steading, Dalilea

In all 35,000 acres: being 16 miles by 3 and two-fifths.[98]

In 1773, Callert is shown diagrammatically on a map as having a peind roof, over a three-bay, single-storey house with two chimney stacks, one at the apex of each pean.[99] In 1843 there is little change: 'Much attention is paid to the management of sheep farms... Wedders from here are considered in the south country markets second only to wedders reared on the farm of Auch in Glenorchy...';[100] and 'There is not much arable land in this parish... There is not one acre out of 300 cultivated or capable of cultivation in this parish'.[101]

In 1870, Callert is described as:'A neat substantial dwelling house with pleasure-ground garden, situated on the north side of Lochleven and distant about 3 miles from North Ballachulish. Property of the heir of the late Campbell of Monzie'.[102]

The contemporary Ordnance Survey map shows the barn detached from the other buildings.[103] At this stage it was probably a woolbarn over a smearing house. By 1903, the scatter of buildings to the south of the barn have developed into a courtyard steading.[104] The former smearing house appears to have been converted to a stable and tack room. The cast iron fittings and hit-and-miss type ventilators in the new steading are stamped "Walker Iron Foundry, York". This firm flourished from circa 1825 to 1923. The Walker Foundry, Walmgate, York is reckoned to be the foremost of several iron works based in York in the nineteenth century and provided gates for the British Museum and Kew Gardens. The windows and ventilators at Callert are the furthest north of any of the known Walker Foundry products.[105]

The woolbarn is further altered at this time by the addition of the 'Wedding Clock' and bell tower at the apex of the south gable. This probably dates from 1901 and is a present to the younger generation of the owner's family. The clock is possibly the work of William Potts and Son, who were specialist in elaborate devices of this type. Their work includes many clocks for railway stations and town halls and even automated types featuring life-size figures to strike the bells. A Potts clock may be seen in an arcade in Leeds where Robin Hood and his merry men strike the bells. Potts of Leeds have been contacted regarding the Callert clock but they have been unable to trace an order. This can be explained by the company's practice of selling a proportion of their mechanisms through agents.[106]

The building was surveyed on 15 October 1984 by Ray Marshall and Adrian Neville and comprises a tall, two-storey block with twentieth-century additions to the north and south gables. The original woolbarn measures 19.5 metres by 7.2 metres and was obviously remodelled circa 1900: the bell-cote, east-facing louvred window, hit-and-miss ventilators in the stable, and the use of RSJs to support the floor all support this supposition. The ground floor comprises two stables, now much altered, and a central tack room. The south stable has been reduced to provide access to the bell-cote. The tack room has a lower ceiling than either of the stables and may reflect the original height of the smearing house. The room under the bell-cote, the tack room and other internal partitions are all lined with match-boarding.

The upper storey, still used as a barn, comprises a single volume apart from a small enclosure containing the ladder to the bell-cote. The west elevation has a series of six slit ventilators in the masonry, each with three stone slab ties to provide stability to the wall. The east elevation has windows in place of the slits. These have a segmental arch externally, but timber safe-lintels internally. Each opening contains adjustable timber-louvred ventilators. Access to this floor is provided by a wide opening in the centre of the west elevation. This also has a segmental arch. The opposing window has a solid timber shutter rather than adjustable louvres.

Externally the building is harled and whitewashed. There is a corrugated-iron shed on a masonry base against the north gable and a crude lean-to against the south. The south gable also supports the Wedding Clock and an art-nouveau belfry. Two cast-iron rooflights light the ladder compartment under the belfry.

Keppoch, Kilmonivaig, Inverness-shire (NM269809)

This structure may have provided the model for the other woolbarns in the district as it was originally built as a barracks for government troops in the mid eighteenth century.[107] Its position, surrounded by sheep fanks and attached to a later agricultural steading confirms its later use as a woolbarn. In 1842, John McIntyre reports: 'The hills and glens of this parish afford the most excellent pasture for sheep and black cattle... particularly the former, upwards of 100,000 sheep are reared every year... Messrs McDonell of Keppoch are supposed to have... near 100 square miles under sheep'.[108] He also observes: 'No improvements in agriculture have taken place in this parish to any considerable extent'.[109]

A plan of Bunroy Farms[110] contemporary with the description shows the building with a small extension against the south gable. To the north of the barracks/woolbarn, and slightly offset from it stood another structure of equal width but only two-thirds the length. This building had been demolished prior to the first edition of the Ordnance Survey in 1870.[111] It is replaced by an east/west-oriented block of approximately the same area. This develops into an almost enclosed courtyard on the east side of the barracks/woolbarn.[112]

The building was surveyed by Fraser Middleton and Lawrie Orr. The barracks/woolbarn is a long two-storey, rectangular structure with blue-slated gabled roof and harled masonry walls (Figure 9.6). It measures 27.4 metres by 6.85 metres excluding the 5.75 metres by 6.15 metres gabled projection against the south gable. This projecting structure is now used as a garage.

The building gives the impression of having been restored from a ruined shell with new floor levels, new fenestration and changes in the internal planning.

The ground floor is subdivided into four irregularly-sized apartments by three masonry cross-walls. These are obviously insertions as there are no bonding stones between these and the outer walls. The small room at the north end contains a large fireplace opening spanned by a segmental arch. This may have been the kitchen fire for the barracks and later the fireplace required for a smearing house. Only two of the ground floor rooms are lit or ventilated; the room second from the north gable having a slit ventilator; the other central room having four slit ventilators plus a shuttered window. Each of these ground floor rooms has an outward opening door into the courtyard. The court passage is constructed in mass concrete.

The building is built into a slope giving ground-level access to the first floor in the north west corner. The large beam supporting this floor has '1900' painted on it in red. The scarcement on the gable over the large fireplace is 4.15 metres above the basement floor. This would provide a reasonable headroom if that fireplace served the kitchen of the barracks: the present floor-to- floor height of 2.5 metres being more in keeping with its possible use as a smearing house. A floor relating to the above mentioned scarcement leaves 2.5 metres to wallhead level which is generous if one considers that the rafters were normally left open at the time of its use as a barracks.

At the south end of the building the first floor level rises by two steps over the south ground floor apartment. The south gable may have been rebuilt as it has a pyramid pattern of slit ventilators in keeping with many of the other barns. The scarcement level on this gable is higher than on the north gable and ties in exactly with the sills of the upper row of slit ventilators. A floor at that level would give a three-storey building with floor-to-floor height of 2.8 metres, 2.5 metres and 1.4 metres to the wallhead but a possible 2 metres to the collars of the couples. This arrangement of floors ties in particularly well with the existing fenestration and there is a 5.4

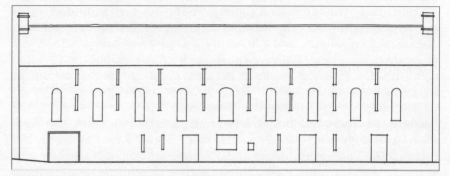

Figure 9.6 Woolbarn (former barracks) Keppoch, from east

metres length of floor abutting the north gable at the height of the south
gable scarcement. The fenestration to the upper volume comprises: alternate louvred windows, with segmental arches to the exterior but timber or
slate safe-lintels to the interior, and slit ventilators, broken to correspond
with the floor at the south gable scarcement level.

The west elevation has two large openings: a central door with a segmental arch, and an opening at the north end, slapped into the cheek of a
slit ventilator and incorporating the space formerly occupied by a louvred
ventilator. This is probably contemporary with the setting up of a horse
engine to drive a small threshing machine. The horse engine, a post-1850
type has its shaft running into the centre of the third bay from the north.
The louvred ventilator at this point is truncated accordingly. On the east
elevation a standard width doorway replaces the central louvred ventilator. It also has a segmental arch suggesting it was constructed at the same
time as the other openings.

The surviving roof of the woolbarn comprises rafters of two sizes: 17.5
centimetres by 7.5 centimetres or 15 centimetres by 10 centimetres. Some
are rough sawn, others dressed. The sarking varies in width but averages
boards of 30 centimetres. The slates are nailed direct to the sarking without any form of felt. The rafters sit on the outer edge of the wallhead. A
cement weathering still surviving on the chimney heads suggests that the
roof may have been thatched in the past.

The gabled building against the south gable is an obvious extension,
built across the symmetrical pattern of ventilation slits without aesthetic
consideration.

Coroghon, Canna, Argyll (NG278055)

In 1796, when the laws against the shipping of wool were still in force,
improved agriculture was introduced to the Small Isles. 'Great oats are
reported to be responding well on Canna but a quantity of meal still has to
be imported.'[113] This success does not appear to be widespread in the
Small Isles since the same report gives the situation on Eigg as: 'The cultivation of grain has been attempted for two years past, but did not succeed.'[114] 'One farm on Eigg was begun to be stocked with black-faced
sheep, about two years ago. They seem to multiply and thrive well.'[115]

Kildonnan, Eigg, Argyll (NM490850)

In 1796, a report on Eigg states: 'the cultivation of grain has been attempted for two years past, but did not succeed'.[116] 'One farm on Eigg was
begun to be stocked with blackfaced sheep, about two years ago. They
seem to multiply and thrive well.'[117]

Conclusions

The physical surveys carried out to date mainly concentrate on those structures considered to be woolbarns although adjoining sheep fanks were included on those sites where they physically touched the woolbarn structure. A number of Lochalsh sheep cots have been surveyed in the past but under the guise of their subsequent function of field barns, used to make hay in the wet climate of Lochalsh, but now recognised for their original function of sheepcots. These were created in areas where there was a large fox population to protect vulnerable ewes and small lambs during the lambing season. The barn at Balmacara owned by the National Trust for Scotland provides a readily accessible example which still retains some of its original stake-and-rice (wattle) walling.

Much has still to be done before a complete picture will emerge. It is hoped that this will be achieved before this interesting, but temporary, phase of Scottish agricultural history becomes so fragmented that valuable evidence is lost.

Notes and references

1. Handley, J.E., *Scottish farming in the eighteenth century* (London, n.d.).
2. Anderson, J., *An account of the present state of the Hebrides and western coasts of Scotland* (Edinburgh, 1785), pp 121–3.
3. Ibid., pp 123–5.
4. 'Farms, kelp shores and coals', advertisement, *Caledonian Mercury*, 12 March 1771, No. 7641 (back page).
5. Grant, W., and Murison, D., *The Scottish National Dictionary* (Edinburgh, 1971), pp ix, 6–7.
6. *Caledonian Mercury*, 12 February 1766, No. 6798. Advertisement, no heading, refers to the Borders.
7. Fraser, A., 'The parish of Kilmalie', *Statistical Account of Scotland*, 8 (Edinburgh, 1793), p 427.
8. McNicol, D., 'United parishes of Lismore and Appin', *Statistical Account of Scotland*, 1 (Edinburgh, 1791), p 488.
9. Campbell, A., 'Parish of Ardnamurchan', *Statistical Account of Scotland*, 20, (Edinburgh, 1798), p 293.
10. Ibid.
11. Fraser (1793) op. cit., p 426.
12. Ibid., p 427.
13. Lees, J.C., *Inverness* (county histories of Scotland) (Edinburgh, 1897), p 259.
14. Clerk, D., 'On the agriculture of the county of Argyll' *Transactions of the Highland and Agricultural Society*, 4th series, 10, pp 1, 47.
15. Ibid., p 96.
16. Anon., 'Designs of farms buildings drawn up under the direction of a Committee of the Highland Society of Scotland', *Transactions of the Highland Society of Scotland*, n.s. p 2 (1831), pp 365–9 (plus plates).
17. Ibid., p 387.
18. Wheeler, C., *Historic sheep stations of the South Island* (Wellington, Auckland and

Sydney, 1968).

19. SRO GD 221: 1872, 'Specifications of barn and smearing house to be erected at Skirinish Farm, Skye, 1872'.
20. Anthony Buckley, shepherd, Dalilea, provided the basic information which was supported by a number of other shepherds on Lochaber, Angus and Perthshire farms.
21. Logan, J., *Gaelic gatherings* (Inverness, 1848), p 76.
22. Macdonald, W., 'Agriculture of Inverness-shire', *Transactions of the Highland and Agricultural Society* (1872), p 275.
23. Ibid., p 277.
24. Ibid., p 278.
25. Caird, Professor J.B., 1985, verbal information.
26. Gaskell, P., *Morvern transformed* (Cambridge, 1968), p 181.
27. Macdonald (1872), op. cit., p 278.
28. Lees (1897), op. cit., p 272.
29. McLean, D., 'Parish of the Small Isles', *Statistical Account of Scotland*, 17 (Edinburgh, 1796), p 274.
30. Fenton, A., and Walker, B., *The Rural Architecture of Scotland* (Edinburgh, 1981), pp 46–8 and 78–9; O'Malley, R., *One horse farm* (London, 1948), facing 51.
31. Mackenzie. G.S., *Treatise on the Diseases and Management of Sheep*, Inverness, 1809, opposite title page; Walker, B., and McGregor, C., *Earth structures and construction in Scotland: A guide to the recognition and conservation of earth technology in Scottish buildings* (Edinburgh, 1996), pp 36–7.
32. O'Malley (1948), op. cit.
33. Scott, W.B., The Nativity (oil painting, National Gallery of Scotland) NG2396.
34. Walker and McGregor (1996), op. cit.
35. Mackenzie (1809), op. cit.
36. Burstow, F., manuscript report and verbal information.
37. Fenton and Walker (1981) op. cit., pp 78–9. Horrocks, H., *The National Trust for Scotland Guide to over 100 properties* (Edinburgh, 1995), p 17.
38. McNicol (1791), op. cit., p 483.
39. Ibid., p 488.
40. Ibid., p 497.
41. SRO: RHP 3091, 'Achnacoan Shealling'.
42. OS Namebook : Argyll.
43. OS 1875, (6″ map), surveyed 1870.
44. Clerk , op. cit., p 17.
45. Horrocks (1995), op. cit., p 35.
46. McLeod, N., 'Parish of Morven', *Statistical Account of Scotland*, 20, (Edinburgh, 1794), p 265.
47. Ibid., p 266.
48. Ibid., p 270.
49. Gaskell (1968), op. cit., p 52.
50. Ibid., pp 66–7.
51. Ibid.
52. OS 1875, (6″ map), surveyed 1872.
53. Gaskell (1968), op. cit., p 181.
54. Clerk, op. cit., p 18.
55. OS 1900, (6″ map).

56. Gaskell (1968), op. cit., p 181.
57. Ibid.
58. Ibid.
59. Ibid.
60. Ibid.
61. Ibid.
62. OS Namebook: Argyll 71. 43.
63. Clerk, op. cit., p 19.
64. Gaskell (1968), op. cit., p 160.
65. Typescript document held by Dr Hemmings, Glencripesdale.
66. Harrods Ltd., n.d., cutting held by Dr Hemmings, Glencripesdale.
67. Personal observation in the countryside around Stains and Graz, Austria.
68. OS Namebook : Argyll 72. 32.
69. Ibid.
70. OS 1878 (6" map), surveyed 1872.
71. Clerk, op. cit., p 12.
72. Verbal information from the owner.
73. Beaton, E., 'The bank barns and combination steadings of Lochaber district', 1884, Historic Scotland (typescript), p 17.
74. Clerk, A., 'Parish of Ardnamurchan', *Statistical Account of Scotland*, 7 (Argyll), (Edinburgh and London, 1845), p 125.
75. OS Namebook: Argyll 2. 1.
76. OS 1872 (25" map).
77. OS 1875 (6" map), surveyed 1872.
78. OS 1896 (25" map).
79. Clerk, op. cit., p 19.
80. Anon (1831), op. cit.
81. OS Namebook: Argyll 9. 8.
82. OS 1875 and 1900.
83. Clerk, op. cit., p 19.
84. Personal observations on the ground and in farming programmes on BBC TV in the 1980s.
85. OS Namebook: Inverness 10. 91.
86. OS 1872 (6" map).
87. OS 1901 (6" map).
88. Donaldson, M.E.M., *The Country of Clanranald* (Paisley, 1934), p 364.
89. OS Namebook: Inverness 10. 107.
90. OS 1875, surveyed 1872.
91. Anthony Buckley, verbal information confirmed by visual inspection.
92. Fraser (1793), op. cit., pp 423–4.
93. Ibid., p 432.
94. Ibid., p 408.
95. Ibid., pp 423–4.
96. Ibid., p 424.
97. Ibid., p 427.
98. Ibid., p 425.
99. SRO – RHP 3,423, 'Part of the farm of Callert, 1773'.
100. McGillvray, D., 'Parish of Kilmallie', *Statistical Account of Scotland*, 14, (Edinburgh and London, 1843), p 120.

101. Ibid., p 123.
102. OS Namebook: Inverness 38. 16.
103. OS 1873 (6" map), surveyed 1870.
104. OS 1903 (6" map).
105. Correspondence between Ray Marshall and Castle Museum, York.
106. Correspondence between Ray Marshall and Potts of Leeds.
107. Beaton, op. cit., p 24; Stell, G., verbal information.
108. McIntyre, J., 'Parish of Kilmonivaig', *Statistical Account of Scotland*, 14, (Inverness), (Edinburgh and London, 1842), p 504.
109. Ibid., p 511.
110. SRO – RHP 10,482, 'Plan of Bunroy Farms' (mid nineteenth century).
111. OS 1872 (6" map), surveyed 1870.
112. OS 1903 (6" map).
113. McLean, D., 'Parish of Small Isles', *Statistical Account of Scotland*, 17, (Argyll), (Edinburgh and London, 1796), pp 273–4.
114. Ibid., p 273.
115. Ibid., p 274.
116. Ibid., p 273.
117. Ibid., p 274.

10

The Role of the Horse on Irish Farms

MERVYN WATSON

THE HORSE HAS HAD a long and significant role in Irish agriculture. During the Middle Ages horses supplanted oxen as the principal draught animal for ploughing.[1] Although the quality of Irish horses had been recognised for centuries[2] by the early nineteenth both horses and their use by Irish farmers were often adversely criticised by observers. Wakefield writing in 1812 commented, 'The condition of the working horse in Ireland is altogether miserable… Bad feeding and hard working keep them in a state of wretchedness hardly to be conceived'.[3]

Ironically, horse-powered technology became a major element of improved agriculture in the nineteenth century and the horse remained the main source of draught power on Irish farms well into the twentieth century. In recent years there has been a revival of interest in the working horse among farmers. This is particularly evident at rural events such as local ploughing matches or farming shows. As a result the role of the horse has taken on a new dimension in Irish farming life.

Breeds

Although the origins of indigenous breeds of Irish horse are obscure, authorities argue that early Irish texts distinguish between two main categories of horse used by farmers (*boaire*). These are the work horse (*capall fognamo*) and the riding horse (*ech immrimme*). Farmers of high social status (*boaire febsa*) were expected to own both a work horse and riding horse whereas farmers of lower rank (*ocaire*) had a horse which was used for both work and riding.[4] In the case of farmers of higher social status it is a matter of conjecture if the horses used for work and riding were of different types or the same type with different functions.

It is difficult from early Irish writings to attribute precise physical characteristics to particular types of horse. However, skeletal remains from archaeological evidence suggest that a small type of domesticated horse existed in Ireland which stood thirteen to fourteen hands high and had strong Arab features. It has been argued that these small horses or ponies were the descendants of a form of wild horse, *Equus caballus celticus* (Figure 10.1) and the antecedents of extinct types and surviving breeds of native Irish horse.[5] During the middle ages a small light Irish horse called the Hobby (Figure 10.2) was known and exported throughout Europe. Although it was in the theatre of war that the Hobby was esteemed as a light cavalry horse,[6] its stamina and mettle gained it high repute as both a saddle and pack animal. Some writers have argued that the Hobby was the foundation stock of more recent breeds and types of Irish light horse and pony. Interestingly, a shared characteristic between the Hobby and more recent native equines used by farmers was their ability to perform a variety of tasks and double up as a riding horse and work horse.[7] In early Irish literature small Irish work horses or ponies are often referred to as *'gerranes'*. Post-Norman times saw the term pass into English in the form of 'garron'[8] and it occurs frequently in more recent written sources.

Early nineteenth-century descriptions of native garrons (Figure 10.3) or small work horses, although not always complimentary, often share similar characteristics, particularly size, hardiness, and agility. In 1804 Sir Charles Coote's account of Irish garrons in County Armagh describes them as having slender bones, remarkable for speed and hardiness, and as being reared in the mountainous districts.[9] In 1814 the Rev. George Sampson remarked:

Figure 10.1 *Equus caballus celticus*: celtic pony as identified by J.C. Ewart. From Wallace, R., *Farm livestock of Great Britain* (Edinburgh, 1923), plate 133.

Figure 10.2 A horseboy holds a Hobby while his Irish lord prepares to go on a cattle raid.
From Derricke, J., *Images of Ireland*, 1581.

> The strains of horses distinguishable in this county (Londonderry) are first
> the native garron of the mountainous country; these are thinly made up, in
> general have crooked hams seldom exceed 14 hands, are often much lower;
> the prevalent colours are bay and sorrel. This breed have, for the most part,
> a gentle head and aspect, with nice shanks.[10]

The Rev. John Dubourdieu's 1814 survey of county Antrim observed,

> There is a very hardy, strong, though small, race of horses,... much in use
> on the northern and north-eastern coast, and in the mountains. They are
> active and sure-footed, but few of them exceed fourteen hands high, and
> many are much lower. In shape, their defects are, want of height and length
> before, and, behind, their hams approach too close; but their backs and
> limbs are excellent, and their paces far above what would naturally be
> expected from their apparent strength, being equal to support a journey of
> equal length with a horse double their bulk, when not unmercifully
> loaded.[11]

Hely Dutton, in 1824 claimed that Connemara 'has long been famed for its
breed of small hardy horses'.[12]

As well as the shared characteristics of size, hardiness and agility, the
above nineteenth-century descriptions suggest that small native horses
were found mainly in marginal, mountainous areas. In 1901, the
Department of Agriculture and Technical Instruction (DATI) in its assess-

ment of the Irish horse breeding industry, identified two principal areas which possessed small horses 'deserving of special mention'. These were the bleak moorlands of western Galway and Mayo, home of the Connemara pony, and the mountainous districts of north Antrim which produced the Cushendall.[13]

Although native horses of particular types possessed similar characteristics, their breeding was carried out by farmers at an informal level and was based on local and individual needs. As a result horses from a specific area, as well as sharing features, often had a wide diversity of characteristics within a type. The Connemara was such a case. J.C. Ewart's study commissioned by DATI in1900, to assess the potential of the Connemara for improvement, argues that due to the absence of a selective breeding programme and years of uncontrolled cross breeding or 'blending' of native horses with introduced animals there was not a 'single distinct strain' of Connemara pony. Instead he estimated that there were five categories or types of Connemara which he referred to as the Andalusian, (Figure 10.4) the Eastern, the Cashel, the Clydesdale and the Clifden. Ewart felt that of the five types the Andalusian and the Clifden were of particular interest. The Andalusian he claimed, represented the original or old breed of Connemara and the Clifden 'the best kind of the Connemara… well worth preserving, not only because it was well adapted for the country, but also because it would be invaluable for crossing with other breeds'. The Andalusian was described as standing '12 to 13 hands high; some are black others are grey or chestnut but the most char-

Figure 10.3   Ploughing with native garrons near Hillsborough, County Down, 1783. Detail from print by W. Hincks.

Figure 10.4 Andalusian-type of Connemara pony taking home seaweed for fertiliser, in overloaded pardogs (creels with opening bottoms), c.1910. (From R.J. Welch collection, NMGNI, Ulster Museum.)

acteristic specimens are of a yellow dun colour'. Although only slightly higher than the Andalusian, standing 13.2 hands at the withers, Ewart describes the typical Clifden as being heavier and stouter, and very different in build. Ewart postulates that these differences in confirmation may have resulted either from cross breeding, or the Andalusian and Clifden having different aboriginal ancestors. While Ewart saw the need for the standardisation of type through a breeding programme based on selected stallions and mares, he was also aware that any attempts at improvement must not destroy the essential qualities of hardiness, stamina and docility inherent in the native Connemara. These qualities, Ewart believed, were shaped by the natural and working environment within which the Connemara had to survive.[14] However it was not until 1923 that Ewart's recommendations were acted upon with the setting up of the Connemara Pony Breeders' Society, and the opening of the Connemara Stud Book. As result, it has been widely exported throughout the world and Connemara Pony societies successfully established abroad.

Like the Connemara, the recently extinct Cushendall pony (Figure 10.5) was a product of its natural and working environment. In 1904, DATI noted the Cushendall and Connemara ponies as being striking examples of how 'horses become modified through adapting themselves to their surroundings' and 'admirably calculated to live and thrive and do useful work under the circumstances and amidst the surroundings in which they have been evolved'.[15] As with the Connemara, the local farmers in north Antrim bred the Cushendall at an informal level and to suit local needs, crossing native ponies with imported animals to varying degrees of success. In the nineteenth century this included ponies from the Highlands of Scotland and in this century, bloodstock, Shires and Irish Draught. Unlike the Connemara, no official stud book was ever opened or breeder's society formed for the Cushendall pony. However, despite the lack of a selective breeding programme, a typical Cushendall was said to have been small in stature, standing around fourteen hands high, with an Arab head and possessing the essential qualities of hardiness, surefootedness and strength. It is claimed that the demise of the Cushendall was due to the decrease in tillage and spread of the tractor after the Second World War.[16] While these are major factors contributing to the end of its use by local farmers, additional factors, which will be discussed later, related to the implementation of a selective breeding programme and its role as a working horse also contributed towards the disappearance of the Cushendall.

The value of a selective breeding programme and officially recognised stud book in helping to conserve breeds is aptly illustrated by the recent revival of the Kerry Bog pony (Figure 10.6). Referred to by locals as the 'old pony', and reputed to have been taken in large numbers by the British

Figure 10.5 Cushendall pony pulling a slide car in the Glens of Antrim, c.1918. (From W.A. Green collection, UFTM, WAG 236.)

KERRY
BOG PONY
ALMOST EXTINCT BREED
Contact: Kerry Bog Village,
Glenbeigh, Ring Of Kerry,
Ireland (066) 69184

Figure 10.6 Postcard publicising the Kerry Bog pony (photograph courtesy of J. Mulvihill)

army to serve as a pack animal during the Peninsular Wars, the Kerry Bog pony is described as ten to eleven hands high, with a dished Arab-like face, chestnut coloured with flaxen mane and tail or liver chestnut with black mane and bay or grey tail, and having a docile temperament.[17] By the early 1990s it was said to be on the edge of extinction, but the dedicated efforts of John Mulvihill from Glenbeigh, County Kerry, in the southwest of Ireland, changed the fortunes of the Kerry Bog pony. After the chance discovery of a stallion and locating a suitable mare, Mulvihill was determined to save the Kerry Bog pony by establishing a stud farm. Part of his strategy to achieve this and conserve the pony as a distinct breed included blood typing to identify genetic markers for future breeding, official recognition by registering the breed with the Irish Horse Board, the opening of a stud book to record lines of breeding and the formation of the Kerry Bog Pony Society. Mulvihill has been successful in implementing these elements of his strategy and the Kerry Bog pony looks safe from extinction. However, another important factor of Mulvihill's strategy to save the pony involved a significant change, which will be discussed later, to its working role on the farms and bogs of County Kerry.

With regard to larger working horses, Ireland's most famous surviving breed is the Irish Draught (Figure 10.7). The first 'authentic reference' to the Irish Draught is reputed to come from the end of the eighteenth century. It is claimed that increased tillage also 'increased demand for heavy horse labour' among Irish farmers.[18] Heavy horses from England and Scotland were imported but it was found they did not suit the needs of the majority of Irish farmers, who required a hardy multipurpose animal. Instead it is argued the best type of horse suited to Irish farming practices of the period evolved through the selection and breeding of heavier types of native horse by the farmers themselves. The horse produced was said to be a 'medium sized farm horse of excellent quality' capable of a range of work and described as rarely exceeding 15.3 or 16 hands high, with strong clean legs, plenty of bone and substance, short back, strong loins and quarters and having a strong neck and smallish head.[19] As well as being a versatile farm horse, a valuable characteristic of the breed was the suitability of mares for crossing with thoroughbred stallions to produce the famous Irish hunter.

During the nineteenth century, breeding of the Irish Draught remained at local level and in the hands of individual farmers. Due to a depression in the agricultural sector and an accompanying decrease in tillage the latter half of the century saw a decline in the number of 'typical' Irish Draught horses. This, coupled with the informal system of breeding and the resulting progeny, became a matter of concern for officialdom. In 1901, DATI, assessing the potential for the development of the hunter breeding industry in Ireland noted,

Figure 10.7 Irish Draught stallion, Prince Henry V, sire of four Irish Draught stallions, 1904 (UFTM L2853/6)

Quite a large percentage of the mares by which Irish hunters are produced
are the property of small farmers... Unfortunately for the country, the
breeding of these 'old Irish' mares has not hitherto received the attention
which it merited. Numbers of them have a dash of thoroughbred blood in
them but the majority are got by sires of such mixed breeding that from the
standpoint of pedigree they are but mere mongrels.[20]

Such was the decline of the Irish Draught, its improvement was considered a question of national concern, and its restoration vitally important
for the future of the horse-breeding industry of the country.[21] However, to
produce the Irish Draught to a standard which suited both the needs of the
small farmer and hunter breeder, required a move from an informal system of breeding operated at the level of individual farmers, to a formally
organised system of selective breeding controlled at national or government level. In 1904, DATI initiated a special horse improvement scheme
under which subsidies of £50 per annum were offered in respect of
approved stallions of the Irish Draught and Hunter type. Unfortunately,
due to the small number of stallions originally selected, breeders were
often required to bring their mares long distances to be served and as a
consequence the scheme was discontinued in 1915.[22] Although only mod-
erately successful, the scheme did produce a number of animals of desirable quality for further breeding and also showed that there was sufficient
stock available to firmly establish the breed.

The impetus to establish the breed on more permanent lines came, not
at national level, but at international level and involved a divergence of
roles for the Irish Draught. With the onslaught of the First World War,
tillage in Ireland increased and the demand for strong active draught horses grew. The demand, however, was not restricted solely to the sphere of
agriculture. In the theatre of war, the army also had urgent need of strong
active draught horses for field artillery purposes. It was recognised that
the horse best suited to both the needs of Irish farmers and the army was
the versatile Irish Draught and once more attention was focused at government level on its development. In 1917, DATI opened a Book for Irish
Draught horses and in that year department inspectors had 372 mares and
44 stallions for registration. By 1938, the number of registered stallions had
risen to 183.

The spread of the tractor after the Second World War heralded the
demise of the working farm horse and was reflected in the number of registered Irish Draught stallions, which fell from 187 in 1944 to 63 in 1978.
The continued survival of the Irish Draught has seen a move away from
its central role as a general purpose farm horse, and will be discussed later.

Despite attempts to introduce heavy horses such as Clydesdales, and
Shires, their use on Irish farms was limited. In terms of improving native
animals through interbreeding, the resulting crosses, as discussed earlier,
were found to be unsatisfactory and their adoption as a working farm
horse was restricted to a few areas. Early nineteenth-century observers

Figure 10.8 Pair of Clydesdales at recent ploughing match held at the Ulster Folk and Transport Museum (UFTM L2896/9)

argued that the generally small size of farms, along with increased upkeep in terms of feeding, made the use of heavy horses an uneconomic proposition to the average impoverished tenant farmer. At the start of the twentieth century the counties noted for heavy horses were Dublin, Louth, Antrim, Down and Derry. In recent times heavy horses, particularly Clydesdales, have enjoyed a revival of interest amongst farmers in the north of Ireland (Figure 10.8). However, the revival has involved a significant change of role for heavy horses.

Uses and changing role

The significance of the horse in Irish agriculture was highlighted by the nineteenth-century improver Baldwin, who estimated that there were upwards of 500,000 horses in Ireland, two-thirds of which were used for agricultural purposes.[23] The ability to perform a wide range of tasks and survive in harsh conditions were key characteristics of native horses, which ensured their use as working farm horses from early times well into this century. Commenting on the jobs carried out by the Connemara, J.C.

Ewart describes the pony working variously as a pack horse, riding horse and cart horse and using an array of local farm implements.

> Without a pony the peasant farmer in the west of Galway is all but help-less... The work of the ponies varies with the season of the year. At one time they may be seen climbing steep hillsides heavily laden with seaweed, seed corn, or potatoes; at another time they convey the produce to market.
>
> Sometimes it is a load of turf, oats, or barley; at other times creels crowded with a lively family of young pigs.
>
> Returning from market each pony generally carries two men one in front and the other on the pillion behind... In Clifden and other centres, as on the larger holdings and some of the small farms close to the main roads, cars, turf, and other carts take the place of the pack-saddle and pillion.[24]

However, the continued survival of the Connemara has resulted in it changing roles, from that of a working animal to that of a riding animal, exported and bred abroad. Ironically, the successful export of the modern Connemara has caused a decline in the numbers of brood mares at home and is a source of worry for those authorities who are afraid that the Connemara 'will cease to be distinctively Irish'. This current concern supports Ewart's earlier view that the harsh conditions of its native environment shaped the essential qualities of the Connemara pony.

The Cushendall pony, like the Connemara, was a hardy multipurpose animal capable of performing a range of tasks. Local farmers from the Glens of Antrim who worked with the Cushendall said it was 'an all round pony, you could plough with him, cart with him, or if you wanted a bit of pleasure, you could put him in a trap and drive'.[25] A better size for pulling locally made slide cars and wheel cars, the Cushendall was also said to be more manoeuvrable in the small sloping fields of the Glens than the larger Clydesdale or Shire, when using 'improved' implements and techniques such as swing ploughs for lea ploughing and drill culture for potato cultivation.

As mentioned earlier, the spread of the tractor and a decrease in tillage were major factors which contributed towards its disappearance. However, I would suggest that the failure to develop the versatile characteristics of the Cushendall through a selective breeding programme, and the establishment of an alternative role for it, such as that of a high-class riding pony, were also contributory factors to its demise. Consequently, when its principal function as the source of draught power on the farm was made redundant by the tractor, the Cushendall pony's extinction was more probable.

Known as the 'maid of all work', the Kerry Bog pony was also a hardy multipurpose animal used for a range of work on the small farmsteads of the area. In recent times it has been particularly celebrated for its work in the bog, where it was used for bringing home turf for domestic fuel. The 'original' method of transporting the turf is claimed to have been 'in baskets placed on crudely constructed wheel-less slides, which consisted of two shafts made from holly or birch trees... Later, small wheeled carts came into use, particularly in less boggy areas'.[26] Depending on the type of terrain and the suitability of the method of transport for those conditions, this suggests that the Kerry Bog pony was used with both local and improved forms of transport.

However, an important factor in the continued survival of the Kerry Bog Pony is not its re-emergence as a work horse. As well as being used as the logo for the Kerry Bog Village Museum, Mulvihill's and the Kerry Bog Pony Society's ultimate aim is to set up a 'heritage bog workshop', housing a range of crafts and craft workers, with the Kerry Bog pony as 'central character and symbol'.[27] Consequently its past role as a working animal has changed to that of a heritage icon.

The Irish Draught, like the above-mentioned native horses, was a hardy multipurpose animal, able to 'rough it' in all weathers with little feed. Kept mainly by small farmers it was said to have been used 'for every class of work on their holdings – for ploughing or harrowing one day, for hauling heavy loads of farm produce the next, and on the third, perhaps, for driving to market at an eight or nine miles an hour trot'.[28] However, the survival of the Irish Draught was not due to its role as a general purpose farm horse but because of its role as the foundation stock for the Irish Hunter. Conversely the demise of the Irish Draught as a working horse has had implications for its continued survival as the foundation stock of the Irish Hunter.

The loss of its direct economic role as a working farm horse, coupled with the growing demand for half-bred horses for competitive and leisure riding made it more profitable for Irish farmers to cross Irish Draught mares with thoroughbred stallions rather than Irish Draught stallions.[29] In recent years, authorities worried by this breeding trend and the possible extinction of the foundation stock of Irish Draught mares have set up various bodies and schemes to encourage farmers to mate Irish Draught mares with Irish Draught stallions.

As discussed earlier, the use of introduced heavy horses such as Clydesdales and Shires was limited mainly to the north eastern areas of the country. They were kept on larger farms in districts where heavier tillage was practised, and near cities where heavy haulage was carried on. The above distribution pattern of heavy horses was reinforced in the earlier part of this century by DATI which delimited the areas in which Clydesdales and Shires could be registered to the 'province of Ulster, the counties Louth and Dublin, and the district within a radius of ten miles of Cork city'.[30] As with other working horses, the use of heavy horses for farm work declined with the increased use of the tractor.

In recent years, however, there has been renewed interest in working horses at agricultural shows and events. One type of event which has enjoyed a significant revival among the farming community is the horse ploughing match. They became widespread during the nineteenth century, when they were regarded by landlords and farming societies as a means for the encouragement of new farming techniques by promoting the use of improved plough types and tillage practices through competition.[31]

It has been argued that the revival of horse ploughing matches has given the matches a symbolic significance in which the horse plays a central role. Although the horses are a public attraction in themselves at matches, it is their contextual use in association with past farming methods which gives the matches their particular symbolic significance and frames the role of the horse. Its role has shifted from that of a working animal to an animal used for leisure pursuits which reflect and maintain a link with a past way of life.[32]

With modern agricultural practices under attack for polluting the environment and modern tractors criticised for compacting the land, some devotees of the working horse not only see it as having a symbolic linkage with the past, but take the view that its resurrection on the farm is essential for the future of sustainable farming. Murt Fitzgerald from west Cork who works the family farm with Irish Draught horses, like his father and grandfather before him, regards the draught horse as the 'power unit of the future' and is of the opinion: 'There should... be at least one horse on every farm to supplement the tractor and do the many jobs that the horse does best... I think we must get back to a more natural and sustainable type of food production – and the draught horse (in my case the Irish Draught horse) is a fundamental part of that re-think'.[33]

Notes and references

1. Lucas, A.T., 'Irish ploughing practices part 2', *Tools and Tillage*, 2:2 (1973), p 67.
2. Smith, B., *The horse in Ireland* (Dublin, 1997), p 68.
3. Wakefield, E., *An account of Ireland statistical and political,* vol. 2 (London, 1812), p 352.
4. Kelly, Fergus, *Early Irish farming* (Dublin, 1997), pp 89–90, 96.
5. Watson, M., 'Cushendall hill ponies' *Ulster Folklife*, 26 (1980), p 13.
6. Smith (1997) op. cit., p 68.
7. Wallace, R., *Farm livestock of Great Britain* (Edinburgh, 1923), p 507.
8. Kelly (1997) op. cit., p 91.
9. Coote, C., *Statistical survey of the county of Armagh* (Dublin, 1804), p 291.
10. Sampson, G., *A memoir explanatory of the chart and survey of the County of Londonderry* (London, 1814), p 182.
11. Dubourdieu, J., *Statistical Survey of the County of Antrim* (Dublin, 1812), p 334.
12. Dutton, H., *Statistical and agricultural survey of the County of Galway* (Dublin, 1824), p 113.
13. 'The Irish horse breeding industry', in Coyne, W.P. (ed.) *Ireland industrial and agricultural* (Dublin, 1902), p 329.
14. Ewart, J.C., 'The ponies of Connemara', in Coyne (1902) op. cit., pp 332–41.

15. 'The horse in Ireland', Department of Agriculture and Technical Instruction *Journal*, 5 No. 1 (1904), p 19.
16. Watson (1980), op. cit., p 12.
17. 'Kerry Bog pony', Kerry Bog Village Museum, promotional leaflet, c.1995.
18. Hanly, J., *Mixed farming a practical text in Irish agriculture* (Dublin, 1924).
19. Smith (1997), op. cit., p 276.
20. Coyne (1902), op. cit., p 327.
21. 'The horse in Ireland' (1904), op. cit., p 28.
22. 'Notes and memoranda', Department of Agriculture and Technical Instruction *Journal*, 8 No. 3 (1918), p 369.
23. Baldwin, T., *Introduction to Irish farming* (Dublin 1874), p 81.
24. Ewart (1902) op. cit., p 349.
25. Watson (1980), op. cit., p 13.
26. 'Kerry Bog pony' (1995), op. cit.
27. Coleman, D., 'The Kerry Bog pony', *The Chase Journal*
28. Coyne (1902), op. cit., p 327.
29. Smith (1997), op. cit., pp 278, 298.
30. O'Donovan, P. J., *The economic history of live stock in Ireland* (Dublin, 1940), p 382.
31. Watson, M., 'Backins, hintins, ins and outs and turnouts: a study of horse ploughing societies in Northern Ireland' (MA dissertation, QUB 1991, p 11).
32. Ibid., pp 29–30.
33. O'Molloy, A., 'Power unit of the future: the Irishmen who stick by their native draught breed', *Heavy Horse World* 12, 1, England 1998, p 18.

11

Concealed Horse Skulls:
Testimony and Message

Eurwyn Wiliam

ALAN GAILEY'S EXAMINATION OF THE NATURE of tradition, drawing on the thoughts of Vansina, Shils and others in addition to his own, contrasted the subjective and interpreted 'message' inherent in an oral tradition with the objective testimony of an object.[1] As Gailey put it:

> … a pot dug from an archaeological site, a plough in a collection of agricultural implements, a vernacular dwelling in the landscape, is not a message. It bears direct testimony to the age when it was made and used. It is an objective record of the cultural performance that created it, whereas one has to objectify an oral performance so that it can become testimony.[2]

He recognised, though, that some objects, such as works of art, were created primarily to be interpreted.[3]

However, there is also a class of object which seems to transcend the boundary between these two forms of testimony. This occurs when an object, either natural or created for a particular purpose, is then subjected to a secondary use. A case in point might be when a shoe, once worn, could be further rendered useless by slashing it with a knife and, together with other left-footed shoes of varying sizes, be bricked up in a fireplace.[4] Here we have an item offering objective testimony of its original existence also suggesting a far more subjective and interpreted 'message' about its secondary existence. It was designed and used as a shoe, and speaks for itself and to us about the materials, craft technology and fashion of a past age; but we can only guess at the rationale underlying its secondary use, and the testimony it offers is clouded by our own interpretation, affected by that of our predecessor folklorists and our own frequent subliminal wish for a deeper meaning.

In this paper I wish to look at another class of object which fits into this latter, third category. It is almost exactly a century since attention was drawn in the ethnological literature to the practice of burying horse skulls under house-floors in the British Isles.[5] Intermittent interest continued to be shown in the practice until S. O'Súilleabhaín's major examination in the 1930s of the phenomenon in Ireland was published, which linked the burial of horse skulls in dwelling-houses to the practice of burying horse skulls in churches, with a view to improving their acoustics. Since many houses in which skulls had been found could be shown to have been linked to music-making and dancing, O'Súilleabhaín concluded that improving the acoustics was the major rationale for such burials in Irish dwellings, but that this was a secondary motive, and was a rationalisation of the forgotten primary motive of foundation sacrifice designed to keep the house safe from evil.[6]

This view was challenged by Sandklef, who cited copious Scandinavian evidence that horse skulls were buried under threshing-floors to improve the echo, against a background of farmers fearing loss of status in the community if they were not seen (and heard) to have produced a large amount of corn to thresh.[7] Sandklef went on to implicitly criticise O'Súilleabhaín's interpretation of the Irish evidence, noting that scholars should not impose their own meanings if the material itself did not provide that testimony.[8] Two papers in the 1960s added to the examples known from Wales and further British cases have been noted since.[9] Buchanan, Harris and Gailey have added examples from Northern Ireland to O'Súilleabhaín's list.[10] Of the Welsh papers, that of J.D.K. Lloyd in 1969 laid the foundation of a corpus comparable to O'Súilleabhaín's.[11] Much of this literature has suggested links between the traditions exemplified in these historical examples and the practice of burying horse skulls in building foundations and in storage pits known from the British and wider, Celtic, Iron Age.[12]

Additional examples of horse skull burials have come to light in Wales since Lloyd's paper, bringing the total number of discoveries to over two dozen. It thus seems opportune to re-appraise the evidence here, particularly since it links two of Alan Gailey's major interests, traditional dwellings and folk customs. This paper could also serve as a small contribution to the debate between those more traditional folklorists who have interpreted an apparent correlation between past and present practices as a result of cultural continuity, and those, on the other hand, who would see such an interpretation as somewhat naive evolutionism.[13]

Since this paper provides an opportunity to create an up-to-date corpus of horse skulls and allied discoveries of animal bones from Wales, those examples noted by Lloyd or otherwise known by the time of his 1969 article are briefly summarised here.

1. Poyston, Haverfordwest, Pembrokeshire
    Horse skulls found under floor, 1900.[14]
2. Jordanston, Pembrokeshire

Twenty horse skulls found under floor, 1901. All replaced by owner.[15]
3. Dolfor Hall, Radnorshire
   Reported in 1910 that 'some 80 years ago' [1830s] when old hall, then 200 years old [1630s] being restored. Four horse skulls in a flagstone vault under kitchen paving, one to each corner of the vault and all facing north.[16]
4. Chapel, Brechfa, Breconshire
   'Several' horse skulls found in the ceiling 'and horses' skulls are still occasionally found when repairing churches'.[17]
5. Montgomeryshire
   Four horse skulls reported in 1936 from an unspecified Montgomeryshire location.[18]
6. Calvinistic Methodist Chapel, Caerfarchell, Pembrokeshire
   New chapel built in 1827. Willie Lewis, a sailor and member of the congregation, told to find two skulls 'to kill the echo'. He obtained four, and they were buried in the foundations; it is not reported what effect they had.[19]
7. Llandaff Cathedral, Cardiff, Glamorgan
   Horse skulls variously reported as 'embedded in the choir stalls of the south aisle' or 'two horses' skulls... found during some repair work... in the 1930s, I believe in the floor'.[20]
8. Lygan-y-wern, Halkyn, Flintshire
   Two horse skulls, one light, one dark, found under the floorboards of the dining room of the pre-1700 house in 1965. Replaced.[21]
9. Gunley, Forden, Montgomeryshire
   Twenty-four skulls, mostly of horses but with a few oxen, found under the floor joists in 1965. They had been carefully placed on half-inch thick flat split stones. One was saved for the Powysland Museum, Welshpool.[22]
10. Hendre Arddwyfaen, Llangwm, Denbighshire
    Horse skull found in the ceiling, placed there 'to dispel the spirits'. Complete skeleton of one or two horses also buried under the floor.[23]
11. Beulah Congregational Chapel, Cwm Nant-yr-eira, Montgomeryshire
    At least one horse skull placed under the floor to help the acoustics of this chapel when built by Iorwerth Peate's grandfather in 1876.[24]
12. Monmouthshire
    Discovery of a horse skull reported by T. M. Owen.[25]
    Since Lloyd's 1969 article a number of fresh discoveries have been made, as well as some previously unreported cases. These may be briefly enumerated:
13. Trefwrdan Uchaf, Nevern, Pembrokeshire
    Under a flat stone slab found at some depth below a cowhouse floor in 1968, a 'complete but crumbling' horse skull was found.[26]
14. Plas Pentre, Llwyn Mawr, Llangollen, Denbighshire
    Bones regarded as being those of a goat by their discoverer Mr Dewi P.

Jones were found in 1968. Two piles of bones were found at foundation level outside the house, but more in a square hole nine inches below floor level just inside one gable.[27]

15. Pentrefoelas, Denbighshire
A horse skull in a house.[28]

16. Plas Cottage, Heol Meidrim, Llangeitho, Cardiganshire
During the restoration of a clay-walled structure in 1976, Mr Emlyn Evans discovered two horse skulls, one under the kitchen floor and one under that of the parlour. He was not familiar with any custom of burying horse skulls, and threw them with the builders' rubble into a stream.[29]

17. Tanyrhiwiau, Ffair Rhos, Cardiganshire
Mr Ian Hughes, whilst lifting the floor of the home of a brother and sister, Mr Tom Owen and Mrs Florence Edwards, in 1976, found the skull of a horse, later identified as that of a ten-year old animal.[30]

18. Glyn Cuch, Pembrokeshire
Four or five horse skulls were found in a house in 1979.[31]

19. Garth Fawr, Rhos y Garth, Llanilar, Cardiganshire
While demolishing a clay wall between the cowshed and the barn in 1982, Mr Rowland George come across the skulls of five horses which fell out of the wall. Four of the skulls were large and one smaller (Figure 11.1).[32]

20. Kemeys Cottages, Kemeys Commander, Monmouthshire
A skull described as a 'boar's head' was found under the floor of this

Figure 11.1 Horse skulls discovered at Garth Fawr, Lledrod, Cardiganshire, 1982 (MWL 35/29, 909, photograph courtesy of Arvid Parry Jones).

property in 1982.[33]

21. Rhosdyrnog, Talywern, Machynlleth, Merioneth

   A number of items were discovered in 1991 in a small room under the roof and next to the chimney stack. These included a decayed horse skull, some horse bones, several iron items including a scythe blade, an iron bar and chain and four barrel hoops. In addition, there were several small boys' shoes – all of the right foot – a girl's shoe (left) with a brass buckle, and a man's right shoe. All the shoes were slashed or otherwise rendered useless.[34]

22. Wern-newydd, New Quay, Cardiganshire

   When the floors of this late medieval house (where Henry Tudor stayed overnight on his way to Bosworth) were lifted in the 1920s or 1930s, a number of animal skulls were found. The discoverer was certain that they were not horse skulls, and described them as 'buffalo skulls' – perhaps ox skulls?[35]

23. Ebenezer Independent Chapel, Newport, Pembrokeshire

   Three horse skulls were discovered circa 1958 under the floor of this chapel, and were regarded as having been buried to improve the acoustics, in a similar manner to the brass pan placed in a canopy above the pulpit.[36]

24. Manmoel, Bedwellty, Monmouthshire

   When Cyrus Meredith was sent to a farmhouse to recuperate as a child before the First World War, he saw a sheep skull in the dairy. He was told not an any account to touch the skull, as it was very old and was there to keep the devil and evil spirits away from the house.[37]

25. Castelldraenog, Llanboidy, Carmarthenshire

   Sometime at the beginning of the twentieth century, bones which appeared to be human were found two feet under the parlour floor. They were identified by the local doctor as those of a small pony, though some in the locality thought this had been said to quell rumours.[38]

26. Modrydd, Libanus, Breconshire

   A single horse skull was found in December 1992 by Colin Powell, son of the owners Mr and Mrs B. Powell, in the middle of the living-room floor and immediately below the floor flags. It was enclosed in a tight cist formed of stone slabs. New concrete floor laid but skull preserved in situ.[39]

   The practice has seen at least one conscious revival in Wales recently:

27. Tŷ Crwn, Cae'r Delyn, St Hilary, Glamorgan

   A horse skull was buried under the threshold of a reproduction Iron-Age round house, erected using authentic materials and methods in 1997.[40]

The only dated occurrences of the examples listed above refer to the two chapels, Caerfarchell (No. 6) in 1827, and Cwm Nant-yr-eira (No.11) in 1876. The discovery at Dolfor Hall (No. 3) appears to have been made about 1830. Dolfor Hall and Modrydd (No. 26), at least, date to the seventeenth century, while, by their nature, most of the other houses listed would be expected to date to the eighteenth or nineteenth centuries. We can postulate, therefore, that most if not all of the Welsh evidence refers to the late post-medieval period, which accords well with the other British and Irish testimony.

Horses were highly regarded in Wales in this period. It was a time when the country was becoming increasingly industrialised – indeed, if one uses the yardstick of more people being employed in industry than in agriculture, it became the first industrialised country in the world in the 1840s – with a consequent increased demand for horses as the prime instrument of motive power on the farm. It had not always been so. Early horses were small in stature and not as strong as oxen. Equally, until the invention of the rigid horse-collar about the tenth century AD, they could not pull with all their strength and weight.[41] The laws of the Welsh king Hywel Dda, probably codified in the tenth century, mention draught mares as being of equal value to a cow, but it is quite clear that horses were meant to be ridden and not normally used as plough-animals.[42] By about 1300, however, the average farmer in north-west Wales had two oxen, three cows, a horse and smaller animals. The horse was used together with the oxen to draw the farming implements. By the sixteenth century mixed plough teams, of oxen and horses, are recorded in Caernarfonshire and Pembrokeshire, though in Anglesey in the 1630s, Robert Bulkeley, a gentleman farmer, possessed no horses. In 1748, however, another Anglesey Bulkeley wrote, 'Today I began to plow anew with oxen after I had disused them for above twenty years'.[43]

The native Welsh horses of the eighteenth century, especially the hill ponies (*merlynnod*), were regarded as light and weak, and so unsuitable for heavy draught work. A somewhat larger breed, formed from a cross between the native type and English horse, provided draught horses ideally suited to small, steep highland farms, where the strength and weight of a heavy horse would be of no advantage. The gentry and wealthier farmers used black English horses, which the agricultural commentator Walter Davies regarded as excellent for both coaches and wagons. In the early eighteenth century there were only two major types of English draught horse – the black old English and the Suffolk. The black horse was later improved to become the Shire, a heavy, powerful animal, but slow and cumbersome. The Suffolk also was renowned for its pulling power. A third type, the Clydesdale, was a lighter and more active horse, more suited to hill farms, and it also had the added advantage of a longer working life. It was particularly well-suited to pulling sleds and two-wheeled carts. These three formed, almost exclusively, the range of nineteenth-century work horses, with the Shires being commoner in the eastern and lowland districts, and the Clydesdale and their local crosses being more common in the highlands.[44]

By the time of the general reviews of the state of agriculture made to the Board of Agriculture in 1794 it is clear that horses alone were used to plough over much of north Wales, but with mixed teams surviving elsewhere except for the extreme south-east where ox teams persisted. Even as late as the middle of the nineteenth century, however, many small farmers did not possess a horse, and even some 100-acre holdings had only one. In such cases two neighbours would act in concert.[45]. By the end of the century, the use of horses on Welsh farms had increased considerably, and 126,000 horses of all kinds were recorded on farms in 1870, rising to a peak of 184,000 in 1921. The increase in the number of work horses coincided with the more general use of implements such as the self-binder and the mower, as the old hand processes were replaced in order to meet the needs of increased production at a time when young men were increasingly leaving the land to seek more lucrative employment in industry.[46]. By the 1920s Wales was producing a substantial surplus of horses for sale.

Horses were treated with greater care than cattle because they provided the prime source of motive power, and in many ways the success of the farm depended on the quality and health of its horses. It is, perhaps, indicative of the fact that horses, and particularly stallions, were regarded as higher in status that they were universally called by prestigious-sounding English names like 'Captain' or 'Duke', even in areas which were still predominantly Welsh-speaking, in contrast to the mundane, descriptive, and invariably Welsh names put on cattle on the same farms. Oxen also had been treated with respect and the vestiges of this which survived into the nineteenth century seem to be a mixture of honour to economic dependence mixed with the ox's traditional role as witness to the birth of Christ. In addition to being the prime work animal on the farm, horses provided pack animals for traders, and became increasingly important as the early industrial revolution gained speed, not displaced until the steam engines of the early nineteenth century. They also provided mounts for the gentry, the clergy and others in a better-than-average economic position. Farmers, too, aspired to own a riding-horse. This is reflected in the literature of the nineteenth century, such as in Daniel Owen's novel *Gwen Tomos* (1893), where a young farmer aspiring to become accepted by the gentry as one of themselves is led into a situation where his prized and coveted animal is killed in a hunting accident. The status of the horse reflected on those who worked with them. On small farms the farmer himself could manage a pair of horses as well as carrying out the other main tasks. On a larger farm, however, a man was needed to work each additional pair of horses, and working with the horses was his only task. He was a *gwas*, a farm servant, an unmarried man who in west Wales would sleep in the stable loft so as to look after his charges, and of superior status to the married farm labourer (*gweithiwr*) who was equally skilled in other but less prestigious areas of farm activity such as hedging or ditching.

The role and significance of the horse in rural society, in terms of asso-

ciated customs as well as work practices, has been well chronicled by
Evans.[47] He accepted that burying horse skulls under the floor, as well as
placing other horse bones elsewhere within the fabric of a building,
derived from foundation-sacrifices to keep away evil[48]. Evans saw links
with Epona, the Celtic horse goddess, and with the horse as a messenger
and symbol of death, citing the *Mari Lwyd* (Grey Mary) ceremony of south-
east Wales as a relic of such customs.[49] Aldhouse-Green has summarised
the evidence for the sacrificial deposition of horse remains in the Celtic
world in a recent paper.[50] She notes numerous examples of horse burials
in the British Iron Age, associated with shrines, settlements and graves. At
South Cadbury, Somerset, for example, a small rectangular building
included pits containing the skulls of cattle and horses, carefully deposit-
ed the right way up. At the great hill-fort of Danebury, likewise, many
chalk-cut grain pits included horse-skulls. She drew attention to the fact
that horse remains were often associated with situations which could be
described as liminal – associated with boundaries or thresholds – and that
some scholars have seen horses as creatures that straddled two worlds, the
civilized and the settled on the one hand, and the areas outside on the
other. The horse was a symbol of an aristocratic warrior elite, its sexual
vigour endowing it with symbolism redolent of fertility and prosperity.
Epona, the horse-goddess, was venerated above all as a divinity associated with domestic prosperity and well-being, but could also be associated
with the passage of life and death[51]. The burial of horse skulls should also
be seen within a wider tradition of deposition in early Britain, from burial
in Neolithic wells to prestige goods in many contexts in the Bronze and
Iron Ages.[52] Rich metalwork was destroyed, prior to deposition, perhaps
in order to preserve its restricted role or as votive offerings with the associated prestige that destroying valuables would bring,[53] and an element of
this latter motivation may very well have been present in horse skull offerings and burials also.

The many horse-related customs in Wales in particular, and in the
British Isles and Ireland generally, have been much discussed and need not
detain us here.[54] Suffice, however, to note the *Mari Lwyd*, which was associated with Christmas and the New Year, when a horse's skull covered
with a white sheet and decorated with ribbons was taken from door to
door by a man concealed under the sheet and accompanied by a party of
wassailers[55]. It is quite clear that there was a whole canon of horse-related
beliefs and practices, of which skull-burying was only one. There has long
been an accepted view that there must be a link between the practices of
the Iron Age and 'survivals' such as the *Mari Lwyd*. Such reasoning, however, has been recently challenged by Wood, who has argued that the theoretical approach of seeking to find such a link is a relatively modern
phenomenon[56]. She holds that:

... the lack of evidence over long periods of time... has to be accounted for by something more specific than folk memory... There is little hard evidence before the end of the eighteenth century, yet only a century later, these customs had been transformed into a threatened heritage, the remnants of pagan customs hundreds of years old.[57]

Similar cases of apparent continuity, on examination, have proved not to be entirely conclusive. One example of such apparent continuity of primitive practice is represented in the sixty or so corbelled pigsties which are known to have existed in Wales in the eighteenth and nineteenth centuries and which Iorwerth Peate suggested, somewhat tentatively, were the descendants of a megalithic building culture that had once held sway over much of Europe.[58] If such were the case, one would expect a spread of examples through time if the type had existed for centuries or millennia, with a concentration of survivors at the end of the timescale but with earlier examples as well. In this case, it seems possible that the introduction of major domical structures into Britain, first by the Normans and then in the Renaissance, could have provided the necessary impetus to ensure the survival or even the re-introduction of corbelled pigsties at a time when Wales, in common with the other Celtic countries, was busy re-inventing itself and its traditions.[59]

The same fundamental question has to be asked about the burial of horse skulls. We have seen that there are well-attested cases in the pre-Roman Iron Age and in the Roman period. Thereafter there is an almost total gap in the record until the examples recorded in the folkloristic literature, most of which appear to date from the eighteenth and nineteenth centuries, though some of the buildings in question might well be a century or so earlier in date. Substantial numbers of medieval buildings have been excavated in Great Britain and Ireland since the Second World War, including a fair number in Wales, and buried horse skulls do not feature as a common phenomenon. The only case cited in Merrifield's detailed study is the four skulls found beneath the doorway of a house in the fourteenth-century deserted village of Thuxton, Norfolk.[60]

The fact that the overwhelming majority of finds seem to date from the late post-medieval period does not prove that there is a gap in the testimony. With the inexorable growth in the population after the demographic shock of the Black Death, more houses were built in each century than during the preceding one, and particularly so during the population explosions of the sixteenth and nineteenth centuries.[61] Likewise, the rate of attrition of historical buildings (and their inherent testimony) will have increased in a similar proportion. It is therefore entirely reasonable to expect more discoveries dating to the later period than to earlier centuries, and the testimony for horse-skull burial to date is not in itself incompatible with a continuously-surviving custom of deposition, though the apparent gap from the Roman period onwards still exists and has to be accounted for.

As we have seen, O'Súilleabháin's study, confirmed by later work by

Buchanan, Harris and Gailey, makes it clear that in Ireland horse skulls were commonly buried for their acoustic properties in dwellings as well as in churches.[62] Although the number of Welsh examples of buried horse skulls is smaller, there is no recorded oral assertion from Wales that skulls were buried in houses for their acoustic properties. The case is different with churches and chapels, where skulls are attested as being buried to aid the resonance.[63] There is presumably some link between this custom and the late-medieval practice of placing clay pots high up in church wall as well as under floors, in a revival of earlier classical practices reported by Vitruvius.[64] It is reasonably easy to rationalise the need for acoustic enhancement in the Irish tradition, given that many of the houses where horse skulls have been found are also attested as being *ceilidh* centres, where singing and dancing were common.[65] Wales, too, had an active home-based culture before the Methodist Revival but it seems to have been based more on a quieter, story-telling and community activity genre, such as the *noson weu* (knitting evening), at least within the last few centuries, although there were also occasions – usually seasonal – when noisy variants of customs such as wassailing took place.[66]

A find some five years ago at the Portway Hotel, Staunton-on-Wye, Herefordshire, may serve to throw some light. There, a horse skull was found encased in a slate 'casket' under the floorboards, together with a heavy green bottle. Inside the bottle was a note reading 'When this house was rebuilt in 1870, from underneath this floor was taken 40 horses heads placed there about the year 1800 by order of Sir John Cotterell Bart, supposed for some musical purpose'.[67] As a hotel, this case might provide a mainland link to the clear Irish testimony of burial for acoustic reasons. This might also provide a reason for the multiple burials of horse skulls. One or two skulls should have sufficed for apotropaic reasons, but large numbers would fit happier with an acoustic reason for their burial. Of the twenty domestic finds in Wales eleven are single, two double, four are of four or five skulls, while one is of twenty skulls and one of twenty-four.

Excepting nation-wide catastrophes such as the Black Death, the number of places of worship would have remained both fairly low and fairly constant throughout the Middle Ages. New, dissenting, congregations would have come into being from the sixteenth century onwards, with a steady rise in the number of non-conformist chapels being built. With the Methodist and allied movements of the eighteenth century, still more places of worship would have been erected, until the growth of industry and population in the nineteenth century resulted in as many as 5000 chapels and a number of churches being built or substantially rebuilt in Wales. Unlike the Middle Ages, too, the new denominations placed great emphasis on the word, spoken and sung. This was the age of the great preachers, with the pulpit rather than the altar or communion table the focus of the building, and it was also the age of the great male-voice choirs which contributed so much to the musical education of the Welsh nation.[68]

Resonance and good acoustics were thus probably of particular concern to chapel-builders and their commissioning congregations.[69]

But how easy was it for these builders and others to obtain horse skulls? In fact, it seems that horse skulls would have been fairly readily available to anyone who had a need for them. In normal circumstances, when not faced by extremes of climate, being worked unnaturally hard, or subject to being sacrificed or eaten, horse mortality is of the order of 5 per cent of the population in any one year.[70] By the latter half of the nineteenth century, when the British horse population was approaching its peak, horse deaths in Wales may have numbered some 5000 animals every year. In the very likely event that not all these skulls would be used every year, the potential number available to those prepared to go to the trouble of slaughtering a horse or exhuming a dead one would be many tens of thousands. They were thus not a scarce commodity, though their concentration in some communities would make them scarcer in some areas than in others.

Like many customs, no contemporary explanations survive of the rationale behind these activities. However, it is certain that nineteenth-century Britain saw more social changes than ever before, with the heavy industrialisation of the previous century being carried on at an accelerated rate, resulting in massive population growth and urbanisation. Those movements in themselves set great strains on the countryside, depopulation and a call for increased productivity among them, and all happening at a time of religious and political ferment. At a subconscious level, therefore, it is hardly surprising that some people at least may have been choosing to perpetuate or revive customs that afforded them some comfort and a link to a rapidly-disappearing past.

We do not really know why our ancestors – our relatively recent ancestors, in many cases – chose to bury horse skulls in buildings, and we will never do so. Nineteenth-century testimony relates to the wish for acoustic improvement in chapels, and vague references to 'good luck', 'preserving the luck of the house', or 'keeping the Black Lady at bay', usually noted at the time of discovery in domestic contexts.[71] Today, folklorists are frequently unwilling to accept the more mundane explanations given for human activity, and wish for a deeper, 'more meaningful' reason, ideally one that fits in with an unbroken evolutionist view of history. No contemporary documentary evidence, and hardly any oral testimony, survives to affect our interpretation, which is clouded only by the views of our predecessors.

As I have attempted to demonstrate in another context,[72] it may be that we have here a custom, weakened by no longer serving its original function and with that function metamorphosed over time, rejuvenated and given a new imperative by fresh factors. These new factors in this case would have been the fresh importance accorded to the acoustics of religious buildings from the mid eighteenth century onward, allied to the building of many more such structures at any one time than ever before, on the one hand, and the growing importance of the horse in the agricultural revolution of the nineteenth century, on the other, resulting in more horses being reared in Britain than at any other time in history. A dying – perhaps dead – custom may have then been rejuvenated to meet the needs of a new age, in exactly the same way as many other customs of rural origin gained new life through industrialisation and urbanisation.

The last word, however, should go to Mrs Anne George of Llanilar, where five skulls were discovered in 1982. 'Although we don't believe in these traditions [of keeping the 'Black Lady' at bay], she said, 'you never know what can happen, so we decided to re-bury the skulls last week...'.[73]

Notes and references

1. Gailey, A., 'The nature of tradition', *Folklore*, 100: ii, (1989), pp 143–61.
2. Ibid., p 149. R.J. Moore-Colyer, 'On the ritual burial of horses in Britain', *Folk Life*, 32, (1993–94), pp 58–65, provides a similar international context and chthonic explanation.
3. Ibid.
4. Merrifield, R., *The archaeology of ritual and magic* (London, 1987).
5. See, for example, the indexes to *Folklore*.
6. O'Súilleabháin, S., 'Foundation sacrifices', *Journal of the Royal Society of Antiquaries of Ireland* 75, (1945), pp 45–51.
7. Sandklef, A., 'Singing Flails', *Folklore Fellows Communications* 136, (1949), pp 27–72.
8. Ibid., p 72.
9. Brown, M.S.,'Buried horse-skulls in a Welsh house' *Folklore* 77 (1966), pp 64–66; Lloyd, J.D.K., 'A discovery of horses' skulls at Gunley', *Montgomeryshire Collections* 61 (1969), pp 133–5; Hayhurst, Y., 'A recent find of a horse skull in a house at Ballaugh, Isle of Man', *Folklore* 100:1 (1989), pp 105–9.
10. Buchanan, R.H., 'A buried horse-skull', *Ulster Folklife* 2 (1956), pp 60–1; Harris, K.M., 'Buried horse-skulls: a further note', *Ulster Folklife* 3 (1957), pp 70–1; Harris, K.M., 'More buried horse-skulls', *Ulster Folklife* 4 (1958), pp 76–7; Gailey, A., 'Horse skulls under a County Down farmhouse floor', *Ulster Folk Museum Year Book 1969/1970*, pp 13–4.
11. Lloyd (1969), op.cit. note 9.
12. Aldhouse-Green, M., 'The symbolic horse in Pagan Celtic Europe: an archaeological perspective', in S. Davies and N.A. Jones, (eds) *The horse in Celtic culture* (Cardiff, 1997), pp 1–22, provides a useful recent overview.
13. As recently expressed by, for example, Wood, J., 'The horse in Welsh folklore: a boundary image in custom and narrative', in S. Davies and N.A. Jones, (eds) op.cit., pp 162–3. For a recent populist interpretation, see Jones, T. Ll., *Hen Gof. Ysgrifau Llên Gwerin* (Llanrwst, 1996), pp 39–43.
14. Grove, F., 'Horses' heads', *Folklore* 12 (1901), pp 348–9.
15. Ibid.
16. Leather, E.M., *Folklore* 24 (1913), p 110.
17. Phillips, T.R., *The Breconshire Border* (Talgarth, 1926), p 103.
18. Isaac, E., *Coelion Cymru* (London, 1938), p 158.

19. Ibid.
20. Evans, G.E., *The pattern under the plough*, London, 1966, p 198; and letter from I.C. Peate to J.D.K. Lloyd, 4 March 1968, in Museum of Welsh Life, St Fagans (MWL) archives.
21. Brown, M.S., 'Buried horse-skulls in a Welsh house', *Folklore 77* (1966), pp 64–66.
22. Lloyd, J.D.K., 'A discovery of horses' skulls at Gunley', *Montgomeryshire Collections* 61 (1969), pp 133–5.
23. Ibid., pp 133–4; complete skeletons MWL Tape 4066.
24. Ibid., p 134.
25. Ibid.
26. Letter from I. Mathias, Cardigan, to I.C. Peate, 21 January 1968, MWL archives.
27. Letter from D.P. Jones to R. Gwyndaf, 13 January 1968, MWL Archive 1498/2.
28. Ex inf. my colleague R. Gwyndaf, 22 January 1975.
29. Letter from Mrs K. Morris, Llangeitho, to author, 11 October 1976, in MWL archives.
30. *Y Barcud* 5 September 1976.
31. Ex inf. Rev. T. Jones, 18 April 1979.
32. *Y Cymro*, 12 October 1982; *Cambrian News*, 15 October 1982; MWL film UC 61, copy of BBC Wales TV news item transmitted 15 October 1982.
33. Ex inf. Mrs Griffiths, Cwmbran, 27 October 1982.
34. Ex inf. Mrs Wigley, owner, 16 January 1991; *Y Faner* 24 May 1991.
35. Ex inf. my former colleague W. Jones (son of the discoverer), 20 September 1978.
36. J. Thomas, Newport, recorded 3 July 1970 on MWL Tape 2905.
37. Ex inf. the late Mr C. Meredith, Tredegar, 13 April 1975.
39. Letter from M. John, Llanboidy, to author, 7 March 1974, in MWL archives.
39. Photographic record by Brecon Museum and by R. Gwyndaf, MWL, February 1993. A recognised dowser, the late Mr A. George of Aberystwyth, claimed, using his dowsing techniques, that the skull was 364 years old. Mr and Mrs Powell believe the house to date from the 1620s–1630s. A coincidence, or more?
40. By Dafydd Wiliam (the author's son) and colleagues.
41. *The Cambridge economic history of Europe* (Cambridge, 1941), p 134.
42. Richards, M., *The laws of Hywel Dda* (Liverpool, 1954), pp 88–90.
43. Wiliam, E., *Traditional farm buildings in north-east Wales 1550–1900* (Cardiff, 1982), p 160.
44. Ibid., p 161.
45. Jenkins, D., *The agricultural community in south-west Wales at the turn of the twentieth century* (Cardiff , 1971), p 46.
46. Ashby, A.W. and Evans, I.L., *The agriculture of Wales and Monmouthshire* (Cardiff, 1944), pp 35–7.
47. Evans, G.E., *The horse in the furrow* (London, 1960); *The pattern under the plough* (London, 1966).
48. Evans (1966), op. cit., p 199.
49. Ibid., pp 194–5.
50. See note 12, 1–5; also Merrifield (1987), op. cit., pp 47, 54.
51. Ibid., pp 2–3, 13.
52. Ross, A., 'Shafts, pits, wells? Sanctuaries of the Belgic Britons', in J.M. Coles and D.D.A. Simpson (eds), *Studies in ancient Europe* (Leicester, 1968), pp 255–85;

Ross, A., and Feacham, R., 'Ritual rubbish? The Newstead pits', in J.V.S. Megaw (ed.), *To illustrate the monuments* (London, 1976), pp 230–7.

53. Bradley, R., *The social foundations of prehistoric Britain* (London and New York, 1984), pp 96–127.

54. Eg, Thompson, E.P., *Customs in common*, (London, 1991), pp 467–538; Cawte, E.C., *Ritual animal disguise* (Cambridge, 1978); Ifans, R.L, *Sêrs a Rybana. Astudiaeth o'r Canu Gwasael* (Llandysul, 1983).

55. Owen, T.M., *Welsh folk customs* (Cardiff, 1959), pp 49–63.

56. Wood (1966), op. cit., pp 162–82.

57. Ibid., p 166.

58. Wiliam, E., 'The re-invention of tradition: an architectural example from Wales', in H. Cheape (ed.), *Tools & traditions: studies in European ethnology presented to Alexander Fenton* (Edinburgh, 1993), pp 180–4.

59. On this see E. Hobsbawm and T. Ranger (eds), *The invention of tradition* (Cambridge, 1983).

60. Merrifield (1987), op. cit., p 118.

61. Brunskill, R.W., *Illustrated handbook of vernacular architecture* (London, 1970).

62. O'Súilleabháin (1945), op. cit.

63. Ebenezer, Newport, Pembs; Caerfarchell, Pembs, 1827; and Beulah, Cwm Nant-yr-eira, Mnts., 1876.

64. Merrifield, op. cit., pp 121–5.

65. O'Súilleabháin (1945) op. cit. and Gailey (1969–70), op. cit.

66. Roberts, P., *The Cambrian popular antiquities* (London, 1815); Owen, T.M., *The customs and traditions of Wales* (Cardiff, 1991).

67. *Hereford Times*, 8 July 1993.

68. Morgan, T.J., *Diwylliant Gwerin* (Llandysul, 1972).

69. Jones, A., *Welsh chapels*, revised edn (Stroud, 1996), pp 106–17.

70. Levine, M.A., 'Mortality models and the interpretation of horse population structure', in G. Bailey (ed.), *Hunter-gatherer economy in prehistory* (Cambridge, 1983), pp 23–46.

71. '*cadw y Ladi Ddu bant*' quoted about No. 19, Llanilar, *Y Cymro* 12 October 1982.

72. Wiliam (1993), op. cit.

73. *Cambrian News*, 15 October 1982. And see the postscript reprinted by R. Gwyndaf, 'The past in the present: folk beliefs in Welsh oral tradition', *Fabula* 35, 1994, p 247, recording Mrs George's flight to Canada before the skulls had been re-buried, and how a warning was received of a terrorist bomb on the plane on which she was due to return. This caused her to think that she had received a 'little reminder that the skulls had not yet been re-buried'.

12

The Christmas Rhyme Chapbook Tradition in Ireland

PAUL SMITH AND MICHAEL J. PRESTON

Introduction

THE RELATIONSHIPS BETWEEN SEASONAL performances of traditional plays and commercially printed chapbooks containing such texts pose complex questions. For example, many assumptions are packed into the culturally important question: 'To what extent did chapbook texts influence the mummers?' In our work, often jointly with Georgina Boyes,[1] we have attempted to address the various components of such a question, in part by following up research by Alex Helm[2] and Alan Gailey[3] with a concentrated search which has resulted in our locating additional examples of chapbooks and relevant information. Here we report on this research, which has allowed us to establish the probable printing relationships among the Christmas Rhyme chapbooks printed in Ireland.[4] We hope that the results we describe and summarise here will provide researchers with the information to determine the kind and extent of the relationships between this group of chapbooks and the traditional plays performed in Ireland.

The existence of Irish printings of chapbooks containing traditional play texts has long been known. Towards the middle of the nineteenth century, the Irish antiquarian Thomas Crofton Croker (1798-1854) commented, when discussing the elusive 1685 manuscript account of 'mumming and masking' in Cork,[5] '... and for the benefit of the antiquaries I beg to state that a half penny Edition, under the title of 'Christmas Rhymes,' is still printed and... sold by Charles Dillon, Castle Street, next to the Exchange.'[6] The number and range of Irish chapbooks containing traditional play texts has, however, never been fully established. As a consequence, pioneering studies of Irish traditional drama, such as E.R.R. Green's 1946 essay, 'Christmas Rhymers and Mummers,'[7] while noting the existence of chapbook texts, were weakened by uncertainty concerning what the chapbook tradition involved.

> In the east of Ireland chapbook texts seem to have been very widely used. From Ballynahinch and Castlebellingham come traditions of the Rhymes being hawked around, and sold in the shops, 'as a sort of ballad.' In 1872 Christmas Rhymes chapbooks were being sold in Belfast at a halfpenny each. The *New Christmas Rhyme Book* consists of fifteen pages, illustrated by fourteen cuts, one of them on the cover. The chapbook was published some time in the latter part of the last century, but the cuts have a much more venerable appearance.[8]

The lack of specific knowledge about the chapbooks and their interrelationships meant that only tentative conclusions could be put forward when discussing sources of, and influences on, oral texts, 'I *imagine that we should rather* attribute it [literary fragments in traditional texts] to the influence of chapbooks [emphasis ours]'.[9] More recently, however, studies by Alex Helm and Alan Gailey have focused attention on the printing histories of Belfast chapbooks containing traditional play texts: 'The Belfast chapbook is contemporary with its English counterparts, being dated on typographical evidence to c.1850, and it was still on sale in 1913'.[10]

To date, eight distinct printings of Christmas Rhyme chapbooks have been identified, and their imprints, together with the approximate dates of their production, are set out as follows:

1. Joseph Smyth and David Lyons (c.1803-18): Belfast, printed and sold, wholesale, by Smyth & Lyons.
2. Joseph Smyth (c.1810-50): Belfast, printed and sold, wholesale, by J. Smyth.
3. Charles Dillon (c.1824–41): Cork, printed and sold by Charles Dillon, Castle Street, next to the Exchange.
4. R.J.E. Tiddy reprint (pre-1916): Belfast, reprinted in Tiddy (1923).[11]
5. W.H. Patterson reprint (pre-1872): Belfast?, reprinted in Patterson (1872).[12]
6. John Nicholson (1) (1890–92): Belfast, printed for the book sellers by J. Nicholson, Cheapside, Church Lane, Belfast.
7. John Nicholson (2) (1890–1913): Belfast, printed for the book sellers by J. Nicholson, Cheapside, Church Lane, Belfast.
8. John Nicholson (3) (1890–1903/04): Belfast, printed by J. Nicholson, 26 Church Lane.

Because none of these chapbooks bears a date, the approximate dates of their publication have been based primarily on biographical information concerning their printers. Wherever possible, these dates have been further delimited by the use of contemporary observations and even annotations on the chapbooks. For example, in the case of one John Nicholson (2) chapbook, it is known from comments by Colm O'Lochlainn that this was 'purchased in 1913 in Belfast from the printer,'[13] and one of the extant copies of John Nicholson (3) is annotated 'Bought 14/12/03 at N's.'[14] Such annotations, however, must always be treated with care. Another copy of Nicholson (3) has on the cover the note 'Circa 1881' (see Figure 12.1).[15] In this instance, as will be seen, other evidence indicates that John Nicholson was not printing at that address at that date. Instead then, perhaps, some annotations reflect a perceived date of printing, based on the appearance of the chapbook rather than any tangible evidence.

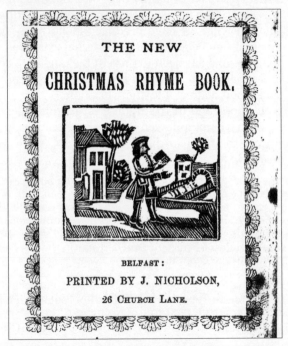

Figure 12.1   Front cover of John Nicholson's *The New Christmas Rhyme Book* [c.1890–1903] (QUB Library, Hibernica Collection, hp PN6110.C5 NEW)

It is perhaps realistic to think that 1913 represents almost the end of the printing history of these chapbooks, and perhaps also the beginning of the end of a reasonably active performance tradition. Times were changing, and the First World War was about to erupt in Europe. In fact, J.R.R. Adams refers to Nicholson's *The New Christmas Rhyme Book* as 'probably the very last chapbook proper to be printed in Ulster'.[16] In a similar vein, Professor Byers had commented in 1904, 'I am afraid this custom is now largely a thing of the past',[17] a sentiment echoed by John J. Marshall in 1923.[18]

Having acquired copies of all known examples of the chapbooks containing traditional play texts which have been printed in Ireland, as well as published reproductions (sometimes even purchasing an item if necessary),[19] we had to devise a method of studying these materials in a systematic way. Fortunately, there is a long tradition of studying printed texts, as described by Philip Gaskell in *A New Introduction to Bibliography*,[20] but most research in that area has assumed an authored text. However, even if the traditional play texts in chapbooks were authored at some time, they were printed as anonymous. Thus the goal of our study was not, 'to provide the principles and materials for a critical edition which will represent as nearly as possible the author's intentions for his text'. It was, rather, 'the establishment of the relationship of the surviving [chapbooks] to each other (in the form of a *stemma* or family tree)' without making the assumption that 'their evidence can be used to reconstruct the features of the lost original'.[21] Although what we have produced could allow one to reconstruct an 'original', if one believes that an original existed in the sense of an authored text, our goal has been to present the range of variation in the chapbook texts so that oral texts could be compared to a specific printed tradition with a known degree of textual variation.

While Gaskell's book and the tradition it represents have much to recommend them, we have not followed it slavishly because our experiences sometimes indicate the need to differ from what Gaskell suggests. For example, he asserts that

> Editions of the hand-press period are usually easy to identify. Resetting by hand, even when the compositor follows the spellings and abbreviations of printed copy word for word and line for line, always result in identifiable differences of spaces between the words, and the random pattern of damaged types is likewise different. With practice, two very similar settings can be told apart at a glance when copies are laid side by side, something that is usually easy to arrange with the aid of photocopies.[22]

While Gaskell's statement is generally true, in practice it is not always so easy to identify different type-settings when the pages are small, woodblocks are re-used, and the printer may have gone to some effort to imitate an earlier edition.

In pursuing this study, we have gone beyond comparing 'copies ... laid side by side'. We have also made use of a Hinman collating machine, invented by Charlton Hinman specifically for the study of the many surviving copies of Shakespeare's First Folio, but which has far broader applications.[23]

A Hinman collator uses technology of the 1950s, and its operation may be readily described. In essence, corresponding pages from two copies of a single edition are lighted by individual sources and their images reflected by mirrors so that they can be superimposed. If they are from the same edition, they should be identical in every respect – including layout, type, and 'glitches', in addition to verbal content – so that the viewer of the superimposed images sees a single image. The two light sources are connected to an alternating switch so that, when activated, one light goes on when the other goes off. The speed of this switching is controlled by the operator of the machine. At moderate speed this alteration makes any difference between the two images appear to 'jump' or 'flicker', and so highlights them by apparent movement. For example, if an 'e' has been changed to an 'a', there will be a distinct flicking as first one letter and then the other appears. Other changes during printing, such as inserting or removing letters or words, will result in that part of the line seeming to jump back and forth as the images alternate. Thus the operator of the machine can scan the page, looking at each line for such highlighted items, and note whether they are the result of in-press changes, or merely the result of physical damage to the page itself.

Such technology can be readily applied to chapbooks, although we found it took some adaptation because one can rarely work with the original printed items as Hinman was able to do. Instead, one is faced with working with photocopies which are rarely perfect copies, there being a certain amount of distortion involved in the use of that technology. Fortunately, a Hinman collator allows its operator to raise or lower one copy, and this is frequently sufficient to correct a situation such as when the photocopy machine has simply enlarged or reduced the copy evenly by a very small percentage. Unfortunately, some photocopy machines tend to elongate the image, and photocopies of photocopies are correspondingly more difficult to work with. Thus one must employ a certain amount of 'windage'. Nonetheless, we have found a Hinman collator to be a useful device.

In addition to using a Hinman collator, we supplemented this work with a simpler technology available to almost everyone. We have used photocopy machines to produce transparencies designed for overhead projectors, and laid them over a presumably identical photocopied page. We have even placed two transparencies of corresponding pages on top of each other on an overhead-projector and projected that image in imitation of a Hinman collator. These uses of transparencies do not provide one with the advantage of alternating light sources, and the resultant 'jumping' of differences between the two images, but they are useful in working with different copies of the apparently 'same' chapbooks, in order to determine if they are identical copies, or even corrected reprints. In particular instances, the use of transparencies seems to be more efficient than using a Hinman collator, which is at times over-precise for the task at hand.

A proposed printing history

The oldest of the eight Christmas Rhyme chapbooks identified to date was printed by Joseph Smyth and David Lyons,[24] probably between 1803 and 1818. The chapbook produced some years later, probably after 1810, by one member of this partnership, Joseph Smyth (see Figure 12.2), appears to have been printed from the standing type of the Smyth and Lyons edition. A very few minor corrections, such as the change in line 83 from 'be' to 'he', were made for this second printing. The essential differences

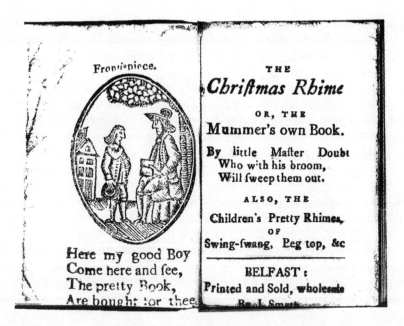

Figure 12.2 Title page of Joseph Smyth's *Christmas Rhime* chapbook [c.1810–50]

between the two printings are the shifting of some type, the repositioning of woodcuts, and the change in the designation of the printer. The source of the text contained in these chapbooks is as yet unknown, but Joseph Smyth had working relationships with printers in other parts of Ireland, such as Dublin, and certainly as late as 1845 he maintained connections with printers in Manchester, a city where many chapbooks containing traditional plays are known to have been published.

Apparently no Christmas Rhyme chapbook survives from the time between the printing of the Joseph Smyth chapbook and the earliest edition by John Nicholson. However, chapbook texts from this intervening period were reprinted in 1923 by R.J.E. Tiddy,[25] identified as coming from a Belfast chapbook, and in 1872 by W.H. Patterson,[26] identified as having been performed in the Belfast area. Furthermore, at least one chapbook supposedly printed by Charles Dillon of Cork may have been produced.[27] The reprinted items present a number of problems. Patterson, for example, displays a certain vagueness in his description of the text: 'The following are the Rhymes which, of course, have to be committed to memory by the different performers... The words are printed in little books which are sold at a halfpenny each'.[28] It is not totally clear from these statements whether the text that follows was taken from the printed version or from the oral tradition. Having said that, we do know that Patterson was not referring to the Nicholson (1) chapbook which he sent to the Folklore Society in December 1892,[29] because Nicholson does not appear to have commenced printing in Belfast until 1890.[30] Consequently, quite what Patterson was quoting from in 1872 remains uncertain.

Similarly, the headnote to the play reproduced by Tiddy expresses reservations regarding the reliability of his informant:

> The communicator of this text wrote that it was copied from a small leaflet called 'The Christmas Rime,' printed in Belfast. This seems to be inaccurate, an almost identical version being given in The New Christmas Rhyme Book, Belfast, printed for the Booksellers by J. Nicholson, Cheapside, Church Lane, Belfast.[31]

In addition, the accuracy of these texts must be questioned, since both were recopied at least once prior to being reprinted, and consequently some transcribing errors may well have occurred. Nonetheless, these two reprints contain crucial textual evidence linking the Smyth and Lyons and Joseph Smyth chapbooks with those of John Nicholson.

Tiddy's text appears to be closely related to the earlier Smyth and Lyons and Joseph Smyth chapbooks since it contains several identical readings: for example, lines 4 'in' and 12 'Knight'. In contrast, it also has affinities with the later Nicholson chapbooks: for example, the omission in line 65 of the stage direction 'Answer' and the spelling 'Beelzebub' in line 106. In addition, Tiddy's reprint contains a number of unique readings: in lines 6 'youth' and 21 'gallant', among others. Although some of these may be attributed to copyist's or printer's errors, there are too many variant readings to make this a reasonable possibility. It seems likely, therefore, that the chapbook reprinted by Tiddy was not the source of the later Nicholson editions, but rather a now-lost parallel descendant from the Joseph Smyth text.

Patterson's reprint, on the other hand, appears to be a more probable intermediary between the Joseph Smyth and the John Nicholson chapbooks. This text agrees in some respects with the earlier chapbooks: for example, in lines 72 'broke' and 76 'come'. However, it shares with the later printings the substitutions in lines 10 and 12 of 'St' for both 'Prince' and 'Knight'. The history of a single reading 'set' in line 72 of the Joseph Smyth chapbook illustrates this probable relationship. 'Set' becomes 'fit' in Patterson, representing an apparent misreading of the archaic long 's' of the earlier version coupled with a 'sense' correction of the vowel. The further rationalisation to 'fix' in the Nicholson chapbook demonstrates the likely association among the three printings. From this we deduce that, despite the occasional similarities between the texts reprinted by Patterson and Tiddy, the play documented by Patterson appears to be the possible source for the later Nicholson chapbooks.

Interestingly, Tiddy and Patterson give transcriptions of only the texts and do not indicate if there were woodcuts in the original printed versions, as there presumably were. If looked at in comparison with either the earlier or later Irish chapbooks, this appears to be a striking omission because, especially in the early chapbooks, the woodcuts seem to provide a visual representation of the characters speaking and thus take the place of the names of the speakers of parts as found in literary dramatic texts. Instead, what one finds in both Tiddy's and Patterson's texts is that the name of the speaker of each part is given.

Who printed Tiddy's and Patterson's originals is a question worth considering, although no conclusion can be reached at this time. *The Belfast and Province of Ulster Directory for 1852*[32] indicates that Alexander Mayne took over from Joseph Smyth, 'Alexander Mayne, printer and publisher (Late J. Smyth's)'. Adams additionally connects Mayne and Nicholson, although the connection is less specific than one might wish.

> Towards the end of the century one Belfast printer, following in the footsteps of Alexander Mayne, Joseph Smyth's successor, specialized in the production of street ballads... J. Nicholson's sheets were intended to be cut up, and the ballads bear Nicholson's imprint at the foot.[33]

It would certainly be reasonable for Mayne to reprint items published earlier by Joseph Smyth, and so Mayne is a logical possibility as the printer of Patterson's original and perhaps Tiddy's. Mayne would have no reason to change the title, and so *The Christmas Rime*, the title that Tiddy objected to, would have been appropriate for him to use. Alternative contenders as printers of the Tiddy and Patterson originals include the stationer James Moore, who worked from 1845 to 1877 out of various premises in Belfast, including 26 Church Street – Nicholson's eventual premises. Also, James Moore's widow, Mrs Moore, who continued to do business at that address until it was taken over by John Nicholson around 1890,[34] is a possibility. Unfortunately, it is not known if Nicholson 'inherited' any of Moore's stock or, for want of a better term, 'intellectual properties'. If he did, however, as Adams notes, Nicholson was 'a good business man',[35] and it is plausible that he inserted 'new' into the title of *The New Christmas Rhyme Book*. To document such an account, however, will require that additional evidence be found.

The exact relationship among the Nicholson chapbooks is complex. The simplest explanation is that Nicholson (1) is most closely related to the Patterson reprint in that they agree in lines 19 'rock' and 56 'can', while Nicholson (2) and Nicholson (3) have 'block' and 'who can'. Similarly, Nicholson (1) and Nicholson (2) often agree, differing from Nicholson (3), as in lines 4 'at the' and 120 'Gentlemen and ladies'. Thus it might be maintained that Nicholson (1) was set from the chapbook reprinted by Patterson, that Nicholson (2) was set from Nicholson (1), and Nicholson (3) from Nicholson (2). Unfortunately, this proposition appears to be contradicted by a number of irregularities, primarily the indistinct periods and commas and the rare disagreement in capitalisation, as in lines 48 'mince' and 49 'Oven'. In spite of any concessions for the quality of the printing, such minor evidence must be considered. Thus, rather than a simple linear association, it seems best to suggest that at least two as yet unlocated intermediate printings may have existed.

The textual history of the chapbooks, which coincides with their tem-

158 From Corrib to Cultra

poral distribution, is reinforced by two further considerations. First, there
is the continuity of titles in the chapbooks. The Smyth and Lyons and the
Joseph Smyth chapbooks are both entitled *Christmas Rime*. Nicholson's
'new' in the title certainly acknowledged his awareness of earlier *Christmas
Rime* books and may well have implied his indebtedness to them.
Furthermore, the woodcuts Nicholson used throughout appear to be generally imitative of those in the Smyth and Lyons and the Joseph Smyth
printings of three-quarters of a century earlier. This may in part account
for Green's comment that Nicholson's woodcuts 'have a much more ven-
erable appearance'[36] than was consistent with his date of printing.

The relationships outlined above represent our understanding of the
textual relationships among the Irish chapbooks traced to date, specifically those produced by Belfast printers. The originals of the chapbooks
reprinted by Tiddy and Patterson must at present be viewed as unlocated
items which could contain the solution to some textual problems. Overall,
the similarity among the known texts and the apparent copying of cuts in
earlier Smyth and Lyons chapbooks for John Nicholson's publications suggests a continuous printing history of a single 'Belfast version' which,
through successive printings, was available as a potential influence on the
oral versions of traditional plays throughout the nineteenth and into at
least the early twentieth century.

Beyond this 'Belfast version' there are a number of tantalising references, most of them sufficiently vague to be of little help in reconstructing
any relationship among the various printed versions, or even in docu-
menting the fact that particular chapbooks ever existed. As yet, a search
for the Cork version printed by Charles Dillon in the second quarter of the
nineteenth century has proved fruitless. It is perhaps appropriate to note,
however, that Alan Gailey, in 'Mummers' and Christmas Rhymers' plays
in Ireland: the problem of distribution,'[37] does not record any plays from
the Cork area. Since we surmise that plays were not generally printed or
sold in areas where plays were not performed, this allusion to a chapbook
appears to be an anomaly. Several possible explanations, however, may be
offered.

First, although there may have been no plays performed around Cork,
chapbooks may have been printed in Cork either for sale elsewhere, or
perhaps in an attempt to generate new sales. Unfortunately, to date no evidence has come to light that Dillon had trading arrangements with printers or publishers elsewhere in the country. Certainly there are reports from
areas not currently known to produce such items of the use of chapbooks
containing traditional play texts.[38] For example, Bryan Jones reported that
in 1916 in Braganstown near Castle Bellingham, County Louth, '... ballad
singers used to hawk broadsheets of mumming rhymes at Christmas
time'.[39] Similarly, Richard Hayward points to the use of such chapbooks in
Larne early in this century.[40] Second, it may be that plays were performed
in this region but, since the distribution of the documentation of plays is a

function of the distribution of collectors rather than performances, they still await collection. Cawte, Helm and Peacock certainly found this to be the case when they were analysing the spatial distribution of traditions they had indexed, 'The pattern is also modified by differing intensities of collection, as when a collector increased our collection of Buckinghamshire plays by 35%.'[41] Third, this 'chapbook' may prove to be a 'literary' production for antiquarians and others interested in oral and literary traditions. Finally, there remains the possibility that Crofton Croker may have 'invented' the reference. At present we have insufficient evidence to support any of these alternatives.

Other similarly unverified or ambiguous accounts of possible chapbook traditions are known, such as that provided by William Pinkerton in 1866 who quotes, with an unknown degree of accuracy, from 'the printed version'.[42] Is this a chapbook he is citing, or a printed version of an oral text? If a chapbook, is it from Belfast, or elsewhere in Ireland? The short section of text printed differs considerably from all of the Belfast chapbook versions located so far and, for the present, must be considered an intriguing reference requiring further investigation.[43]

Although we have brought our study to a conclusion, clearly we do not mean to imply that there is no more to be learned about the history of chapbooks containing traditional play texts in Ireland. We believe that we have outlined *the*, or *a*, Belfast tradition, but it is still possible that other printings within the Belfast tradition may exist, as well as editions which may document the existence of as yet unverified chapbook traditions elsewhere in Ireland.

Acknowledgements

The authors would like to take this opportunity to thank the following individuals who spent time and trouble in answering our many questions and making materials available to us: William S. Campbell of Hearst Magazines, Eílís Ní Dhuibhne, Dr Christopher Cawte, Timothy Collins, Dr Alan Gailey, Linda Greenwood, Mary Kelly, Peter Millington, James Mosley, the late Peter Opie, M. Pollard, Steve Roud, Hugh Shields, Ron Shuttleworth, Heather Stanley, Anne and Peter Stockham, and the librarians of Belfast Public Libraries, Trinity College Library, City of Dublin Public Library, The Queen's University of Belfast Library, University College Dublin, and the National Library.

We would also like to thank the Librarian of The Queen's University of Belfast Library for giving us permission to reproduce a facsimile of the title page of John Nicholson's The New Christmas Rhyme Book from the Hibernica Collection (hp PN6110.C5 NEW) (see Figure 12.1).

Notes and references

1. See Preston, M.J., Smith, M.G., and Smith, P.S., 'SLF research projects: traditional drama. Project 1: A classification of chapbooks containing traditional play texts,' *Lore and Language* 1.7 (1972), pp 3–5; Preston, M.J., Smith, M.G., and Smith, P.S., 'SLF research projects: traditional drama. Project 1: A classification of chapbooks containing traditional play texts: interim report,' *Lore and Language* 2.4 (1976), pp 5–7; Preston, M.J., Smith, M.G., and Smith, P.S., 'The peace egg chapbooks in Scotland: an analytic approach to the study of chapbooks,' *The Bibliotheck: A Scottish Journal of Bibliography and Allied Topics* 8.3 (1976), pp 71–89; Preston, M.J., Smith, M.G., and Smith, P.S., *An interim checklist of chapbooks containing traditional play texts* (Newcastle, 1976); Preston, M.J., Smith, M.G., and Smith, P.S., *Chapbooks and traditional drama: an examination of chapbooks containing traditional play texts, part I, Alexander and the King of Egypt Chapbooks*, CECTAL Bibliographical and Special Series, No. 2 (Sheffield, 1977a); Preston, M.J., Smith, M.G., and Smith, P.S., 'The lost chapbooks,' *Folklore* 88 (1977b), pp 169–71; Smith, Georgina, *Chapbook sources of British traditional drama: the mummers' play as popular culture*, Folklore Preprint Series, 6.6, Bloomington, Indiana, 1978; and Smith, Georgina, 'Chapbooks and traditional plays: communication and performance,' *Folklore* 92 (1981), pp 208–18.
2. See Helm, Alex, *The chapbook mummers' plays: a study of the printed versions of the north-west of England* (Leicester, 1969), pp 17, 38–9.
3. See Gailey, Alan, 'The folk-play in Ireland,' *Studia Hibernica* 6, 1966, pp 113–54; *Christmas rhymers and mummers in Ireland* (Leicester, 1968), pp 16–17, 40–43; *Irish folk drama* (Cork, 1969), pp 9, 43; 'A missing Belfast chapbook: the Christmas Rime, or, the mummers' own book,' *Irish Booklore* 2.1 (1972), pp 54–8; 'The Christmas Rhime,' *Ulster Folklife* 21 (1975), pp 73–84; 'Chapbook influence on the Irish mummers' play,' *Folklore* 85 (1974), pp 1–22.
4. For a discussion of the history and taxonomy of this group of chapbooks see, Boyes, Georgina, Preston, M.J., and Smith, Paul, *Chapbooks and traditional drama: an examination of chapbooks containing traditional play texts, Part II: Christmas rhyme books* (Sheffield, 1999).
5. Croker, T.C., *Recollections of Cork*, MS1206, Chap. 9, ff. 11–12, Trinity College Library, Dublin. This manuscript must have been compiled between 1826 and 1854 because it contains quotations from William Hone, *The Every-Day Book*, 2 Vols. (1826–27), and Croker died in 1854. For a discussion of the 1685 manuscript, see Tom Pettitt, 'Cork revisited: a reconsideration of some early records of the mummers' plays,' *Traditional Drama Studies* 3 (1994), pp 15–30.
6. Croker, ff.12. Unfortunately no copy of this chapbook has been located.
7. Green, E.R.R., 'Christmas rhymers and mummers,' *Ulster Journal of Archaeology* 9 (1946), pp 3–21.
8. Ibid., p 6.
9. Ibid., p 5.
10. Gailey (1968), op. cit., p 40.
11. Tiddy, R.J E, *The mummers' play* (Oxford, 1923), pp 141–3.
12. Patterson, W.H., 'The Christmas rhymers in the north of Ireland,' *Notes and Queries* Ser. 4, 10, 21 December 1872, pp 487–8.
13. O'Lochlainn, Colm, 'Christmas rhymers and mummers,' *The Irish Book Lover* 16, July-December 1928, p 126.

14. Ulster Folk and Transport Museum Archive. A facsimile of the title page appears in McClelland, Aiken, 'Irish chapbooks,' *Ulster Folklife and Transport Museum Year Book*, 1971/72, p 24.

15. Queen's University Belfast Library, Hibernica Collection (hp PN6110.C5 NEW).

16. Adams, J.R.R., *The printed word and the common man: popular culture in Ulster 1700–1900* (Belfast, 1987), pp 160–61.

17. Professor Byers, *Sayings, proverbs and humour of Ulster* (Belfast, 1904), p 31.

18. Marshall, J.J., *Popular rhymes and sayings of Ireland*, second series, (Dungannon, 1923), p 18.

19. Preston, Smith and Smith (1977b), op. cit., pp 169–71.

20. Gaskell, Philip, *A new introduction to bibliography* (Oxford, 1972), repr. 1974.

21. Ibid., p 336.

22. Ibid., p 313.

23. Hinman, Charlton, *The first folio of Shakespeare: the Norton facsimile* (New York, 1968); and Gaskell (1972), op. cit., p 357.

24. Marshall, J.J., 'Notes on old Belfast printers,' *Quarterly Notes* [Belfast Municipal Museum and Art Gallery], 1936, pp 17–18, comments:

> Smyth & Lyons, 115 High St. Before 1819 the partnership was dissolved. David Lyons setting up in Smithfield, where he printed The Irishman newspaper for 'honest Jack Lawless' during the run (1819–1826) of that lively sheet. He probably died or gave up business between 1826 and 1830.

> Joseph Smyth, the senior partner had his printing office 34 High Street, where he continued till sometime about 1850, as he has disappeared from Henderson's Directory for 1852.

Evidence contained in the various editions of John Anderson's Catalogue of Early Belfast Printed Books 1694–1830, and the subsequent supplements, indicates that this summary of the relationship between the two printers is essentially correct. From the various entries in Anderson, it appears that Joseph Smyth was working alone from 1799–1803. However, from 1803 to 1818 Joseph Smyth and David Lyons were working in partnership, but, to confuse the issue, items were appearing, certainly from 1810 onwards, bearing their individual as well as joint imprints. In addition, both were involved in working with other parties. For a further discussion of this relationship and the types of materials they printed see Adams (1987), op. cit., pp 137–56, 194–99. All of this makes it very difficult to establish a printing date for these two editions of the Christmas Rhime. Certainly there is no record of items bearing the Lyons imprint after 1826. A discussion of the relationship between these two chapbooks is also to be found in Gailey (1975), p 74.

25. Tiddy (1923), op. cit., pp 141–3.

26. Patterson (1872), op. cit., pp 487–8.

27. See Croker, ff.12. It has proved almost impossible to uncover any details regarding Charles Dillon and his printing activities. Pigot & Co., *City of Dublin and provincial directory* (1824), list him as printer and bookseller at 12 Castle Street, Cork. Dillon is given as the printer of Patrick Dunn's *Pious Miscellany* (1841), being at this time at 19 Great George Street, Cork. Finally the *Cork county and city directory* (1844) lists a Charles Dillon at 34 Great George Street, Cork.

28. Patterson (1872), op. cit., p 487.

29. 'Proceedings at the Evening Meetings – Wednesday, December 21, 1892,' *Folklore* 4 (1893), p 120.

30. The first record of John Nicholson is as a printer and stationer at 26 Church-Lane, Belfast, in 1890 (see *The Belfast and Province of Ulster directory for 1890*, (Belfast, 1890), p 391). An annual entry for Nicholson at this address, up until 1919, is to be found in both *The Belfast and Province of Ulster directory* and also in the various editions of *Kelly's directory of stationers, printers, booksellers, publishers, papermakers, &c*, London. No entry is to be found for John Nicholson in the Belfast directories for 1920, and it is taken that he was no longer in business. For further information on Nicholson, see Adams, op. cit, (1987), pp 160–1, and MacLochlainn, Alf, 'Belfast printed ballad sheets,' *Irish Booklore* 1, 1971, pp 21–3.

31. Tiddy (1923), op. cit., p 141.

32. *The Belfast and Province of Ulster directory for 1852* (Belfast, 1852), p 117.

33. Adams (1987), op. cit., p 160.

34. Communication from Mary Kelly, Assistant Librarian (Special Collections) The Library, The Queen's University of Belfast, 12 November, 1997.

35. Adams (1987), op. cit., p 160.

36. Green (1946), op. cit., p 6.

37. Gailey, Alan, 'Mummers' and Christmas rhymers' plays in Ireland: the problem of distribution,' *Ulster Folklife* 24 (1978), pp 59–68.

38. References to their use outside the Belfast and Cork areas include: Ballynahinch, County Down, *Department of Irish Folklore* MS 1087, 18; Dungiven, County Derry, *Ulster Folk and Transport Museum Archive* 664036; Carrickfergus, County Antrim, *Ulster Folk and Transport Museum Archive* 664064. We are indebted to Dr Alan Gailey for providing these details.

39. Jones, Bryan, 'Christmas mumming in Ireland,' *Folklore* 27 (1916), p 301.

40. Hayward, Richard, 'Christmas rhymers,' *Ulster Illustrated* 5.5–6 (1957/8), p 10.

41. Cawte, E.C., Helm, A., and Peacock, N., *English ritual drama: a geographical index* (London, 1967), p 31.

42. Pinkerton, William, 'Anonymous ballads,' *Notes and Queries* Ser. 3, 11, 17 February 1866, p 143.

43. This in itself presents a daunting task, as the Pinkerton material in the R.M. Young Collection in the Public Record Office of Northern Ireland (PRONI) 'contains 92 separately listed items largely described as notebooks containing historical notes, extracts etc.' (Correspondence from Heather Stanley, PRONI, 15 July 1998.)

13

Royal Arch, Royal Arch Purple and
Raiders of the Lost Ark:
Secrecy in Orange and Masonic Ritual

Anthony D. Buckley

THIS ESSAY IS CONCERNED WITH Orange and Masonic ritual in England and Ireland. Secrecy, however, is very widespread in human affairs. So I shall begin with an anecdote from studying medicine among Yoruba herbalists in Nigeria.[1]

At that time, I was trying to find out about the number three. I knew that among the Yoruba, three was associated with the secret society called Ògbóni. I had been told, for example, that if you put three spots in the corner of an envelope, then the postman might deliver the letter without insisting on a stamp. I knew that three was important, but I could persuade nobody to talk about it. One day, I asked one of my main informants to tell me about the number four but he just chuckled and said, 'if I tell you about four, I shall have to tell you about three'.

Eventually, a man who worked near to where I had an office took me on one side. 'I understand', he said secretively, 'that you are trying to find out about the number three'. And then he said, 'The three stones of the hearth will not spill the soup (aàrò métạ kìí dọbẹ̀ẹnú)'. He explained that this proverb showed how the earth supported the world. And I also worked out that you had to use three stones in a fireplace so you could rest a round cooking pot on it without spilling the soup. And there, abruptly, the conversation ended.

Suddenly, I realised that the proverb was very profound indeed. Though it took me many years to put the pieces together, I felt, at least in principle, that I understood how Yoruba herbalists understood both the cosmos and the human body.

But the strange thing is this, that this proverb, 'The three stones of the hearth will not spill the soup' was not a secret at all. It was actually very well known. But by hearing it as though it were a secret, I learned just what an important saying it was. To use an idea of Elizabeth Tonkin's,[2] the fact that it was secret gave the idea 'power'.

Secrecy is ubiquitous in all human societies. There is confidentiality in all but the most fleeting of relationships. Information is often shared with some, and hidden from others. Secrecy is also found in drama, and it has a special place in ritual.

This article will attempt two things. First, it will imitate Alan Gailey's survey of *Irish folk drama*,[3] looking at some traditional dramas which are essentially very similar to each other, drawing out differences and similarities. The dramas dealt with here are the Royal Arch rituals found in English and Irish Freemasonry, and the rite of the Royal Arch Purple Order, associated with the Orange Order.

Second, the article will make use of the fact that there is a well-known adventure film, *Raiders of the Lost Ark*, whose plot is remarkably similar to one of the motifs found in these rituals. My aim in comparing some important rituals with a popular film, is to consider the nature of ritual. More specifically, and developing some of Robinson's ideas,[4] I want to explore the ritual secrecy which is so characteristic of not only the Royal Arch and Royal Arch Purple rituals, but also more generally among the groups I call 'brotherhoods'.[5]

It will be suggested that, in these rites, as more generally in social relationships, secrecy has the function of symbolising the boundary between insiders and outsiders, in this case emphasising bonds of fellowship. It will also be argued, more importantly, that secrecy can be intrinsic to the dramatic structure of the ritual itself. Without the secrecy, the rite would lose much of its purpose.[6]

Though here the discussion will be confined to a very few rituals, the list of organisations with secretive rituals is, in fact, very long indeed. For example, a nineteenth-century source gives details of more than 600 such secretive brotherhoods in America.[7] In nineteenth and early twentieth century Ireland, there were friendly societies such as the Ancient Order of Foresters, the Irish National Foresters, the British Order of Ancient Free Gardeners and the Independent Order of Odd Fellows; temperance groups like the International Order of Good Templars and the Independent Order of Rechabites; convivial societies like the Royal Antediluvian Order of Buffaloes and the Freemasons themselves; and the politico-religious organisations like the Ancient Order of Hibernians and the Orange Order.[8] From the eighteenth century too there were the so-called agrarian secret societies, Oak Boys, Steel Boys, Defenders, Ribbonmen and others also characterised by ritual secrecy.[9]

There are, of course, many rituals in the British Isles which are *not* secret, the major exceptions here being the ritual practices of most Christian churches, and of other world religions, such as Islam, Hinduism or Buddhism. Nevertheless, one can say that very many of the rituals found in eighteenth, nineteenth and twentieth century Britain, Europe and America – perhaps the majority – have contained ritual secrets.

The rituals described here differ in important respects, but they nevertheless bear a close family resemblance to each other. Specifically, each rite contains at least one of two separate types of story. One type of story comes from the Book of Exodus and tells of the Israelites wandering through the desert. The other type of story is what Jones calls the 'crypt legend', telling of the discovery of an ancient text – the Bible or some part of it – in a previously unknown crypt.[10]

The Royal Arch Purple rite is almost entirely based on the first of these stories, the wandering of the Israelites in the desert, and it contains only a hint of a connection with the story of the crypt. The Masonic Royal Arch rite found in England consists almost entirely of a version of the second story, but it does contain a hint of desert wanderings. And the Royal Arch degree worked by Irish Masons contains quite full versions of both stories.

As a non-member of these different bodies, I rely on published materials for my analysis. My understanding of the Irish Royal Arch depends largely upon Jones's study of the Royal Arch.[11] It is fortunate that the English Royal Arch has been revealed to the curious by a number of 'exposés', of which I have found Hannah's *Darkness Visible* particularly useful.[12] My analysis of the Royal Arch Purple depends upon Cargo's delicate exposition,[13] and more generally upon the work by Kilpatrick, Murdie and Cargo which has, indeed, opened up the field for study.[14]

One advantage of studying this particular set of rituals is that the second of these story-types, the crypt legend, has also been used as the pivotal idea in the now classic movie *Raiders of the Lost Ark*,[15] directed by Steven Spielberg. Gailey has suggested, in his discussion of the Mummer's play, that ancient rituals can 'survive' in the modern world by becoming theatrical or quasi-theatrical forms of drama.[16] Spielberg's film is undoubtedly one such transformation.

This happy coincidence between a well-known adventure film and an important set of rituals allows this discussion to focus on a distinction between what I shall call *theatrical* presentations – drama in the normal sense, whether on stage or screen – and those dramatic presentations which are properly called *rituals*. By engaging in a comparison, I shall tease out the role of secrecy in both theatrical drama and ritual, and specifically explore why so many rituals are secretive.

The Royal Arch Purple and the exodus through the desert

Though it is, undoubtedly, part of the same family of rituals as the Masonic Royal Arch, Kilpatrick argues convincingly that the Royal Arch Purple ritual has its proximate origins not in Freemasonry, but in the rites of the Boyne Society,[17] a body set up in the early eighteenth century to celebrate the victory of King William at the Boyne.

The Royal Arch Purple degree is one of a sequence of degrees open to members of the Orange Order. An Orangeman who has taken the two Orange Order degrees of Orange and Purple is free to enter the organisationally separate Royal Arch Purple Order. He may then choose to pass through the eleven degrees of yet another organisation, the Royal Black Institution.[18]

The narrative which is the basis for the Royal Arch Purple degree is almost entirely taken from the biblical story of the Exodus. It has only the faintest echo of the second of the other type of narrative under consideration, the story of the crypt. Cargo's account of the ritual[19] takes care not to reveal too much of what is going on – and I shall try to follow his example. Cargo gives an informative list of the biblical texts read out during the ritual and these spell out much of the narrative.

The rite begins with the preparation of the candidate before his entry to the chapter room. Here the candidate is blindfolded ('hoodwinked'), and his shoelaces are undone. Perhaps one or both shoes are taken off. His belt may also be removed or unbuckled. As well as this, the candidate is likely to be frightened by lurid stories and allusions. He may have been told that he will have to 'ride a goat'. He might be advised to put butter behind his knees, and have no holes in his socks. He might be asked if he suffered from heart trouble or had a back injury. He will also have to remove any sharp objects from his person (informant's description).

Blindfolded, slipshod, and a little apprehensive, the candidate now enters the body of the hall, and is greeted by the word 'profane'.[20] Also, it appears from an oblique reference that a sword is pointed towards the candidate's heart, to indicate the seriousness of the obligation he is taking.[21] The candidate is now asked to declare his trust in God and to promise to keep secret what is to be revealed to him, even should he be threatened by some terrible danger.[22]

There now follows the main part of the ritual, called 'the travel'. The word 'travel' is open to several possible readings. It seems to be derived from the French *travail* (work) thus linking it to the Masonic expression 'working' – ie, performing – a 'degree'. The closely related English term 'travail', however, suggests that it may also refer to the fact that the ritual is something of an ordeal for the candidate.[23] The word may also refer, however, to the fact that, as in the Irish Royal Arch, it involves a lot of 'walking all around'.[24]

Cargo's account continues: 'Many of the things that happen during this travel remind us of the sufferings of God's people and the likelihood that we may fall from grace but that with His help we can conquer even death'.[25] The journey around the room is 'a metaphorical journey... through the desert' (informant's description), accompanied by an interjection of biblical texts.[26]

The travel begins with an allusion to the departure of the Children of Israel from Egypt (Exodus 13, 15-18) and to the way that they eluded both the Egyptians and the land of the Philistines by miraculously crossing the Red Sea. There is a mention too of the fecklessness of the Israelites which led to their being condemned to wander in the wilderness for forty years (Numbers 14, 11-12, 26-28, 33). There now follows an incident reminiscent of the Irish Masonic Royal Arch, an encounter by Joshua with the angelic Captain of the Host. In the story, the Captain of the Host instructs Joshua to 'loose the shoe from off thy foot; for the place whereon thou standest *is* holy' (Joshua 5, 13-15). Thus, one imagines, the candidate is instructed to remove his already untied shoe, or perhaps the only one that still remains. Recitals from the psalms (Psalm 107, 4-8, 12-15; Psalm 46, 43-45) now acquaint the candidate with the discomforts of the desert. It is probably at this moment that the most publicly well-known part of the rite takes place, for the candidate finds his feet bitten by 'serpents'. An informant tells me that there may be other events which upset the harassed candidate.

Cargo tells us that there next takes place the 'advancement'. This 'reminds us of the tribe of Reuben, the tribe of Gad and the half tribe of Manasseh who, although their inheritance was assured on the other side of Jordan advanced in the vanguard of the army when crossing the river to assist their brethren to secure the Promised Land'.[27]

At the end of these desert meanderings, the ritual comes to a dramatic conclusion. Cargo speaks obliquely about this final and spectacular part of the ceremony. The blindfolded candidate is introduced to the idea of a ladder, whose three steps are named respectively 'Faith', 'Hope' and 'Charity'. He is also told the story of Jacob's ladder, the ladder which, in a dream, allowed Jacob to meet God and be promised the land of Canaan (Exodus 13, 15-18).

The candidate now experiences the sensation of falling, and he is told that this fall signifies a ' "fall from grace" by disobedience from God which can only be remedied by seeking forgiveness'.[28] Finding himself flat on the floor, his hoodwink is at last removed. Then, in a manner not unlike that of the third degree ritual in Freemasonry, he is lifted to his feet and taught the formalised embrace called the Five Points of Fellowship: Hand to Hand, Foot to Foot, Knee to Knee, Breast to Breast, Hand to Back.

The Royal Arch Purple degree therefore, focuses almost exclusively upon a sojourn in the desert. As the candidate emerges from the wilderness, he joins in a 'link and chain' (in the manner of *Auld Lang Syne*). Thus he is:

> ... brought to the realisation that the true light can only be found in the Trinity... and that every day living will and can be enhanced by the help of those in the chain of fellowship who had received that Purple in the darkness of ignorance and brought it to the true light of understanding.[29]

The Masonic Royal Arch in England: the descent into the crypt

We turn now to the English and then the Irish Royal Arch degree as found in Freemasonry. This degree has, as its central feature, a descent into a crypt. The Royal Arch degree in Freemasonry has existed since at least the eighteenth century. It is now one of the commonest forms of ritual found in America, Europe and elsewhere. The degree is available to those who have been initiated through the basic three degrees of Craft Masonry. It is also associated with another degree, that of Mark Master Mason. The crypt legend is the other main type of story found in the Royal Arch type of ritual, and it seems to have considerable antiquity. It tells how a group of people, searching among the ruins of an ancient building – usually the Temple in Jerusalem – come upon an entrance to a deep crypt. When one of their number is lowered by a rope into the vault, a bible (or a portion of it) is discovered.[30]

In the English Royal Arch, this descent into a crypt is added on to the story of the building of the Second Temple of Jerusalem by Zerubbabel after the Babylonian exile. This story is biblical, and it is recounted at some considerable length in the books of Nehemiah, Ezra and Haggai. In this rite, three individuals, Zerubbabel the Governor, Joshua the High Priest and the Prophet Haggai, are credited with the rebuilding of the Second Temple of Jerusalem. It is these figures, addressed as 'Most Excellent Zerubbabel', 'Excellent Joshua' and 'Excellent Haggai' who are the main officers (the 'Principals') in an English Royal Arch chapter.[31]

In the English Royal Arch, the hoodwinked candidate is guided around towards the west of the chapter room by an officer called the Principal Sojourner. This comparatively brief journey is almost certainly a faint shadow of the sojourn in the desert found in the Royal Arch Purple and in the Royal Arch in Irish Freemasonry.

From here, the candidate advances towards the sacred shrine in the east. There, the candidate is invited to pretend with a crow bar, to wrench a stone from the floor (this stone is here represented pictorially on a floor-cloth). Unlike in Irish Masonry, the candidate is only symbolically lowered into the vault. In fact, he kneels down on a small stool.[32] He then gropes around until he finds 'something like a scroll of vellum or parchment' which 'for want of light' he is unable to read.[33]

Next the candidate is guided to lever up a second keystone and again he is symbolically 'lowered' into the vault to the accompaniment of a reading (Haggai 2, 1-9). Thence, he is taken to the altar where he makes a vow upon the volume of the sacred law. The candidate is then brought to his feet, and at last the hoodwink is removed. Having thus come 'into the light', the candidate reads aloud the scroll on which are written the opening three verses of Genesis, and which concludes 'And God said, let there be light, and there was light'.[34]

The Principal Sojourner now tells the whole story to Zerubbabel (the first officer of the chapter) and to the assembled brethren, speaking on behalf of the initiate:

Principal Sojourner... Resuming our labours... our progress was here impeded by the fragments which had fallen during the conflagration of the former Temple. These we cleared away, and arrived at what appeared to be solid rock; accidentally striking at it with my crow, I remarked a hollow sound... Aware of who had been the Architect[35] of the former Temple, and that no part thereof had been constructed in vain, we determined to examine it further, for which purpose we wrenched forth two of the archstones, when a Vault of considerable magnitude appeared to view...

My companions then tied this strong cord or lifeline round my body by which to lower me into the Vault... I was then duly lowered into the Vault. On arriving at the bottom I felt something like the base or pedestal of a column, with certain characters engraven thereon, but for the want of light I was unable to decipher their meanings. I then... found this scroll of vellum or parchment, but from the same cause was unable to read its contents. I therefore signalled with my right hand, and my Companions drew me up, bringing the scroll with me. On arriving at the light of day we found from the first words therein recorded that it was a part of the long-lost Sacred Law, promulgated by our Grand Master Moses at the foot of Mount Horeb in the wilderness of Sinai. The possession of this precious treasure stimulated us to further exertions; we therefore enlarged the aperture by removing the key-stone, and I descended as before. The sun by this time had gained its greatest altitude, and darted its rays with meridian splendour into the Vault, enabling me clearly to distinguish those objects I had before so imperfectly discovered. In the centre of the Vault stood a block of white marble, wrought in the form of the Altar of Incense, a doubled cube. On the front were engraven the initials of the three Grand Masters who presided at the building of the former Temple, that is Solomon, King of Israel, Hiram King of Tyre, and Hiram Abiff[36] – with certain mystic characters, and a veil covered the Altar. Approaching with reverential awe I raised the veil, and there beheld on a plate of gold that which I humbly conceived to be the Sacred and Mysterious Name of the True and Living God Most High. I carefully re-veiled it, retired with all respect and reverence, gave the agreed-on signal, and was again drawn up. With the assistance of my Companions I closed the aperture...[37]

The Principal Sojourner on the candidate's behalf at first declines to state what he has seen on the plate of gold, since:

'it was not lawful for anyone to pronounce the Sacred and Mysterious Name of the True and Living God Most High, save the High Priest, nor him but once a year, when he entered the Holy of Holies and stood before the Ark of the Covenant to make propitiation for the sins of the people'.[38]

Zerubbabel nevertheless instructs the candidate to speak the Sacred Name to the scribes Ezra and Nehemiah (other officers of the chapter), who in turn report that what he has learned is correct. The candidate is then invested into the degree, and is taught how properly to recite the Sacred Name of God.

Zerubbabel now explains that the candidate has found the secret information lost at the building of Solomon's First Temple. The Third, Master Mason's degree ritual, through which the candidate has already passed, has already explained that the premature death of the master builder, Hiram Abiff, has led to the loss of certain secret information and this had prevented Solomon's Temple being perfect. According to the legend dramatised in the Royal Arch degree, this lost secret is now restored.

The Masonic Royal Arch in Ireland: the two stories united

In Ireland, the Masonic Royal Arch degree puts versions of both of these stories together. According to Jones, the hoodwinked Exaltee is first taken through the biblical story of the Exodus through the desert in a similar but not identical manner to the Royal Arch Purple. It then makes him descend into a crypt where he discovers a sacred text. This part of the ritual is similar, but again not identical, to that found in the English Royal Arch rite.

The Irish Royal Arch starts in much the same way as the Royal Arch Purple rite of the Orange system, the hoodwinked Exaltee (candidate), his knees bared, his feet slipshod, with a cable-tow around his waist, is admitted to the chapter by giving the Past Master's word and sign. He is then led by a conductor on a meandering journey which tells the story of the Israelites' Exodus through the desert.[39]

This Masonic version of the Exodus, however, differs somewhat from that of the Royal Arch Purple. The incidents chosen from the Bible are different in each case. Importantly too, the candidate's desert journey in the Royal Arch is punctuated by a passage through a series of veils. The veils have different colours: blue, denoting friendship; purple (a union of blue and scarlet) denoting unity and concord; scarlet, denoting fervency and zeal; and white signifying purity.[40] Each veil is presided over by a 'Captain', who allows the candidate to pass only when he has uttered an appropriate password. At each veil, a biblical text is read out, each referring to an incident in the life of Moses.

Jones tells us that this part of the modern Irish Royal Arch ceremony is similar to that found in an older English one.[41] The narrative is therefore significantly different from that found in the Royal Arch Purple:

> The scripture reading was from Exodus iii, 1-6, referring to the burning bush, following which the thirteenth and fourteenth verses of the same chapter were read, including the words 'I am that I am'. At the second veil the candidate gave a password already received and met the emblems of the Serpent and Aaron's Rod, and the relevant Scripture (Exodus iv) was read. Suitably entrusted, he was now enabled to pass the Guard of the Third Veil; here the Scripture reading, from Exodus iv, told of the miracles of the leprous hand and of the water poured upon the dry land and turning into blood. He now heard the words 'Holiness to the Lord,' and was shown the Ark of the Covenant containing the tables of stone, the pot of manna, the table of shew-bread, the burning incense, and the candlestick with seven branches, and was now qualified to enter as a sojourner and candidate for Exaltation. During the veils ceremonies he received passwords and signs enabling him to pass the successive veils and finally to present himself as a sojourner.[42]

It is at the end of this journey in the desert that the Irish Royal Arch degree takes up the motif of the crypt. However, just as the Exodus story in Irish Masonry differs from the Exodus story in the Royal Arch Purple, so the crypt legend in Irish Masonry differs significantly from that found in English Masonry.

In Ireland, the crypt story tells not of the building of the Second Temple under Zerubbabel. Rather it speaks of the repair of Solomon's original temple by King Josiah (2 Kings 22, 3–13 and 2 Chronicles 34, 8–21).

The relevant biblical accounts tell how Josiah, having purged the land of Judah of idolatry (2 Chronicles 33), decided to repair Solomon's Temple. Workmen were paid and began work, and in the ruined temple, a book was found:

> Hilkiah the priest found a book of the law of the Lord given by Moses. And Hilkiah answered and said to Shaphan the scribe, I have found the book of the law in the house of the Lord. And Hilkiah delivered the book to Shaphan. And Shaphan carried the book to the king (2 Chronicles 34, 14-16).

The Irish Royal Arch ritual's narrative is an expansion of this brief biblical story and indeed, the King, the High Priest and the Chief Scribe (Josiah, Hilkiah and Shaphan in the Bible), are the 'principals' – the chief officers in Irish Royal Arch Masonry. However, the ritual also weaves into this story elements from the crypt legend absent in the biblical accounts.

The Exaltee is first of all told that he is searching for something which is lost. He is also told that he should search for the truth. He is then admitted to the council chamber, where sit the three principal officers of the chapter, the Chief Scribe, the High Priest, and the Excellent King behind the Captain of the Host.[43]

The Exaltee, together with two other Companions, asks the King's permission to repair the temple. He is given tools to help him with this task. Symbolically, the pick roots out from the mind all evil thoughts; the shovel clears away from the mind the rubbish of passion and prejudice; and the crowbar raises a person's desires above the interests of this life, the better to prepare for the search after knowledge and the reception of truth and religion. The three craftsmen, one of whom is the Exaltee, now stand on what is represented to be part of the foundations of the temple. They clear away the rubbish and they raise a stone slab which gives entrance to an arched vault.[44]

The ritual now continues much as before, but with this rather spectacular variation: The Exaltee is actually lowered into the vault, and there he makes certain discoveries, among them being the squares of the three Grand Masters; ancient coins of Israel and Tyre; a medal bearing the interlaced triangles and the triple tau; a plate of gold on which is engraved the sacred Tetragrammaton; a cubic stone on which has been sculpted certain initial letters; and lastly, a copy of the Sacred Law.[45]

Raiders of the Lost Ark: ritual and theatrical drama

It will be seen that, despite elements of fun and horseplay, the different Royal Arch and Royal Arch Purple rituals do have a certain gravity. Freemasons, I gather, treat some of their rituals more seriously than they do others. I have been told, for example, that Irish Masons often regard their first degree rather light-heartedly. Other degrees, however, are treated with some reverence. A Masonic informant tells me, for example, that when you go through the third degree, 'you feel yourself to be touching something very old and very mysterious'. 'Nobody', he says, 'mocks the third degree'. And the same is certainly true of the Royal Arch which all sympathetic commentators write about with some awe. Orangemen too seem to regard the Royal Arch Purple as having great significance beyond its undoubted horseplay. As an Orange colleague said to me with understated feeling, 'It's a great wee ritual'.

The next narrative, the film *Raiders of the Lost Ark*, in contrast, has no such theological pretensions, but it is none the worse for this, for it does constitute a good adventure story. I want now to look at this film, drawing comparison between ritual and theatrical forms of drama. The aim will be to gain a better understanding of the nature of ritual, and especially of ritual secrecy.

The central episode in Spielberg's *Raiders of the Lost Ark* is provided by the same basic crypt legend found at in the Royal Arch rituals. The story in this case tells of a modern archaeologist, Indiana Jones, played by the actor Harrison Ford, who journeys to the Holy Land in search of the lost Ark of the Covenant. This Ark, of course, was an elaborate box containing the Mosaic Law, and it prefigures the Ark containing the Torah, found in every synagogue to this day. So the story remains faithful to the idea of a descent into the crypt and the discovery of a sacred text.

The film also contains motifs found in the crypt legend of the Masonic Royal Arch rituals. As in the rituals, the hero searches with some friends in the desert. As in the Royal Arch, there is much digging around in the debris of a sacred place. Also, the sun coming through the roof of an underground vault, manages to illuminate the otherwise hidden knowledge. Once the stone has been lifted, Jones is lowered deep into a second vaulted crypt where, as fire falls from heaven,[46] he discovers the lost Ark. Here, rather like the Royal Arch Purple candidate, Jones finds himself amid serpents which, with some difficulty, he manages to evade.

The ritual and the film, of course, differ in important respects. In the film, the actors and the audience are physically separate, the one putting on a performance for the edification and entertainment of the other. In the ritual, in contrast, the actors put on the show for themselves, being, so to speak, their own audience. In the film, too, the hero has a chequered relationship with an attractive woman but he rescues her from danger and wins her affection. There is also an array of bad people – especially Nazis

– who are also searching for the Ark, who hope to harness its powers for their evil cause. Bad people and attractive women are, of course, absent from the ritual.

Despite these obvious differences, there is, both in the Masonic rituals and in the film, the common idea of a central character who is lowered or who falls into a crypt-like place where, amid difficulties of various kinds, he discovers a sacred scripture. Both the ritual and the film, of course, are metaphorically related to more commonplace events in real life. The play and the ritual are both 'set aside', are placed 'in quotes'[47] so they may imprecisely evoke, for example, the conflict between good and evil, the quest for and discovery of knowledge and truth, the search for the sacred, the emergence from darkness into light, etc. These concerns, found both in the rites and in the film, are also real-life concerns. However, as is often the case with symbols, it is left to the individual to interpret precisely what this real-life good or evil, power or knowledge might be.[48]

An important point is that, although the Spielberg film is peculiar in that it makes use of a legend found at the heart of a well-known ritual, in other respects it is not peculiar at all. Whatever the origin of the story, *Raiders of the Lost Ark* is, quite, simply, a ripping yarn. It tells how a lone (male) individual confronts evil and other dangers and difficulties, and how he overcomes these difficulties by discovering information which was hidden. This even more basic theme, underlying the crypt legend itself, is the basis for countless popular stories, novels, films and television programmes. A very similar pattern is found, for example, in another genre of story close to the adventure story and the thriller, namely the detective story, where the emphasis is less upon the personal difficulties of the hero as on the search for hidden information. Indeed, a major point which arises out of this brief comparison between these rituals and this film is that there can often be a remarkable similarity between the rites of passage of brotherhoods (of which the Royal Arch is almost an archetype) and typical stories of adventure and detection.

The most crucial difference between the ritual and the film, however, concerns the relationship between the characters being portrayed and the actors who do the portraying. It has to do with the fact that in both film and ritual, the actors are involved in *make-believe*, but that the make-believe has a slightly different quality in each case.

The first point to make here is that everyone knows, for example, that *Raiders of the Lost Ark* is fiction, that the people on screen are not *really* Indiana Jones, or archaeologists, or Nazis, etc. And similarly, in the rite, everyone knows that the initiate and those around him are not *really* sojourners in the desert or Zerubbabel or the chief scribe or whoever. Harrison Ford and his supporting actors, but also the initiate and his brethren in the rite, all go home to their quite normal households at the end of their respective performances.

There is, however, an important difference between the actors in the film and the participants in the rite. I am thinking here especially – but not exclusively – of the leading actor in the film, Harrison Ford, and the candidate for initiation in the ritual. In the ritual, the real life status of the initiate is central to the ritual's action. In the film, this is not the case. One can say, I suppose, that the status of the actor on the screen, Harrison Ford, was transformed by his having participated in the film. No doubt Mr Ford gained hugely, both financially and in professional prestige, through having been an actor in *Raiders of the Lost Ark*. In the play or film, however, the transformation of the actor is strictly peripheral to the action of the play. The transformation of Harrison Ford's life, to the extent that it happened at all, is not what the film is about. It happened, as it were, 'backstage',[49] away from the film's action.

The transformation of the initiate, on the contrary, takes place with quite a different emphasis. In the ritual, the transformation of the hero – the initiate – happens *down*-stage. It is not at all peripheral or incidental. It is at the *heart* of the action. Transforming the real life status of the ordinary person who is acting his heroic part is what the action of the ritual is about.

In the ritual, we may not forget that the initiate has *two* personalities both at once and that *both* of these personalities are transformed. Importantly, the ritual *depends* on the initiate being continually seen to remain an ordinary everyday person. He must consistently remain an actor-playing-a-character, with the actor, as much as the character, at the front of the stage, in the centre of the action. In the theatrical drama, the events portrayed have to do with the trials and tribulations of the character Indiana Jones, not the actor Harrison Ford. The events in the rite, in contrast, portray events in the lives of both the character and the actor. They are intended to have an impact on the actor's real-life relationships. What is being dramatised is his transition from one real-life status to another.

Secrecy

We may turn now to the central issue of this article, the question of secrecy. This question is important, since not only the Royal Arch and Royal Arch Purple rituals, but the rituals of very many brotherhoods – Odd Fellow, Rechabite, Good Templars, Buffalo and other, as well as Masonic and Orange – have also contained secret elements.

Robinson speaks of three aspects to the secrecy of brotherhoods: of the secrecy of initiation rituals, involving catechisms or 'lectures'; of the secrecy of the organisation's official histories or ideologies; and of the use of secret handshakes, passwords, and other signs of recognition.[50] The focus of the present discussion is upon rituals of initiation, though my remarks apply to all of Robinson's categories.

I want here to consider two elements to ritual secrecy. One has to do with the symbolism of companionship, or social proximity; the other is concerned with the dynamics of ritual or drama.

Concealment and companionship

First of all, ritual secrecy should be seen as just a special case of secrecy in general. Secrecy – by its presence or absence – has the very general role of differentiating comparatively close from comparatively distant relationships. It is a widespread, if not universal, feature of human life that insiders to a relationship of whatever kind, will share information which they keep secret from outsiders.

This kind of secrecy can be either pragmatic or symbolic, though the two are often intertwined. Indeed, it seems plausible to regard the symbolic use of secrecy, as a means of differentiating social proximity from social distance, as originating in more pragmatic considerations.

First of all, knowledge and skill can be a form of property,[51] and this intellectual property is constituted in major part by secrecy. In very many contexts, people will sell their privileged access to specialised knowledge and special techniques or skills. This is not confined to Europe. I have myself argued, for example, that Yoruba healers keep their medicinal recipes secret largely because, if they became freely available, the valuable knowledge implicit in the recipe could be used by anybody.[52] The same principle is found in western law: patents, copyright, performers' rights, codes against plagiarism, industrial secrets; all these ensure that particular information should be used only by those with the right to use it. Clearly, secrecy is not the sole element in legal restrictions on the use of information, but it is very important. If others discover our knowledge or techniques, they can use them for profit.

Another element here is strategy and tactics. If one is engaged in competition – or, in extreme cases, in crime or warfare – then one does not want to reveal one's strategy or tactics to the opposition. In the case of military information, breaches of confidentiality bring the severest penalties. But all situations of conflict require a degree of discretion.

Conversely, if it is important that certain others should *not* have ready access to personal, political, professional or military secrets, it is often also important that yet other people should be taken into one's confidence. There is a need to share information in order to co-operate with others, whether this be in one's private or professional dealings. More than this, one must talk through one's difficulties (or whatever kind) with others as a way of solving one's practical difficulties. Understanding, knowledge, skill are rarely wholly individual enterprises. Rather, one gains knowledge and skill by collaborating with others.

It is plain that even where symbolic considerations are few and where pragmatic considerations predominate – for example, in business or military secrets – a pragmatic need for secrecy places secrecy de facto at social boundaries and tends to make the secrecy as such a symbol of boundaries. By its very nature, secrecy divides those who know from those who are kept from knowing. It is a small step from this to use secrecy in a wholly

symbolic way, merely as a boundary marker, in contexts where it is unconnected to pragmatic concerns.

Secrecy and openness, therefore, usually stand at the boundary
between proximate and distant relationships. The sharing of knowledge,
skills or even messages between individuals or within a group is contrasted with the non-sharing of such knowledge, skills or messages. The revelation of otherwise secret or confidential information to another implies
trust, a reliance on the other not to disseminate the information across a
relevant boundary. In part, as we have seen, this trust may have a pragmatic basis, but it is often merely symbolic, for the sharing of information
or the refusal to share can symbolise the boundary between insiders and
outsiders.

This kind of thing is very widespread. It exists, for example, in gossip,
where private opinions are expressed in the expectation, not always
realised, that the information will not be repeated.[53] Most obviously it
exists in the intimate relationships of family life. A man may address his
wife privately as 'my squidgy poo', but he is unlikely to tell his colleagues
in the office about it. Nor will he speak of their sexual practices, or even of
the satisfaction he gains from playing cribbage or from walking through
the park with his wife. It is not that there is any pragmatic reason for keeping these matters secret. If revealed, his acquaintances will not be sur-
prised or dismayed. Rather, the information is kept secret precisely to con-
vey a sense of intimacy between the individuals who share it.

Secrecy and the dynamics of ritual and dramatic practice

Although the most obvious purpose of secrecy in brotherhoods such as the
Masons, Orangemen, Odd Fellows, etc, is to point up the boundary
between insiders and outsiders, this is not its only function. In the Royal
Arch Purple and Royal Arch degrees, it is essential to the thrust of the
story that the candidate be kept in the dark about what will happen next.

The hoodwinked candidate must not know in advance the tribulations
he will encounter. He may have heard he must 'ride a goat', and, as he
begins the travel through the rite, he may wonder if this is not indeed true.
He may come to wonder whether the things snapping at his feet are not
indeed serpents. Then, as he finds himself hanging in the air, trusting only
in his brethren and in God, he may well wonder, with some justice, what
on earth is happening to him. Because of the secrecy, the candidate's
adventure is a traumatic ordeal. Without it, it would all seem tame indeed.
When, at the end, he discovers the truth, the revelation to him is the more
significant because it was initially hidden.

But secrecy is not just a part of *ritual* drama. It is also found in the *theatrical* dramas found in theatres and cinemas. In theatrical drama, however, it is not the *actor* who must be kept in the dark about the forthcoming
events: it is the *audience*. Newspaper critics, for example, will hide details

of a play or film from potential audiences. *Some* things they *may* talk about. Critics may tell their readers whether a film or a play is worth going to see. They may tell about the actors and the quality of their performances, of the directing, and the sets and the special effects. They will also, however, go to considerable lengths to *avoid* giving their public certain information. In particular, they will avoid giving detailed information about the play's development and especially about its dénouement. To reveal too much of a play's plot will 'give the game away' and 'spoil the story'. In some genres of play more than others, but in all to some degree, the fact that the plot is unknown to the audience has some considerable importance. Even in well-known plays, such as those by Shakespeare, the audience must effectively *pretend* not to know. They must suspend their knowledge of how the play will turn out if they are to understand and enjoy it.

Typically, in detective mysteries – Poirot, Whimsey, Frost, Morse – as in mere adventure stories such as *Raiders of the Lost Ark*, the story's hero remains ignorant of the truth until he has confronted a succession of difficulties. Often the audience must share in the hero's ignorance. Sometimes it is just the audience who is ignorant. In the *Inspector Morse* detective series, for example, until the final episode, the author kept from his audience the first name of the eponymous hero whom everybody addressed simply as 'Morse'. This name, however, remained so closely guarded, that many avid fans (including myself) who did not see the final episode still do not know what the character's name actually was.

The crucial difference between the ritual and the theatrical drama in these cases is not, therefore, the presence or absence of secrecy. In theatrical drama, there is no point at all in hiding the dramatic events from the actor(s) since the collaboration of the actors is necessary for the performance. To have kept Harrison Ford in ignorance of his script would have destroyed the film. Instead, the drama must be kept secret from the audience. In the ritual, in contrast, it is the actor-playing-the-character who is hoodwinked and to whom the truth in the story is dramatically revealed.

Conclusion

I have here drawn a comparison between a well-known film and an important set of rituals, taking advantage of the fact that both make use of the crypt legend motif. My aim was to highlight certain features of a typical rite of passage, and examine in particular the role of ritual secrecy. The argument is that in ritual, secrecy can act as a symbolic means of binding participants together in a bond of intimacy and fellowship. As well as this, however, and perhaps more importantly, secrecy can often be an essential feature of the presentation itself. In much the same way that the success of a theatrical drama often depends on nobody giving away the plot to a potential audience, so in certain rites of passage it is important not to give away the plot to potential candidates.

I began by saying how information which I encountered among the Yoruba was for me made more powerful by the very fact that it was hitherto kept secret, an idea which I took from Elizabeth Tonkin's discussion of masks.[54] And indeed this is what happens in both theatrical drama and in ritual. In the theatre, the impact of the play is made greater by the fact that one does not know what is going to happen next. So too in the ritual.

This is put into words to the newly exalted candidate in the English form of the Masonic Royal Arch by the Most Excellent Zerubbabel. He says:

> When you were raised to the Third Degree, you were informed that by the untimely death of our Master Hiram Abiff the secrets of a Master Mason were lost... These secrets were lost for a period of nearly five hundred years, and were regained in the manner which has just been described to you, *somewhat in a dramatic form, the more forcibly to impress on your mind the providential means by which those ancient secrets were regained.*[55]

Much of the basic story-material included in much of the narrative of each rite is well known or at least accessible by virtue of its being contained in the Bible. Many of the ideas embodied in the ritual too are readily available. Secrecy is, therefore, not only a means of drawing men together into a form of brotherhood, it is also the means of impressing onto the mind important ideals using a dramatic form.

Notes and references

1. Buckley, A.D., *Yoruba medicine* (Oxford, 1985), pp 118–19 et passim.
2. Tonkin, J.E.A., 'Masks and power' *Man* (NS), 14 (1979), pp 237–84.
3. Gailey, R.A., *Irish folk drama* (Cork, 1969).
4. Robinson, P.S., 'Hanging ropes and buried secrets', *Ulster Folklife*, 32 (1986), pp 3–15.
5. Buckley, A.D. and Anderson, T.K., *Brotherhoods in Ireland* (Cultra, 1988).
6. In deference to the members of these different bodies, I have attempted to be discreet in my revelations.
7. Stevens, A.C., *The cyclopedia of fraternities: a compilation of existing authentic information as to the origin, derivation, founders, development, aims, emblems, character, and personnel of more than six hundred secret societies in the United States, supplemented by family trees of groups of societies comparative statistics of membership, charts, plates, maps and the names of many representative members* (New York and Patterson NJ, 1899).
8. Buckley, A.D., 'On the club: friendly societies in Ireland', *Irish Historical Studies*, 24 (1985), pp 39–58; Buckley and Anderson (1998), op. cit.
9. Bartlett, T., 'Select documents 38: defenders and defenderism', *Irish Historical Studies*, 24 (1985), pp 338–9; Bigger, F.J., *The Ulster land war of 1770 (the Hearts of Steel)* (Dublin, 1910); Donnelly, J.S. 'The Rightboy movement', *Studia Hibernica*, 17–18 (1978), pp 120–202; Donnelly, J.S. 'Hearts of Oak, Hearts of Steel', *Studia Hibernica*, 21 (1981), pp 7–73; Moody, T.W. *The Fenian Movement* (Cork, 1969); Robinson (1986), op. cit.; Williams, D. (ed.), *Secret societies in Ireland* (Dublin, 1973).

10. Jones, B.E., *Freemasons' book of the Royal Arch*, revised edn (London, 1980), 126ff.
11. Ibid.
12. Hannah, W., *Darkness visible: a revelation and interpretation of freemasonry* (London, 1963).
13. Cargo, D., 'The Royal Arch Purple Degree', in C.S. Kilpatrick, D. Cargo, and W. Murdie, (eds) *History of the Royal Arch Purple Order* (Belfast, 1993).
14. Kilpatrick, C.S., Cargo, D., and Murdie, W. (1993), op. cit.; Kilpatrick, C.S., 'The Arch Purple story: the origin of the Loyal Orders and Degrees'. (Paper read to the Orange Lodge of Research 18 February 1995); Kilpatrick, C.S., 'Black, Scarlet, Blue, Royal Arch Purple or any other colour', *Ulster Folklife*, 42 (1996), pp 23–31. More generally, I have also received much private help, especially from David Cargo, Cecil Kilpatrick and Philip Robinson, but also from Linda Buckley, Roger Dixon and others for which I am very grateful indeed.
15. *Raiders of the Lost Ark* (1981) is a Paramount Picture, written by George Lucas and Philip Kaufman, screenplay by Lawrence Kasdan, directed by Steven Spielberg. It is a Lucasfilm Production.
16. Gailey (1969), op. cit., p 7.
17. Kilpatrick, C.S., 'The period 1690–1911', in Kilpatrick, Cargo, and Murdie, (eds) (1993) op. cit., pp 9–55, passim, Kilpatrick (1995) op. cit., p 13.
18. Buckley, A.D., and Kenney M.C., *Negotiating identity: rhetoric, metaphor and social drama in Northern Ireland* (Washington, 1995), Chapter 11.
19. Cargo (1993), op. cit.
20. Ibid., p 191.
21. Ibid., p 198.
22. Ibid., p 192.
23. Kilpatrick (1995), op. cit., p 3.
24. Cargo (1993), op. cit., p 193.
25. Ibid.
26. Ibid., p 194.
27. The reference here is to the crossing of the Jordan by these tribes in fulfilment of their promise to Moses as related in Joshua 4, 12 (David Cargo, private note). It may well be that the story of these tribes is not dealt with thoroughly in the Royal Arch Purple, because it is the topic for a whole degree ceremony, that of the Royal Gold degree in the Royal Black Institution.
28. David Cargo, private note.
29. Cargo (1993), op. cit., p 193.
30. This idea – of a person being lowered into a vault and discovering a sacred text – has been added on to a variety of narratives other than the ones found in Masonic ritual. For example, it has been added on to the story of the attempted rebuilding of the Third Temple at Jerusalem by the Roman Emperor Julian the Apostate. (See Johnston, S.P., 'Seventeenth century descriptions of Solomon's Temple', *Ars Quatuar Coronatorum Transactions 12 (1899)*, pp 139–40; Jones (1980), op. cit., 126ff). This same story – shorn, however, of the crypt element – is also found in Gibbon, E. *The history of the decline and fall of the Roman Empire* (London, 1993), pp 117–23.
31. Hannah (1963), op. cit., p 151.
32. Ibid., p 161.
33. Ibid., p 162.
34. Ibid., pp 163–5.
35. God, or perhaps Hiram Abiff, the Master Mason.

36. These three men are the ones in Masonic tradition, and, indeed, implicitly in the biblical account itself, most directly responsible for the building of the First Temple.
37. Hannah (1963), op. cit., pp 168–9.
38. Ibid., p 170.
39. Jones (1980), op.cit., 195ff.
40. Ibid., p 199.
41. Ibid.
42. Ibid., p 197.
43. Ibid., p 215.
44. Ibid., pp 215–6.
45. Ibid., p 216.
46. See the coincidence with Johnston (1899) op. cit., pp 139–40.
47. Sperber, D., *Rethinking symbolism*, (Cambridge, 1975). See also Tonkin, J.E.A., 'Cunning mysteries' in S. Kafir (ed.), *West African masks and cultural systems*, (Sciences humaines, 126), Terveuren, Musee Royale de l'Afrique, 1988, p 241. Goffman, E., *Frame analysis* (Harmondsworth, 1975), uses the less felicitous term 'keyed' to refer to the same idea.
48. Buckley, A.D., 'Introduction: daring us to laugh: creativity and power in Northern Irish symbols' in A.D. Buckley (ed.), *Symbols in Northern Ireland* (Belfast, 1998), pp 10–12. Turner, V.W., *The ritual process, structure and anti-structure* (London, 1969), pp 41–42. Not all of the rituals, however, are 'multivocal' or 'polysemic'. For example, the Royal Arch Purple rite spells out pretty clearly the need to seek forgiveness, trust one's brethren and trust in God.
49. Goffman, E., *The presentation of self in everyday life* (New York, 1959).
50. Robinson (1986), op. cit., p 9.
51. Harrison, S., 'Ritual as intellectual property' *Man* (NS), 27 (1992), pp 225–44.
52. Buckley (1985), op. cit., pp 179–80.
53. MacFarlane, W.G., 'Gossip and social relationships in a Northern Ireland village' (doctoral thesis, Department of Social Anthropology, Queen's University, Belfast, 1978).
54. Tonkin (1979), op. cit., pp 237–84.
55. Hannah (1963), op. cit., (my emphasis).

14

Changing Attitudes in the Diet
of the Scots over 300 Years

ALEXANDER FENTON

THE AIM OF THIS PAPER IS TO LOOK at a selection of aspects of food in a historical and cultural context for Scotland, including survival strategies, and to
consider how, in broad ways, eating habits and attitudes to them have
changed over the last 300 years. The health implications are also examined

It is a matter of importance to consider attitudes at different periods in
time, since these affect actions and reactions. Learned attitudes do not
necessarily coincide with those of the people in general, but at all times
attitudes are conditioned by the prevailing state of knowledge and by the
changing means and rates of access to advances in knowledge. The following quotation from a manuscript recipe book of 1692 may well shock the
sensitivities of the present day, though clearly it was not a matter of special
comment in the late seventeenth century:

> Take a peck of Garden shell snails, wash them weell in small beer, and put
> them in ane hot oven till they have Done making a noise, then take them
> out, and wipe them well from the green froth that is upon them, and bruise
> them shells and all in a Stone mortar, then take a quart of earth worms
> Scower them with salt, slit them and wash them well with water, from ther
> filth and in a Stone mortar beat them to pieces, then lay in the bottome of
> your Distilled pot Angelica, tuo handfulls and tuo handfulls of Celandine
> upon them, to which put tuo quarts of Rosmarie flowers, bears foott,
> Agrimonie, red Dock roots, bark of Barberries, Bettonie, wood Sorrell of
> each tuo handfulls Rue one handfull, then lay the snails and worms on the
> top of the herbs and flowers then pour on three gallons of the strongest ail;
> and let it stand all neight, in the Morning put in three ounces of Cloves beat-
> ten six penny worth of beatten Saffrone, and on the top of them six ounces
> of shaved harts horne then set on the Limbeck and close it with paste, And
> so receive the water by pints which will be nine in all, the first is the
> strongest, wherof take in the morning tuo spoonfulls in four spoonfulls of
> small beer, and the like in the afternoon: yow most keep a good diet, and
> use moderate exercise to warm the blood.[1]

This was to cure consumption, ie pulmonary tuberculosis, and dropsy, the stopping of the stomach and liver, and it could be distilled with milk for weak people and children, with harts' tongues and elecampane.

The volume was compiled in Scotland for or by a family of a reasonably high social level. There are two interrelated messages to be drawn from it. The first is that when we look at the story of a nation's eating habits, we must not be too much influenced by the concepts and attitudes of the present day. What is totally unacceptable to us may have passed with little comment, even with approbation, in earlier days, as this recipe or cure indicates.

The second message is that this delectable melange of snails and worms and herbs and ale was regarded as appropriate at high social levels – it was 'The admirable and most famous Snaill water'. This, in the late seventeenth century, was still before the days when more rational understanding of the virtues of herbs and other living entities had begun to be broadcast in sources such as the Edinburgh *Pharmacopoeia* of 1699. But though better understanding progressed quickly in the eighteenth and nineteenth centuries, this was primarily among the better-educated members of the population, though even so, some cures were too well established to be discarded by them. In the early 1700s, jaundice was cured in Shetland by putting the powder of snail shells in a drink, the cure taking three or four days. 'They first dry, then pulverize the Snails; and it is observable, that tho this Dust should be kept all the Year round, and grow into Vermine, it may be dry'd again, and pulveriz'd for that use'.[2] Snail tea also remained a known remedy among upper class ladies for long after. For example, a manuscript of Anne Susanna Hope, of Hopetoun House in Midlothian, in 1786, provided the following recipe: 'Snail Tea. 20 Snails put into a Pint of Water let it boil till it is reduced to a Tea Cup Full strain it add to it a Pint of Milk and some brown sugar. A Tea Cup full to be taken Night and Morning'.[3]

Folk medicine long continued to play a strong role for most people, in towns as well as in the countryside – also because of the real cost of medical care – so that we may find (to continue with snails) that in Orkney, rickets were treated by drinking a snail and its shell dissolved in vinegar.[4] In Fife, black slugs 'masked' in a teapot with water and salt supplied an oil that was useful for rubbing, and white slugs placed in a jelly-bag along with a quantity of salt dripped an oil that was administered like cod-liver oil for those suffering from phthisis, ie consumption. The same cure was known in England.[5] You could also rub a slug on a wart then stick it on a thorn to decay, a practice known in Fife as also in parts of the Highlands into recent times.[6] In Shetland, little over a century ago, a snail in its shell or the shell alone was put into the drinking water as a remedy for jaundice in cattle,[7] and the same was true for curing people in Uist. Warts, chronic rheumatism, lung diseases, whooping cough, jaundice, tubercular swellings, rickets and cold sores were all thought to benefit from snail-oil or the direct application of snails,[8] and in such beliefs we see the fingers of the past poking firmly into more recent times. This was not, however, a straight historical sequence, for the phenomenon touches on different social classes at different times and questions of eating habits and health are inextricably related to questions of social class. Exploration of dietary habits and of 'folk medicine' beliefs can provide a useful touchstone to attitudes at different times and at different social levels.

Spring hunger

Food habits, at whatever level, were never fixed and fossilised. It is, of course, true that since the late eighteenth century, as can be judged from the parish-by-parish entries in the *First Statistical Account of Scotland* of the 1790s, the spread of industrialisation and urbanisation increasingly has been eroding dependence on local, home-grown foodstuffs. Sir Robert Sibbald, in writing of famine, noted in 1699 that God had placed the Scots in the midst of a great variety of food,[9] but in those days there was no tele-vision chef such as Nick Nairn to show how to exploit natural foods to their full potential (the role of such 'experts' in spreading knowledge about foodstuffs, and in some degree conditioning public taste, has recent-ly been examined for France by Saadi Lahlou, a statistician and social psychologist,[10]) and much of what could be got was only seasonally avail-able.

Among the ordinary folk of the countryside, 'spring hunger' was a real phenomenon, and spring was one of the points in the year when the inci-dence of human mortality was likely to peak. It has been recorded in Denmark that it was a habit of the young folk in spring to go to the fields of growing rye and twist off little bunches of the green shoots that had not yet ripened into straw, leaving the roots in the ground. They then nibbled the soft green tubes of the stalks, which had for them a glorious taste after a somewhat barren period.[11] This is very reminiscent of the practice by young folk in Scotland – even in my own time – of digging up with their knives 'arnuts' or 'lucy-arnuts' (Bunium flexuosum), and eating the sweet-ish tasting tubers. Poor folk did the same in times of hunger, adding other wild plants to the menu, such as 'myles', Chenopodeia, edible forms of goosefoot. The Maclagan MSS in the School of Scottish Studies of the University of Edinburgh record that parts of several wild plants were eaten in the Highlands: the leaves of wild sorrel (*sabhadh*), the roots of the silverweed (*briosglan*), wild skirret (*brisgean*), the roots of wild liquorice (*cairmeal*) and of arnuts (*braonan*), and water cress (*biolar*).[12]

Another form of hunger food was the coalfish, caught from the shores, which could be dried and beaten up to be eaten like bread by the poor when other resources failed, or in the hungry time in spring when the cere-al crops had been pretty well used up and the new crops were not yet ready. Whelks and limpets from the rocks could also serve as stand-by foods for the poor in emergency times.[13] It is extraordinary how the instinct to use such roots and other foods from the wild can remain in the mind, appearing seasonally or in times of distress, and perhaps going back to the hunter-gatherer period of prehistory. But for the time being, I want to concentrate on the major food resources.

Seasonality

Seasonality of supply, to which the phenomenon of spring hunger is due, is a feature of earlier times that has almost completely vanished, due to the scale of the food industry, and the regular provision of so much international variety that, according to the sociologists, the problems of choice can lead to considerable stress or at least insecurity for the individual consumer. This can also be in part a result of the loss of the old familiar food canon, and from the break-up of the more traditional forms of family and community life within which the individual was socially embedded. There has been from the late eighteenth century a growing clash between the traditional and the industrial, and nowadays this also involves the range of novelty with which people are faced and to which they respond according to their age, social grouping and the like. Allied to this is a tendency towards taking a new look at traditional forms of food, and making them into prestige products, as markers of regional identity that are encouraged by the tourist authorities, and that can become subject to mass-production also.[14] The oatcakes found on the breakfast tables of good quality hotels, often in round tins decorated with motifs from the Highlands – even though oatcakes are more of a Lowland phenomenon – is one example, as also is the promulgation of shortbread as one of the 'tastes' of Scotland. Seasonality was a phenomenon that had to be reckoned with in earlier days, and which impinged on questions of health. Obviously there were fluctuations in the supply of milk due to the normal drying up of the cows before calving, and in the supply of cereal grains in the crofting areas especially, where cropping was on a relatively small scale and the yields might not serve the communities for more than nine months in any year. In the remoter communities seasonality of supply was a correspondingly more serious matter, and this is a point made vivid for us at the present day by the innumerable stone cleits in St Kilda, where the islanders hung birds garnered from the cliffs, or mutton from the sheep that ranged the hill-slopes, to dry in the salt sea air that blew through these open-work constructions.[15] The stone skeos of Shetland had a similar purpose. Law cases of the early seventeenth century show that fish, cheese, meat, butter and fish were kept in them – and were not infrequently stolen from them.[16] The use of such structures extended the period over which foodstuffs could be stored, using the drying power of the wind, though a comment by George Low in 1774 again makes us think of the question of contemporary attitudes: 'Nothing can smell stronger than a number of these skeos placed near one another'.[17]

Among other shifts to which people were driven in the hungry days of winter and spring when little milk was to be had was the bleeding of cattle. They could be bled once or twice a year. The blood was boiled, thickened with oatmeal – like a very wet black pudding mixture – poured into containers and eaten with a little milk. According to Captain Burt in the 1720s, the blood was boiled into cakes, and the practice was said to be adopted when the oatmeal supplies were low.[18] Somewhat earlier, in 1699, when the Welsh antiquary, Edward Lhuyd (he was keeper of the Ashmolean Museum in Oxford), was travelling in Scotland, he noted that: 'In the time of scarcity they launce their cows neck and make meat of their Blood; *with butter or milk when boyld in time of dearth'*.[19]

It should not be thought that the ordinary folk were the only ones who felt the impact of seasonality. The diet of the higher classes might frequently include salmon and trout, and wild fowl in plenty, as well, of course, as cereal products including wheaten bread, but for much of the year, according to Captain Burt, in the 1720s, they were hankering after beef, mutton, veal and lamb. 'There is hardly any such Thing as Mutton to be had until August, or Beef till September – that is to say, in Quality fit to be eaten; and both go out about Christmas'. He is speaking, of course, of fresh meat.[20]

Salting and scurvy

From Martinmas, 11 November, beef was salted everywhere,[21] to be stored in tubs and barrels. This was known as the 'mart', a word which does not come from 'Martinmas', as is sometimes thought, but from Gaelic 'mart', early Irish 'mart', a cow for killing, so the custom has a good Highland ancestry. Not only was the procedure carried out to provide the family with occasional animal food, but it was also an element in the payment of rents in kind, which in turn would condition the nature of the diet of those who received such payments. Other animals besides cattle could be salted as marts – and in fact, goats' flesh, so treated, was called the 'poor man's mart' in the Highlands.[22] In view of present-day inhibitions about the use of too much salt, the question may be raised of what the intake of salt in salt butter, salt meat and salt fish did to the health of our ancestors. The eating of such foods was generally – and until surprisingly recent times – allied to an unwillingness to eat very much in the way of vegetables and fruit (which was in any case very seasonal, even if it could happen that apples were kept for longer covered with oatmeal in the meal girnel). In my own time I have heard salad referred to as 'rabbits' food', and not infrequently. One health consequence was the prevalence of scurvy, common among sailors who spent long periods at sea, but also among some of the land-based population. It was sometimes known as 'bastard scurvy', described in 1701 as 'a kind of leprosy'.[23] Martin Martin, in speaking of Shetland about the same period, reported that:

> The Disease that afflicts the Inhabitants here most, is the Scurvy, which they suppose is occasion'd by their eating too much Salt-Fish. There is a distemper here call'd Bastard Scurvy, which discovers it self by the falling of the Hair from the Peoples Eyebrows, and the falling of their Noses, &c. and as soon as the symptoms appear, the Persons are remov'd to the Fields, where little Houses are built for them on purpose, to prevent Infection. The principal Cause of the Distemper is believed to be want of Bread, and feeding on Fish alone, particularly the Liver: many poor families are sometimes without Bread, for three, four, or Five Months together. They say likewise that their drinking of Bland, which is their universal Liquor, and preserv'd for the Winter as part of their Provisions, is another Cause of this Distemper. This Drink is made of Buttermilk mix'd with Water... The Isles in general afford a great Quantity of Scurvy-grass, which us'd discreetly, is found to be a good Remedy against this Disease.[24]

Knowledge of the use of scurvy-grass as a cure, as well as of brooklime, cress and strawberry leaves, had been passed from the Dutch to the English already by the late sixteenth century, as a matter of fact,[25] but there appears to have been only a slow spread of the remedy.

Lack of vitamin C led to swollen, spongy and bleeding gums, a feeling of weakness and a dry, livid skin, which people thought was a form of leprosy and so in places like the island of Papa Stour in Shetland in the late eighteenth century there was a colony of sufferers, housed outside the main settlement area and fed by grace and favour of their fitter relatives and friends. Brand saw the ruins of a hut for sufferers within half a mile of Lerwick.[26]

Scurvy, however, was far from confined to the lower social levels. It is significant that the manuscript recipe collection of 1692, already mentioned, contains seven cures for the scurvy out of a total of 145 recipes and cures. One is reminiscent of the rye shoots that Danish boys nibbled: 'Take the green blads of wheat befor it be shott and drink the juice of it with vinegar or claret wine in the morning continouing some dayes This hath cured those that had the whol body covered with black spots of the scurvey'.[27]

But as cogent evidence of the little understanding people had of the true causes, one of the other recipes included the instruction that 'as for the ordering of your diet it may be as it is at other tyms only forbear fish, fruit, milk [all of which would have greatly helped the condition] and all salt meats'.[28]

There seems to have been a higher incidence of this disease of malnutrition in the subsistence areas of Scotland, as can be realised from stray observations. For example, when Samuel Johnson and James Boswell visited the western island of Coll, Boswell had to share a bed with the young son of the family: 'I have a mortal aversion at sleeping in the same bed with a man; and a young Highlander was always somewhat suspicious as to scorbutic symptoms... Upon inspection, as much as could be without his observing it, he semed to be quite clean'.[29] The *Old Statistical Account* of the 1790s records scurvy in the parish of Arngask, Perthshire, for example, where it was considered to be due to too much use of oatmeal.[30] People did not realise that it was due to lack of fresh vegetables and fruit.

The greening of the countryside

In fact, the brassica, kail, was the main form of green that was regularly eaten, certainly from the fifteenth century, though not necessarily with the conscious knowledge that it was an anti-scorbutic. It was so widespread in the kailyards and in the everyday diet of Scotland that already by the sixteenth century the name had been generalised to mean broth made with vegetables and by the nineteenth century it could refer to a main meal, dinner. It could be a major element in broth, along with barley; it could be boiled with oatmeal; or it could be served on its own along with butter and milk.[31] Even Samuel Johnson realised its importance: 'They cultivate hardly any other plant for common tables, and when they had not kail they probably had nothing'.[32] And if the kail pot should happen to boil dry, the smell of burning kail – which I experienced once when I went to visit the blacksmith at Tollo in Banffshire – is one of the worst and most clinging smells on earth.

Other green crops of an early vintage – though classed more as grain crops – were pease and beans. By the fifteenth century they were already integrated into the food system, though pease in particular, especially in the form of pease-meal, had a reputation as a poor man's food. Legislation of the fifteenth and seventeenth centuries requiring farmers to sow a certain quantity of pease, suggests that those in authority felt a need to ensure food supplies for the people. It could also form an important part of the wages paid in kind to farm servants, even well through the nineteenth century.

In the course of the eighteenth century, as the countryside became enclosed – at least in the Lowland areas – and as farming improvements proceeded over a wide front, major innovations began to establish a dietary scene that survived until well through the twentieth century. The turnip that had earlier been an estate garden crop became a field crop, and was a basis for the foddering of livestock in byres throughout the winter, so that fresh meat began to be available all the year round. By the time of the *Second Statistical Account of Scotland* of the 1840s, butchers' shops were spreading in the small towns and fresh meat could be bought at least for special occasions or for the Sunday dinner. Typically, this was boiling beef, boiled in broth with kail and other vegetables. The broth was the first course, and the beef, which had been taken out, was the second course. Turnips were used not only to feed stock, but also figured in the broth and with the meat course. However, this was the case primarily in the more Lowland areas, and what really affected the diet of the west and north was the coming of the potato.

The pastoral areas

In pre-potato days, roughly before 1750, the Highland areas were predominantly pastoral – as they still are – and this meant that the everyday diet tended to be based on flesh to some extent, and of course inshore fish, but even more on the milk and cheese of sheep and cows. Sir Thomas Craig wrote in 1605 that in years of bad Lowland harvests, when cereals were in short supply, the Highlands could supply them with cheese, and that the Highlanders themselves lived solely on cheese, flesh and milk.[33] Milk, of course, had to be consumed almost at once, either as it came or frothed up with a very common instrument, a 'fro-stick'. In Lowland Scotland a mixture of cream and whey was often whisked up in this way, and sprinkled with oatmeal, in a manner perhaps reminiscent of the dessert dish sometimes eaten nowadays as 'crannachan'.[34] In the Highlands, the dish of thickened milk or whey was called 'oon' (from Gaelic *omhan*). But milk in its processed form, as cheese, could keep for a long time, or as butter or especially salt butter, for a shorter period. Travellers in the Highlands were frequently offered cheese but were not always impressed. James Boswell, for instance, when journeying with Samuel Johnson in the 1770s, got local cheese at Raasay House in the Hebrides and commented: 'It is the custom over all the Highlands to have it; and it often smells very strong, and poisons to a certain degree the elegance of an Indian [ie, luxurious] breakfast'.[35] Cheese was also a feature in the payment of rents in kind, and was therefore an article of trade as well as an item of home consumption, though in fact, as a trade or rental item, it may at times have come into the category of lobsters or salmon or even shellfish in recent times, little eaten at home but turned into ready cash instead. Hard cheese is, of course, being discussed here. There were also soft cheeses, with a much shorter keeping span, of the 'crowdie' variety, which could be mixed with butter. This is the basis for the entirely modern product, 'Caboc', the name of which is reminiscent of both Gaelic '*cábag*' and Lowland Scots '*kebbock*'. It is a 'double cream cheese' rolled in pinhead oatmeal, made by Highland Fine Cheeses Ltd, and sold in a tartan box. This is an example of how modern commerce can apply aspects of tradition to a new product that is entirely suitable for modern living conditions, which include the possession of refrigerators, as a reconstruction or perhaps re-invention of tradition.

The potato

With the eighteenth and nineteenth century population increase in the Highland areas, which led in part to the well-known Clearances, the traditional and highly seasonal food supplies were stretched well beyond their limits. The produce of pasture and arable could not cope, and in such a situation the coming of the potato was a godsend. Though people had at first to be persuaded of its value – for the growing of potatoes intruded a strange element into the rotational system of cereal crops – it soon came to play a dominant role in the diet beyond the Highland Line, leading to a great reduction in the oat and bere crops, so that when the potato blight struck in the 1846, havoc ensued. The use of the potato was not, of course, confined to the Highlands. It spread in the Lowlands too from the 1750s, though by the 1790s it was far from being standard everywhere. By the 1840s it was eaten in 95 per cent of the parishes of Scotland. Farmers around the main towns were growing potatoes for the urban market, even for export to the hungry maw of London and other major English ports. In some areas potatoes were replacing a decline in the growing of oats, and in others had come to replace the formerly widespread Lowland crop, pease. By the late eighteenth century, they had become not only a main dietary element in the Highlands but also played the same role for the poorer people in the towns of Scotland. And blight or no blight, they had come to stay, as an almost inevitable accompaniment to the main course at every meal.[36]

Cereals

Cereals, however, were the primary basic elements in the diet of the majority. The daily meals of a typical Aberdeenshire farmer in 1782, before the adoption of the potato, show that the family might as well have been vegetarian. Breakfast was of porridge made by boiling oatmeal in water, and eaten with milk or with ale when milk was scarce, or of brose made of chopped cabbage or kail left overnight. They then had oatcakes and milk, or ale or small beer if milk was lacking. Dinner in the middle of the day was of two courses: 'sowens' or flummery made from the steeped husks of oats, and again oatcakes eaten with milk or kail. Supper during winter was of kail-brose, with a second course of kail eaten with oatcakes; in summer there was generally only one course, porridge and milk, or oatcakes and kail or milk. The kail was prepared by being cut up small, boiled with salt and water, and thickened with a little oatmeal. Kail brose was oatmeal put into a wooden dish, the brose '*caap*', into which the boiling liquid from the kail was stirred. There could, incidentally, also be neep-brose, made with the juice from boiled turnips, but the most common dish by far among the farm servants as well as the farmers' families was plain brose made with boiling water and supped with milk. In the 1782 Aberdeenshire account, a special treat was at harvest time, when instead of sowens, dinner could be of a thick broth of barley and turnip.[37]

These elements, it seems to me – oatmeal in the form of porridge, brose, sowens and oatcakes, kail, milk and occasionally barley broth and turnips – are what the generality of Scots lived on up to the end of the eighteenth century. There is no mention of meat in this account, and no mention of wheaten bread or as yet of potatoes. But change was near, at first with potatoes and then with an increasing amount of meat, itself a basis for an increasing use of broth, though the continuing use of oatmeal in full degree, and of bere meal to a diminishing degree in the Lowlands, was to remain until well into the twentieth century.

The nutritionist Maisie Steven, was in no doubt that the rural people's larder made them a 'sturdy and vigorous race', and that 'the diet of the Scots rural workers was in most respects a highly nourishing one'. She attempted to make an estimate of the nutritional value of the rural diet, presumably for the nineteenth or early twentieth century, and concluded that with potatoes, oatmeal, kail, turnips, barley, butter, cheese, milk and ale, an average male agricultural worker's intake could be protein, 67.8 g; K Cals 2494; calcium, 500 mg; and iron 14.27 mg. This compares well with the Department of Health and Social Security recommendations of 1979 for a very active man of protein, 84 g; K Cal 3350; calcium 500 g; and iron 10.0 g.[38]

Of course this is no more than an estimate, and though it may have approximated to the situation at the level of the farmer and his family, it may not have been such a good fit when applied to the farm labourers. There evolved after the agricultural improvement period of the later eighteenth century three basic forms of farm employment. First, there were the married servants living in tied houses, many of which had gardens for kail, rhubarb and berry bushes, receiving allowances of milk, potatoes, and oatmeal as part of their wages, and sometimes – in some areas – permission to keep a pig as well as poultry. Perhaps these could come close to Maisie Steven's average picture, but single men were less well off. Second, in many parts of the country the bothy system developed, first in the south-east, then in Fife and Angus, and spreading in part to the north-east, Easter Ross, Cromarty and Caithness. In the bothies, the men largely looked after themselves and it is little wonder that the custom grew of having water brose supped with milk three times a day, for breakfast, dinner and tea. There is the tale of an interested enquirer who asked a farm servant what he had for breakfast. 'Oh, brose'. And for dinner? 'Brose'. And for supper? 'Jist brose'. He asked the question, 'Isn't that boring?' and back came the answer, 'Weel, fa (who) wid get tired o his mait?' This is an extreme example but it borders on the truth, and the eating of too much oatmeal was said to produce a skin eruption popularly known as the 'Scotch fiddle'. In fact it was really scabies or the itch, due to a tiny burrowing mite,[39] and all the indications are that a diet of oatmeal, supported with milk, may have been monotonous, but was not too bad. A third main form of farm servant accommodation, in the medium-sized farm areas of the north-east and of West Central Scotland, was the 'kitchie' system, where the men slept in the chaumer but had their food in the farm kitchen, when there may have been expected to be a little more variety, though much depended on the good- or ill-nature of the farmers' wives, many of whom had a passion for home economics to an advanced degree.[40]

The levelling of regional variety

There is a clear impression that because of the increasing social differentiation between farmer and servant after the onset of what is popularly called the Agricultural Revolution, there was a levelling out of what had been a greater range of regional variety, with conditions of farm service and the nature of wages in kind having a strong effect. When R. Hutchison wrote his 'Report on the dietaries of Scotch rural labourers' in 1869,[41] he found a marked degree of uniformity between the diets of those dwelling inland or on the coast, whether in the Highlands or the Lowlands. This sameness was based on oatmeal – or in the Highland areas often also beremeal – milk and potatoes. Later writers, however, see the situation as going a step further. A.H. Kitchin and R. Passmore, in their book *The Scotsman's food*, commented that 'the plain and simple diet of the Scottish peasant has been remarkably stable throughout the centuries', though they also acknowledged 'the disappearance of many distinctive habits and customs'.[42] The economic historian, Professor Roy Campbell, saw the modern history of diet in Scotland as 'fundamentally that of the rejection of oatmeal as its leading item', leading to 'a decline in the standards of nutrition of the people... The history of diet in Scotland is, therefore, the story of an exercise in choice that must be regretted by the nutritionist'.[43] Such change, he thought, took place between the 1790s and the outbreak of the First World War in 1914, though at different rates depending on whether the broad group was rural worker, city-dweller, or from the Highlands and Islands. It was considered that oatmeal held its ground best in the country districts, though supplemented by tea, bread and occasional fresh meat from after the middle of the nineteenth century. Bread and butter, jam and tea had largely displaced the more traditional foodstuffs in the cities, as they also did in certain classes, notably the cottar bairns, in the countryside. The potato was the staple food in the north and west, till the time of the potato famine, after which that too began to be replaced by less nutritious products.

Roy Campbell was not entirely accurate in his view of the disappearance of oatmeal. The Board of Trade carried out an investigation into workmen's diets in 1904, including 455 returns from Scotland,[44] which showed that oatmeal was still a staple. In Argyll, for instance, breakfast was of porridge, tea, bread and butter, scones and oatcakes; dinner was of broth, fish and potatoes, with butcher's meat occasionally and on Sundays; tea was of bread, scones, oatcakes, tea, butter and jam; and supper of porridge and milk, bread, butter and jam. There was thus a greater variety to complement the basics, and indeed from my own experience in the 1950s and 1960s in the north-east of Scotland I can vouch for the fact that such a dietary range was then still perfectly well known; in other words, there was a high – but decreasing – cereal consumption, with a low figure for fat and meat. In 1956, Scotland was top of the British league in the National Food Survey for cereal consumption, at 82 oz per head per week. But by 1975, Scotland had taken second place to the north of England, the figure having fallen to 62 oz. It is also relevant to note that the results of surveys carried out under Sir John Boyd Orr at the Rowett Research Institute, Aberdeen, make it appear that rural diets were relatively better than those in the towns, at least for the poorer strata.[45] It would therefore be of much interest to establish the areas of origin of those who have suffered from the cardiovascular problems that are very common in Scotland. Has it been more of a disease of the towns than of the countryside? And if so, do we then try to bring back the 'good Scots diet'?

This paper has looked at changing attitudes, the elimination of the seasonality factor, the lack of understanding of fruit and vegetables as a source for keeping certain ills at bay, the impact of the Agricultural Revolution and the differences in diet between town and country. It has touched on the increasing interest, largely between the wars, of official interest in the health of the nation, and on the difficulties brought about by the incredible range of dietary choices that lie before us, even in the most remote parts of the country. As often as not, we no longer even know what are the ingredients of our foodstuffs. But in terms of what may or may not constitute a healthy diet, which is one of the great preoccupations of the present day, it is essential to examine in detail the historical background to the country's eating habits, looking at them region by region, and relating them on the one hand to forms of land use and proximity to the sea and rivers, and on the other to the state of housing, sanitation, water supply and the like in both town and country. There is also the important question of attitudes. How, for example, can people in general be educated into accepting government recommendations of the type that to eat five portions of fruit and vegetables a day is health promoting? There is also the question of 'social embeddedness'. The break-up of the old family and community cohesion, not least in dietary habits, opens up a whole new area of study, but for that, a thorough knowledge of the historical background will continue to be essential.

Notes and references

1. Manuscript recipe collection begun in 1692, kindly lent by Alasdair Dunlop: item 59.
2. Martin, Martin, *A description of the Western Islands of Scotland,* first edn 1701 (Edinburgh, 1981), p 374.
3. *Tocher,* 4 (Winter, 1971), p 107.
4. Leask, J.T.S., *A peculiar people and other Orkney Tales* (Kirkwall, 1931), p 72.
5. Buchan, David, (ed.), *Folk tradition and folk medicine in Scotland: the writings of David Rorie* (Edinburgh, 1994), pp 39, 40, 105, 245 (the source dates from 1904).
6. Ibid., pp 100, 243 (the source dates from 1914), Beith, Mary, *Healing threads: traditional medicines of the Highlands and Islands* (Edinburgh, 1995), p 184.
7. Jakobsen, Jakob, *An etymological dictionary of the Norn language in Shetland,*

(1908, 1928), (Lerwick, 1984), s.v. *Gulsa*.

8. Beith, (1994), op. cit., pp 184–5.
9. Burnett, John, *The Scots in sickness and health* (Edinburgh, 1997), p 12.
10. Lahlou, Saadi, 'Experts, industriels, médias, consommateurs, institutions: comment les représentations des acteurs et le marché se co-construisent', in I. Giachetti, (ed.), *Identités des mangeurs Images des aliments* (Paris, 1996), pp 123–50.
11. Riismoller, Peter, *Sultegrænsen* (København, 1971), p 22.
12. *Tocher*, 17 (Spring 1975), p 18.
13. Fenton, Alexander, *The Northern Isles: Orkney and Shetland* (Edinburgh, 1978; new edn, East Linton 1997), p 528.
14. See, eg Warde, Alan, *Consumption, food & taste: culinary antinomies and commodity culture* (Sage Publications, 1997).
15. See, eg Buchanan, Meg, (ed.) *St Kilda: The continuing story of the Islands* (HMSO, 1995).
16. Fenton (1997), op. cit., p 160.
17. Low, George, *A tour through the islands of Orkney and Shetland* (Kirkwall 1879), p 90.
18. Burt, Edward, *Letters from a gentleman in the north of Scotland to his friend in London*, first edn. 1754; (Edinburgh, 1974), pp 11, 131.
19. Campbell, J.L., (ed.), *A collection of Highland rites and customes copied by Edward Lhuyd from the manuscript of the Rev James Kirkwood (1650–1709) and annotated by him with the aid of the Rev John Beaton* (Ipswich, 1975), p 7.
20. Burt (1754, 1976), op. cit., pp 1, 120–1.
21. Ibid., p 121.
22. Ramsay, J, *Scotland and Scotsmen in the 18th century* (Edinburgh and London, 1888), pp 11, 535.
23. Brand, J, *A brief description of Orkney, Zetland, Pight-land-Firth and Caithness* (Edinburgh, 1701, 1703), p iv.
24. Martin (1701, 1981), op. cit., pp 373–4.
25. Stead, Jennifer, 'Navy blues: the sailor's diet, 1530–1830', in C.A. Wilson (ed.), *Food for the community: special diets for special groups* (Edinburgh, 1993), p 72.
26. Brand (1701, 1703), op. cit., p 72.
27. MS recipe collection, 1692, op.cit.: item 130.
28. Ibid.: item 124.
29. Pottle, F.A. and Bennett, C.H., *Boswell's journal of a tour to the Hebrides with Samuel Johnson, LL.D 1773* (Melbourne, London, Toronto, 1963), p 254.
30. Steven, Maisie, *The good Scots diet: what happened to it?* (Aberdeen, 1985), p 66.
31. Fenton, Alexander, 'The greening of the Scottish countryside', *Acta Ethnographica Hungarica*, 40 (1–2), (1995), pp 223–6.
32. Johnston, Samuel, *A journey to the western Islands of Scotland* (London, 1775; Oxford, 1979), p 24.
33. Craig, Sir Thomas, *De Unione Regnorum Britanniae Tractatus* (Edinburgh, 1909), pp 184, 447.
34. For a recipe, see Lockhart, G.W., *The Scot and his oats* (Barr 1983), p 45.
35. Pottle and Bennett (1963), op. cit., p 135.
36. Fenton (1995), op. cit., pp 232–6.
37. Douglas, F., *A general description of the east coast of Scotland* (Paisley, 1782), pp 168–70.

38. Steven (1985), op. cit., pp 21, 23.
39. Boog-Watson, W.N., 'The Scotch fiddle', *Scottish Studies*, 15 (1971), pp 141–5.
40. Fenton, Alexander, *Scottish country life* (Edinburgh, 1976, reprint 1977), pp 186–9 of revised edn (East Linton, 1999) pp 295–9.
41. Hutchinson, R., 'Report on the dietaries of Scotch rural labourers', *Transactions of the Highland and Agricultural Society of Scotland II* (Sec 4), (1869), pp 1–29.
42. Kitchin, A.H. and Passmore, R., *The Scotsman's food: an historical introduction to modern food administration*, (Edinburgh, 1949), pp 25, 57.
43. Campbell, Roy, 'Diet in Scotland; an example of regional variation', in T.C. Barker, J.C. McKenzie, and J. Yudkin, (eds) *Our changing fare, two hundred years of British food habits* (London, 1966), p 60.
44. *Second series of memoranda, statistical tables and charts*, PP 1905 (Cd 2337), LXXXIV.
45. Oddy, Derek, 'The paradox of diet and health: England and Scotland in the nineteenth and twentieth centuries', International Commission on Research into European Food History Conference Paper, Aberdeen, 1997, in A. Fenton, (ed.) *Order and disorder: the health implications of eating and drinking* (East Linton, 2000), pp 45–63.

15

Food-provision Strategies on the Great Blasket Island: Livestock and Tillage

PATRICIA LYSAGHT

Tine, bia agus éadach na trí ní a bhfuil an bráca go léir á leanúint...
[Fire, food and clothes are the three needs that bring all the drudgery...][1]

THE ECONOMY OF THE GREAT BLASKET ISLAND was based on the land and the sea. Here, the land of the Great Blasket as a main source of food for the Islanders will be discussed.[2] The focus, therefore, will be on livestock production and tillage, the main land-based economic activities on the Island, but the practice of hunting and gathering on land as a supplementary form of food provision will also be dealt with.

It is evident both from the comments of outsiders[3] and from the descriptions of Island life by the Islanders themselves,[4] that while women and older children might work on the land and gather shore food, it was the men only who fished the sea. It was also the male members of the community, both men and young boys, who went hunting and gathering on land and cliff.

While a two-meal system of food consumption known as *bia na maidine* ('morning food') and *bia na hoíche* ('night food') seems to have been general on the Island in the late nineteenth century,[5] a three-meal system incorporating a midday meal (*bia lár an lae*) is also recognised in the early twentieth century.[6]

The Islanders had adapted to the harsh Blasket environment and had developed a range of skills, including an intimate knowledge of their surrounding physical landscape, as the abundance of place-names shows,[7] which they deployed on land, sea, cliff and shore, in order to secure a livelihood for themselves and their families. Here we shall consider how they made the most of the limited land resources of the Great Blasket Island as part of their endeavour to make a living on the Island. In that context, the Great Blasket must not be considered in isolation but as the most important of a group of islands known collectively as the Blasket Islands, which formed an economic and social unit. The economy of the Great Blasket, not least in relation to livestock rearing, was closely linked to the natural resources of the surrounding islands of the Blasket group. This cluster of islands and its economic and social interrelationship will now be introduced.

I

The Blasket archipelago

The Blasket Islands, consisting of seven islands and several islets and rocks, lie off the the Dingle peninsula, County Kerry, in the south-west of Ireland. Although relatively inaccessible, small and economically and strategically unimportant, the group of islands formed a parcel of land and as such had a landlord since the Middle Ages. Prior to the failed Desmond rebellion of 1583 when they were confiscated by the Crown, the islands formed part of the estates of the Earl of Desmond. The Ferriters (*na Feiritéaraigh*), an important Anglo-Norman family, held lands in Kerry, including the Blaskets, from the Earl of Desmond. The townland and parish of Ballyferriter (*Baile an Fheirtéaraigh*) in the Dingle peninsula are named after them. They were chieftains of the Blasket Islands and paid an annual rent of two hawks for the lease of the islands to the Earl of Desmond. In maps and documents from the sixteenth and seventeenth centuries the Blaskets are sometimes referred to as 'Ferriter's Islands'.[8] It would seem that the Ferriters lost their lease of the Blasket Islands in the early seventeenth century and that the Islands thereafter passed through several hands until they were eventually purchased by Sir Richard Boyle, later Earl of Cork.[9] For much of the eighteenth century and almost all of the nineteenth century the islands were leased to the Hussey family of Dingle, who acted as land agents for the Earl of Cork and they remained part of that earl's Cork and Orrery estates until they were eventually purchased by the Congested Districts Board[10] in 1907. The Blasket Islanders were, therefore, tenants, subject to rent, and were to remain so until the 1920s when they had the opportunity to purchase their holdings under a native government.[11]

The Islands

An Blascaod Mór (The Great Blasket) or *An tOileán Tiar* (The Western Island), an island of just over a thousand acres,[12] was inhabited from at least the eighteenth century until 1953–54 when it was finally evacuated.

It is the largest of the Blasket Islands and it is also the focus of this paper. It is about 5 km long and 1 km at its widest point. The island village – *An Baile* – was located on the eastern side of the island where the basic requirements necessary for a permanent settlement – shelter, fresh water and a means of subsistence – were available. It was sheltered to some extent by the mountain ridge which forms the Blasket from the prevailing westerly wind. It also had several freshwater springs, and most of the island's tillage land was also adjacent to the village. In addition, the village was located within sight of the mainland, just above the Island harbour (*Caladh an Oileáin*), which provided access to it. These were factors of both physical and psychological importance for the Islanders because they depended on the mainland for trade and a range of other services.

There is a sea journey of 5 kilometres across the often treacherous waters of The Sound (*An Bealach*) from the mainland harbour, *An Fhaill Mór* (The Great Cliff) at *Dún Chaoin* (Dunquin), to the tiny Great Blasket harbour, a small natural cove and the only safe landing place of the Island. In the 1840s a breakwater to protect the landing place was built by the Dingle and Ventry Missionary Association, a Protestant proselytising organisation which gained a foothold on the Great Blasket in 1839–40 when it built the first school on the Island. This breakwater, which benefited the Islanders as well as the mission, had been partially swept away by high tides and stormy seas by 1850, by which time the mission's influence on the Island was effectively at an end.[13] It was not until almost forty years later (1893–98) that a breakwater and slip were constructed by the Congested Districts Board and further improved by the board in 1910. Despite these improvements the Blasket Island harbour could only accommodate a few small boats of shallow draught, such as keel-less currachs, at the one time. In addition only one currach could pull along the slipway at a time and low tide was to be avoided when possible. Thus, boarding and landing from these crafts was difficult, as was, for example, the task of loading and unloading animals, fish, seaweed and a variety of supplies from the mainland.

Inis na Bró (Quernstone island), an island of 102 acres,[14] lies off the southernmost tip of the Great Blasket and is separated from it by The Great Sound (*An Bealach Mór*). Like the Great Blasket the remains of a promontory fort points to Iron Age settlement on this island. Although it was the least accessible of the Blasket Islands, there was small-scale habitation there until the middle of the nineteenth century – the Census of Population for 1851 records that one family consisting of two males and two females lived there. It would seem that this island provided summer grazing for sheep, from the Great Blasket and for half-grown lambs from another island, *Inis Mhic Fhaoláin*, to its south.[15] The Islanders also made frequent visits there to hunt rabbits and seabirds, and the deep, extensive caves of its shoreline which had a large seal population, were a rich hunting ground for the Islanders.[16]

Inis Mhic Fhaoláin, an island of 171 acres,[17] is the most southerly of the
Blasket Islands, and after the Great Blasket, the once most often visited. A
sea-journey of about a quarter of a mile across the Narrow Sound [*Bealach
Caol na hInise*], separates the island from *Inis na Bró* to its north.[18] The
remains of what was probably an early monastic site and a cemetery indicate that the island was inhabited at an early period, and families are also
intermittently reported as living on the island in the nineteenth and early
twentieth centuries.[19] The island was farmed, growing potatoes, oats and
vegetable crops, and was also stocked with sheep.[20] There was strong and
relatively frequent contact, weather permitting, between the Great Blasket
Island and *Inis Mhic an Fhaoláin*. The Blasket Islanders were wont to undertake the boat journey of about 10 kilometres from the harbour of the Great
Blasket to *Inis Mhic Fhaoláin*, in order to put livestock out to grass for fattening and also to hunt for rabbits on land and seals in the many island
caves.[21] There were also close family links established by marriage
between the Great Blasket community and the families on *Inis Mhic
Fhaoláin* – in the nineteenth century, four daughters of the Ó Gaoithín family of the island married into the Great Blasket[22] and the 'Islandman'
Tomás Ó Criomhthain of the Great Blasket, had also probably intended to
marry a daughter of the O'Daly family of *Inis Mhic Fhaoláin*.[23] In times of
stress or emergency, fires were lighted by the people of *Inis Mhic Fhaoláin*
to attract the attention of the Blasket Islanders.[24]

An Tiaracht (westerly isle), is, as its name indicates, the most westerly
island of the Blasket group. It is essentially a great rock about 200 metres
in height with little vegetation. Consequently it was the only island of the
Blasket group which was not used by the Islanders for summer grazing for
livestock.[25] Nevertheless, this high and precipitous rock featured in the
economy of the Blasket Islanders as a place for hunting puffins. The flesh
of these seabirds was used for food and their feathers for bedding and
quilts.[26] Evidence of the importance of the puffins (and other seabirds) as
a source of food and bedding was the value placed on the island by the
Earl of Cork when it was purchased by the Port of Dublin Corporation in
the nineteenth century in order to erect a lighthouse there.[27]The purchase
price was £200 with a further £75 for Miss Clara Hussey's interest as lessee of the island from the Earl of Cork.[28]

Inis Tuaisceart (northern island), an island of 186 acres,[29] lying about
five miles norh of the Great Blasket,[30] is the most northerly of the Blasket
Islands.[31] It has early Christian remains with an associated field system
which was probably still in use until the latter half of the nineteenth century, when there was still one family living on the island.[32] *Inis Tuaisceart*
also provided grazing for livestock, especially sheep, from the Great
Blasket which, from the late nineteenth century onwards, were transported by currach from the island harbour.[33] The caves around the island also
had a large seal population.[34]

Beiginis (Little island) consisting of some thirty-six acres of land, lies close to the north-east side of the Great Blasket and it is protected by it from the harsh westerly winds. Unlike the other islands of the Blasket group it is flat and its 'cliffs' rise scarcely 10 metres above sea level. It is a fertile, accessible island with lush grass and it, too, was important for the Great Blasket economy. Livestock from the island, including sheep, were put there for fattening in preparation for the markets on the mainland. The main drawback of the island was that it did not have an adequate supply of fresh water and this militated against any substantial human habitation there. As it had a good supply of grass suitable for cows a 'milk house' was built there by the landlord in the early nineteenth century, and dairymen looked after the cows and ran the dairy on behalf of the landlord. This enterprise appears to have ended, however, later on in the nineteenth century when a dairyman was drowned while bringing drinking water by currach from the Great Blasket.[35]

Lying behind Beiginis is *Oileán na nÓg* (Island of the Young Animals?). This island was uninhabited but newly-weaned lambs from the Great Blasket were put out to grass there.[36]

The Great Blasket Island community

According to official data, the population of the Blasket Islands as a whole never reached 200 persons. While some of the other islands of the Blasket group were also inhabited at various periods, the main population was, as we have seen, on the largest island, the Great Blasket.[37] The official census data record the number of persons living on this island in the nineteenth and early twentieth century as follows: 128 (1821), 153 (1841), 97 (1851), 98 (1861), 138 (1871), 148 (1881), 139 (1891), 151 (1901), 160 (1911), and 150 (1925). While the Island population decreased by some 30 per cent during the decade 1841 to 1851 which included the period of the Great Famine, it is difficult to determine, in the apparent absence of relevant records, what proportion of that population decrease was due to famine-related deaths rather than to emigration. What is evident, however, is that the decline was less and the recovery swifter than on the mainland, due, perhaps, to the assistance provided by the Dingle and Ventry Missionary Association, the shipwrecks of the 1850s, the protection from 'famine fever' probably afforded the Island by its isolation, and the absence of evictions common on the mainland.[38]

Around 1916, when the fishing was good and the Island was at the height of its economic strength, there appears to have been 176 people living on the Island.[39] Since the early twentieth century, especially with the decline of the island fishing economy after the end of the First World War, emigration to the USA – increasingly intensified by the process of chain emigration by which a family member already established in the USA provided the passage money for a sibling – was the major cause of population decrease on the islands.[40] In 1930 the population of the Great Blasket had declined to 121 people. In 1938 there were 106 persons on the Island, while in 1947 there were only 50 people left. In 1953, the year the Island was being evacuated, there were only 22 persons, mainly older persons, still living on the Island. The decline in the number of prospective currach[41] crews as the young men emigrated gave an increased sense of isolation to the remaining community on the Great Blasket. A fatal blow to the Islanders' morale was the closure of the primary school by the Irish Department of Education in 1941 as there were only three pupils attending the school and there were no prospects of adequate numbers in the future.[42] As the Islanders had become more dependent on the mainland for essential supplies as their population declined and became progressively older, the difficulties experienced by them in securing foodstuffs and other household necessities during the Second World War, also encouraged them to leave the Island.[43] During the 1940s, therefore, more and more of the remaining inhabitants of the Great Blasket began to settle on the mainland, mainly in Dún Chaoin and the surrounding areas where many of their relatives lived, with the final evacuation of the Island taking place in 1953–54.

In its heyday, however, the Great Blasket community was a vigorous, closely-integrated one. The presence of a core group of families on the Island since at least the early eighteenth century gave stability to the Island community. The extended network of family ties, created through intermarriage over the generations, was a cornerstone of Island society and it was reflected in the clustering of the houses in the village and in the undifferentiated system of landholding which pertained until the early twentieth century.

As was the case with some of the other west-coast islands and fishing communities in the last century,[44] the Great Blasket had a 'king', *Rí an Oileáin* (The Island King). This 'king' was a nominal leader who acted as an independent spokesman, both in relation to internal Island affairs and in the Islanders' dealings with outside authorities. Such an independent and authoritative voice was necessary in the close-knit Island community, especially for the upholding of the common good on which the lives and livelihood of the Islanders as a whole depended, in such precarious surroundings and circumstances, and also for dealing with officialdom as a consequence of the Island's relative independence vis-à-vis the mainland.

The last Island 'king' was Pádraig Ó Catháin, whose grandfather had also been 'king' of the Island and apparently a man of considerable substance by Island standards as he was said to have possessed five cows. Ó Catháin, thus, came of an old and respected Island family. But he seems to have earned the right to the kingship of the Island by virtue of his physical, intellectual and social qualities. He was physically strong and courageous, a skilled seaman, and fully literate in both the Irish and English languages – a necessary qualification for an Island spokesman. He was the first Island postman, and thus, as well as delivering the mail, he brought, and read, the newspapers, and disseminated and interpreted news from the mainland. He also ferried most of the important early visitors to the Island and many of them lodged with him. But he was also a man of the people in that his general mode of life was similar to theirs. In the words of Tomás Ó Criomhthain 'he was both King and mariner when the call came, as well as being just as handy at planting potatoes and carrying manure for them'.[45] He was, thus, a man who was considered to be both noble and humble; he had the respect of the community as well as being of the community. He was also the childhood companion, life-long friend and brother-in-law of the 'Islandman' Tomás Ó Criomhthain.[46]

Mutual assistance was a cornerstone of economic endeavour and social interaction on the Island. This is stressed in an account of Island life by Máire Ni Ghaoithín[47] (born 1910) who states: '*Áit dob ea na hoileáin go dteastódh cabhair ann. Bhí mórán rudaí ná féadfá a dhéanamh as duit féin ann. Chaitheadh beirt ar an gcuid is lú a bheith chun naomhóg a chur síos agus suas...*' ('Help was needed on the islands. There were many things that you could not do on your own. At least two people were needed to launch and beach a currach.')[48] And again she states: '*Ní mhaireadh aoinne as féin san oileán, faoi mar a deir an seanfhocal "ar scáth a chéile a mhaireann an saol"*'. ('Nobody would survive on his own on the island, and as the proverb says, "the world lives on mutual assistance"'.)[49]

While land cultivation and some shore tasks such as collecting seaweed and shellfish for manuring purposes, could be, and often were, carried out individually, other activities, such as the provision of food from wild nature by hunting or fishing, the transport of animals between the islands, and sheep-shearing, were performed by groups of Islanders.[50]

The Islanders also required the assistance of the mainland population in their efforts to secure a livelihood. Here the extended family network reaching out to the mainland was of vital importance. Some of the Islanders, especially the girls, 'married out' of the island having found marriage partners in the parishes of Dunquin or Ballyferriter. But mainlanders also 'married into' the island. The wife of the Island 'king', for example, came from nearby Dunquin on the mainland[51] as did the wife of Tomás Ó Criomhthain's brother.[52] Peig Sayers, who gained the reputation as the major Blasket Island storyteller, can also be mentioned in this connection. She came originally from Baile Viocáire, Dunquin, on the mainland and, in 1892 at nineteen years of age, she married into the Great Blasket where she spent the next fifty years of her life.[53] New alliances with mainland families created in this way not only ensured that the Island families did not intermarry too closely within themselves, but also provided important additional channels of support for the Island community.

Although the Blasket Islanders were, thus, in the words of Tomás Ó Criomhthain, 'close of kin and much intermarried' with the people of the contiguous mainland, they always considered themselves different from them, and, on occasion, even engaged in bitter strife with them in relation to the Islanders' primary source of livelihood – fishing.[54] Whatever their sense of independence and of being a separate community, however, there was, of course, an unavoidable economic dependence on the mainland as the Island did not have sufficient natural resources to be self-supporting. Assistance with the movement of animals in and out of the Island was of primary importance, as was the handling of fish at Dunquin and the provision of transport to Dingle. Fishing equipment, wood for boat or currach building, withies for making lobster pots, for example, and land cultivation and sea-harvesting equipment, were bought on the mainland. This was the case also in relation to bread-making ingredients, and food items such as tea and sugar, which had become basic elements of the diet of the islands by the late nineteenth century. And, of course, tobacco, which was viewed almost as a necessity of life by the Islanders, was purchased on the mainland.

Such fundamental facilities as those provided by the church, medical and legal professions, were also available only from the mainland.[55] As the Island was without a priest, church or cemetery the Blasket Islanders were baptised, married and buried on the mainland.

II

The provision of food – hunting, tillage and livestock

Hunting

On the limited land resources of the Island, livestock was raised and crops were cultivated, but the Islanders also augmented their diet with rabbit meat, and, in season, with the flesh of sea-birds.[56] The island had a high rabbit population which was eagerly hunted by the young and older men of the community. Tomás Ó Criomhthain talks enthusiastically of rabbit hunting with his friend Pádraig Ó Catháin, who later became the Island 'king'.[57] He also tells of rabbit-hunting expeditions which he made with his uncle and others to *Inis Mhic Fhaoláin*,[58] a practice which continued to the dying days of the Blasket Island community as is evident from the account of Island life written by Eilís Ní Shúilleabháin in 1940.[59] While the Islanders viewed rabbit hunting – an activity which provided an essential fresh meat supplement to their largely fish and salt-food diet – also as a from of sport, Robin Flower was repelled by it. Here is his reaction to a hunting scene which he witnessed on *Inis Mhic Fhaoláin* described in *The Western Island or the Great Blasket*, his book about his time on the Blasket Islands:

> Off ran the dogs, snuffing and burrowing in the crumbling soil along the cliff edge. Soon it was plain that they were on a hot scent, and the men fell to digging out the hole till they came on a hapless rabbit crouching terrified

in the last cover. A twist of the hand finished him, and the dogs were away to another hole. I soon grew weary of this monotonous sport, and drifted away over the island out of sound of the slaughter.[60]

Ferrets as well as dogs were used to hunt rabbits, but slings made of copper wire were also fixed on the rabbit tracks at night to trap them. These traps had to be checked in the early morning to prevent birds or wild cats from eating the rabbits.[61]

The most vivid account of bird-hunting on land is that given by Muiris Ó Súilleabháin in his account of hunting thrushes on Hallowe'en night. About 100 were caught and these were subsequently plucked, roasted and eaten by the group of young people as a kind of ceremonial feast.[62]

Tillage

In relation to the cultivation of crops and animal rearing, the island economy resembled the formal food economy of the mainland. These activities were, of course, carried out on a much smaller scale because of the limitations imposed by the Island's size, topograpy, soil quality, the rundale system of landholding, the difficulties involved in transporting animals to and from the mainland, and because of the emphasis which was placed on labour-intensive fishing for the achievement of livelihood and household support and as an important source of income.

The extent of tillage land on the island was severely limited. The Island consisted of just over 1100 acres of land, only about sixty acres of which was cultivated, amounting to roughly one-eighteenth of the total acreage.[63] The non-arable land, which was held in common, included mountain pasture and peatland and each tenant had a share of each.[64]

The arable land was adjacent to the Island village on the eastern side of the Island. The individual family holdings of this land were apparently small. In 1907 when the Congested Districts Board purchased the Island, no tenant had access to more than four acres of arable land, but there is evidence in Griffiths Valuation of the mid nineteenth century (1850) of somewhat larger arable holdings. The reduction in size of such holdings in the course of the nineteenth century probably arose from an increase in population – apart from the famine years – partly consisting of migration from the mainland, in the course of the nineteenth century. This movement to the island was probably due in the first instance, to the development of the Island fishing industry as a result of the adoption of the large seine fishing boats which required a crew of eight, in the early nineteenth century. Other factors which probably brought people to the Island during the nineteenth century were land agitation and famine conditions on the mainland.[65]

Although there were about sixty acres of arable land on the Island it is not clear how much of this land was actually cultivated each year. Apart from the necessity to 'let out' some of the land, that is, to allow it to remain fallow in order to enable it to regenerate, another factor of relevance in relation to the extent of tillage on the Great Blasket was the system of land-holding on the Island. This deserves special mention.

Prior to the purchase of the Island by the Congested Districts Board in 1907, the Islanders, as tenants, held their tillage land under the medieval rundale system of scattered unfenced strips in large open fields – a method of land use which still persisted in other agriculturally marginal districts in western Ireland in this century.[66] The allocation of the land in the Great Blasket was from west to east and the rundale system in operation gave each tenant a mixture of the three distinguishable qualities of land in three separate areas on the Island. Strips of exposed land faced the shore, behind them were the fertile plots further inland, leading finally to the steep, rough land of mountain pasture and peatland held in common. Both the lower and middle levels were consistently cultivated, mainly with pota-toes and oats. The various tillage plots were identified only by stone mark-ers set at both ends with a couple of beds between them. On the whole, this system seems to have worked well, although it required the time-con-suming herding of animals during the crop-growing season to keep them away from the cultivated fields. As a result of heavy rain, however, or of young boys playing pranks, the plot markers were sometimes shifted or removed, and this could lead to disagreements among tenants.

The Great Blasket was purchased by the Congested Districts Board from the landlord in 1907 and the land was reallocated over the next ten years so that each person knew his own plot and had it fenced. The revised system seems to have met with the general approval of the Islanders, prob-ably because the board maintained the principal element of the existing rundale system in allocating to each holder a number of scattered plots, rather than contiguous fields, thus ensuring a reasonable mix of land qual-ity. The reorganised holdings were larger than the previous ones and there was also access to the strand. In this way there was only minimal disrup-tion of the Islanders' farming practices.[67]

The principal crops cultivated on the island were oats and potatoes. According to the Island writers referring to the nineteenth and twentieth centuries, oats (and to some extent, also, potatoes) was used for animal fodder, but it is probable that it was also formerly used as a principal bread and porridge grain, as was the case elsewhere along the west of Ireland before the use of wheat flour became common.[68] Potatoes, sown from around mid-March, usually after St Patrick's Day if the weather was favourable, to early April, were the principal Island crop and the primary staple food. As such, the merits of the different varieties of early and late potatoes, the various stages of their cultivation, and their quality, taste and abundance, are mentioned by Island writers.[69] The sense of expectation and excitement at the digging of the new crop, and the evaluation of the potato in the diet vis-à-vis bread, is well expressed in a diary entry by Tomás Ó Criomhthain in his book *Allagar na hInise*. The incident he refers to occurred in late June in the year 1920. It was around midday. The people were in their gardens digging new potatoes for dinner (midday meal) and they were commenting on the crop. Tomás met a woman who had just dug a supply of potatoes and the following conversation ensued: 'I have dug potatoes today that are as good as any I've dug for the last seven years', said she. 'And I'll have them, and fish, for dinner every day from now on. They are much better for me and my children than [having] that heavy bread three times today, and black water [ie tea] without milk or sugar', said she.[70]

Several failures of the potato crop during the nineteenth century were still remembered: in the 1840s during the Great Famine, and also in the 1879, 1886 and 1890 due to unseasonal heavy rainfall and cold in the summer months, when the Islanders had to seek relief from the authorities.[71] As a consequence of this, and because of the central role of the potato in the Islanders' diet, the effects of frost, strong winds, or a prolonged period of heavy rain, and especially blight, on the growing crop was a constant source of worry to them – although it was sprayed with copper sulphate to prevent blight as was the practice on the mainland. This fear is expressed by Tomás Ó Criomhthain in a number of his dairy entries in the 1920s when patches of blight had appeared on the crop.[72]

Corn and potatoes, and the other root crops cultivated on the Island, such as cabbage and turnips, were grown in ridges. This cultivation technique, formerly common in the west of Ireland, and persisting there to some extent even today, was particularly suitable in an area of heavy rainfall such as the Great Blasket, as it facilitated drainage and, by raising the roots of the crop above the ground, protected them from rotting. The remains of these ridges are still observable on the tillage land of the Great Blasket and *Inis Mhic Fhaoláin*. On the southern slope of the Great Blasket where place-names attest to the existence of cultivation in former times, there are large cultivation ridges in a stone-walled enclosure called *Garraí an Choirce* (The Oat Garden). These ridges are from six to seven feet wide and have been identified by the Islanders as oat ridges.[73] The principal implements used in crop cultivation in ridges were: a spade to cut and turn the sod and to dig the furrow; a fork to spread the farmyard manure or seaweed on the ridge; and a shovel to cover the planted ridge with soil.[74] The kinds of fertilizers available to the Islanders were farmyard manure, seaweed and shellfish, which, collectively, provided nitrates, phosphates, potassium and lime for the soil.[75] However, there was an immense amount of labour involved in carting the manure uphill to the fields from farmyard, sea and shore, in backbaskets or in panniers slung on donkeys. Here is a description, dating to the 1870s, given by Tomás Ó Criomhthain, then a young man of twenty-two and just married, of his own efforts to collect seaweed as manure for the potato crop:

> I set to work with keenness. Away I went to the strand to get seaweed for
> manure so that we could have more potatoes to rear pigs on. We had two
> cows at this time. At daybreak, stripped of everything but my drawers,
> with a rake to gather the weed, out I'd go up to my neck in the sea; then I
> had to carry it up to the top of the cliff, carry it to the field and spread it...[76]

In March 1921, as an older man, he observes and comments on the kind
and amount of labour involved in collecting seaweed for the potato crop.
Black seaweed, which was applied fresh, was the type commonly used at
the actual planting of the potatoes. Here is his description of the collecting
process:

> Well, there is a spring tide running and the currachs of the village are afloat,
> two men in some and three in others. They have ropes and sickles to reap
> the black seaweed for manure. But the potatoes have not been planted yet
> and the seaweed cannot be spread until the seed potatoes are in the ground.
> So, one old woman is busy spreading seaweed and heaping up the ridge,
> while another is planting seed potatoes.[77]

Máire Ní Ghaoithín also describes the practice of wading into the sea, in
water up to one's waist, during a spring tide, to collect this variety of seaweed. When the weed was cut it was gathered into a bundle and tied tight-
ly with a rope. It was then pulled ashore over rocks and stones, where it
was then hoisted on one's back, and brought some distance up along the
strand from the water's edge, to protect it from being carried away by the
flowing tide. When the required amount was gathered, the seaweed was
then packed into panniers mounted on a donkey and brought to the tillage
plot. Here it was discharged from the panniers and spread on the ridges,
where the seed potatoes had been set. The earth was shovelled on top so
that the weed would rot and thus act as a valuable fertilizer.[78]

Red seaweed was also used as a fertilizer for the potato crop. This,
however, was collected during the winter months and spread on the
ground where a spring crop of potatoes was to be sown. The seaweed was
covered with earth so that it would rot and, thus, be absorbed into the soil.
This method of fertilizer application was know as *sean leasú* (old/pre-fer-
tilizing), while the newly-scattered black seaweed was called *ath-leasú*
(second fertilizing).[79]

Collecting shellfish (especially mussels) from the rocks to provide lime
for the potato crop was an onerous, but necessary task. While such shellfish were gathered on the Island foreshore, the Islanders also went as far
as *Leac na nIascán* ('Shellfish/Mussel Flag') *Inis na Bró* in search of them.[80]
They had to be knocked off the rocks with an iron implement, collected in
bags and, after unloading them from the currachs at the Island slipway,
they then had to be loaded onto donkeys for transfer to the tillage fields
where they were scattered on the ridges at the first earthing of the potato
crop.[81] Artificial manure (guano) appears to have been used only to a limited extent, at least in the 1920s,[82] as it was considered an expensive commodity which had to be brought from Dingle. On the other hand, natural

fertilizers from the farmyard and the sea, were readily available even if their provision and application took a lot of time, energy and labour.[83]

The main household vegetables were cabbage and turnips. People who kept visitors had a wider range of vegetables, such as carrots, parsnips, cauliflower, onions, beetroot, lettuce and radishes.[84] As there were no fruit bushes or trees on the island, there was none of the kinds of fruit available on the mainland growing in the Island. Apples were purchased on the mainland to make apple cakes, and it was on the mainland that the Islanders sometimes collected blackberries. An Island author, Máire Ní Ghuithín, tells that a visitor to the Island once brought loganberry bushes but they did not survive the windy and salty climate. However, some whortle berries (*fraocháin*) and juniper berries (*samhanna*) – which were very sour and required a lot of brown sugar to make them palatable – grew on the Island shrubland and pies were made of these.[85] Rhubarb, however, which was also brought from the mainland and manured with seaweed, was a great success.[86]

Livestock

Livestock rearing was an important part of the Island economy in the nineteenth and twentieth centuries. The Islanders grazed cows, calves, sheep, goats and donkeys on the Island commonage which was called *an buaile* ['the booley']. According to the Griffiths Valuation House Book (1850) the Island families possessed thirteen cows at that time,[87] while in 1907 the Commissioner of the Congested Districts Board noted the existence of twelve cows on the Island. Island tradition also asserts that there was formerly a larger number of cows on the Island and that butter was made for the market in Dingle. Calves were also reared for sale. Both of these activities required cow's milk, and goats were, therefore, important for the provision of milk, especially for children. From the early twentieth century, most households had only one cow and, therefore, little butter was made, even for home consumption. Instead, butter was bought on the mainland when possible. Some families that kept visitors might keep a second cow for the provision of the extra milk required during the summer months.[88]

Keeping a large number of cows on the Island was troublesome and labour intensive. The provision of winter fodder was problematic as hay was not saved on the Island until the reorganisation of the landholding system in the twentieth century, the cows previous to that time having been fed in winter on oats and potatoes.[89] As cows were valuable livestock they required a lot of attention. It was necessary to herd them carefully in order to keep them away from the crops, and from falling over the cliffs when they grazed on the mountain pastures. Particular attention was accorded to them while they were in calf in the spring.[90] In addition, cows had to be brought to the mainland for insemination. The transport of cows in the seine boats or currachs was a difficult and time-consuming task as each cow had to be loaded and unloaded twice. Up to eight men were required on each occasion, and the Islanders might also have to depend on the assistance of people on the mainland to haul the cow in and out of the currach at the jetty in Dunquin. Gunwales were often damaged in the process. Two men had the heavy task of rowing the currach which contained the cow, and another currach with its complement of three rowers accompanied it in case it capsized.[91]

The Islanders also raised young cattle which were sold on the mainland. The practice of transhumance (*buailteachas*), or the sending of cattle to summer grazing, either on the Great Blasket itself, or, because of the limited grazing available there, to the neighbouring islands of the Blasket group, played a vital role in the raising of cattle. It was also an integral part of the Island economy.

While livestock such as milch cows and dry stock had a fundamental place in the island economy, sheep were also important. According to the report of the Congested Districts Board's commissioner in 1907, there were 200 sheep on the Island at that time. In fact the Blasket Island group as a whole, because of the steep gradient, was more suitable for sheep rearing rather than cattle raising. The number of sheep which the Great Blasket Island could graze was regulated at the rate of twenty-five sheep for each cow. Sheep were easier to handle than cattle, especially in relation to transportation in the currachs, and they also provided wool. In addition, they were a good source of income. In 1919 a pair of sheep fetched £6. The Islanders' view at that time of the value of sheep is pithily expressed in the following statements: 'Any man without a stock of sheep is not worth talking about – one to shear, one to sell and one to eat. They cost nothing to keep and they will always bring in the penny.'[92] While fresh beef – which the Islanders seldom had – was probably the most highly prized meat, it was mutton, rather than beef, which was the meat traditionally eaten by the Islanders at Christmas. A sheep was slaughtered for the festival, and this, was, therefore, one of the relatively few occasions when the Islanders ate fresh meat on an extended basis, as then the remainder of mutton was preserved by salting.

It would appear that pigs were only occasionally kept on the Island, probably because of the Island's limited, and often unreliable, supply of potatoes and oats necessary to feed them, and also because of the difficulty of preventing them from trespassing on the unfenced crops. One notable occasion when piglets were reared on the Island was in 1890 when the Islanders, fearing that the large supply of yellow meal (Indian meal) provided by the Relief Committee in Dingle would go mouldy, bought a supply of bonhams on the mainland and fed them on the meal. Needless to say, no further supply of meal was sent to the Island![93] One of the Island writers, born in 1910, states that she did not see pigs on the Island.[94]

Fowl, particularly hens, were kept on the Island. Hen eggs were an important part of the diet and the hens were also a source of fresh meat.

Geese and turkeys.[95] were also kept to some extent. Apart from providing fresh meat, the geese, which were plucked twice a year, were a source of much-needed feathers and down for bedding.[96]

Conclusion

In the concluding chapter of his description of daily life on the Great Blasket Island in the latter half of the nineteenth century and the first quarter of the twentieth century, Tomás Ó Criomhthain characterised the Island as follows:

> This is a crag in the midst of the great sea, and again and again the blown surf drives right over it before the violence of the wind, so that you daren't put your head out any more than a rabbit that crouches in his borrow in Inishvickillaun when the rain and the salt spume are flying...97

Having spent all of his life on the Island, Ó Criomhthain was fully aware of the harshness of the physical environment and the difficulties involved in gaining a livelihood on that exposed, isolated island off the south-west coast of Ireland. It was necessary at all times to make the most of nature by reaping the bounty of the land, cliffs, sea, and shore.

Compared with the vastness of the surrounding sea, the Island was small and its land resources were very limited. This treeless ridge of bog and mainly mountain pasture contains just over 1000 acres. The population was always low, and, in favourable years, the arable portion of the Island, though small, provided the Islanders with the basic crops – potatoes and oats. Despite the hardship involved in procuring manure, especially seaweed, for the crop, potatoes were the most important staple food of the Islanders, Consequently, all stages of the sowing process are discussed by the various Island writers, particularly by Ó Criomhthain in his book *Allagar na hInise*. As the blight posed a constant threat to the growing crop, this was a continual source of worry to the Islanders.

Corn, especially oats, was also grown, and the latter was probably still used as a principal bread grain in the course of the nineteenth century. Both corn and potatoes were sown in ridges in times gone by, a form of cultivation which enabled drainage of the soil to take place and thus to protect the crop.

The hunting of rabbits was an important supplementary aspect of the provision of food as it provided fresh meat in an otherwise predominantly fish diet. Rabbits were hunted on the Great Blasket and on a number of the neighbouring islands.

Livestock, especially cows, calves and sheep, were also important in the Island economy, and, despite the difficulties involved in transporting animals in the currachs, the grass resources of most of the other islands of the Blasket group were used for summer grazing for these animals.

The islanders were also economically dependent on the mainland as it was there that they sold their surplus fish catch and and brought their livestock to the markets. And as time went on the Islanders became more dependent on shop provisions which could be purchased mainly in Dingle village.

As the Island population declined due to emigration, the tasks of the cultivation of the land and the raising of livestock became increasingly difficult for the remaining population. These factors, as well as those connected with the fishing industry, and many more concerned with other aspects of Island life, combined to rob the Island of viability and led eventually to its desertion in the 1950s.

Notes and references

1. Ó Criomhthain, Tomás, *Allagar na hInise*, 1928, p 70. All further references to *Allagar na hInise*, the diary written during the years 1918 and 1923 by Tomás Ó Criomhthain (1855–1937) fisherman, farmer and stone mason, and a native of the Great Blasket Island, County Kerry, Ireland, are from the new edition of the work edited by Pádraig Ua Maoileoin and published in 1977. The first edition appeared in 1928 and extracts from it, translated into English by Tim Enright, were published in book form by Oxford University Press: O'Crohan, Tomás, *Island Cross-Talk. Pages from a Diary* (Oxford, 1986); hereafter referred to as 'Enright'. *Allagar II*, edited by Pádraig Na Maoilleoin (Baile Átha Cliath, 1999), was not yet published when this article was written.

2. The harvest of the cliffs as a seasonal food resource for the Blasket islanders is dealt with by Patricia Lysaght in 'Food-provision strategies on the Great Blasket Island: Sea-bird fowling', in Patricia Lysaght, *Food from nature: Attitudes, strategies and culinary practices* (Uppsala 2000), pp 333–63. (*Acta Academiae Regiae Gustavi Adolphi LXXI.*)

3. See in this connection the discussion of the historical background of the Great Blasket Island community in Stagles, J. and R., *The Blasket Islands: next parish America* (Dublin, 1980), and the historical articles about landlord and tenant relations and the schools on the Great Blasket island, by Seán Ó Dubháin and Seán Ó Mainín, respectively, in A. Ó Muircheartaigh (*eag./*ed), *Oidhreacht an Bhlascaoid* (The Heritage of the Blasket) (Baile Átha Cliath, 1989), pp 9–44. See also the 'Notes' by Séamus Ó Duilearga in S. Ó Duilearga (*eag./*ed) *Seanchas Ón Oileán Tiar* (Lore from the Western Isle) (Dublin, 1956). This lore was collected by Robin Flower during the years 1920–25, from Tomás Ó Criomhthain and edited by Séamus Ó Duilearga.

4. This paper is based mainly on the descriptions of life and livelihood on the Great Blasket Island given by the following Island writers: Tomás Ó Criomhthain, Máire Ní Ghaoithín/Guithín and Eilís Ní Shúilleabháin. The books referred to in this context are: (a) Tomás Ó Criomhthain (1855–1937) II: *Allagar na hInise* – see note 1; *An t-Oileánach* (Baile Átha Cliath, 1967), (fourth printing); first published in 1929 and translated by Robin Flower 1934. Here the Oxford University Press edition of Flower's translation (O'Crohan, T., *The Islandman*, Oxford, 1951), hereafter referred to as Flower (1951), is used; (b) Máire Ní Ghaoithín/Guithín, born in the Great Blasket (1910): *An tOileán a Bhí* (The Island that Was) (Baile Átha Cliath, 1978), and *Bean an Oileáin* (A Woman of the Island (ie, The Great Blasket)) (Baile Átha Cliath, 1986); and (c) Eilís Ní

Shúilleabháin (born in the Great Blasket c. 1911), *Letters from The Great Blasket* (Cork/Dublin, n.d.), dealing with the years 1931–42 while she lived on the Island, and describing her life on the mainland until 1951.

Also referred to is the important collection of essays in the Irish language about the heritage of the Island edited by A. Ó Muircheartaigh and detailed in the previous note, and the historical survey of the Blasket Islands by J. and R. Stagles mentioned in note three above.

A useful synthesis of the descriptions of livelihood and household support on the Great Blasket in the nineteenth and twentieth centuries, given in the books written by the Islanders, and the books and articles written about the islands by outsiders from the nineteenth century onwards, is provided by Criostóir Mac Cárthaigh as part of a heritage report on The Blasket Islands presented prior to the setting up of a Visitor's Centre in Dunquin: Mac Cárthaigh, C., *The Blasket Islands: a heritage report* (Dún Chaoin, 1990), pp 1–103 (typescript).

For a bibliography of works by Island writers see: Mac Conghail, M., *The Blaskets: people and literature* (Dublin, 1994), pp 168–9 (first published 1987). For an additional bibliographical perspective see also Uí Laoithe-Bheaglaoich, C., *Liosta Leabhar*, in *The Blasket Islands: a heritage report* (Dún Chaoin, 1990), pp 182–201 (typescript).

5. Ó Criomhthain (1967), op. cit., p 40.; Flower (1951), op. cit., pp 31–2.
6. Ní Ghaoithín (1978), op. cit., p 76.
7. See in this connection Tomás Ó Criomhthain's commentary on the place-names of the Blasket island group: *Dinnsheanchas na mBlascaodaí* ('Placename Lore of the Blaskets') (Baile Átha Cliath, 1935).
8. Ó Dubháin (1989), op. cit., pp 14–15; Stagles (1980), op. cit., pp 25–6.
9. Ó Dubháin (1989), op. cit., p 15, who states, on the evidence of the Lismore Papers, that the Ferriter lease of the Blasket Islands was lost in 1622 as a result of an earlier mortgage transaction.
10. The Congested Districts Board was established by the British government in 1891 after a particularly severe period of deprivation along the west coast of Ireland in 1890. Its function was to investigate and then, where possible, to improve the conditions of the poorest parts of Ireland. There were eighty-four such congested districts along the Atlantic seaboard of Ireland, extending from Lough Foyle in the north to Youghal in the south. For an account of the Boards activities in Ireland, see Micks, M., *History of the Congested Districts Board for Ireland* (Dublin, 1925).
11. Ó Dubháin (1989), op. cit., pp 15–16, 27.
12. The figure of 1132 acres is given by Stagles (1980), op. cit., pp 82–5.
13. Ibid., pp 43–8, 53–4. Several shipwrecks off the Blaskets in the year 1850 are said to have rescued the Islanders from starvation and from the charity of the Dingle and Ventry Missionary association.
14. Ó Duilearga (1956), op. cit., p 256.
15. Ó Criomhthain (1977), op. cit., pp 81–2; Ní Ghaoithín (1978) op. cit., p 84.
16. MacConghail (1994), op. cit., p 31, and Stagles (1980), op. cit., p 122.
17. Ó Duilearga (1956), op. cit., p 256.
18. Ní Ghaoithín (1978), op. cit., p 84.
19. According to the Census of Population Reports there were three people living on *Inis Mhic Fhaoláin* in 1841, while in 1851 there were eight people residing there, and by 1901 the number had dropped to six.

20. Ó Duilearga (1956), op. cit., p 185; Stagles (1980), op. cit., pp 118–21.
21. Ó Criomhthain (1967), op. cit., p 112, Flower (1951), op. cit., p 97.
22. Ní Ghaoithín (1978), op. cit., p 83.
23. For an account of his romantic interest in the daughter of the O'Daly family and his later arranged marriage, see Ó Criomhthain (1967), op. cit., pp 107, 123–5, 127–8; Flower (1951) op. cit., pp 103, 109–10,112–13, 128–30, 144–6.
24. Ní Ghaoithín (1978), op. cit., p 84; Ó Duilearga (1956), op. cit., p 186,
25. Stagles (1980), op. cit., p 122; Duilearga (1956), op. cit., pp 254–5.
26. Lysaght (2000) op. cit., pp 342–55, and see note 96.
27. The date of purchase of the island is given as 15 September 1864. A lighthouse was erected there in 1870 and the fog horn operated until May 1987. This was the last light which emigrants saw on their journey from Queenstown, County Cork, to America. This lighthouse is now automatic (Stagles (1980), op. cit., pp 122, 125, Mac Conghail (1994), op. cit., p 32).
28. Mac Conghail (1994), op. cit., p 32; Ó Duilearga (1956), op. cit., pp 254–5. In his autobiography,Tomás Ó Criomhthain tells of the running battle which the crew of a boat from Dunquin fought with those guarding Clara Hussey's interest in the birds on the Little Skellig rock, as they sought to confiscate the Islanders catch of young gannets (Ó Criomhthain (1967), op. cit., pp 167–9; Flower (1951), op. cit., pp 150–2). For references to Little Skellig (*An Sceilg Bheag*) and Skellig Michael (*Sceilg Mhichíl*), see Ó Duilearga (1956), op. cit., p 246; and Lavelle, D., *Skellig Island:Outpost of Europe* (Dublin 1977).
29. Ó Duilearga (1956), op. cit., p 254.
30. Ibid., p 253.
31. It is also sometimes colloquially known as *An Fear Marbh* (The Dead Man), because when seen in the distance it seems to resemble a dead man laid out at a wake (Ní Guithín (1986), op. cit., p 88).
32. This married couple, named Ó Catháin, who lived in a *clochán*, or early Christian corbelled structure, was tragically cut off from assistance from the Great Blasket during a six-week period of bad weather in the 1860s. The husband died and his wife was in a state of extreme distress when rescued (Mac Conghail (1994), op. cit., p 32).
33. Ibid., p 49, for a description of the awesome task of bringing sheep on and off the island in the absence of a suitable harbour.
34. Ó Duilearga (1956), op. cit., p 253.
35. Stagles (1980), op. cit., pp 128–9; Ó Duilearga (1956), op. cit., pp 251–2.
36. Mac Conghail (1994), op. cit., p 33.
37. For the extent of the population on the other islands of the Blasket group in the nineteenth century, see the Census of Population for the various years, and also cf. Ó Duilearga (1956), op. cit., pp 262–3.
38. Stagles (1980), op. cit., pp 48–50.
39. According to Tomás Criomhthain in a letter to Robin Flower; see in this connection, Mac Conghail (1994), op. cit., p 34. Cf. also Ó Duilearga (1956), op. cit., p 263.
40. For the effect of this pattern of emigration on Tomás Ó Criomhthain's family, see Ó Criomhthain (1967), op. cit., p 76, Flower (1951), op. cit., pp 64–5, For a similar kind of emigration in the Ó Gaoithín family from *Inis Mhic Fhaoláin*, see Ní Ghaoithín (1978), op. cit., pp 83–4.
41. These craft made of a framework of laths and covered with tarred canvas are

known as *naomhóga* in the Dingle peninsula.

42. The school was built about 1866. At the time when the school was closed there was only one young child in the Island and the family in question left the Island for the mainland in 1942. (Ní Shúilleabháin (n.d.), op. cit., pp 81–2 (3.2.1940), 86 (6.2.1941).

43. See Eilís Ní Shúilleabháin's descriptions of the difficulties of life on the Island in the late 1930s and early 1940s, in Ní Shúilleabháin (n.d.), op. cit., 78ff.

44. See in this connection Ó Danachair, C., 'An rí (the king): an example of traditional social organisation', *Journal of the Royal Society of Antiquaries of Ireland*, 3 (1981), pp 14–28.

45. Flower (1951), op. cit., p 203; Ó Criomhthain (1967), op. cit., 222.

46. Mac Cárthaigh (1990), op. cit., pp 53–4; Ó Danachair (1981), op. cit., pp 21–22.

47. In her later work (1986) op. cit.., her surname appears as 'Guithín'.

48. Ní Ghaoithín (1978), op. cit., p 88.

49. Ní Ghuithín (1986), op. cit., p 36.

50. Stagles (1980), op. cit., p 90.

51. Ó Criomhthain (1967), op. cit.,p 97; Flower (1951), op. cit., p 84.

52. Ibid., p 76; ibid., p 64

53. Peig and her poet-son, 'Maidhc File' returned to live on the mainland in 1942 (Mac Conghail (1994), op. cit., p 161).

54. See in this connection Tomás Ó Criomhthain's statement that although both communities were closely interrelated that 'they were always at odds over the fishing'. (Ó Criomhthain (1967), op. cit., p 165; Flower (1951) op. cit., p 148). See also his vivid description of the fight between the Islanders and the boats from Dunquin for the school of porpoises which was lured ashore on the Island's White Strand (Ó Criomhthain (1967), op. cit., pp 14–15; Flower (1951), op. cit., pp 7–9).

55. Mac Cárthaigh (1990), op. cit., p 61.

56. For sea-bird fowling see Lysaght (2000), op. cit.

57. Ó Criomhthain (1967), op. cit., pp 72–4; Flower (1951), op. cit., pp 62–3.

58. Ibid., pp 127–8; ibid. pp 112–13

59. Ní Shúilleabháin (n.d.), op. cit., p 85. See also the account of a rabbit-hunting expedition to *Inis Mhic Fhaoláin* by Maurice O'Sullivan, in *Twenty years a-growing* (Oxford, 1992), pp 124–8. Irish original *Fiche Bliain ag Fás* by Muiris Ó Súilleabháin (Baile Átha Cliath, 1933), pp 169–74. Translated by Moya Llewelyn Davies and George Thomson, 1933.

60. Flower, Robin, *The Western Island or The Great Blasket* (Oxford 1946), p 115 (first published 1944).

61. Ní Ghaoithín (1978), op. cit., p 82.

62. O'Sullivan (1992) op. cit., pp 88–92.

63. Stagles (1980), op. cit., pp 82–5.

64. The task of transporting the turf to the house was, however, a time-consuming and laborious one and it was often performed by the girls or women. This is mentioned by Tomás Ó Criomhthain who tells of his mother carrying turf in a creel on her back even when he was eighteen years of age. (Ó Criomhthain (1967), op. cit., pp 265, 266; Flower (1951), op. cit., pp 244, 245). It involved a return journey of five miles, the outward half of the trip being uphill, carrying a back basket, or leading a donkey with side creels, to bring home turf as often as it was required (Ó Criomhthain (1977), op. cit., pp 273–4, p 274; Enright, op.

cit., p 107). Scraws and brushwood, particularly furze bushes, were also col-
lected on the hillside, for fuel. It was while performing this task that Peig
Sayer's son, Thomas, fell over a cliff and lost his life. (In her autobiography,
Peig Sayers gives the date of the accident as Friday, 20 April, 1920.) (Sayers, P.,
Peig (Baile Átha Cliath, 1936), p 213, pp 213–17. Translated by MacMahon, B.,
Peig: the autobiography of Peig Sayers of the Great Blasket Island (Dublin, 1973), pp
180–4). The incident is also mentioned by Tomás Ó Criomhthain in his diary (Ó
Criomhthain (1977), op. cit., p 196; Enright, op. cit., p 79.)

65. Mac Cárthaigh (1990), op. cit., p 17.
66. Evans, E.E., *Irish folk ways* (London 1972), pp 23–26 (fifth impression).
67. Stagles (1980), op. cit., pp 79–92.
68. For example, Tomás Ó Criomhthain, b. 1856, states (1967) op. cit., p 40; Flower
    (1951), op. cit., pp 1951, 32) that in his youth bread made of Indian meal was
    eaten as a substitute for potatoes, while 'wheat-flour' was eaten during the
    period in which he was writing (1920s).
69. See, for example, her appreciation of the different kinds of potatoes expressed
    by Máire Ní Gaoithín (1986), op. cit., pp 36–7.
70. Ó Criomhthain (1977), op. cit., pp 217–18. Author's translation.
71. Tomás Ó Criomhthain was born a decade after the commencement of the Great
    Famine (1845–50) and lived through the other failures or partial failures of the
    potato crop during the nineteenth century – failures which were also wide-
    spread on the mainland. For details of the relief work carried out by the Dingle
    and Ventry Mission Association, a Protestant organisation which gained a
    foothold in the Great Blasket in 1839–40, during the Great Famine years, which
    included the dispensing of soup and Indian meal stirabout to the children of
    the Island, see Stagles (1980), op. cit., pp 43–50. For official relief measures
    taken by the authorities to relieve distress in the 1870s, 1880s and the 1890s, see
    Seán Ó Dubháin, 'Báillí agus Callshaoth' [Bailiffs and Contention'], in Ó
    Muircheartaigh (1989), op. cit., pp 18–27.
72. See in this connection his diary entries by Tomás Ó Criomhthain (1977), op. cit.,
    pp 213–15. Cf. Enright (1986), op. cit., pp 81–3.
73. Stagles (1980), op. cit., p 85. Cf. Evans (1972), op. cit., pp 141–2.
74. For a detailed description of the construction of ridges or 'lazy-beds', see Evans
    (1972), op. cit., pp 142–6.
75. Seaweed is a valuable fertilizer for plants as it is rich in potassium, it has a
    nitrogen content equivalent to that of farmyard manure and about twice the
    amount of potassium. However, it is deficient in lime and has only about a
    third of the phosphorus content of farmyard manure. See in this connection:
    Fenton, A., *The shape of the past 2: essays in Scottish ethnology* (Edinburgh, 1986),p
    48.
76. Ó Criomhthain (1967), op. cit., pp 162–3; Flower (1951), op. cit., p 146.
77. Enright (1986), op. cit., p 114; Ó Criomhthain (1977), op. cit., p 277.
78. Ní Guithín (1986), op. cit., p 37.
79. Idem.
80. Mac Cárthaigh (1990), op. cit., p 24. In a diary entry for September 1922 Tomás
    Ó Criomhthain describes two currachs full of of dead seals as lying 'as low in
    the water as they would be at manuring time in the spring when loaded with
    mussels'. (Enright (1986), op. cit., p 202; Ó Criomhthain (1977), op. cit., p 349.).

81. Ó Criomhthain (1977), op. cit., pp 86–7; Enright (1986), op. cit., p 15. It is not clear from the literature whether or not the shells were broken or burnt prior to their being applied to the ridges. It appears from a diary entry by Tomás Ó Criomhthain that shellfish might also be scattered on a field as a form of pre-manuring for an early crop of potatoes – see Enright (1986), op. cit., p 79; Ó Criomhthain (1977), op. cit., p 196.

82. Eilís Ní Shúilleabháin refers to the difficulty of getting this manure during the Second World War. This would indicate an increased use of this fertilizer in the intervening decades. (Ní Shúilleabháin (n.d.), op. cit., p 89, [4.4.1942].)

83. Ó Criomhthain (1977), op. cit., pp 86–7, Enright (1986), op. cit., pp 15, 202.

84. Ní Ghuithín (1986), op. cit., p 36.

85. Ibid., pp 31–2.

86. Ibid., p 37.

87. Two more cows were owned by the Protestant minister Rev. Thomas Moriarty, and a further twenty-five cows by Edward Hussey, Esq. The recorder for the Griffith Valuation states: '40 cows this Island'; – see in this connection, Séamus Ó Duilearga (1956), op. cit., pp 262–3.

88. Mac Cárthaigh (1990), op. cit., pp 24–5.

89. Ní Ghaoithín (1978), op. cit., p 81.

90. Ní Shúilleabháin (n.d.), op. cit., p 75, referring to 1938.

91. Ní Ghaoithín (1978), op. cit., p 82; Mac Conghail (1994), op. cit., pp 48–9, 58 (illustration).

92. Enright (1986), op. cit., p 52; Ó Criomhthain (1977), op. cit., pp 144–5.

93. Ó Criomhthain (1967), op. cit., pp 220–26; Flower (1951), op. cit., pp 201–7.

94. Ní Ghuithín (1978), op. cit., p 82.

95. Ní Ghuithín (1986), op. cit., p 34, refers to her mother and aunt roasting geese and turkeys. It is not clear to what extent geese and turkeys were reared on the Island. For a description of a prank played on an old man by putting the schoolmaster's goose down the chimney, see Enright (1986), op. cit., pp 89–90.

96. Feathers of seagulls, cormorants and puffins were also used for bedding – Lysaght (2000) op. cit., pp 342–55. Robin Flower in his book *The Western Island or The Great Blasket*, p 107, discusses the merits and demerits of 'mattresses stuffed with the feathers of seabirds,' as follows: 'This mattress is beautifully soft when you go to bed at night, but by morning your weight has worked through the feathers, and the hardness of the boards begins to make itself felt'.

97. Ó Criomhthain (1967), op. cit., p 264; Flower (1951), op. cit., p 243.

16

The Dutch in Shetland:
Their Influence on the History, Trade, Folklife and Lore of the Islands

VENETIA NEWALL

THE FIRST ACCOUNT SPECIFICALLY inspired by Dutch activities in Shetland was published in the mid eighteenth century by Dr John Campbell, who had spent several years in the islands. Dr Campbell, a Scot, evidently disliked the Dutchmen, an attitude not shared by the Shetlanders, but his comments are sometimes interesting. Referring to early June, he says:

> About this time the Dutch, to the number of ten or eleven hundred busses [a type of boat], have wet their nets upon the coast, which they are obliged to do against the eleventh of June, by an express act of the States-General of the United Provinces; then they come into Bressay Sound to buy stockings; they have for convoy two or three ships of war, each carrying ten or twelve guns; these ships, when they cast anchor, fire these guns as a signal for the inhabitants all round the country and isles to come in, which they accordingly do, when the Coupmen [a word of Dutch origin, with a sense akin to 'brokers'] come ashore with bags of money, and buy them all up at ten shillings per score... [They] continue fishing till the beginning of September, during which space they load sundry items, carry the fish to Holland, where it sells at an exorbitant rate... afterwards when they are served, they send to other lands all over Europe... yea, they have even the assurance to dispose of the fish at our own markets...[1]

Peter Jamieson, in his Shetland 'pen-pictures' entitled *The Viking Isles*,[2] gives a vivid description of the summer foy day at Scatsta in July 1612. Using only a reasonable amount of imagination, and basing his account on contemporary documents, he shows realistically the good-natured relations which existed between the Dutch and local people. The day ended in tragedy, which explains its mention in legal proceedings of the period, but this was coincidental to the Dutch presence. In any case, these 'foys', or festivals, tended to be rowdy events: the Dutch fair at Lerwick had to be disbanded thirteen years later. Aided by a certain amount of intelligent guess-work, Jamieson suggests the type of goods which the Dutch might have provided on these occasions – 'fine cloth, spices, snuffs, "Eastern ware", skilfully-woven baskets, tin-ware... spirits and tobacco'. With much the same method he also provides us with hints of the Dutch-English dialect which may have been spoken.

'Tinkst du dat?' a modern Lerwick man will reply, if you suggest that some of his words sound foreign. That the phrase sounds distinctly Dutch may be coincidental, but it serves as a ready reminder of the islands' former close links with the Netherlands. Certainly, while the Shetland dialects have been much adulterated with mainland Scots-English, the expression is still far from 'Do you think so?' taught at school, and the very separateness of the islands itself owes much to Dutch influence. The old photographs of Amsterdam or Antwerp, decorating local pubs and cafés fifty years ago, have faded and been replaced; now Norwegians are the most usual foreigners in the capital's streets. But centuries of contact with the Netherlands are not obliterated. Visiting the Shetland Room in Lerwick's palatial modern museum, soon after it was opened in 1966, the first map to strike the eye was by Iohannis van Keulen of Amsterdam – a curious, inverted projection, with the north coast of Scotland upside-down at the top, and then in descending order the Orcades (Orkney), Hitlandt (Shetland) and Fero (Faroe). The three outlying Shetland isles best known to the Dutch are named: Fayerhil (Fair Isle), Ielle (Yell) and Onst (Unst).

Bergen was probably the place through which the continental North Sea ports first had contact with the Northern Isles. These had been settled prior to AD 800 from Scotland and Ireland, but at about that date the Vikings arrived in all three archipelagos, the Nordreyjar as they called them. For almost five centuries, Shetland was then linked to Scandinavia, until 1195 as part of the Norse Earldom of Orkney, then for nearly two centuries, along with Faroe, as an outlying part of Norway. Through their tenure of Orkney, the Scoto-Scandinavian rulers who followed already owed allegiance to the Norwegian crown, but in 1397 this was transferred to Denmark. In 1474, shortly after the Scottish annexation, the Bishop of Orkney became lessee under this new suzerainty, but only until 1488, when the former overlordship effectively ended.

Hamburg and Bremen merchants were trading with Bergen by the mid twelfth century, and they probably also sailed to the Northern Isles. Certainly, Shetland traders must have dealt with them at Bergen. To mark the importance of Shetland commerce, one of the harbour entrances there is called Hjeltefjord, after Hjaltland. It means 'High Land', the Viking name for the islands, van Keulen used a version on his map. The document providing evidence of the earliest Hanseatic trade, is dated 1567; and some of the individuals it mentions had been connected with Shetland since 1501 and their ancestors before them.

In fact the Danes, at least since 1470, had been diligently fostering

Hanseatic links with Iceland, still further to the north, mainly to counter English encroachments in the North Sea area. On the long and difficult journey from the continent, through storm-swept seas, the three intermediary archipelagos must often have provided essential shelter. England and Denmark had been at war for two years, and sporadic skirmishing between the English and Hansamen in the far north continued for the next six decades. Between 1511 and 1514, English vessels are recorded plundering Hansa ships on the northern route, but the Hanseatic merchants, mostly from Bremen and Hamburg, were not daunted and, especially after 1520, pressed on with increased sailings to Iceland. In summer 1532, a Hansa force of 280 men destroyed the English base there, though it was another twenty-seven years before the Danes, with Scottish help, dislodged them from Vestermannaeyjar.

Anglo-Danish rivalry was not continuous, and in 1518 and 1522 Christian II was trying to pawn Iceland to Henry VIII. Christian was following his earlier namesake, who ceded Orkney, Shetland and his nominal sovereignty over the Hebrides and Man, to the Scots in a similar pledge half a century earlier. Henry refused the offer; so did Amsterdam, Antwerp and the Waterlandische towns of north Holland in 1517 and 1519. But, even the offer of such a formal link must have fixed the Dutch focus firmly on the north. And from 1523 to 1531 Christian II, whose claim to the Danish throne received support in Lübeck and the north, lived as an exile in the Netherlands. Effective Danish control had lapsed, but Denmark was to lay claim to Orkney and Shetland for another two centuries.

The official pro-Hanseatic attitude contrasted strongly with isolationism of the early fifteenth century. In 1413 the Danish Crown forbade Icelanders to deal with foreigners, apart from their customary trade contacts; four years later Bergen merchants banned direct Hanseatic contacts with Orkney, Shetland and the Faroes. A complaint in 1514, almost a century later, that Hamburgers, Bremers, Amsterdamers and other Dutch merchants, were trading with Shetland and the Faroes fell on deaf ears. James V of Scotland complained in 1540 that Flemings, Frieslanders and Hollanders were fishing too close inshore, but met with no greater success.

Hanseatic discrimination drove the Dutch north. Until 1384 they, the Icelanders, English, Normans, Flemings, Frieslanders and others, participated in the Scania fisheries, and the great annual Hanseatic salting enterprise, which brought an army of fish gutters from across Europe. Lübeck, doyen of Hanseatic cities, owned the Lüneberg salt mines, which provided the essential second ingredient of salt herring. But the outsiders began importing their own salt, *baiesalt* from south-western France, picked up before the journey north to the Hanseatic fish-wharves.

By 1384 and the Hanseatic legislation against immigrant labour, the Netherlanders were learning the basic salting technique. The fish is gutted, and its gills and entrails, except for the soft roe, are discarded; then it is barrelled in brine. They gradually built up a fleet of fast, deep-water fishing vessels, the *haringbuizen* first mentioned in 1405, which contrasted with the Hansa's shallow-water craft. These developments foreshadowed the great Dutch fishing industry, and its concentration on the North Sea. It seems the northern isles were soon recognised as an invaluable shelter and revictualling post, even as a factory station.

Bergen's fortunes reached a low ebb at this time; it was sacked in 1394 by the Vitalien Brethren, pirates from Gotland. But *Friedenschiffe* were organised by the Hansa, with help from the Teutonic Knights, to see their North Sea catch safely into Bergen, and the deadline for their arrival was Martinmas (11 November). Thirty-four years later the pillage was repeated by a 'Dutch' buccaneer, Bartolomäus Voet. He was killed in 1435 by Hanseatic forces, but Bergen was now reduced to a satellite of Lübeck.

The exact date is unknown, but the Netherlanders were well established in Bergen's fishing grounds before this; the Scots had attacked Dutch fishing boats in the North Sea in 1410. Their large and efficient fleet went far afield at the end of the fishing season, delivering the catch throughout much of northern Europe. They broke the Hanseatic stipulation that Baltic deliveries must be in exchange for wheat bought by Hansamen further east, and soon had a larger corner in the west German trade: North Sea herrings were taken to Deventer, where a huge fish market grew up, and from there by lighter to Cologne for further sale.

In the old records and in some of the Shetland place-names there is often confusion as to the origin of the merchants. Citizens of the Netherlands, though occasionally described as Hollanders, are often indiscriminately classed with the Hansa people as Dutch, a word deriving from *deutsch*, which had not yet acquired its modern meaning. For example, a seventeenth-century list naming ten 'Dutch merchants' in Shetland, describes five as 'Breamers' (from Bremen), three as 'Hamburgers'. The two remaining, Baivn Hultrop and Allexander Joly, may or may not have been Hollanders – no details are provided.

Scottish influence in Shetland did not become apparent until the concluding decades of the fifteenth century. In 1468-69 both Orkney and Shetland fell to the sovereignty of James III in pawn against the failure to pay Margaret of Norway's dowry. The value put on Shetland was 8,000 Florins; it has never been redeemed. If the sum were offered today, an interesting legal position might arise. Scotland annexed the islands in 1472 and largely abolished the traditional Norwegian system of government in 1564 but these were arbitrary acts. Even today the law of the northern isles differs slightly from Scottish practice.

The new status of the islands made little difference to the Dutch. If anything, it strengthened their position. Three hundred miles from Edinburgh, the islands were remote from the new centres of power. 'We got nothing from Scotland but dear meal and drunken ministers' was a popular saying, and although at the end of the fifteenth century the Fowde of Shetland, Sir David Sinclair, commanded the Palace Guard at Bergen, links with Norway also dwindled. The field lay open for continental traders and Dutch (Hollander) fishermen. Oddly enough, at the turn of the same century the short sea link between the inshore islands and Scotland was also in the hands of a Dutchman, Jan de Groot, who ran the ferry over the Pentland Firth to Orkney. He is credited with the construction of a curious octagonal house; the foundations still exist. The story goes that he willed his land to be divided equally between his eight offspring – which implies that he was influenced by the traditional Norse laws of the islands – and the building was planned to avoid disputes between them. It had eight doors, and contained an eight-sided table, so that each could enter through a front door, and sit at the head of the board. The place is still called John O'Groats after him, and is well known as the *ultima Thule* of Great Britain (*ultima Thule* being an ancient term to describe the remotest place on earth). Shetlanders dispute this, claiming for Lerwick's motto *Dispecta est Thule*.

Thule it must have seemed to the Dutch sailors, but the richness of the waters around its coast made it an ideal fishing ground and their technique for curing herrings enabled them to exploit it fully. By the mid sixteenth century, barely more than a century after the trade became well established so far north, anything from 500 to 2000 Dutch *busses (haringbuizen)* were engaged in it annually. Some were over 80 tons, with crews of fifteen to twenty men. They spent most of the summer around the islands; a favourite harbour was Bressay Sound, or Buss Haven as they called it, to the east of Shetland mainland. In 1600 the seat of government was established at Scalloway, six miles away on the west coast. Soon Scalloway market wives were coming over the mountains to trade with the Dutchmen. The sailors met them on the high ground above the Sound, and it became Hollanders Knowe (hill), as it is today.

The architecture of Scalloway castle, supposedly cemented with a mixture of blood, egg and lime, shows Dutch influence. As Eric Linklater says: 'both Muness and Scalloway preserve, with an heroic obstinacy, something of the elegance in the design to which they were built',[3] even though both are now ruined, and Muness partly demolished. Earl Patrick built Scalloway, using forced labour, and Muness, constructed on Unst for the Earl's kinsman, Lawrence Bruce, dates from 1598, the same period. Dr Douglas Simpson plausibly suggested that 'nothing is more likely, than that Earl Patrick should have lent his own master mason to Lawrence Bruce for building Muness', though the reverse may be true, since Bruce had long been settled in Shetland when Patrick Stewart arrived, and his castle could be slightly earlier.

It would be rash to assume that the master mason was Dutch. Scalloway's gun turrets, with their supposedly Dutch influence, and imported Dutch brick at Muness are the only real evidence. But there is a tradition that Muness was destroyed by one Hakki of Dikkeram, in the seventeenth century. Dikkeram sounds like a Dutch name deriving from Dijk-van Dijk, Dijkman, Dickema, Dikker, Dikkerboom, and many others, which still exist today, while Hackrey is an old local expression for a tough or uncouth person. As a first name, of course, Hakki usually derives from the Norse, Hakon. Sandy Breamer is less problematical: no doubt its origin was Alexander from Bremen. According to a local legend, he outwitted a baffling individual called Black Eric. Half-wizard, half-rogue, Eric's speciality was sheep rustling. He used a magic sea horse called Tangie, and in his many battles with Breamer, owed his escape at least once to Tangie's intervention. Breamer got the better of Eric, but Tangie lifted up both, whirling them around until his master's opponent fainted. But eventually, Breamer overcame his enemy, and Eric was flung from the top of Fitful Head, where he lived in a cave.

The earliest Breamer graves on the islands are from the sixteenth century. They commemorate two men who died towards the end of the century, when Bremen was consolidating its influence in the North Sea. Bremers, and the men of Hamburg and Deventer, had contested Lübeck's influence in the north, and at about this time they gained the ascendancy at Bergen. Had it not been for disasters in the 1570s, during the Dutch revolt against Philip II, Deventer, with its vast wealth founded on North Sea fishing would probably have taken the lead.

The two Shetland Breamers, whose memorials tell us their names, were settled in Unst, less than 400 miles from the Arctic Circle, the Onst of van Keulen's map. Segebad Detken died in 1573, Hinrik Segelcken in 1585, and they were buried in Lund churchyard. From contemporary documents we know that Detken came to Shetland soon after 1520, and the inscription on his tombstone confirms this: he 'carried on business in this country for fifty-two years'.

Despite their preference for Bressay, Netherlanders must have been usual visitors to Unst, long before their modern herring fleet used to congregate around Baltasound, prior to 1914. An account of 1716 records that Danish – eventually Norn, the local pre-Scottish language – was widely used. It adds that several Unst islanders also knew 'English, Norse and Hollands'. A report from a few years earlier speaks of the Unstmen fishing in small boats, four or six men together, and selling their catch to the six continental merchants. It seems curious to read of this cosmopolitan scene in so remote a spot, 200 miles from the nearest Scottish town. The island's name, dating from Viking times, is Norn for 'nearest' – Norn was known there, it is sometimes claimed, until about 1850 – but implies only a relative proximity, for it is nearly as far from Bergen. But there is a belief on the island that Bergen is easily accessible, to the *Finnmen* at least. These people, living on in Shetland in the form of seals, are believed to be the original, pre-Celtic inhabitants. They are able to cross from Unst to Bergen and back between sunset and sunrise, rowing a distance of nine miles with each *warp* (oar-stroke).

Herman Perk of Papa Stour, who features in a popular tale about these *Finns*, was probably a Dutchman, or of Dutch origin, though Herman is also the name of a giant on Unst. One day Herman Perk was stranded on an outlying skerry. A seal rescued him on condition that Perk returned a skin that he had at home. He kept his word and took the sealskin to the shore, where his rescuer's wife was waiting in the form of a beautiful woman. She put on the skin, resumed the shape of a seal, and swam off to Finnmark beside her husband.

Papa Stour, where this took place, was one of several smaller islands frequented by 'Dutch' merchants, ready to brave the forbidding surroundings for such meagre return as they could obtain. Not long after Segebad Detken died on Unst, the Scottish historian George Buchanan described Yell, to the south, as 'so uncouth a place that no creature can live there, except such as are born there. A Breamer merchant, however, it is said, resides here, who imports all foreign merchandise which they require and supplies them abundantly'. Later there were two more merchants: one settled permanently. Perk, with his Dutch name, was probably a resident of Papa Stour, fifteen miles west of Yell, off the opposite side of the mainland.

Beyond this, precise details of foreign traders on the island are lacking, though Papa Stour's Dutch booth is mentioned in written sources, and a little lake called Dutch Loch is thought possibly to mark a former foreign community. Richard Wolfram[4] suggests that the famous local sword dance, has counterparts in Germany – an interesting theory. It was still danced well into the nineteenth century, with straightened iron hoops from herring barrels serving as swords, and in 1892 was consciously revived, though apparently still in the true style. M. Macleod Banks gives a description,[5] as well as Jamieson[6] provides music, together with a shortened account.

Papa Island, further south, has a ruined church, once used by the inhabitants of many small islands round about; in it was a bell and copper basin, given by the merchant Adolphus Westermann, 'who resided some time in this countrey' – certainly from 1680 to 1693. Bujrra nearby and Fair Isle, twenty-five miles off south Shetland, at about that time had Hansa booths, and Johan Dirik Buhrmeister was the trader on Whalsay, off the east coast.

There was also a merchant named Geert Hemelingk, who had achieved notoriety when his ship, the *Pelican*, used by the defeated Bothwell in his flight, was implicated in a murder in 1602. A tragedy of the same period, probably concerning a Dutch sailor rather than one of the traders, is still remembered in Fetlar, the next island. A Burgastoun man, returning home one evening from fishing, found his wife and children all lying dead at home, with wounds on heads and bodies. No culprit was ever traced, and the only clue was a single 'foreign clog' floating in the sea, so it was assumed that the attacker had also perished. Later, another disaster brought Dutch gold to Fetlar; the *Vandela*, said to be from Amsterdam, went down offshore with the equivalent of £20,000 on board; some of it was recovered by local men.

According to another tradition, 3 million guilders and several chests of gold were lost from the 'Carmelan', a Dutch East Indiaman, the *Kermerlant*, which was wrecked off the Out Skerries in 1664. A handsome earthenware gin bottle from the cargo is now in Lerwick museum, and the men of the Skerries salvaged enough to make themselves drunk for three days, or so the story goes. But only four of the crew were rescued.

Bressay, the third sizeable island off the east coast, after Unst and Yell, provided perfect shelter for the Dutch fleet on stormy days. The long sound between it and mainland Shetland is comparatively calm in the strongest gale. But it was to be the populous mainland, not to Bressay, that the Dutchmen turned for trade and entertainment. However, there is an interesting tomb in the abandoned Church of St Mary's, near the east coast of the island. It is the grave of Captain Claes Bruyn of the *Amboina*, which put into Bressay Sound on 24 August 1636, on its way from Surat in India. Many of the crew were ill, and three days later the captain was dead. His tombstone, with the arms of his home county, Waterland in Holland, is the finest of several inside the crumbling ruins.

Another seventeenth century burial is worth noting. It is of a fairly well-to-do man, possibly a small trader, whose body was dug out of a peat bog at Gunnister in 1951. His clothes and belongings were intact, including a two stiver coin of Overijjssel (1681), another from Nymwegen (1690), and a Swedish one-fifth ore piece. The reason for the man's death is not apparent, but, whoever he was, he lived at a time when the Dutch and Hanseatic presence in the islands was still noticeable. Throughout the Mainland, the Hansa merchants had their booths, from Hillswick, the northernmost village, to Bigton in the south, and from Hambrough Haven (Hamburg Harbour) in the east to Sandness in the west, where the little lake at Boosta is still called *De Böd Loch* (The Booth Lake). Though the name has not survived, another inlet mentioned in 1711 was 'called the Dutch pool, because the Dutch and Hamburgh Merchants used to lye there and make merchant Fishes'. The same account says of the islanders, 'besides the Herrings... they are constantly employed in taking Cod and Ling, which they sell to the Hamburgers, Bremeres, Lubecquers' and others, who in exchange supplied 'Hooks and Lines for the taking of Cod and Ling, Nets for the taking of Herring, Brandie and strong Waters of all Sorts; Mead, Strong Beer, Bisket, Wheatmeal, Ryemeal, Barley, Salt, Tobacco, Fruits of all Sorts, Monmouth Caps, and the Courser sort of Cloth and Linen'. Apart from the professional merchants, sailors from the Netherlands brought cheese, barley, peas, salt and, no doubt, spirits; but the only beer to be had in the islands (1701) was 'Hamburgh beer, both strong and small... to be had in plenty, tho at a good rate of 6 sh to 8 sh our pint'. Another delicacy was the 'wheat bread the Hamburgers bring in the month of May... that which they call Cringel Bread'. In texture this is not unlike a Pretzel, but it is ring-shaped.

The Hansamen who came to the islands seasonally usually stayed from early May to the end of summer. During Bergen's supremacy, the fishing season may have begun and ended slightly later, since the actual return of the fleet was awaited at Martinmas. In Dutch times, and practically throughout the seventeenth century, up to 2000 or more boats from the Netherlands, most of them *busses*, came to Bressay Sound. Some accounts place the figure considerably lower, but by any reckoning there were large numbers of Dutchmen in Shetland, and the story that, when all the boats were moored across the sound, it was possible to walk from the Mainland to Bressay, almost three quarters of a mile at Lerwick, is famous.

King James VI, who joined Scotland and England in a personal union in 1603, tried to control the trade, but this did not happen until the reign of his son, Charles I. Under James's rule the Dutch continued to come, often spending weeks or even months in the sound before the season officially opened, and neither he nor his predecessors succeeded in extracting from them the 10 per cent royalty which many thought reasonable. They merely increased their protection in the form of armed vessels – one account speaks of 1500 herring *busses* and a smaller fleet of line fishermen, accompanied by twenty ships of war. By this time Flanders and Zeeland had largely dropped out of the trade, now mainly based on Hoorn, Enkhuizen and De Rijp in West Friesland, though Rotterdam and the smaller ports around the Meuse estuary were also represented. Not only Shetland, but Phayrillt (Fair Isle) and, to a lesser extent, Orkney, were swarming with Dutch fishermen at this period.

Hoorn had a certain claim to primacy in the trade, for the first great herring net was made there in 1416. The actual Dutch curing process was devised by a Zeeland man, thirty-one years earlier. But, as the seventeenth century progressed, an ever-increasing proportion of the catch was channelled through Enkhuizen, and later Rotterdam. By 1630 the total import, practically all from the North Sea, was 13 million gallons of barrelled herring, of which about 10.5 million gallons were re-exported. The trade was worth 10 million florins, and a consistently high-quality product resulted from the many Dutch municipal laws governing its conduct. Processing factories on the Dutch mainland often repacked and preserved the imported fish, as the rough and ready methods employed in Shetland and elsewhere were not always enough to ensure the required standard. Vinegar and seasoning added to the mixture also improved the flavour.

The customary trade-sign of the fish seller was a biblical scene, the miraculous draught of fishes, and the merchants were organised in a powerful guild. The smoked-fish trade had its own guild at Amsterdam. Hoorn, with its eclipse as a fishing centre, became influential in the whaling industry, and the headquarters of the Northern Company was set up in its Hoofdtoren, a beautiful building of 1573. Amsterdam launched the first Dutch whaler in 1612, sixteen years after William Barents's discovery of Spitzbergen on his last voyage, after sailing from the same port. The Northern Company was founded in 1614 to exploit the rich whale fisheries revealed by his journey, and ships from Enkhuizen, Delft and Zaandam joined the fleet.

Eventually Amsterdam, Bremen and Hamburg became the chief whaling bases, and Frieslanders from all parts of the territory – especially the islands off the Dutch, East Frisian, Oldenburg and Holstein coasts – became the mainstay of the crews. In 1634, the French authorities forbade Basque participation in the whale hunt, as mercenary sailors of the Dutch, and within the next four decades the Holstein Frieslanders alone were providing 4000 crew members. A high proportion of the remainder came from the long chain of islands between Texel and Wangeroog. To this day a dialect survives among the elderly on one or two of the islands, in which Frisian is interlaced with English and German words – a relic of whaling days, and reminiscent of the fictitious language devised by Jamieson.

The Frieslanders celebrated one of their greatest annual festivals on *Piadersdai* (21 February). Traditionally 22 February is when St Peter throws a warm stone into the water, ending winter. But in Friesland the occasion used to be marked by great hilltop bonfires; the people danced and sang round them. Until the seventeenth century, a pigeon-Latin chant was used on the remoter islands: *O Jova tuta nei, A vi avoca nei* – 'Jupiter protect me, and guard me from danger'. This is of slight, though coincidental, interest, since the same date was observed at Sandwick in Orkney, until the eighteenth century. Due to the 1752 calendar change it was celebrated on 3 March. No record of any similar event survives in Shetland, and it was, in any case, simply marked as an additional 'Lord's Day', with abstinence from work. This, so it was said, expressed veneration of St Peter, to whom Sandwick parish church was dedicated.

As soon as the festival was over, the Frieslanders set off for Amsterdam or the German ports, for recruitment into the whaling fleet, and within a month many of them were in Shetland, en route northwards. The season lasted until July. The Northern Company ceased to exist in 1642, and no effective means of controlling the industry was ever enforced. This is why the Spitsbergen whale fisheries were exhausted comparatively quickly.

Charles I finally forced the Dutch to comply with the fixed herring season, beginning with Johnsmas (24 June) each year. An annual tribute was also agreed; a real innovation, since Johnsmas was the technical opening date. Many of the boats seem to have arrived early, but they waited in the sound, and the limits of the season were not infringed. In fact, although they were technically allowed to continue until Martinmas, in practice many did not fish in Shetland waters for much beyond two months.

The tribute paid in the first year was £30,000, some sign of the trade's importance to the Netherlands; but if suggestions that the Shetland catch was really worth £3 million are correct, it was a royalty of only 1 per cent.

Despite clashes between French warships and the Dutch men-of-war escorting the *busses*, fishing continued unabated. Another battle, this time with the English navy, is still commemorated in the name Hollanders Grave, near Hillswick. After a bloody fight, a Dutch ship, *Het Wapen van Rotterdam*, was overpowered, and many of the casualties were buried on shore alongside. However, there was a Dutch revenge; in 1673 the fort built by Cromwell's men at what is now Lerwick, was destroyed by the Dutch navy. Later it was repaired and embellished with a Dutch cannon recovered from Lerwick harbour in 1922, part of the armaments of two Dutch men-of-war sunk in 1640 by Dunkirk pirates. The Flemish port was ruled from 1583 by the Dukes of Parma and the Spaniards, and it became a buccaneers' haven, even after the restoration of French sovereignty in 1646.

Larwyc, the name given on van Keulen's map, was an old Viking word. One of its earlie spellings, Leirvik, means 'Clay Creek', a depressing title first recorded in 1263. Hakon, King of Norway, and his 200 galleys, anchored there on the way to the Battle of Largs, where he was defeated and mortally wounded by the Scots. He died at Kirkwall in Orkney on the way home. Four hundred years later Scandinavian influence in the islands reached its lowest ebb. In 1662, Frederick III of Denmark confirmed the sale of Norway's last estates there to Scottish Lairds. Held until 1661 by the 'Lordis of Norroway' – who were really the Provosts of Bergen Cathedral – they were considerable properties on the south-east mainland.

At that time Lerwick, on its foggy, northern shore, appeared to be embarking on a life of merriment. The place owed its origin, in the early seventeenth century, to a few stone and wooden buildings put up by the Dutch to store their sails and tackle, as well as salt and provisions, no doubt with some resident watchmen. Around this a hamlet evidently grew up. The Sheriff, Sir John Buchanan, a God-fearing Scot, later ordered it to be burned to the ground, on account of 'the great abominatioun and wickedness committit yearlie by the Hollanderis and cuntrie people'. The town's reputation was evidently due to its popularity with local girls. They came from Scalloway and all around, ostensibly to sell 'sockis and otheris necessaris'. Instead they were accused of engaging in 'manifold adultrie and fornicatioun' with the foreigners.

That there were relationships, both romantic and of a less savoury kind, between the young sailors and Shetland girls goes almost without saying. But Netherlands historians tend to credit their own seafaring men with good morals. A contemporary French commentator, writing in about 1670, paints them as stalwart but rather unemotional men: 'Most of their life is passed at sea, away from the everyday world, and denied the practice of any refinements, save only that of patience, which wind and tempest give them ample opportunity to employ. They are certainly brave, yet they give the impression of a bravery which is passive, not active.'

Whether lace-knitting, a typically Shetland craft, reached the islands by way of favours brought by the sailors to please the local girls, or simply from lace imported as an item of trade, is impossible to say. It was probably established there during the eighteenth century, and the designs used are from Flemish and other continental patterns, as well as Madeira – and, later, from the Scottish mainland. This separates the whole style from the mainstream of Shetland's beautiful and elaborate knitting craft, which is Norse in origin and conception.

In 1665 an English fleet visited Lerwick, and the report they brought back mentions only a tiny settlement, with no church. But by the end of the century, 200 to 300 families had moved in, and a church was under construction. It was during this period that the *lodberries*, concealed loading places for unshipping cargo, were installed. They remain an unusual feature of the town, which has many buildings formerly used for storing illicit imports. *Lodberries* are traditionally associated with the Dutch trade, and the local belief is that secret passages lead from many of them to the quay-side warehouses and cellars.

In 1712, 120 years before any Shetlander received the right to vote in British parliamentary elections, a duty was imposed on foreign salt which was an irreparable blow to the foreign traders on whom the islands so heavily depended, particularly to the herring salters. This was soon after the Act of Union between Scotland and England. The Rev. Hugh Leigh, minister of Bressay until 1714, was concerned that trade in the islands had 'greatly decayed... At this day only a few Hamburgers and Bremers use a small Trafficking in it'. While the majority of foreign merchants ceased to come, commerce kept its mainly continental orientation, but it was taken over by the local Lairds. Continental coinage continued to circulate, chiefly from the Netherlands, Scandinavia, Hamburg, Bremen and Lübeck, but also from as far afield as Danzig. Perhaps a Lübeck merchant still had his booth at Sandness, since these coins are mentioned specially on the west mainland. In 1727, an exchange rate for the mark 'lübick', against the Scottish pound, was fixed by Magnus Henderson, Laird of Bressay. Henderson claimed descent from a member of the entourage of Haakon V, a fourteenth-century king of Norway (including Shetland). It was during his reign that the Norwegian court moved from Bergen to Oslo, edged out by privileges granted to the Hansa in the old capital five years before he came to the throne.

Henderson dealt with a Hamburg merchant called Robert Barclay; perhaps he belonged to the well-known Scoto-German Barclay family. Notable in the eastern Baltic, their fame peaked in Prince Barclay de Tolly, the Russians' Commander-in-Chief against Napoleon. Henderson became prominent in the continental trade soon after 1712, and Bressay, along with Busta on the north mainland, played a leading role. Dutch merchants were established at Busta until the mid eighteenth century – Brea, at the head of Busta Voe (fjord) and nearby Scatsta had traders' booths in years gone by.

The new duties, and their strict enforcement, provided the *raison d'être* of the *lodberries*. Constructed as they are, it was, if not easy, at least possible for goods smuggled into the sound by sailors to be unloaded secretly from small boats. Much evidently got past the excise officers. With many Hanseatic merchants gone, and the rest of trade virtually a monopoly of the Lairds, Dutch fishermen had greater openings for doing business with the islanders. Lerwick, which had grown up exclusively around the Great Fishery, as the annual expedition of the Hollanders was called, now became even more dependent. Apart from onshore relaxation, the Shetlanders could still offer the sailors cottage-industry products, formerly bartered with the merchants – 'sokis and otheris necessaris' which, despite Sir John Buchanan's accusation, had indeed been marketed. Stockings, gloves, garters, and a coarse cloth known as Wadmell sold well; so did feathers, seal-skins and hides. At this time, mainly as an aspect of their whaling interests, the Dutch were the main suppliers of leather to most of the continent – Germany, Austria, Hungary, France and, of course, the Low Countries.

The sailors also used Shetland to provision their ships. Tallow and meat could be had; oil and butter were sometimes available, though much went in rent to the Lairds. Records for one particular year in the latter seventeenth century mention the Lordship of Shetland selling 15 tons of butter to Hansa cities, as well as 146 barrels of oil, and this seems to have been an annual export. Bog butter, plentiful in Shetland at an earlier period, and made in Ireland until the end of the eighteenth century, was probably available. As a way of preserving their butter surplus for peasants, it must have been ideal for ships' supplies. Ordinary butter is enclosed in a skin or barrel, and buried in a peat bog. Dug up after a lengthy period, its flavour was distinctive – but not, apparently, unpleasant – and it was thoroughly cured. Forgotten barrels still occasionally come to light, during turf-cutting for fuel.

The lairds took over the local herring trade, and, in exchange for goods brought from the continent, salted most of the catch for export. As a result, the Dutch were able to sell a proportion of their catch to the islanders, in addition to the cheese and cereals which they had always provided. A description of 1766, displayed in the Shetland room at Lerwick, stresses that the town could not exist without the Dutch fishermen; 800 to 900 of their boats were still coming regularly, and six years later, Rev. Low, passing through Shetland, spoke disapprovingly of the 'many thousand barrels caught annually by the Dutch Doggers and others'[7] – a dogger is a type of two-masted fishing vessel from Holland. The same account adds that country folk flocked to the shore to sell the Dutchmen 'loads of coarse stockings' – the most popular item – and 'gloves, night-caps, rugs, and some few articles of fresh provisions'. The stockings sold at six to eight pence the pair, the rugs from sixteen shillings to two guineas (forty-two shillings), according to quality. 'The rugs were a sort of carpet stuff, used sometimes for coverlids for beds, and seemed peculiar to Shetland. They were made of different coloured worsteds, sewed on a coarse ground'.

Already the Great Fishery, its peak some 125 years earlier, had declined considerably since the turn of the century. In 1702, the French attacked the Dutch escort off Fair Isle, and soon after, sank 150 *busses* in Bressay sound. Twenty years later, the attack was repeated, despite a chain stretching from Lerwick to the opposite shore on Bressay, a Dutch precaution to exclude marauders. The end rings on both sides have lasted to the present time, but it was no protection against the French. And so the number of ships journeying north began to dwindle.

'Greenland voyagers' became rarer visitors to the islands. *Het Nieuwe Land*, as Barents had called Spitsbergen on his discovery in 1596, had become so over-fished that few whales were left. Others were partly responsible, but Netherlanders were the main offenders – in 1697 121 Dutch ships were recorded at Klokbay in Spitsbergen, together with fifty-four from Hamburg and fifteen from Bremen. The Frieslanders, a notable part of all these crews, had two vessels in the north, whalers from Emden. An average ship of this type was 100-130 feet long, and up to 32 feet in width.

While Shetland figures as an intermediary staging-post on these voyages, the northern base was established first on T'veere Eylundt (Bear Island), and later transferred to Jan Mayen, in the Greenland Sea, and Amsterdam Island in Spitsbergen proper. At this time it was thought that each was an appendage of Greenland itself – hence the popular name for the whale hunt. 'Whale voyaging', as it was also called, attracted about 14,000 Netherlands sailors, and a sizeable town grew up on Amsterdam Island to cater for them and to process the catch. Smeerenburg (Blubber Town) was predominantly a summer settlement, with shops and inns conducting a lively trade during the season; during some winters, a permanent population remained to look after the buildings: many were factories for processing whale and seal.

With the whales more or less gone, this activity disappeared, and the attentions of British and continental whalers shifted further to the west, to the Atlantic and the waters around Greenland itself. Shetland ceased to be so obvious a port of call en route, though many English and Scottish whalers continued to put in there, if only to make their crews up to strength. Many Shetlanders were by now expert whale fishermen, and ships from the British mainland often made up anything from a quarter to a third of their crew in the islands. In 1800, when the Norn language had already disappeared from virtually the whole archipelago, the entire population of Lerwick could still speak Dutch. Indeed, sixty years later it is still recorded in common knowledge among the local working classes.

Continental currencies remained as common as Scottish until the 1830s when Danish predominated. This may have been because the lairds, devoting their attention to the cod and ling fisheries, had adopted a suitable type of Scandinavian boat. They were called *Haf* boats, and were shipped from Norway in sections for assembly in the islands. During the 1820s, a Lerwick trader brought over some Dutchmen so that local men could learn their herring expertise, but it was unsuccessful. Throughout this part of the century, only three Shetland boats were active in the herring trade.

In 1837, however, a Shetland Fishing Company was founded, with a view to breaking the lairds' monopoly. The commercial connection with Hamburg had lapsed, largely because of disturbed times on the continent, and Leith took its place. In due course, boat-building was taken up locally, and gradually the *Haf* trade came to a close. New managers meant new markets, and the whole nature of the herring business began to change. Through time its British character became more pronounced, though mainland and Manx boats still outnumbered those from the islands. As a result, until quite recently, a seasonal influx of Irish herring gutters was needed, hence the large Catholic church at Lerwick, surprising in a stronghold of northern Protestantism. The Faroese also became involved in the trade. They had only learned herring-curing from the Shetlanders in 1839, and until the present century their fishing industry was still underdeveloped. Their smacks used to pick up Shetland salt-fish from the western coast and carry it to Iberia, the Mediterranean and North Africa, a market which had formerly been a Dutch domain. But the Dutch covered much of the northern continent, and even supplied Brazil.

In the nineteenth century, Scotsmen, mostly lowlander – 'Ooterals' or 'Scottish adventurers' as the Shetlanders called them arrived in the islands in greater numbers. The population, which had been about 10,000 in 1600, rose to 32,000 by 1861, and while there had, of course, been some local natural increase, there was now considerable human influence to induce closer ties with the Scottish mainland. This period also saw the last recorded appearance of the Ranselmen at Lunnasting, the only outstanding evidence of former Norse rule. They were a kind of inquisitor, with authority over suspected thieves and petty offenders, and were last seen in 1836; later only certain idiosyncratic laws remained to set Shetland apart. It must have seemed as though Shetland's special character, dependent on its continental and Scandinavian connections, was bound to disappear.

This did not happen, chiefly because of a revival in the Dutch herring trade. The herring lugger was invented in 1866, and soon 200 of these vessels, mainly from Vlaardingen, were making the journey north. By 1878, this figure is said to have doubled, and boats from Katwijk, Scheveningen and other places along the Holland coast were commonplace at Lerwick. Many crew members were recruited from Marken or other places further afield, and old people in these former Dutch fishing villages still show off treasured souvenirs from their Shetland journeys. Shetland was no mere unknown dot on the map; in 1904, it received a ceremonial visit from a German Imperial fleet. The same year, 800,000 barrels of herring were exported.

As before, the fishing season began with 24 June, and lasted until late autumn. When Queen Victoria's Diamond Jubilee was celebrated in 1897, 500 Dutchmen were present; at the same period the Rev. van der Valk of Scheveningen, who twice accompanied the Dutch fishermen, preached in Lerwick church. A hospital-ship, the *De Hoop,* used to sail with the fleet; as late as 1919, it comprised 600 sailing and sixty-six steam luggers.

Many of the inhabitants, older people especially, continued to speak Dutch. Even Orkney, where Netherlands' influence had been less pronounced, maintained some ties. In the 1860s, it is said, smuggled Hollands gin could be bought over the counter in a Kirkwall bank, and the local lairds traded in contraband direct with the continent. Private-still whisky, much of it apparently brewed on Stroma, which is now chiefly famous for its numerous attractive postage stamps, seems to have been a useful export commodity. In Shetland, at least, barter of local produce for Dutch gin imported by the fishermen continued well into the present century.

In the 1880s a winter festival, Up-Helly-A, regarded locally as the relic of ancient sun worship, took place in Lerwick, as indeed it had long before.[8] But now it was formalised into an annual nationalist demonstration. Today the black raven flag of the Vikings is hoisted each January, a galley is burned in re-enactment of ancient funeral rites, and a patriotic song, 'The Norseman's Home', is sung. The sentiment expressed, of course, is not Dutch. But this does not obscure the fact that, over 500 or more years, Dutch trade kept the country alive; had it not done so, there would by now be no separate historical identity to celebrate. In the mid-nineteenth century, when Shetland's population was over 30,000, the Faroes' was under 5000. If the Dutch fleet had sought herring further north, these figures might well have been reversed, and Shetland, which has not as yet shared the twentieth century Faroese revival, might scarcely be inhabited by now.

After the First World War, Dutchmen became rarer visitors, especially as a result of the depression, and other recent circumstances have been unkind. The population today – 22,522 – is little above half what it was 100 years ago; the rural total is back to the 1600 figure, when no towns existed. Lerwick, in contrast, has never been larger, with a population of 7336; and has been transformed into a capital, with a considerable administrative population and engineers connected with North Sea oil-drilling, it inflates the total. In the Faroes, where fishing has prospered, the opposite has happened. The inhabitants now exceed 35,000, and Shetland delegations visit Torshavn to study what should be done. And indeed they must, for the small islands are already all deserted; Foula, remotest of the larger ones, scarcely has three dozen inhabitants – at the beginning of the century it had 222. Forsaken houses, abandoned farms, rotting shells of fishing boats lying beside dead wharves; these are the monuments to a once active community.

In this sometimes forlorn, decaying atmosphere, the Dutch are not entirely forgotten. On the contrary, they are sadly remembered, symbolic of flourishing times when the islands were busy and full of life. As long as the *Haf* fishing prospered, with the Lammas Foy to bring the season to an end, the Dutch *krook*, with its contents of Hollands gin, was an essential part of the spread. Every Lerwicker likes to tell of the time when you could walk across the sound to Bressay on the Dutchmen's boats, and older people treasure faded local postcards, proving that Dutch fishermen's costume was once part of the everyday Shetland scene. But now Norwegian, not Dutch, is second language in the town. In the June 1975 referendum on whether to remain part of the European Community, Shetlanders echoed their Norwegian cousins across the North Sea, who had earlier voted against membership (for Shetland, the result was 43 per cent for and 56 per cent against). Apart from the Hebrides, one of the two other special Island Authorities in modern Scotland, Shetland was the only British region to do so and, as the BBC remarked on the following day, so demonstrated 'its sturdy independence of the rest of the country'. With the Hebrides it certainly shared special anxieties about continental over-fishing of its waters, but the consciousness of the old Norse link is unique.

In fact, not only were various Norwegian organisations based in Shetland during the Second World War – the fleet at Scalloway, the underground movement at Lunnasting, and a secret radio at Binna Ness – but the majority of fishing vessels putting into the harbours today are Scandinavian. They far outnumber even British ships, and only on Whalsay and Burra is Shetland's own fishing industry still really active. The shop signs are in Scandinavian and Faroese, as well as English; and prices, too, are often given in kroner. At the Seamen's Club, notices are in these languages, along with German and Russian, though the Russians – many of them based around Königsberg (Kaliningrad) seldom land. But, alas, nothing is now in Dutch, and even if it was, there are rarely Dutchmen to read it.

Notes and references

1. Campbell, John, *An exact and authentic account of the Greatest White-Herring Fishery in Scotland, carried on yearly in the island of Zetland by the Dutch only* (London, 1750).
2. Jamieson, Peter, *The Viking Isles* (London, 1933).
3. Linklater, Eric, *Orkney and Shetland* (London, 1965).
4. Wolfram, Richard, *Schwerttanz und Männerbund* (Kassel, 1935).
5. Macleod Banks, M., *British Calendar Customs, Orkey and Shetland* (London, 1946) pp 96–101.
6. Jamieson (1933), op. cit., p 128.
7. Low, Rev. G., *Tour through the islands of Orkney and Shetland in 1774* (London, 1774).
8. Newall, Venetia, 'Up-Helly-A: A Shetland Winter Festival' in *ARV* (Stockholm, 1978); Beenhakker, A.J., *Hollanders in Shetland* (Lerwick, 1973); Reid Tate, E.S., *Some Notes on the Shetland Hanseatic Trade* (Lerwick, 1955).

17

Early Steamship Enterprise in Ireland: The County of Down and Liverpool Steam-Boat Company 1836–39

MICHAEL MCCAUGHAN

I

STEAM COMMUNICATION BETWEEN Britain and Ireland began in 1818 when the Scottish entrepreneur David Napier inaugurated a service between the Clyde and Belfast with the 90-ton paddle steamer *Rob Roy*. A year later in 1819, George Lantry, Belfast owner of a fleet of sailing packets introduced the steamer *Waterloo* on the Belfast-Liverpool route. From 1820 onwards, steamship services rapidly expanded and eclipsed windships as the most expeditious means for passenger and livestock traffic to cross the Irish Sea. By 1835 paddle steamers were providing cross-channel services from a dozen Irish ports to the Clyde, Liverpool, Bristol and Whitehaven, besides services between the several Post Office Packet Stations.[1] (Figure 17.1). In terms of the number of steamship links with Ireland, Liverpool was the most important British port. Connected to the English urban markets and industrial areas by a well-developed inland transport network, Liverpool was both the primary distribution point for Irish labour, livestock and agricultural produce and the major outlet for English manufactured goods being shipped to Ireland.[2] In the north of Ireland, steam communication between Newry and Liverpool was established in 1825, six years after Langtry's pioneering service from Belfast to Liverpool was introduced. A service from Derry began in the late 1820s and in 1835 the Port Rush Steam Navigation Company was formed to provide direct connections between north Ulster and Liverpool.[3]

During the nineteenth century, the steamship developed from a vessel with limited range, coupled with high capital and operating costs, into an efficient and technically advanced form of water transport, capable of profitable, long ocean voyages. In the 1820s and the 1830s the adoption of the steamship as a viable sea-going merchant vessel was pioneered on the short sea and cross-channel routes of the British Isles, and especially in the Irish sea trade (Figure 17.2). Here the necessary conditions for steamship innovation existed. The relatively short distances between ports meant that these early steamships with their inefficient engines and boilers, which required large quantities of coal, were never far from their fuel supplies. Furthermore the weight of engines, boilers and bunkers, together

Figure 17.1 Development of Irish cross-channel services 1820–36. Routes extrapolated from D.B. McNeill's pioneering work, *Irish passenger steamship services*, vols 1 and 2.

with the space they occupied, not only reduced considerably the earning capacity of a steamship, but also resulted in much higher operating costs, when compared to a sailing vessel of similar dimensions.[4] Therefore to be profitable, in the absence of a government subsidy in the form of a mail contract, these early steamships were effectively confined to short sea and cross-channel trades where there was high density traffic, and where there was a market for the carriage of passengers, livestock and other high value, low volume cargoes commanding high freight rates.

Clearly, in the early years of steam navigation, the steamship was expensive to build, to operate and could only carry with profit specialised cargoes in specific trades. However, they did offer one supreme advantage over sailing vessels, for unlike them, steamships were independent of winds and tides. With predictable passage times, not only could they achieve a higher number of voyages per year than windships in the same trade, but they could also operate to fixed timetables, which was of vital importance to the expansion of commerce, industry and trade. Thus, in the early nineteenth century the introduction of steam technology for the transportation of people and goods on land as well as sea, brought about a regularisation of trade that had not existed hitherto. Above all it initiated a transport revolution that not only was a crucial factor in the growth of the nineteenth-century economy and empire, but which contributed substantially to the sweeping social changes affecting the lives of the people of Britain and Ireland during that century.

In the third and fourth decades of the nineteenth century, steam technology was the heroic wonder of the age; the symbol of progress and prosperity. By its application to industry and transport, man's mastery of his material environment had seemingly been achieved. The harnessing of the

Figure 17.2 Printer's block of a typical Irish Sea cross-channel paddle steamer of the 1830s. It was used in the first newspaper sailing notice for the County of Down and Liverpool Steam-Boat Company's 'new and powerful steam-packet', *Victoria. Downpatrick Recorder*, 30 September 1837 (UFTM L1261/3).

elements of fire and water to create mechanical power and propulsion was a marvel, and as the supreme technological achievement of the age, was widely celebrated in the arts. An anonymous poet, for example, gave expression to his wonder of steam at sea in the following verse:

To a Steam Boat[5]

Dark stranger on the teeming map of fate –
    Fabric, thou seem'st a thing alike apart
From aught that man or mystic arts create;
    To me a mystery thou art!
And awe and wonder strike me at thy frame
    Strange birth of motion, water, steam and flame.

Two types of accommodation were offered to passengers in early steamships – cabin or deck.[6] Perhaps surprisingly, more descriptions exist of the conditions under which deck passengers, or deckers, travelled than those of cabin passengers. This is due in the main to the 1849 parliamentary investigation by Captain Denham of the often appalling deprivations suffered by passengers crossing the Irish Sea on the open decks of steamships.[7] Decker traffic was characteristically seasonal in nature and mainly comprised migrant Irish labourers. The two peaks in decker travel was just before and just after the British grain harvest, and although deckers travelled at other times of the year, it was during the annual migration of thousands of Irish harvesters that the worst conditions prevailed. Many steamship companies made no provision whatsoever for deckers, although in exceptionally bad weather they were sometimes permitted the relative comfort of stables or allowed to lie down among the cattle aboard. Often 'passengers and cattle were therefore indiscriminately mixed together; the sea and urine pouring on their clothes from the animals; and they stood in the midst of filth and mire'.[8] Overcrowding was a major problem, exacerbated by the practice of companies paying commissions to their agents in the ports on the amount of business done, and by not placing limitations on the number of tickets issued for any one sailing. As a result, crowds of labourers, wishing to remain together for the voyage, often rushed aboard a particular favourite vessel, leaving a second steamer relatively empty. One captain declared that he had on one occasion brought over 728 deck passengers from Ireland in a vessel of 220 registered tons 'with the holds too full of cattle to admit any of them below'.[9] A Scots newspaper reported in 1838 that the *Foyle* of 136 tons arrived at the Broomielaw with 660 reapers crowded into the steerage, on every inch of deck and even on top of the paddle boxes.[10]

Although this seasonal decker traffic was easily-earned revenue for the steamship companies, the regular carriage of cabin passengers, livestock and general cargo throughout the year was regarded as a more important source of income. In the strongly competitive Irish Sea transport market of the 1830s, the provision of shelter and comfort for fluctuating and unpredictable numbers of deckers was considered subsidiary to the business offered by the regular shipper and cabin passenger, and the profits earned from them.

In stark contrast to deckers, cabin passengers enjoyed a remarkably high standard of accommodation.[11] Although not immune to the terrors of sea sickness, their *mal de mer* could be assuaged by the attendance of stewards and the provision of comfortable berths and water closets. The standard type of accommodation was the communal cabin at the after end of the vessel, although some steamers were fitted with a forward cabin for the use of ladies only. Often individual berths were provided and some steamers also had separate dining rooms. The *Superb*, for example, built in 1826 for the sole carriage of passengers on the Cork-Bristol route, had two cabins for gentlemen with thirty-seven berths, while a single ladies' cabin was fitted with twenty-six berths. The cabins had sofas, lockers, a bookcase and attached water closets.[12] Contemporary illustrations of steamer cabin accommodation depict elegant apartments with prosperous passengers of assured social position. They were, in short, microcosms of early nineteenth-century civilized society.

While it is certain that passenger traffic on Irish steamship routes increased steadily between 1820 and 1840, it is difficult to assess accurately the total numbers carried, due to the lack of reliable evidence. Although records exist for the services maintained by the Post Office Packets, documentation of the private companies is sparse or non-existent. Even in the nineteenth century many companies did not reveal publicly the numbers of passengers conveyed in their ships. Most notably these companies refused to divulge figures to the Railway Commissioners for Ireland, who investigated passenger traffic between Britain and Ireland in 1836. The Commissioners reported that if they calculated the flow of passengers at that date as 'twenty times the number carried by the sailing packets [in 1821], we could scarcely be charged with exaggeration'. Numerically the Commissioners gave an estimate of between 500,000 and 600,000 passenger crossings in 1836, but a recent assessment suggests a total of 363,000 to be a more accurate figure. Of this total, it is calculated that perhaps 78,000 to 103,000 were cabin passengers and between 260,000 and 285,000 were deck passengers.[13]

Although the individual shipowner and entrepreneur played a major role in developing early steamship services, during the 1820s and 1830s steamships were increasingly owned and operated by some form of corporate business enterprise, usually a joint stock company. Attracted by the prospect of quick and substantial profits, venture capital was readily subscribed to these enterprises, many of which, especially in the 1830s, were promoted on a wave of steamship mania, often with little chance of long-term success. This emergent form of corporate ownership clearly related to the speculative nature of such enterprises, and to the requirement for large amounts of capital to construct and operate these technically advanced ships.[14]

The two largest and most important companies were the City of Dublin Steam Packet Company and the St George Steam Packet Company. The City of Dublin Company expanded rapidly after its formation in 1824 with a capital of £50,000, largely subscribed by merchants in Dublin and Liverpool. By 1850 the company was operating a fleet of sixteen vessels and had a capital of £450,000, three-quarters of which was now held by the Dublin merchants. The St George Steam Packet Company was founded in 1821 with capital raised in Liverpool, Cork and Dublin. One of the company's vessels was the cross-channel steamer *Sirius*, which was chartered in 1838 by the related British and Atlantic Steam Navigation Company for what was to become the first continuous steam crossing of the North Atlantic. Like the City of Dublin Company, the St George Company began operations on a combination of Liverpool and Irish capital, but later the Irish element in the capital resources of both concerns became dominant. Significantly the St George Company moved its headquarters to Cork shortly after its formation, and in the 1830s both companies transferred the registration of their steamers from Liverpool to Dublin and Cork.[15]

Although early steamship enterprise in the Irish trade is a sparsely documented and largely uncharted aspect of maritime history, the impression is that in the 1820s and 1830s the majority of steamship services were established not so much by British enterprise alone, but in combination with, and often wholly by Irish entrepreneurs, capitalists and shipowners. It was ironic, therefore, that later in the century, the reduction of sea transport costs brought about by technical advances in steam navigation, coupled with the development of the Irish railway system, contributed substantially to the decline of Irish domestic, small-scale manufacturing industry through the ready and cheap availability of British mass-produced commodities.[16]

If in the 1820s steamship communication was confined to the major ports and Post Office Packet Stations, the 1830s were characterised by attempts by the smaller provincial ports to establish their own steamship links with Britain, and Liverpool in particular, by forming locally-based companies to purchase and operate steamships. In December 1834, for example, Dundalk merchants published a prospectus for a steamboat to sail between that port and Liverpool.[17] Claiming that 'it should not be considered visionary to describe Co. Louth as a comparative Lancashire', and reminding prospective investors that the steamers run by the rival port of Drogheda were expected to pay a dividend of 30 per cent, the promoters proposed that capital should be raised in shares of only £5 each, so that a large number of cattle dealers could be included in the proprietary.

Even in ports where steam communication was well established, albeit with outside concerns, there was a desire to form local companies with local shareholding and local control. For example, despite the competitive nature of existing services from the port of Newry, it was still considered viable in March 1836 to promote the Newry Steam-Packet Company with a capital of £15,000 to be raised in the rather exclusive shareholding of £50 per share.[18] The Company's prospectus claimed that the increasing import/export trade of the port, coupled with improvements in its navigation, rendered additional steam communication absolutely necessary for commercial prosperity. Furthermore, experience of similar undertakings elsewhere proved it to be a very profitable investment for capital. If the prospective investor was still reluctant to subscribe, it was also proposed that the proprietor of one share be entitled to one free cabin passage to and from Liverpool each year, and an additional one for every share he possessed. Although 300 free return passages to Liverpool per annum would seem an undue erosion of company profit, at £50 per share subscribers might have regarded it as a not unreasonable expectation.

Alas, many of these locally promoted companies collapsed within a few years. Founded on a national wave of steamship mania, their subscribers blinded by speculative fervour and technological euphoria, such enterprises often failed because their promoters had no experience in steamship management and had little understanding of the economic conditions necessary for profitable steamship operation. The Port Rush Steam Navigation Company lasted longer than some of its contemporaries, but nevertheless failed after ten years of trading. In November and December 1845 the company was forced to auction its Port Rush premises and steamer *Coleraine*.[19]

II

It was in the prevailing spirit of steam-generated entrepreneurial excitement that in April 1836 the inhabitants of east Down were advised of the imminence of steamboat communication between Ardglass and Liverpool.[20] On 1 June 1836 a prospectus of a joint stock company was published, for establishing steamboat communication between Liverpool, and the County Down ports of Portaferry, Strangford, Killyleagh, Downpatrick, Ardglass and Killough. Capital of £25,000 was to be raised in 5000 shares of £5 each. Patrons of the undertaking were the landlords of the area, Lord Bangor, David Ker, MP, Matthew Forde, Lord Dufferin, A.W. Beauclerk and Andrew Nugent. The various ports were represented by a provisional committee of fifteen local businessmen.[21]

The majority of the inhabitants of Downpatrick and area had probably only seen their first steamship a few years previously, when steam trading to Strangford Lough and the Quoile began about 1832. On 26 July of that year, Aynsworth Pilson recorded in his diary that 'a steam vessel the

Ormrod sailed from the Coil quay with corn, cattle for Liverpool'.[22] Owned in Liverpool, the *Ormrod* was a small steamer of seventy-seven tons and so capable of navigating the narrow Quoile channel. It was possibly to this vessel that Pilson again referred to in his diary for 25 July 1835, when he noted that his son Conway had 'landed a large quantity of reapinghooks and other hardware at the Quoile quay, brought over by a steam vessel from Liverpool'.[23] Shortly afterwards the service ended, when owing to some mishap the steamer was capsized.[24]

This demonstration of the everyday risks of shipping, coupled with the uncharted technical and financial pitfalls of steam navigation, did little to dispel the heady optimism of the promoters of the new company. Indeed some of them, James Maxwell, William McCleery Junior and Hugh Bowden, all merchants and shipowners of Portaferry, were simultaneously organising a steam ferry service across the Narrows between that town and Strangford. The Portaferry and Strangford Steam Boat Company had been formed in April 1835 and on 11 July 1836, six weeks after the prospectus of the proposed cross-channel steamship company was issued, the steamer *Lady of the Lake* began plying between the two ports.[25] Yet the difficulties of operating a profitable, reliable and successful steamship service were not fully appreciated by the promoters of either company, for both operations collapsed three years later in 1839.

However, in the optimistic summer of 1836, failure was certainly not anticipated. The spirit of enterprise, improvement and speculation was abroad. Provincial pride and the desire to acquire a potent symbol of prestige and prosperity was also a powerful incentive to invest in the new enterprise, for in the previous two years locally-based steamship companies had been formed in the northern ports of Newry, Dundalk and Portrush.[26]

Such were the considerations that were in the minds of those who attended a large meeting in Downpatrick on 8 August 1836 to establish the County of Down and Liverpool Steam-Boat Company. The numerous resolutions proposed and agreed to, included:

1. 'That the business of the Company shall be transacted under a Partnership Deed without going to the expense of seeking an Act of Parliament.'
2. 'That the Directors be instructed not to incur any liabilities for the Company beyond the amount of the Shares for which deposits have been, and shall, from time to time be paid, otherwise the Directors themselves be liable, to protect the Company.'
3. 'That the Directors be instructed to make enquiries and report as to the expediency of purchasing or having a steam-boat built or chartered; also, as to the period of commencing business, and as to the selecting and appointing a proper Commander.'

Fifteen directors were appointed, three each representing the five local ports, excluding Strangford. Downpatrick directors were: Hugh Wallace, Arthur Johnston, John Richardson; the Ardglass directors: Joseph Saunders, James Russell, George Hardacre; the Killyleagh directors: Arthur H. Read, John Martin, James Bryden; the Killough directors: Thomas Russell, William Rogan, Joseph Henry [replaced by Hugh Cleland 2.1.37.] and the Portaferry directors: James Maxwell, William McCleery Junior, Hugh Bowden. Mathew Crozier was appointed agent at Liverpool and the Northern Banking Company remained as bankers.[27]

In July and August 1836 notices appeared in the Belfast and Newry press, advertising company shares. The £25,000 capital was to be raised in 5000 shares of £5 each, 'in order that a numerous proprietary may be created, and give the undertaking the benefit of their influence and connexion'.[28] A deposit of five shillings per share was to be made on subscribing and the future instalments were not to exceed ten shillings per share per month; the time for calling for instalments was to be fixed by the directors. Shareholders not paying within the appointed time would forfeit their shares and all previous payments. Already the share list was filled to two-thirds of the capital, and it included the names of the patrons and other landlords, together with the merchants and shopkeepers of Downpatrick, Killyleagh, Portaferry, Strangford, Ardglass, Killough, and the farmers in these neighbourhoods.

The new venture held great attractions for the population of east Down, for an observer noted that:

> ... it enables the countryman to invest his money in a fund, that not only pays him interest, but also affords him an opportunity of sending the produce of his farm to a profitable market, and lastly of getting a free passage (shareholders having that privilege) to Liverpool. Indeed he will be able to purchase the necessary articles for husbandry at first cost and of a better description that he could purchase in the town of Downpatrick.[29]

By early 1837 preparations for the establishment of a steamboat service were well advanced. The directors reported to the shareholders on 2 January that an order for the building of a steamboat had been placed with Coates and Young of Belfast, and delivery had been agreed for early August 1837. The steamer was to have accommodation for at least forty cabin passengers and 150 tons of merchandise. She was to be coppered, fitted out, and to be at least as fast as any steamboat between Belfast and Liverpool. Consideration had also been given to the problem of providing a floating berth for the steamer at the various places from which she was to sail. Ardglass was satisfactory but improvements were necessary at Strangford, Portaferry, Killough and Downpatrick, to permit arrival and sailing at all states of the tide. However, it was anticipated that the necessary improvements would be paid for by the proprietors of the adjoining estates, without expense to the company.[30]

The *Downpatrick Recorder* expressed its approval of the report and gave thanks to the directors, 'for discharging the trust reposed in them with an energy and a prudence which promises the happiest results'. Compliments were paid to the landlords for their generosity in paying for the harbour improvements and a plea was made for the public to buy the remaining shares. The newspaper called upon the community 'to prepare to realise the unnumbered advantages which must arise from this interesting and important project'.[31]

By mid June 1837, the new steamer, to be named *Victoria*, was almost ready for launching. Although the contract for the construction of the steamboat had been made with the Belfast engineering company Coates and Young, the building of the wooden hull had been subcontracted to the shipbuilder Charles Connell and Sons.[32] In order to pay instalments on the purchase price of the ship as work progressed, a series of calls, each of ten shillings per share had been made by the directors on holders of company stock. On 10 June, Robert Denvir Junior, Clerk to the Company, gave notice of the eighth call, which was payable on or before 1 July. Denvir also announced that the half-yearly meeting was to be held at Denvir's Hotel, Downpatrick on Monday 3 July, before which date the shareholders who had not yet signed the partnership deed were required to do so.[33]

The euphoria at that shareholders' meeting can be imagined, for it was generally known that the *Victoria* was to be launched on the following Thursday 6 July at twelve o'clock precisely. The launch took place on the day, but an hour later than planned, and a detailed eulogistic account of the event was given by the *Recorder*.[34]

Meanwhile, plans were being made for the accommodation of *Victoria* at the Quoile and Killyleagh. The existing quayage and depth of water was inadequate for a steamer registering 372 tons burthen on a deck length of 155 feet and a breadth between paddles of 22 feet.[35] At Killyleagh various alternatives were considered, but by August 1837, it was finally decided to extend the existing quay by 150 feet, to be paid for by Lord Dufferin.[36] The Quoile was more problematic. Although there was about 12 feet of water at the Quay at full tide, the extremely narrow channel and shallows made the passage of boats difficult. In fact, it was impossible for vessels exceeding 120 tons to reach the quay at all, except that they were flat bottomed, with a draft of 8$1/2$–10 feet.[37] Patently, *Victoria* could not come up to the quay, even at high tide. Because of the condition of the fords in the Quoile channel, the nearest she could approach was about a mile downstream. Consequently it was decided to build a new quay nearer the Lough. On Monday, 11 September 1837, the local landlord, Mr Ker, accompanied by Hugh Wallace and a number of the inhabitants of Downpatrick, visited the Quoile and selected the site of the steamboat quay. It was to be built at Mr Ker's expense, but as construction was expected to take several months, Mr Ker agreed to erect a temporary wooden quay for the reception of *Victoria*, whose arrival was shortly expected.[38] However, it was not until

May of the following year that work began on the vital link road to con-
nect the newly-completed quay with Quoile Quay about 1 1/4 miles
upstream.[39] The new road was, of course, vital for the easy movement of
goods between Downpatrick and the steamboat. Its cost, from quay to
quay, including two bridges, battery and sea wall was £1500, of which Mr
Ker contributed £1000 and the Grand Jury £500.[40]

On Thursday, 28 September 1837, the new steamer *Victoria* made her
first appearance in Strangford Lough. On the following day she arrived at
Mr Ker's temporary quay, itself still in course of construction, and steam
communication between the Quoile and Liverpool was re-established.
Victoria, the symbol of local prosperity and progress, was the source of
great excitement and the *Recorder* gave a full account of her arrival, in its
most approving manner and with the usual complement of eulogies.[41]

The same issue of the *Recorder* carried the County of Down and
Liverpool Steam-Boat Company's first shipping notice which gave details
of sailings and freight charges. *Victoria*, 370 tons register, 220 HP, with
William Aberdeen as commander, was scheduled to make her first trip
from the Quoile to Liverpool at twelve noon, Saturday 30 September 1837,
calling at Killyleagh and Portaferry. A twice-weekly service was to be
established, leaving Quoile river and intermediate ports every Saturday
and Ardglass and Killough every Tuesday. Sailings from Liverpool would
be on Mondays and Thursdays. Fares were: cabin (including steward's fee)
17s.6d.; deck 4s.; horses £1 each; horses shipped by dealers in lots under
five, 17s.6d.; cattle 7s.6d. to 10s. Freight of other goods was described as
equally moderate. Prospective passengers were assured that no expense
had been spared in fitting up cabins, and in the other arrangements.
Furthermore, there was the all-important advantage of a considerably
shorter passage than from any other port in Ireland. The company then
expressed the hope that these facilities would secure the steady support of
the public.[42]

Initially these hopes were realised, for a week later the *Recorder* reported:

> It gives us sincere pleasure to learn that the prospects of this steamboat are
> of so encouraging a kind. Goods and passengers to an extent much beyond
> what was expected at first, are offering. She left this (Quoile) on Saturday
> evening last and reached Liverpool several hours before any of the boats
> which sailed from Belfast on that day; and her trip back to Ardglass on
> Wednesday, was, we are informed, made in ten hours and a half. She sails
> from Portaferry at five o'clock this evening.[43]

The *Recorder* tactfully did not refer to her arrival at Ardglass a day late, and
this in her first week of operation.[44] This delay presumably caused some
embarrassment to the new Ardglass Forwarding Office operated by company director George Hardacre.[45] Possibly the original timetable was over
ambitious for on 14 October 1837, the beginning of the third week of operations, a revised and reduced service was advertised. Henceforward
Victoria was to sail every Saturday from Strangford Lough and Ardglass,

with a return sailing from Liverpool every Tuesday.[46]

From its inception the new company, anxious for success, had placed strong emphasis on the need for a fast steamer. The chance to demonstrate *Victoria's* speed occurred during the second week of service, when a race from Liverpool was arranged between her and the Belfast steamer *Falcon*. Not only did *Victoria* beat the *Falcon* conclusively over a given distance, but one of her passengers, keen to give the public positive proof of her superiority, started direct for Belfast from Ardglass and reached Donegall Quay, twenty-six miles away, some time before the arrival of the *Falcon*. Thereafter the company began to advertise itself as The County of Down and Liverpool Steam-Packet Company.[47]

By the end of the first month, the success of the new steamboat service seemed assured, at least on the Ardglass sailings. On 28 October 1837 the *Recorder* reported that on the previous Saturday, when leaving Ardglass, *Victoria's* deck was crowded with livestock, principally black cattle. On her return trip she brought chests of tea, bales of woollen goods, lead, copper, tin plates, rosin, tar, pitch and earthenware. In the *Recorder's* opinion the advantages of the steamer to Downpatrick and the surrounding countryside were incalculable.[48]

In late November 1837, the Post Office permitted *Victoria* to carry mail under the same regulations as the Belfast steamboats. A subsidy was not involved, but rather a reduction in postal charges. Under the new regulations a letter posted in Downpatrick, Killyleagh or Ardglass, and marked in the corner 'per steamer from Downpatrick', cost 8d. postage instead of 1s.3d.[49] Predictably this concession was quickly followed by a *Recorder* leader putting forward a case for the establishment of a direct mail service between Liverpool and the North of Ireland. However the appeal went unheeded by the Post Office.[50]

To take advantage of the short sea passage between Ardglass and Liverpool, passengers began to travel from Belfast to cross in *Victoria*. To facilitate these passengers, the departure time from Ardglass was changed, in early December 1837, from six o'clock to seven o'clock in the evening.[51]

For a few months the company seemed to be a success, but by March 1838, there were indications that all was not well. The *Recorder*, for example, refused to publish a letter about the steamer, with the cryptic explanation that although they agreed with the correspondent's remarks, they did not see any good that might result from publishing them. Later that month rumours began to circulate that *Victoria* had been wrecked, or that she had been sold to a Newry company. The *Recorder*, still sympathetic to the enterprise, was happy to refute the rumours.[52]

However, there were signs that the company was in difficulties. Presumably due to berthing problems and to insufficient trade from the Strangford Lough ports, a decision was taken to reduce sailings from there and to institute peak sailings from Warrenpoint. At the beginning of May 1838 a revised timetable was published, advertising sailings from

Warrenpoint to Liverpool every Saturday and from Strangford Lough ports every other Wednesday. The ship would leave Strangford at precisely six o'clock in the evening and call at Ardglass for goods and passengers. The freight charge for horses from Strangford was reduced from 17s.6d. to 12s.6d. in lots not under five.[53]

There was evident concern about the viability of the company, judging by the *Recorder's* reassuring account of the half-yearly meeting of shareholders on Monday 9 July 1838. Although the company had been in considerable debt in March, it was being gradually reduced and was shortly expected to be free from debt. Undoubtedly this return to liquidity was due to the partial transfer of the steamer to Warrenpoint. This was of little practical benefit to Downpatrick and other local merchants, but the *Recorder* assured those who had money invested in the company, that if matters continued as they were doing, investors would obtain good interest for their money, notwithstanding the fears that were earlier entertained for its success.[54]

On 24 November 1838 *Victoria* was advertised to sail from Strangford to Liverpool on Wednesday 5 December at eleven o'clock in the morning. Evidently the ship had sustained some damage, for it was stated that:

> This splendid vessel has resumed this station, after having received a complete repair in every department. Her speed has been increased by improvements in the machinery and houses erected on deck for the comfort of passengers. Her cabins are fitted up in the most elegant style, affording the best accommodation. Close stables on deck for horses. For further particulars, please apply at the Company's Offices, Newry and Downpatrick.[55]

This advertisement was placed for the two subsequent weeks, with the amendment that the ship was unable to call at Ardglass because of damage to the pier during the recent storm. In fact, the great storm of 27 November 1838 had undermined the new lighthouse and it fell into the sea, carrying with it the end of the pier.[56] Thereafter, and perhaps partly due to the Ardglass catastrophe, the steamer appears to have been out of commission until April 1839, when she returned to the combined Warrenpoint-Strangford Lough station.[57]

By the end of 1838, there was mounting dissatisfaction with the quality of the Strangford Lough service provided by the company. An irate open letter of complaint to the directors and manager, was published in the *Recorder* on 8 December. It was written by Robert Henny, who, with a partner, had established a provision market in Downpatrick in November of the previous year, with the inducement of regular steam communication with Liverpool. In scathing terms Henny complained of the steamer's unpunctuality at the Quoile and insufficient time allowed for loading.

> I have never seen her here, except once, at the appointed time, when she came up in splendid style with flying colours and a band on board, for the gratification no doubt of the passengers (where were they?) and her captain... strange to say her captain had no sooner landed than he announced

that he could not stop a moment, not even to ship my goods which were in sight, no nor even to take on board all lying for her there, perhaps days, but mounted his hobby, the paddle box, and off she went, light as a feather to the fancy air of Rory O'More.

In similar vein Henny lambasted the general running of the company and questioned their agents' attention to the Newry station, to the detriment of the Quoile trade. 'No doubt he did this with the view of making money for the company, but whether this was honourable or not, it is hard to say, when a person looks at the prospectus of the undertaking.' Henny concluded his lengthy letter with the avowed intention of 'laying a claim at the next general meeting of shareholders for damages, such as will remunerate me for my present losses, in which I hope to be supported by all who know what it is to be concerned in a dangerous and adventurous trade'.[58]

The half-yearly meeting of shareholders on 8 January 1839 was a depressing affair. Because of expenses incurred through accidents to the boat, the company was in debt, although when it was working the steamer did make money. *Victoria* was currently under repair in Belfast, and it was decided that when she returned to service, she should resume sailing from Warrenpoint every Saturday and from the port of Strangford every alternate Wednesday. Captain Aberdeen felt that this arrangement would enable him to be punctual to the hour at Strangford, and also to keep his time at Warrenpoint without unnecessary exertion. The shareholders, for their part, thought that it would be as cheap to bring goods from Strangford as from the New Quay, owing to the state of the road recently made to it. Furthermore, Killyleagh harbour was not in a fit state to receive the steamer. For easier distribution of goods from Strangford, consideration was given to the idea of a lighter to bring merchandise to Killyleagh and Quoile Quay.[59]

Victoria did not resume operations until April 1839, and during this period of inactivity, the general disillusionment with the steamboat enterprise, was reflected in the correspondence columns of the *Recorder*.[60] On 21 May a special general meeting of the shareholders revealed that the steamer was currently making money, but that nevertheless her debts were considerable. In its report of the meeting, the *Recorder* considered that there was little likelihood of the *Victoria* trading for much longer, as the proprietors were generally in favour of selling her. However, the *Recorder* expressed the view that it was still possible to make a success of steam communication between Downpatrick and Liverpool. Leading local merchants were asked to consider buying the steamer and confine her to the Strangford Lough ports as originally intended. With repairs to the harbours where she formerly loaded and discharged, it was argued that *Victoria* would be a remunerating concern.[61]

At the next half-yearly meeting on 1 July – for which the *Recorder* noted there was no public notice given as usual – the question of selling *Victoria* was not put to the vote. Instead it was resolved that the steamer should continue on the Warrenpoint and Strangford Lough stations, presumably in an attempt to offset some of the debts that had accumulated when the ship was out of service. The meeting was informed that Mr Ker was about to deepen the Quoile channel to enable *Victoria* and other large vessels to approach Quoile Quay.[62]

Victoria continued on station for the remainder of the summer, but there was by now little confidence in the future of the company. At the end of September a number of £5 shares were offered for sale at 30s. each, and on 5 October, the *Recorder* announced that the *Victoria* herself was offered for sale.[63] However, she continued in service for another month, before being sold by auction on 13 November 1839, in the Commercial Buildings, Belfast. The *Victoria* was bought for £5150, by her builders Messrs Coates and Young, who had been paid £13,000 for her just over two years previously. As the debts against the County of Down and Liverpool Steam-Boat Company stood about £5000, the shareholders were left with six pence for every pound invested.[64]

Several reasons can be advanced for the failure of the company. First, there was the difficulty in keeping to a regular advertised timetable, through an underestimation or lack of knowledge of the tidal conditions in Strangford Lough and the Quoile river. Good time-keeping – the essence of a successful steamship operation – was further aggravated by the shortcomings of quays at the Quoile, Killyleagh and Ardglass.

Second, the company suffered from inept management. The principals had no prior experience in steamship management and indeed a number of them had no ship-owning experience whatsoever. In addition, the master of the steamer, Captain Aberdeen, seems to have been singularly unsuited to his command, and the evidence tends to support the contemporary criticism that he was of 'a rash and hot temperament'.[65]

Finally, the cross-channel trade of Strangford Lough ports in the 1830s, though considerable, was of the wrong type to successfully support a regular steamship service. Essentially the ports were importing and exporting bulk cargoes, chiefly coal and wheat, with little in the way of decker traffic.[66] These high-volume, low-value cargoes were much more suited to movement by sailing vessels than to a sophisticated steamship which required regular low-volume, high-value cargoes for profitable operation. In short, a steamship of the 1830s had no chance of economic viability in the cross-channel trade from Strangford Lough. Different circumstances obtained in the trade from Warrenpoint and Newry and it is significant that the *Victoria* seems to have made a profit when operating from Carlingford Lough.

Under new ownership *Victoria* continued in the cross-channel trade between north-west England and Belfast. However, on a foggy night in February 1842, while on passage from Fleetwood to Belfast, she struck a ledge of rocks off Maughold Head near Ramsay in the Isle of Man. The engines were immediately reversed and the vessel backed off. However the pumps could not cope with the water she was making and *Victoria* was run ashore to save the lives of the crew and passengers, who were all landed without accident. She subsequently broke up in stormy weather.[67]

Notes and references

1. See McNeill, D.B., *Irish passenger steamship services*, vol 1, North of Ireland and vol 2, South of Ireland (Newton Abbot, 1969 and 1971). See also Bagwell, Philip, 'The Post Office Steam Packets, 1821–36, and the development of shipping on the Irish Sea', *Maritime History*, 1, (1971), pp 4–28.
2. See, for example, Anderson, B.L. and Storey, P.J.M. (eds), *Commerce, industry and transport, studies in economic change on Merseyside* (Liverpool, 1983).
   Also Hyde, F.E., *Liverpool and the Mersey, an economic history of a port 1700–1970* (Newton Abbot, 1971).
3. *Newry Examiner*, 5 December 1835.
4. For an outline of pioneering paddle steamer development see Greenhill, Basil, 'Steam before the screw' in Robert Gardiner (ed), *Conway's history of the ship – the advent of steam* (London, 1993), pp 11–27.
5. Verse one of an anonymous eight-verse poem from an English journal, published in the *Downpatrick Recorder*, 16 January 1841.
6. For a detailed discussion of accommodation in early steamships see Irvine, H.S., 'Some aspects of passenger traffic between Britain and Ireland, 1820–50', *The Journal of Transport History*, 4, no. 4 (1960), pp 225–41.
7. *Report by Captain Denham on Passenger Accommodation in Steamers between Ireland and Liverpool*, British parliamentary papers, HC, 1849 (339), L1.
8. Ibid., p 402.
9. Ibid., p 402.
10. Irvine (1960), op. cit., p 235.
11. For illustrations of early steamship cabins see Greenhill, Basil, *Travelling by sea in the nineteenth century* (London, 1972), pp 119–22.
12. Irvine (1960), op. cit., pp 230–1.
13. Ibid., pp 237–9.
14. For a technical description of early paddle steamship design and construction see Hedderwick, Peter, *A treatise on naval architecture* (Edinburgh, 1830), pp 377–97.
15. Cottrell, P.L., 'The steamship on the Mersey, 1815–80, investment and ownership' in P.L. Cottrell and D.H. Aldcroft (eds), *Shipping trade and commerce* (Leicester, 1981), pp 146–7.
   For an outline of steamship rivalries on the Liverpool–Dublin service, see Neal, Frank, 'Liverpool, the Irish steamship companies and the Famine Irish', *Immigrants and Minorities*, 5, no. 1 (1986), pp 30–1.
16. Green, E.R.R., 'Industrial decline in the nineteenth century' in L.M. Cullen (ed), *The formation of the Irish economy* (Cork, 1969), pp 92–3.
   See also Cullen, L.M., *An economic history of Ireland since 1660* (London, 1972), pp 146–8.
17. *Newry Examiner*, 31 December 1834.
18. Ibid., 26 March 1836.
19. *Northern Whig*, 22 November 1845.
20. *Newry Examiner*, 9 April 1836.
21. Ibid., 22 June 1836.

22. Pilson, Aynsworth, unpublished diary, Downpatrick, 26 July 1832, PRONI DOD 365/3.
23. Ibid., 25 July 1835.
24. *Ordnance Survey Memoirs*, Box 25, Down III, VI Saul Parish, 1, c.1836.
25. McCaughan, Michael, 'A Strangford Lough steam ferryboat,' *Ulster Folk and Transport Museum Year Book*, (1972–73), pp 17–18.
26. *Newry Examiner*, 26 March 1836.
    Ibid., 31 December 1834.
    Ibid., 5 December 1835.
27. *Belfast Commercial Chronicle*, 24 August 1836.
28. Ibid.
29. *Ordnance Survey Memoirs*, op. cit.
30. *Downpatrick Recorder*, 4 February 1837.
31. Ibid.
32. Ibid., 10 June 1837.
33. Ibid., 17 June 1837.
34. Ibid., 8 July 1837.
35. Ibid.
36. Ibid., 19 and 26 August 1837.
37. *Ordnance Survey Memoirs*, op. cit. and *Downpatrick Recorder*, 11 May 1850.
38. *Downpatrick Recorder*, 16 September 1837.
39. Ibid., 16 June 1838 and Pilson, Aynsworth, op. cit., 25 May 1838.
40. *Downpatrick Recorder*, 5 February 1876.
41. Ibid., 30 September 1837.
42. Ibid.
43. Ibid., 7 October 1837.
44. Pilson, Aynsworth, op.cit., 3 and 5 October 1837.
45. *Downpatrick Recorder*, 30 September 1837.
46. Ibid., 14 October 1837.
47. Ibid.
48. Ibid., 28 October 1837.
49. Ibid., 25 November 1837.
50. Ibid., 9 December 1837.
51. Ibid.
52. Ibid., 24 and 31 March 1838.
53. Ibid., 5 May 1838.
54. Ibid., 14 July 1838.
55. Ibid., 24 November 1838.
56. Ibid., 1 December 1838.
57. Ibid., 12 January, 16 March and 13 April, 1839.
58. Ibid., 8 December 1838.
59. Ibid., 12 January 1839.
60. Ibid., 16 and 23 March 1839.
61. Ibid., 25 May 1839.
62. Ibid., 29 June and 6 July 1839.
63. Ibid., 28 September and 5 October 1839.
64. Ibid., 16 November 1839.
65. Pilson, Aynsworth, unpublished 'Memoirs of Notable Inhabitants of Downpatrick, 1838,' PRONI T2986/2.
66. *Downpatrick Recorder*, 16 January 1839.
67. *Northern Whig*, 15 February 1842.

R. Alan Gailey:
Bibliography to 1996

COMPILED BY ROGER DIXON

1. 'Settlement and population in the Aran Islands', *Irish Geography*, 4 (1959), pp 65–78.
2. 'Aspects of change in a rural community', *Ulster Folklife*, 5 (1959), pp 27–34.
3. 'Glasgow University North Rona Expedition', *Scottish Geographical Magazine*, 75 (1959), pp 48–50.
4. Quaternary deposits at Murphystown Co Down', *Irish Naturalists Journal*, 13 (1959) (with V.B. Proudfoot).
5. 'Settlement and population in Kintyre 1750–1800', *Scottish Geographical Magazine*, 76 (1960), pp 99–105.
6. 'Thatching with mud: Scotland', *Ulster Folklife*, 6 (1960), pp 68–70.
7. 'The role of sub-letting in the crofting community', *Scottish Studies*, 5 (1961), pp 57–76.
8. 'Some Skye shielings', *Scottish Studies*, 5 (1961), pp 77–84 (with M.D. MacSween).
9. 'Mobility of tenants on a Highland estate in the early nineteenth century', *Scottish Historical Review*, 40 (1961), pp 136–45.
10. 'Fossil ice wedge at Poltalloch', *Scottish Geographical Magazine*, 77 (1961), p. 88 and plate 2.
11. 'The thatched houses of Ulster', *Ulster Folklife*, 7 (1961), pp 9–18.
12. 'The evolution of rural settlement in Scotland and beyond', *Ulster Folklife*, 7 (1961), pp 63–5 (with E.E. Evans).
13. 'Traps and snares', *Ulster Folklife*, 7 (1961), pp 74–5.
14. 'Scottish studies', *Ulster Folklife*, 7 (1961), pp 76–9.
15. 'The peasant houses of the south-west Highlands of Scotland', *Gwerin*, 3 (1962), pp 227–42.
16. 'A survey of the antiquities of North Rona', *Archaeological Journal*, 117 (1962), pp 88–115 (with Helen C. Nisbet).
17. 'The evolution of Highland rural settlement', *Scottish Studies*, 6 (1962), pp 155–77.
18. 'Two cruck truss houses near Lurgan', *Ulster Folklife*, 8 (1962), pp 57–64.

19.   'Ropes and rope-twisters', *Ulster Folklife*, 8 (1962), pp 72–82.
20.   'Agrarian improvement and the development of enclosures in the south-west Highlands of Scotland', *Scottish Historical Review*, 42 (1963), pp 46–52.
21.   'The cots of north Derry', *Ulster Folklife*, 9 (1963), pp 46–52.
22.   'The Ulster tradition', *Folk Life*, 2 (1964), pp 27–41.
23.   'The first Ulster Folk Museum outdoor exhibit: The Magilligan cottier house', *Ulster Folklife*, 10 (1964), pp 88–94 (with George Thompson and Desmond McCourt).
24.   'Notes on three cruck-truss houses', *Ulster Folklife*, 10 (1964), pp 88–94.
25.   'A folktale from County Down', *Ulster Folklife*, 11 (1965), p 136.
26.   'Kitchen furniture', *Ulster Folklife*, 12 (1966), pp 18–34.
27.   'The disappearance of the horse from the Ulster farm', *Folk Life*, 4 (1966), pp 51–5.
28.   *Le Théâtre Populaire Européen*, by Leopold Schmidt, *Béaloideas*, 32 (1964), pp 162–5.
29.   'The folk play in Ireland', *Studia Hibernica*, 6 (1966), pp 113–54.
30.   'The rhymers of south-east Antrim', *Ulster Folklife*, 13 (1967), pp 118–28.
31.   'Wilson House County Tyrone: The structure of the house', in *Wilson House County Tyrone* (National Trust Committee for Northern Ireland, 1967).
32.   'Proposals for indexing folk material', *Museum Journal*, 67 (1967), pp 107–8.
33.   'The development of the open-air museum', *Ulster Folk Museum Yearbook*, 1965/1966, pp 5–7 (unsigned).
34.   'A hill-farm from the Glens of Antrim', *Ulster Folk Museum Yearbook*, 1965/1966, pp 8–10 (unsigned).
35.   'The open-air museum and the linen industry', *Ulster Folk Museum Yearbook*, 1966/1967, pp 9–12.
36.   *Christmas Rhymers and Mummers in Ulster* (Ibstock, Leicestershire, 1968).
37.   'Straw costume in Irish folk customs', *Folk Life*, 6 (1968), pp 83–93.
38.   'Edward L. Sloan's "The year's holidays" ', *Ulster Folklife*, 14 (1968), pp 51–9.
39.   'Irish iron-shod wooden spades', *Ulster Journal of Archaeology*, 3rd series, 31 (1968), pp 77–86.
40.   'An English farm wagon from County Fermanagh', *Ulster Folk Museum Yearbook*, 1967/1968, pp 14–16.
41.   *Irish Folk Drama* (Cork, 1969).
42.   'The typology of the Irish spade', in Alan Gailey and Alexander Fenton (eds), *The Spade in Northern and Atlantic Europe* (Belfast, 1970), pp 35–48.
43.   'Irish corn-drying kilns', *Ulster Folklife*, 15/16 (1970) *(Studies in Folklife Presented to Emyr Estyn Evans)*, pp 52–71.

44. 'Damask weaving in the museum', *Ulster Folk Museum Yearbook*, 1968/1969, pp 10–11.
45. 'The Lisrace forge', *Ulster Folk Museum Yearbook*, 1968/1969, pp 18–20.
46. 'A wicker coffin from Ballyshiel Graveyard, Annaclone, County Down', *Ulster Folklife*, 17 (1971), pp 89–90.
47. 'Grinding old people young', *Ulster Folklife*, 17 (1971), pp 95–7.
48. 'Horse skulls under a County Down farmhouse floor', *Ulster Folk Museum Yearbook*, 1969/1970, pp 13–14.
49. 'Cultural connections in north-west Britain and Ireland', *Ethnologia Europaea*, 2/3 (1968/1969) *(Erixoniana I)*, pp 138–43.
50. 'Spade tillage in south-west Ulster and north Connaught', *Tools and Tillage*, 1, No. 4 (1971), pp 225–36.
51. 'A farmhouse from south-west County Fermanagh', *Ulster Folk Museum Yearbook*, 1970/1971, pp 18–21.
52. 'Ulster maypoles', *Ulster Folk Museum Yearbook*, 1970/1971, pp 18–21.
53. 'The last sheaf in the north of Ireland', *Ulster Folklife*, 18 (1972), pp 1–33.
54. 'Further cruck trusses in east Ulster', *Ulster Folklife*, 18 (1972), pp 80–97.
55. 'Towards an Irish ethnological atlas?' *Ulster Folklife*, 18 (1972), pp 121–5.
56. 'A missing Belfast chapbook: The Christmas rime, or, the mummers' own book', *Irish Booklore*, 2, No. 1 (1972), pp 54–8.
56. 'A family spade-making business in county Tyrone', *Folk Life*, 10 (1972), pp 26–46.
58. 'A New Year custom in south-east Ulster', in Walter Escher et al. (eds), *Festschrift für Robert Wildhaber* (Basel, 1973) *(Schweizerisches Archiv für Volkskunde*, 68 (1962)), pp 126–36.
59. *Christmas Mumming in Newfoundland*, Herbert Halpert and G.M. Storey (eds), *Béaloideas*, 37/38 (1969/1970), pp 338–41.
60. 'Comment: On the concept of cultural fixation', *Ethnologia Europaea*, 6, No. 2 (1972), pp 149–51.
61. 'The Rosses, County Donegal, in 1753–1754', *Ulster Folklife*, 19 (1973), pp 20–3 (as editor).
62. 'The flax harvest', *Ulster Folklife*, 19 (1973), pp 24–9 (as editor).
63. *Rural housing in Ulster in the mid-nineteenth century* (Belfast, 1974) (with Victor Kelly and James Paul).
64. 'Chapbook influence on Irish mummers' plays', *Folklore*, 85 (1974), pp 1–22.
65. 'A house from Gloverstown, Lismacloskey, County Antrim', *Ulster Folklife*, 20 (1974), pp 24–48, including appendix II, house with built-in oven, Carrickreagh, County Fermanagh.
66. 'Fews folk drama', *Mullaghbawn Historical and Folklore Society*, 2 (1974), unpaginated (but 36–41).
67. 'Spade-making at the museum', *Ulster Folk and Transport Museum Yearbook*, 1971/1972, pp 16–19.

68. 'Bonfires in Ulster', *Ulster Folk and Transport Museum Yearbook*, 1972/1973, pp 12–14.
69. 'Some transport survivals', *Ulster Folklife*, 21 (1975), pp 10–14 (as editor).
70. 'The Christmas rime', *Ulster Folklife*, 21 (1975), pp 73–84.
71. 'The Scots element in north Irish folk culture: Some problems in the interpretation of an historical acculturation', *Ethnologia Europaea*, 8, No. 1 (1975), pp 2–22.
72. 'The regional responsibility of Ulster's Folk Museum', *Museums Journal*, 75, No. 3 (1975), pp xxxiii–xxxvi.
73. 'A seventeenth-century English house in Ulster', *Ulster Folk and Transport Museum Yearbook*, 1973/1974, pp 1–3.
74. 'Folk drama in the Craigavon area', *Review. Journal of the Craigavon Historical Society*, 3, No. 2 (1976), pp 29–31.
75. 'Some developments and adaptations of traditional house types', in Caoimhín Ó Danachair (ed.), *Folk and farm: Essays in honour of A T Lucas* (Dublin, 1976), pp 54–71.
76. 'Ethnological mapping in Ireland', *Ethnologia Europaea*, 9, No. 1 (1976), pp 14–34 (with Caoimhín Ó Danachair and with a linguistic contribution by G.B. Adams).
77. 'Ploughing by the tail', *Ulster Folk and Transport Museum Yearbook*, 1974/1975, pp 7–9.
78. 'The housing of the rural poor in nineteenth-century Ulster', *Ulster Folklife*, 22 (1976), pp 34–58.
79. 'Vernacular dwellings in Clogher diocese', *Clogher Record*, 9, No. 2 (1977), pp 187–231.
80. 'Vernacular dwellings in Ireland', *Revue Roumaine d'Histoire de l'Art*, 13 (1976), pp 137–55.
81. 'The bonfire in north Irish tradition', *Folklore*, 88 (1977), pp 3–38.
82. 'Ballyveridagh National School', *Ulster Folk and Transport Museum Yearbook*, 1975/1976, pp 1–4.
83. 'The Ballyhagan inventories, 1716–1740', *Folk Life*, 15 (1977), pp 36–64.
84. *Ulster folk ways* (Belfast, 1978).
85. 'The Ulster Folk and Transport Museum and historic buildings conservation in Northern Ireland', *Ulster Folk and Transport Museum Yearbook*, 1976/1977, pp 13–14.
86. 'Mummers' and Christmas rhymers' plays in Ireland: The problem of distribution', *Ulster Folklife*, 24 (1978), pp 59–68.
87. 'A list of north Irish crucks', *Vernacular Architecture*, 9 (1978), pp 3–9 (with Desmond McCourt).
88. 'Vernacular housing in north-west Ulster', in Alistair Rowan (ed), *North-west Ireland: The buildings of Ireland* (Harmondsworth, Middlesex, 1979), pp 87–103.
89. 'Ulster's shop windows', *Ulster Folk and Transport Museum Yearbook* 1977/1978, pp 9–11.

90. 'A byre-dwelling from Magheragallan, County Donegal', *Ulster Folk and Transport Museum Yearbook*, 1978/1979, pp 1–3.
91. 'Sources for the study of Easter as a popular holiday in Ulster', *Ulster Folklife*, 26 (1980), pp 68–74.
92. Recording traditional buildings', *Ulster Folk and Transport Museum Yearbook*, 1979/1980, pp 3–4.
93. 'Ulster and industrial archaeology', *Ulster Folklife*, 27 (1981), pp 81–7 (with W.H. Crawford).
94. 'The Scotch-Irish in Northern Ireland: Aspects of their vulture, in Jack Weaver (ed), *Selected proceedings of the Scotch-Irish Heritage Festival at Winthrop College* (Rock Hill, South Carolina, 1981), pp 33–53.
95. Crucks in Ireland, in N.W. Alcock (ed), *Cruck construction: An introduction and catalogue* (Council for British Archaeology Research Report No. 42, London, 1981), pp 87–92 (with Desmond McCourt).
96. Folk culture, context and cultural change, in Edith Hörandner and Hans Lunzer (eds), *Folklorismus* (Neuseidel/See, 1982), pp 73–103.
97. *Spade making in Ireland* (Belfast, 1982).
98. Bricks and brick-making in Ulster in the 1830s, *Ulster Folklife*, 28 (1982), pp 61–4.
99. Three houses with outshot in north Louth and south Armagh, *Journal of the County Louth Archaeological and Historical Society*, 20, No. 1 (1981), pp 3–9.
100. The museum's archive of sound recordings, *Ulster Folk and Transport Museum Yearbook*, 1980/1981, pp 19–20.
101. Folk-life study and the Ordnance Survey Memoirs, in Alan Gailey and Daithí Ó hÓgáin (eds), *Gold under the furze*, Studies in Folk Tradition Presented to Caoimhín Ó Danachair (Dublin, 1982), pp 150–64.
102. Traditional houses at Riasc, *Journal of the Kerry Archaeological and Historical Society*, 14 (1981), pp 94–111.
103. Scotland, Ireland and America: Migrant culture in the 17th and 18th centuries, *Working papers in Irish studies*, 84/1 (Irish Studies Program, Northeastern University, Boston).
104. *Rural houses of the north of Ireland* (Edinburgh, 1984).
105. The Scotch-Irish contribution to American architecture, in Jack Weaver (ed), *Selected proceedings of the Scotch-Irish Heritage Festival at Winthrop College, II* (Baton Rouge, 1984), pp 53–69.
106. Cultra: From manor land to open-air museum, in *A folk museum for Ireland: Proceedings of a one-day conference* (Dublin, 1984), unpaginated (but 10 pp.)
107. Introduction and spread of the horse-powered threshing machine to Ulster's farms in the nineteenth century: Some aspects, *Ulster Folklife*, 30 (1984), pp 37–54.
108. Local life in Ulster 1843–1848: The statistical surveys of Maurice Collis, *Ulster Local Studies*, 9, No. 20 (1985), pp 120–7.
109. Traditional buildings in the landscape, in F.H.A. Aalen (ed), *The future*

of the Irish landscape (Dublin, 1985), pp 26–45.

110. Indigenous architecture? *Royal Institute of Architects of Ireland*, Bulletin No. 55 (Feb/Mar 1986), pp 24–5.

111. A view of Irish rural housing in the 1840s, in Colin Thomas (ed), *Rural landscapes and communities: Essays presented to Desmond McCourt* (Blackrock, 1986), pp 121–43.

112. Creating Ulster's folk museum, *Ulster Folklife*, 32 (1986), pp 54–77.

113. A relic of seventeenth-century iron-working in Fermanagh, *Ulster Folk and Transport Museum Yearbook*, 1981/1985, pp 18–21.

114. Cultural connections and cheese, *Folk Life*, 25 (1986–87), pp 92–9.

115. Changes in Irish rural housing, 1600–1900, in Patrick O'Flanagan, Paul Ferguson and Kevin Whelan (eds), *Rural Ireland 1600–1900: Modernisation and change* (Cork, 1987), pp 86–103.

116. Illustrations of a flax clove, and a description of its use, *Ulster Folklife*, 33 (1987), pp 94–5.

117. Tradition and identity, in Alan Gailey (ed), *The use of tradition: essays presented to G B Thompson* (Holywood, 1988), pp 61–7.

118. The nature of tradition. *Folklore* 100 (1989), pp 143–61, (Rhind Lecture, Edinburgh, 1987).

119. Migrant culture, *Folk Life*, 28 (1989–90), pp 5–18. (Presidential Address, Society for Folk Life Studies, 1989).

120. '… such as pass by us daily…': the study of folklife, *Ulster Folklife*, 36 (1990), pp 4–22. (The Estyn Evans Lecture, 1989).

121. Obituary: Emyr Estyn Evans (1905–1989), *Folklore*, 101, ii (1990), pp 231–2.

122. Emyr Estyn Evans (1905–1989), *Folk Life*, 29 (1990–91), pp 92–4.

123. Cultural identity and the open-air museum: The challenge of cultural change, (Kulturelle Identität and Freilichtmuseen: Die Herausforderung durch den Kulturwandel), in *Tagung des Verbandes Europaischer Freilichtmuseen. Meeting of the Association of European Open Air Museums, Czechoslovakia, 14 Tagungsbericht* (Roznov p.R., 1991), pp 21–30, Deutsch pp 30–41.

124. A tourist attraction in spite of itself, in David McDowell and David Leslie (eds), *Tourism resources: Issues, planning and management* (Jordanstown, 1991), pp 97–105.

125. Presenting working life in Ulster's Folk Museum, in *A new head of steam*, Proceedings of the Scottish Museum Council's 7th Annual Conference, Glasgow, 1990 (Edinburgh, 1992), pp 45–7.

126. Conflict-resolution in Northern Ireland: the role of a folk museum, *Museum*, No.175, 44, No. 3 (1992), pp 165–9.

127. Ulster's Folk Museum: Interpretation and identity in a regional context, in Elizabeth I. Kwasnik (ed), *British and Bulgarian ethnography: Papers from a symposium in Liverpool, October, 1989* (Liverpool, 1992), pp 24–9.

128. Across 'The Sheugh': Cultural relations between Scotland and

Ireland, in Hugh Cheape (ed), *Tools and traditions: Studies in European Ethnology Presented to Alexander Fenton* (Edinburgh, 1993), pp 43–8.

129. Ulster's museum of popular culture: Formation and development, in N.A. Nikishin and O.G. Sevan (eds), *Towards museums of the 21st century, Museum Bulletin. Journal of Scientific Work* (in Russian), Moscow, 1991.

130. Religion, language and culture: Conflicting national identities in Ireland, in H.L. Cox (ed), *Kulturgrenzen und Nationale Identität* (Bonn, 1993) being also *Rheinisches Jahrbuch für Volkskunde*, 30 (1993–94), pp 135–51.

131. The use of replica buildings and infill creations in Northern Ireland's open air museums, in Stefan Baumeier (ed), *Preserved realities: Maintenance and construction strategies in European open air museums* (published on behalf of the Association of European Open Air Museums, Westfälisches Freilichtmuseum Detmold, Detmold, 1995), pp 144–8: also in German, ibid, pp 140–4.

132. Cultural heritage, education and the folk museum: The experience in Ulster, in *The role of ethnographical museums within a United Europe: Proceedings of the Inaugural Meeting of Ethnographical Museums in the Countries of the European Community, Eugenides Foundation, Athens, 1–5 October 1992* (Greek Society of Ethnographical Museology, Athens, 1995), pp 275–85.

133. The Ulster poets and local life: 1790–1870, in J. Gray and W. McCann (eds), *An uncommon bookman: Essays in memory of J R R Adams* (Belfast, 1996), 159–74.

Editorial work

Ulster Folklife

Assistant to Editor
(R H Buchanan)   5 (1959)–9(1964)
(D McCourt)   10 (1964)–14(1968)
Assistant Editor   15/16(1970)–18(1972)
Editor   19   (1973)–32(1986)

The Spade in Northern and Atlantic Europe (UFTM and Institute of Irish Studies, QUB, 1970) – conference papers (with A. Fenton)
Gold Under the Furze (Dublin, 1982) – essays presented to Caoimhín Ò Danachair (with Daithí Ó hÓgáin)
The Nature of Tradition (Holywood, UFTM, 1988) – essays presented to G.B. Thompson

Other editorial work for UFTM

Annual Reports prior to 1965
Yearbooks 1965–1979
Research monograph by A.D. Buckley, *A Gentle People*
With G.B. Adams, *Ulster Dialects* (1964)
With M. Barry and P. Tilling, *The English Dialects of Ulster* (1986) – papers
by the late G.B. Adams, republished
Information leaflets
Museum guides/handbooks in 1960s and 1970s